GREGG SHORTHAND

Diamond Jubilee Series

GREGG SHORTHAND

John Robert Gregg
Louis A. Leslie
Charles E. Zoubek
Shorthand written by Charles Rader

GREGG 75

Diamond Jubilee Series

GREGG DIVISION
McGRAW-HILL BOOK COMPANY
New York Chicago Dallas San Francisco
Toronto London

GREGG SHORTHAND, DIAMOND JUBILEE SERIES

Library of Congress Catalog Card Number 61-18132

ISBN 07-024591-6

14 15 16 17 18 19 20 DODO-63 8 7 6 5 4 3 2 1

PREFACE

Gregg Shorthand, the Universal System

To most people, the terms "shorthand" and "Gregg" are synonymous. Since its publication in 1888, Gregg Shorthand has been learned and used by millions of people not only in the English language but in many foreign languages as well. Today Gregg Shorthand is truly the universal system of shorthand.

The success of any shorthand system rests on the merits of its alphabet; the Gregg alphabet is the most efficient shorthand alphabet devised in more than two thousand years of shorthand history. The fact that this alphabet, virtually without change, has been the basis of Gregg Shorthand for three-quarters of a century is indeed a tribute to the genius of its inventor, John Robert Gregg.

Gregg Shorthand, Diamond Jubilee Series

This edition of Gregg Shorthand, issued during the Diamond Jubilee year of the publication of the system, has two primary objectives:

1. To enable the student to learn Gregg Shorthand more quickly and easily. This ease of learning is accomplished through the revision of the shorthand system, which reduces the "learning load."

2. To provide for transcription readiness by increased emphasis on vocabulary development, spelling, punctuation, and application of correct principles of grammar – all concurrently with the teaching of shorthand.

Revision of the System

Gregg Shorthand, Diamond Jubilee Series, represents the first revision of the Gregg Shorthand system since 1949. The changes in the system are based on research by the authors, on suggestions of experienced teachers, and on a study of the application of the principles by the stenographer in the office.

The major changes in the system concern:

Brief Forms. Those brief forms with a low frequency of business use have been eliminated; the words they represented are now written in full. The outlines for some brief forms have been modified for easier joining and greater legibility. A few new brief forms have been added.

In all, there are now 129 brief forms representing 148 meanings.

Phrases. An analysis of the notes of hundreds of students and stenographers revealed that many phrasing principles that had been taught were very seldom applied. These have been eliminated.

Word Beginnings and Endings. The word beginnings and endings that are infrequently used or that apply only to a limited number of words have been omitted.

Principles. Those word-building principles that had presented both teaching and learning problems have been eliminated or modified. Among these are the rules governing the formation of the past tense, the omission of final *t* and *d*, and the writing of *o* on its side before *r* and *l*.

In addition, many minor, but troublesome, points of theory have been eliminated or modified in order to obtain even greater consistency of outline.

As a result of these changes, the student will complete the principles sooner and thus be ready earlier for the second phase of his shorthand program – shorthand skill development.

Building Transcription Skills

Spelling and Punctuation. A very popular and helpful innovation in an elementary shorthand manual was introduced in 1949 in the form of "marginal reminders," which taught the student spelling and punctuation concurrently with shorthand. This new edition retains this helpful learning device with three slight, but useful, modifications:

1. The punctuation marks are encircled in color in the shorthand plates of the Reading and Writing Practice; in addition, the reason for their use is given above the circle. Thus, the student is saved the many eye movements that were previously necessary when the reason was given in the left margin of the page.

2. The words singled out from the Reading and Writing Practice for spelling attention are now syllabicated. Thus, the student is better able to learn correct word division as well as correct spelling.

3. Only one principle of punctuation is presented at a time in each lesson rather than several, as in the previous edition of *Gregg Shorthand.*

Business Vocabulary Builder. Beginning with Chapter 2, each lesson contains a Business Vocabulary Builder consisting of several business words or expressions for which meanings are provided. The expressions are selected from the Reading and Writing Practice. The Business Vocabulary Builder helps to overcome a major transcription handicap – a limited vocabulary.

Similar-Words Drill. These drills teach the student the difference in meaning between similar words that stenographers often confuse: for example, *it's, its; their, there; accept, except.*

Spelling Families. An effective device for improving spelling is to study words in related groups, or spelling families. In *Gregg Shorthand, Diamond Jubilee Series,* the student studies six of these families.

Common Word Roots. A mastery of some of the more common Latin and Greek word roots is an effective device for the student wishing to increase his command of words. In *Gregg Shorthand, Diamond Jubilee Series,* the student studies five of these common word roots.

Grammar Checkup. In a number of lessons, drills are provided on rules of grammar that stenographers often apply incorrectly. Examples illustrating the correct applications of these rules are given in the Reading and Writing Practice.

Transcription Quiz. Beginning with Lesson 57, each lesson contains a Transcription Quiz consisting of a letter in which the student has to supply the internal punctuation. This provides him with a daily test of how well he has mastered the punctuation rules presented in earlier lessons.

Organization of Textbook

Gregg Shorthand, Diamond Jubilee Series, is organized into 3 parts, 10 chapters, and 70 lessons. These 70 lessons provide ample material for a typical semester.

PART 1: *Principles* — Chapters 1 – 8. Each chapter contains six lessons — the first five lessons are devoted to the presentation of principles, and the sixth lesson is a recall. The last of the new principles is presented in Lesson 47.

PART 2: *Reinforcement* — Chapter 9. Chapter 9 contains eight lessons, each of which reviews intensively the principles in one of the chapters in Part 1.

PART 3: *Shorthand and Transcription Skill Building* — Chapter 10. This chapter consists of 14 lessons, each of which is designed to strengthen the student's grasp of a major principle of Gregg Shorthand. In addition, each lesson continues to develop the student's vocabulary and to improve his ability to spell, to punctuate, and to apply rules of grammar correctly.

Organization of Lessons

In *Gregg Shorthand, Diamond Jubilee Series,* the order of presentation of principles has been reorganized to introduce as early as possible the most frequently used alphabetic characters, brief forms, and word-building principles. Because of this reorganization, smooth, natural connected shorthand practice material is available in the very early lessons. In addition, the principles have been distributed more equally among the lessons, so that the student is not confronted with a lengthy assignment one day and a very short one the next.

Brief forms are presented in groups of nine and never in two consecutive lessons.

Reading and Writing Practice

All the shorthand practice material in the Reading and Writing Practice is completely new, fresh, and up to date. A careful balance of business letters and interesting, informative articles has been maintained. Two new features have been introduced into the Reading and Writing Practice:

1. A brief-form letter at the beginning of each lesson in which a group of brief forms has been introduced. This letter contains one or more uses of all the brief forms, or their derivatives, of the lesson.

2. An occasional "Chuckle" that both teacher and students will enjoy as a relief from business material.

Other Features

Chapter Openings. Each chapter is introduced by a beautifully illustrated spread that not only paints for the student a vivid picture of the life and duties of a secretary but also inspires and encourages him in his efforts to acquire the necessary skills.

Student Helps. To be sure that the student gets the greatest benefit from each phase of his shorthand study, he is given step-by-step suggestions on how to handle it when it is first introduced.

Reading Scoreboards. At various points in the text, the student is given an opportunity to determine his reading speed by means of a scoreboard. The scoreboard enables him to calculate the number of words a minute he is reading. By comparing his reading speed from scoreboard to scoreboard, he sees some indication of his shorthand reading growth.

Recall Charts. In the last lesson of each chapter in Part 1, a unique recall chart is provided. This chart contains illustrations of all the theory taught in the chapter. It also contains illustrations of all the theory the student has studied up to that lesson.

Check Lists. To keep the student constantly reminded of the importance of good practice procedures, an occasional check list is provided. These check lists deal with writing shorthand, reading shorthand, homework, proportion, etc.

The authors and publishers wish to express their gratitude for the suggestions, advice, and encouragement they have received from so many teachers "on the firing line." They are confident that because of this help all teachers will derive even greater satisfaction from their teaching and will obtain better results than they have ever obtained before.

The Publishers

CONTENTS

YOUR PRACTICE PROGRAM

To make the most rapid progress in your study of shorthand, you must practice efficiently. By practicing efficiently, you will achieve two important results: first, you will get the greatest benefit from the material on which you practice; and second, and no doubt very important to you, you will be able to complete each lesson in the shortest possible time.

To begin with, choose a quiet place in which to practice—and resist that temptation to turn on the radio or the television set! Then follow these easy steps:

Reading Word Lists

1. With the type key exposed, pronounce and spell aloud—if possible—each word and shorthand outline in the list, thus: *see, s-e; fee, f-e.* By reading aloud, you will be sure that you are concentrating on each word as you study. Repeat this procedure with all the words in the list until you feel you can read the shorthand outlines without referring to the type key.

The student studies the word lists by placing a card or slip of paper over the key and reading the shorthand words aloud.

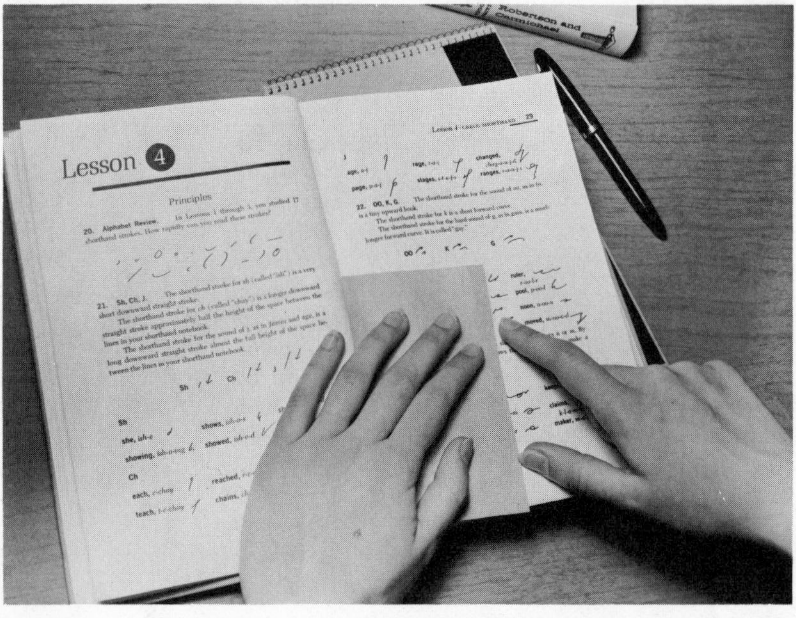
Lesson 4
Principles

2. Cover the type key with a card or slip of paper. Then spell and pronounce aloud, thus: *s-e, see; f-e, fee.*

3. If the spelling of a shorthand outline does not immediately give you the meaning, refer to the type key. Do not spend more than a few seconds trying to decipher an outline.

4. After you have read all the words in the list, read them again following the suggestions in paragraphs 2 and 3. This second reading should be easier for you, and you should not have to refer to the key so often.

5. In reading brief forms and phrases, it is not necessary to spell.

Reading Letters and Articles

Before you start the Reading and Writing Practice, have a pencil and a blank piece of paper or a card handy. Then:

1. Read the shorthand aloud.

2. When you come to a shorthand outline that you cannot read, spell it. If the spelling gives you the meaning, continue reading. If it does not, write the outline on your sheet of paper or card and continue reading. Do not spend more than a few seconds trying to decipher the outline.

3. After you have gone through the entire Reading and Writing Practice in this way, repeat this procedure if time permits. On this second reading you may be able to read some of the outlines that escaped you on your first time through. When that happens, cross that outline off your sheet or card.

4. Finally—and very important—at the earliest opportunity ask your teacher or your classmates the meaning of the outlines that you could not read.

Remember, during the early stages your shorthand reading may not be very rapid. That is only natural, as you are, in a sense, learning a new language. If you do each day's lesson faithfully, however, you will find that your reading rate is increasing almost from day to day.

Writing the Reading and Writing Practice

Before you do any writing of shorthand, you should give careful consideration to the tools of your trade — your notebook and your pen.

Your Notebook. The best notebook for shorthand writing is one that measures 6 by 9 inches and has a vertical rule down the middle of each sheet. If the notebook has a spiral binding, so much the better, as the spiral binding enables you to keep the pages flat at all times. The paper, of course, should take ink well.

Your Pen. If it is at all possible, use a fountain pen or a good ball-point pen for your shorthand writing. Why use a pen for shorthand writing? It requires less effort to write with a pen; consequently, you can write for long periods of time without fatigue. On the other hand, the point of a pencil soon becomes blunt; and the blunter it gets, the more effort you have to expend as you write with it. Pen-written notes remain readable almost indefinitely; pencil notes soon become blurred and hard to read. Pen-written notes are also easier to read under artificial light.

Having selected your writing tools, you should follow these steps in working with each Reading and Writing Practice:

1. Read the material you are going to copy, following the suggestions given under the heading, "Reading Letters and Articles," on page 11. Always read the Reading and Writing Practice before you copy it.

2. When you are ready to start writing, read a convenient group of words from the printed shorthand; then write the group, reading aloud as you write.

3. As you copy from the printed shorthand, you may be able to decipher some of the outlines that you wrote on your sheet of paper or card when you first read the material. When that occurs, cross the outlines off your list.

4. Remember that in the early stages your writing may not be very rapid, nor will your notes be so pretty as those in the book. With regular practice, however, you will soon become so proud of your shorthand notes that you won't want to write any more longhand!

Lesson 9

The student reads the Reading and Writing Practice, writing on the card any outlines that he cannot read after spelling them.

When copying, the student reads a convenient group of words aloud and then writes that group in his notebook. Notice how he keeps his place in the shorthand with his left index finger.

PRINCIPLES

PART 1

Shorthand—Door Opener to Careers

You have your own reasons for learning shorthand. Everyone does. Maybe the title of secretary appeals to you, and you know that shorthand is an absolute "must" if you are to earn that title. Maybe you have your heart set on becoming a shorthand reporter. Or maybe you have some personal reason for wanting to acquire shorthand skill.

One very big reason why many people study shorthand is that shorthand opens doors that might otherwise remain closed to them. How can shorthand open doors? Let's cite an example. Janet Greene has considerable talent in art and is very anxious to get into advertising, where she can put her talent and training to use. But Janet found out quickly that competition is keen in this field, and jobs for beginners are not easy to get. After pounding the pavement and being given the "No Help Wanted" treatment time after time, she asked a personnel counselor, "How do I go about getting into advertising?" The answer was direct: "Study shorthand and develop a good stenographic skill. You can always get a job as a stenographer—a good-paying job, too. Get your foot in the door of an advertising agency by working there as a stenographer. Then, when you have made a niche for yourself, let it be known that you have artistic talents and ambitions. Chances are that the opportunity to employ those talents will be given to you."

Good advice!

Every year countless young women—and men—use their shorthand skill to open doors to varied and interesting careers. They may be careers in art, in television, in medicine, in publishing, or in management. Competition is very keen in these fields, but many people find shorthand the magic key that opens the door wide.

Even the young lady who isn't really interested in a career—only in the title of "Mrs."—finds shorthand and secretarial training valuable. Thousands of young women continue to work even after they are married—to help earn money for a new home, to save for vacation travel, or to help meet unexpected expenses.

Chapter 1

Lesson 1

GREGG SHORTHAND IS EASY TO LEARN

If you can write longhand, you can write Gregg Shorthand – it's as simple as that!

The strokes you will use in writing Gregg Shorthand are the same as those that you have been accustomed to writing in longhand. Actually, in some ways Gregg Shorthand is easier to learn than longhand. Skeptical? Well, just this one illustration should convince you. In longhand there are many different ways to express the letter *f*, all of which you had to learn. Here are six of them:

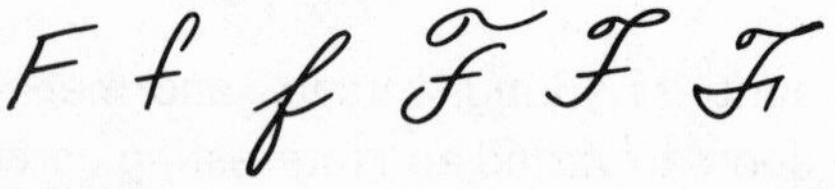

In Gregg Shorthand there is only one way to write *f*, as you will discover in this lesson.

Practice regularly and your shorthand skill will develop rapidly!

Principles

GROUP A

1. **S-Z.** The first stroke you will learn is the shorthand *s*, which is one of the most frequently used letters in the English language. The shorthand *s* is a tiny downward curve that resembles the longhand comma in shape.

Because in English *s* often has the sound of *z*, as in *saves*, the same downward curve is used to express *z*.

S-Z 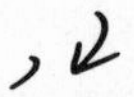

2. A. The next stroke you will learn is the shorthand *a,* which is simply the longhand *a* with the final connecting stroke omitted.

A 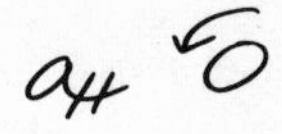

3. Silent Letters Omitted. In the English language, many words contain letters that are not pronounced. In shorthand, these silent letters are omitted; and we write only the sounds that are actually pronounced in a word. For example, in the word *say,* the *y* would not be written because it is not pronounced. For the word *face,* we would write *f-a-s;* the *e* would be omitted because it is not pronounced, and the *c* would be represented by the shorthand *s* because it has the sound of *s.*

What letters in the following words would not be written in shorthand because they are not pronounced?

day	**eat**	**main**
mean	**save**	**steam**

4. S-A Words. With the strokes for *a* and *s,* you can now form two words.

say, *s-a*  **ace,** *a-s* 

Notice that the *c* in *ace* is represented by the shorthand *s* because it has the *s* sound.

5. F, V. The shorthand stroke for *f* is the same shape as the stroke for *s* except that it is larger—about half the height of the space between the lines in your shorthand notebook.

The shorthand stroke for *v* is the same shape as *f* except that it is much larger – almost the full height of the space between the lines of your shorthand notebook. Note the difference in the sizes of *s, f, v.*

S  **F** 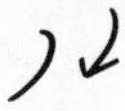 **V** 

F

safe, *s-a-f*  **face,** *f-a-s*  **safes,** *s-a-f-s* 

V

save, *s-a-v*  **vase,** *v-a-s*  **saves,** *s-a-v-s* 

6. E. The shorthand stroke for *e* is a tiny circle. It is simply the longhand *e* with the two connecting strokes omitted.

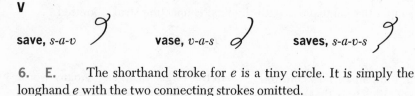

E 

see, *s-e*  **sees,** *s-e-s*  **ease,** *e-s* 

fee, *f-e*  **fees,** *f-e-s*  **easy,** *e-s-e* 

Notice in pronouncing the word *easy* that the *y* sounds like *e;* therefore, in shorthand it is represented by the *e* circle.

Suggestion: At this point, take a few moments to read the procedures outlined for practicing word lists on page 10. By following those procedures, you will derive the greatest benefit from your practice.

GROUP B

7. N, M. The shorthand stroke for *n* is a very short forward straight line.

The shorthand stroke for *m* is a longer forward straight line.

N  **M** 

N

see, *s-e*  **say,** *s-a*  **vain,** *v-a-n* 

seen, *s-e-n*  **sane,** *s-a-n*  **knee,** *n-e*

Notice that the *k* in *knee* is not written; it is not written because it is not pronounced.

M

may, *m-a* 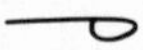 **mean,** *m-e-n* **same,** *s-a-m* 

main, *m-a-n*  **name,** *n-a-m*  **seem,** *s-e-m* 

me, *m-e* **aim,** *a-m*  **fame,** *f-a-m* 

8. T, D. The shorthand stroke for *t* is a short upward straight line. The shorthand stroke for *d* is a longer upward straight line.

T  **D** 

T

eat, *e-t*  **team,** *t-e-m*  **seat,** *s-e-t* 

tea, *t-e*  **neat,** *n-e-t*  **stay,** *s-t-a* 

D

day, *d-a*  **need,** *n-e-d*  **aid,** *a-d* 

date, *d-a-t*  **made,** *m-a-d*  **saved,** *s-a-v-d* 

9. Punctuation and Capitalization

period  **paragraph**  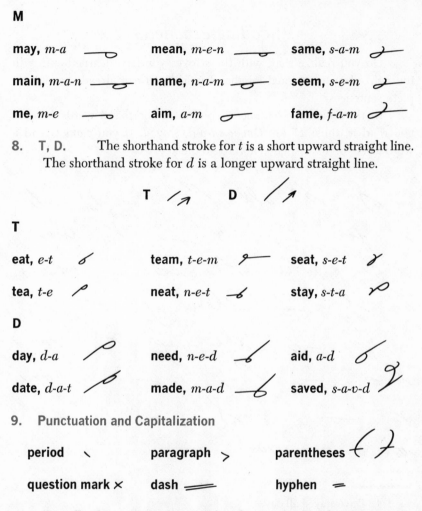 **parentheses** 

question mark  **dash**  **hyphen**

For all other punctuation marks, the regular longhand forms are used.

Capitalization is indicated by two upward dashes underneath the word to be capitalized.

Dave  **Fay**  **May** 

Reading Practice

Do you realize that, with the strokes you have learned and with the help of an occasional longhand word, you can already read complete sentences?

In the following sentences, spell each shorthand word aloud as you read it, thus: *D-a-v, Dave; s-t-a-d, stayed.* If you cannot read a word after you have spelled it, refer to the key.

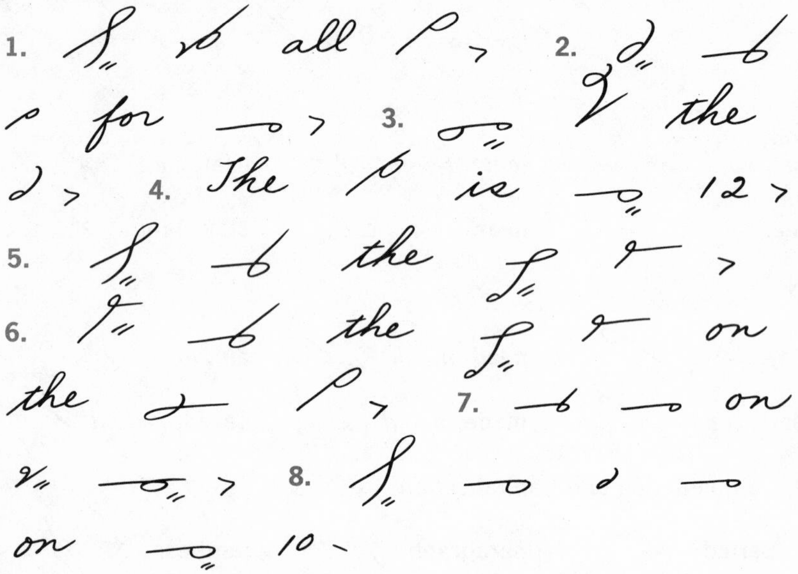

1. Dave stayed all day.
2. Fay made tea for me.
3. Amy saved the fee.
4. The date is May 12.
5. Dave made the Navy team.
6. Dean made the Navy team on the same day.
7. Meet me on East Main.
8. Dave may see me on May 10.

Lesson 2

Principles

10. Alphabet Review. In Lesson 1 you studied the following nine shorthand strokes. How quickly can you read them?

11. O, R, L. The shorthand stroke for *o* is a small deep hook.

The shorthand stroke for *r* is a short forward curve.

The shorthand stroke for *l* is a longer forward curve about three times as long as the stroke for *r*.

Note how these shorthand strokes are derived from their longhand forms.

O
R
L

O

no, *n-o*  **sew,** *s-o*  **own,** *o-n* 

snow, *s-n-o*  **foe,** *f-o*  **tone,** *t-o-n* 

tow, *t-o*  **phone,** *f-o-n*  **dome,** *d-o-m* 

dough, *d-o*  **note,** *n-o-t*  **stone,** *s-t-o-n* 

Notice in the words in the third column that the *o* is placed on its side when it comes before *n, m.* By placing it on its side when it precedes *n, m,* we can make a much easier, faster joining.

R

ray, *r-a*  **ear,** *e-r*  **free,** *f-r-e* 

rate, *r-a-t*  **dear,** *d-e-r*  **fair,** *f-a-r* 

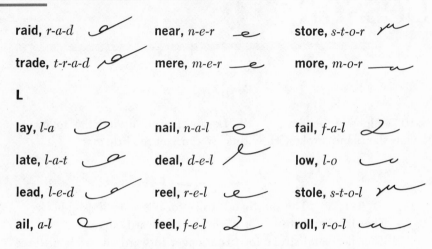

raid, *r-a-d* 	**near,** *n-e-r* 	**store,** *s-t-o-r* 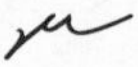
trade, *t-r-a-d* 	**mere,** *m-e-r* 	**more,** *m-o-r*

L

lay, *l-a* 	**nail,** *n-a-l* 	**fail,** *f-a-l* 
late, *l-a-t* 	**deal,** *d-e-l* 	**low,** *l-o* 
lead, *l-e-d* 	**reel,** *r-e-l* 	**stole,** *s-t-o-l* 
ail, *a-l* 	**feel,** *f-e-l* 	**roll,** *r-o-l* 

12. H, -ing. The letter *h* is simply a dot placed above the vowel. With few exceptions, *h* occurs at the beginning of a word.

Ing, which almost always occurs at the end of a word, is also expressed by a dot.

H

he, *h-e* 	**hair,** *h-a-r* 	**hole,** *h-o-l* 

-ing

heating, *h-e-t-ing* 	**heeding,** *h-e-d-ing* 	**hearing,** *h-e-r-ing* 

13. Long Ī. The shorthand stroke for the long sound of *ī,* as in *my,* is a large broken circle.

I 

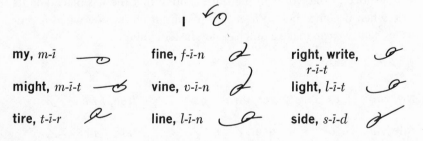

my, *m-ī* 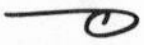	**fine,** *f-ī-n* 	**right, write,** *r-ī-t* 
might, *m-ī-t* 	**vine,** *v-ī-n* 	**light,** *l-ī-t* 
tire, *t-ī-r* 	**line,** *l-ī-n* 	**side,** *s-ī-d* 

14. Omission of Minor Vowels. Sometimes a vowel in a word is slightly sounded or slurred. Such a vowel may be omitted if it does not contribute to speed or legibility.

reader, *r-e-d-r*  **total,** *t-o-t-l*  **later,** *l-a-t-r* 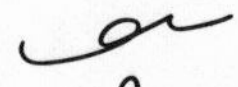

meter, *m-e-t-r*  **heater,** *h-e-t-r*  **even,** *e-v-n* 

Reading Practice

With the aid of a few words in longhand, you can now read the following sentences. Remember to spell each shorthand word aloud as you read it and to refer to the key when you cannot read a word.

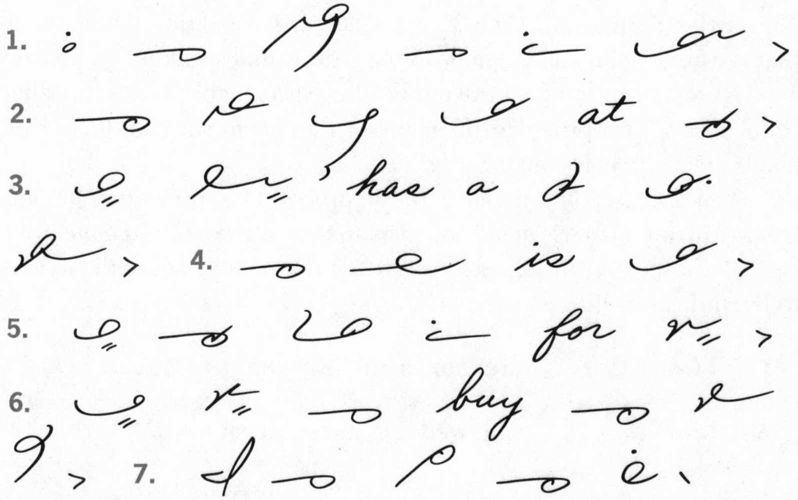
1.
2.
at
3.
has a
4.
is
5.
for
6.
buy
7.

1. He may drive me home later.
2. My train leaves late at night.
3. Ray Taylor has a fine writing style.
4. My mail is late.
5. Ray might fly home for Easter.
6. Lee Stone may buy my steel safe.
7. I may dye my hair.

Lesson 3

Principles

15. Alphabet Review. How rapidly can you read the following shorthand strokes that you studied in Lessons 1 and 2?

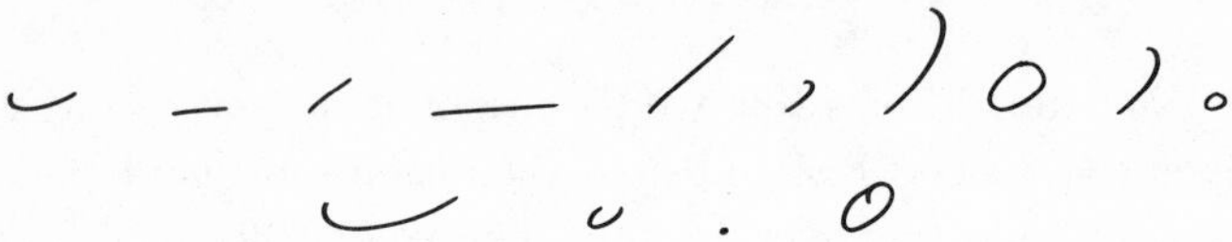

16. Brief Forms. The English language contains many words that are used again and again in all the writing and speaking that we do.

As an aid to rapid shorthand writing, special abbreviations, called "brief forms," are provided for many of these common words. For example, we write *m* for *am, v* for *have.*

You are already familiar with the process of abbreviation in longhand–*Mr.* for *Mister, memo* for *memorandum, Ave.* for *Avenue.*

Because these brief forms occur so frequently, you will be wise to learn them well!

I		**are, our, hour**		**am**	
Mr.		**will, well**		**it, at**	
have		**a, an**		**in, not**	

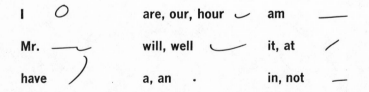

Notice that some of the strokes represent more than one word. You will have no difficulty selecting the correct word in a sentence; the sense of the sentence will give you the answer.

17. Phrases. By using brief forms for common words, we are able to save writing time. Another device that helps save writing time is called "phrasing," or the writing of two or more shorthand outlines together. Here are a number of useful phrases built with the brief forms you have just studied.

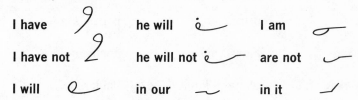

I have  **he will**  **I am** 

I have not  **he will not**  **are not** 

I will  **in our** **in it** 

18. Left S-Z. In Lesson 1 you learned one stroke for *s* and *z*. Another stroke for *s* and *z* is also used in order to provide an easy joining in any combination of strokes—a backward comma, which is also written downward. For convenience it is called the "left *s*."

At this point you need not try to decide which *s* stroke to use in any given word; this will become clear to you as your study of shorthand progresses.

S-Z 

eats, *e-t-s*  **ties,** *t-ī-s*  **sales,** *s-a-l-s* 

readers, *r-e-d-r-s*  **names,** *n-a-m-s*  **days,** *d-a-s* 

files, *f-ī-l-s*  **most,** *m-o-s-t*  **writes,** *r-ī-t-s* 

19. P, B. The shorthand stroke for *p* is the same shape as the stroke for *s*, given in paragraph 18, except that it is larger—approximately half the height of the space between the lines in your shorthand notebook.

The shorthand stroke for *b* is also the same shape, except that it is much larger—almost the full height of the space between the lines in your shorthand notebook. Both *p* and *b* are written downward.

Notice the difference in the sizes of *s, p,* and *b.*

S  **P**  **B** 

P

pay, *p-a*

pays, *p-a-s*

pairs, *p-a-r-s*

spares, *s-p-a-r-s*

price, *p-r-ī-s*

please, *p-l-e-s*

plane, *p-l-a-n*

people, *p-e-p-l*

hopes, *h-o-p-s*

opens, *o-p-n-s*

paid, *p-a-d*

pains, *p-a-n-s*

B

bay, *b-a*

base, *b-a-s*

boats, *b-o-t-s*

brains, *b-r-a-n-s*

blames, *b-l-a-m-s*

blows, *b-l-o-s*

neighbors, *n-a-b-r-s*

beat, *b-e-t*

beam, *b-e-m*

Notice that *pr, pl, br, bl* are written with one sweep of the pen without a pause between the *p* or *b* and the *r* or *l*.

Reading Practice

You have already reached the point where you can read sentences written entirely in shorthand.

Suggestion: Before you start your work on the Reading Practice, read the practice procedures for reading shorthand on page 11. By following those procedures, you will get the most benefit out of the Reading Practice.

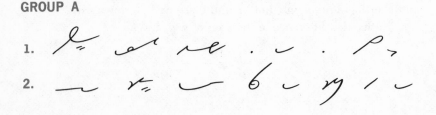

GROUP A

1. 

2. 

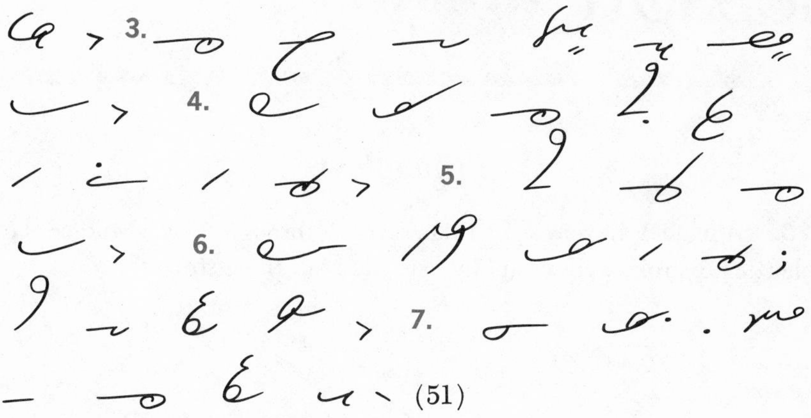
3.
4.
5.
6.
7.

(51)

GROUP B

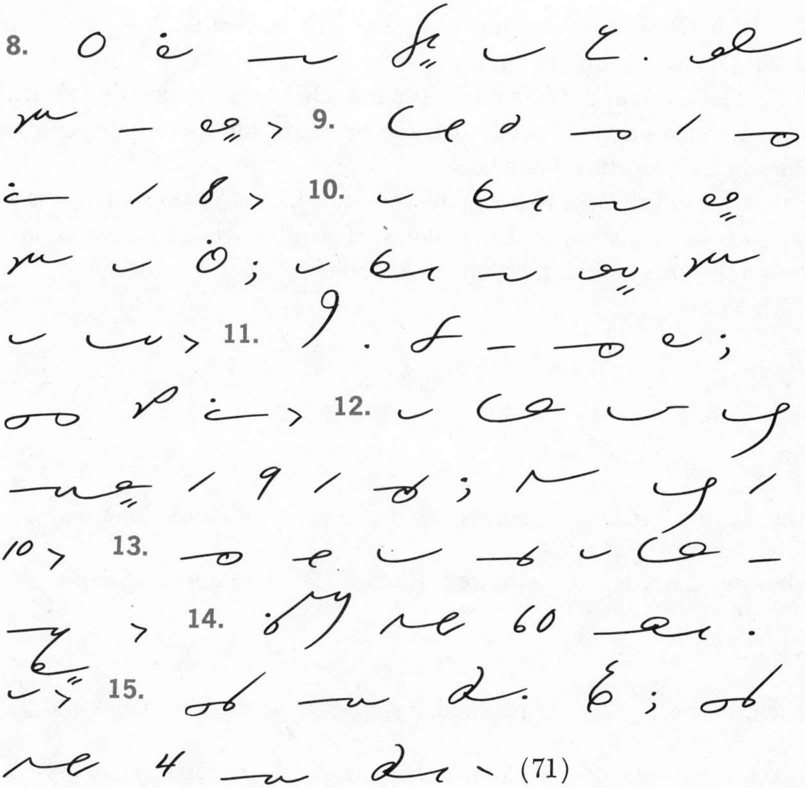
8.
9.
10.
11.
12.
13.
14.
15.

(71)

Lesson 4

Principles

20. Alphabet Review. In Lessons 1 through 3, you studied 17 shorthand strokes. How rapidly can you read these strokes?

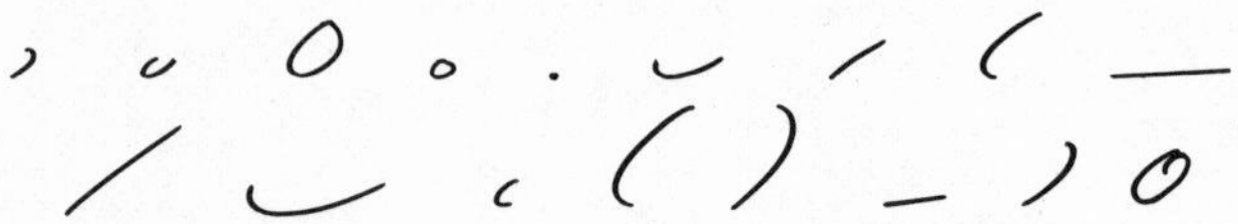

21. Sh, Ch, J. The shorthand stroke for *sh* (called "ish") is a very short downward straight stroke.

The shorthand stroke for *ch* (called "chay") is a longer downward straight stroke approximately half the height of the space between the lines in your shorthand notebook.

The shorthand stroke for the sound of *j*, as in *James* and *age*, is a long downward straight stroke almost the full height of the space between the lines in your shorthand notebook.

Sh  **Ch**  **J** 

Sh

she, *ish-e* 	**shows,** *ish-o-s* 	**shades,** *ish-a-d-s* 
showing, *ish-o-ing* 	**showed,** *ish-o-d* 	**shaped,** *ish-a-p-t* 

Ch

each, *e-chay* 	**reached,** *r-e-chay-t* 	**chairs,** *chay-a-r-s* 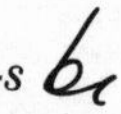
teach, *t-e-chay* 	**chains,** *chay-a-n-s* 	**cheaper,** *chay-e-p-r* 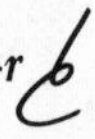

J

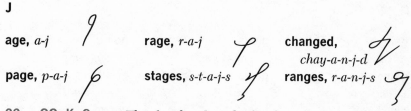

age, *a-j*  **rage,** *r-a-j*  **changed,** *chay-a-n-j-d* 

page, *p-a-j*  **stages,** *s-t-a-j-s*  **ranges,** *r-a-n-j-s* 

22. OO, K, G. The shorthand stroke for the sound of *oo*, as in *to*, is a tiny upward hook.

The shorthand stroke for *k* is a short forward curve.

The shorthand stroke for the hard sound of *g*, as in *gain*, is a much longer forward curve. It is called "gay."

OO  **K**  **G** 

OO

to, two, too, *t-oo*  **fruit,** *f-r-oo-t*  **ruler,** *r-oo-l-r* 

doing, *d-oo-ing*  **room,** *r-oo-m*  **pool,** *p-oo-l* 

shoe, *ish-oo*  **true,** *t-r-oo*  **noon,** *n-oo-n* 

who, *h-oo*  **drew,** *d-r-oo*  **moved,** *m-oo-v-d* 

Notice that *oo* is placed on its side when it follows *n* or *m*. By placing it on its side when it follows these letters, we can make a smoother joining.

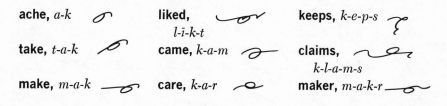

K

ache, *a-k*  **liked,** *l-ī-k-t*  **keeps,** *k-e-p-s* 

take, *t-a-k*  **came,** *k-a-m*  **claims,** *k-l-a-m-s* 

make, *m-a-k*  **care,** *k-a-r*  **maker,** *m-a-k-r* 

G

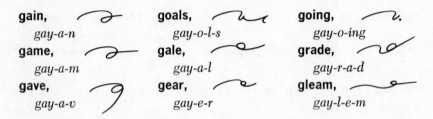

gain,  *gay-a-n*
goals, 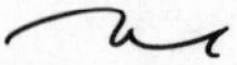 *gay-o-l-s*
going,  *gay-o-ing*
game,  *gay-a-m*
gale,  *gay-a-l*
grade,  *gay-r-a-d*
gave,  *gay-a-v*
gear,  *gay-e-r*
gleam,  *gay-l-e-m*

Notice that *kr* and *gl* are written with one smooth, wavelike motion; *kl* and *gr* are written with a hump between the *k* and the *l* and the g and the *r.*

Reading Practice

The following sentences contain many illustrations of the new shorthand strokes you studied in Lesson 4. They also review all the strokes and brief forms you studied in Lessons 1 through 3.

Read these sentences aloud, spelling out each outline that you cannot read immediately.

GROUP A

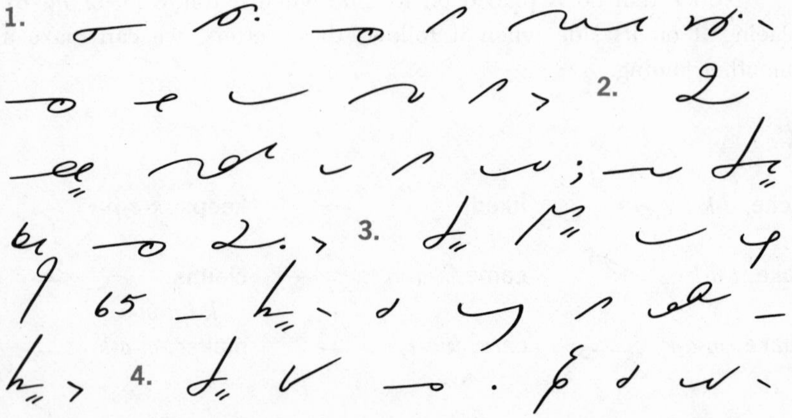

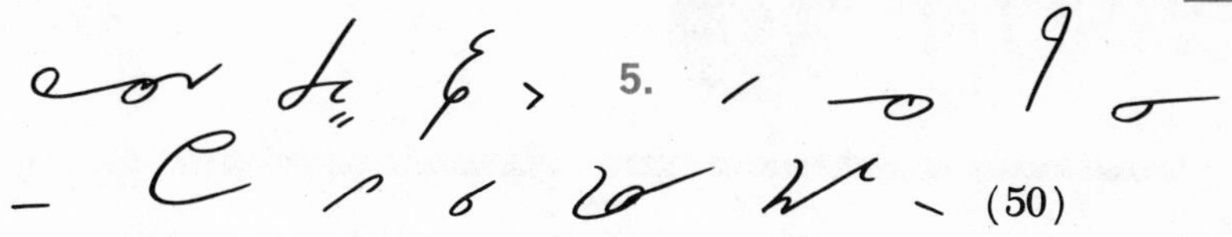
5.

(50)

GROUP B

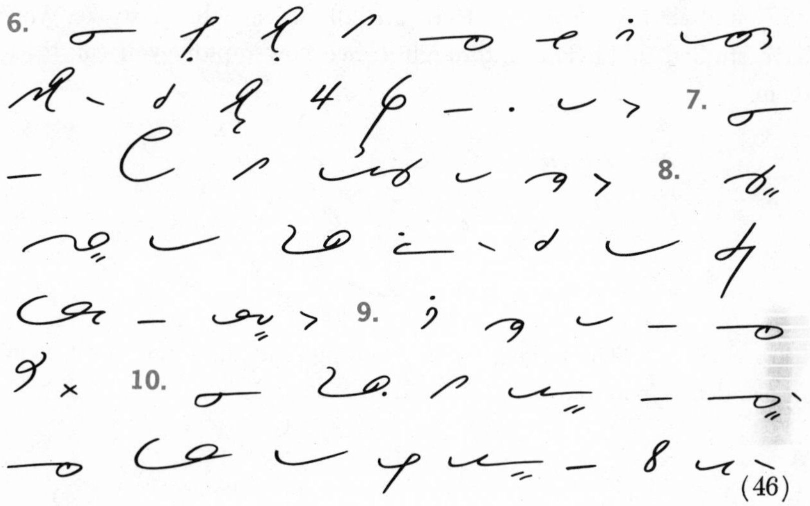
6.
7.
8.
9.
10.

(46)

GROUP C

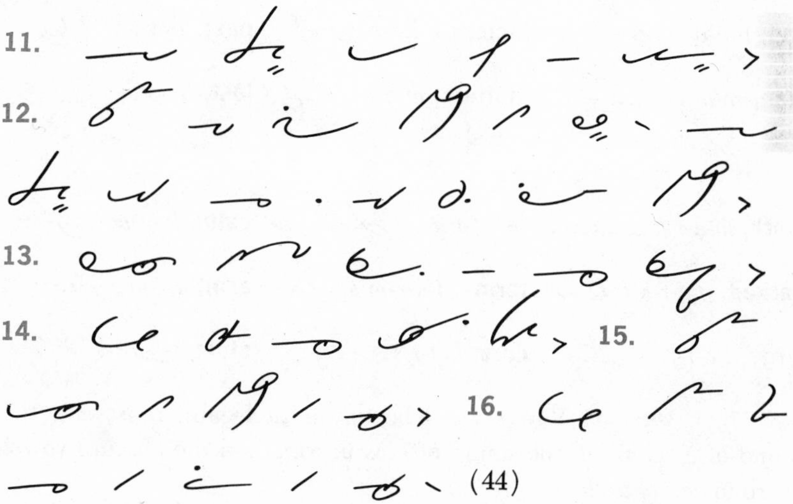
11.
12.
13.
14.
15.
16.

(44)

Lesson 5

Principles

23. Alphabet Review. Here are all the shorthand strokes you have studied in Lessons 1 through 4. See how rapidly you can read them.

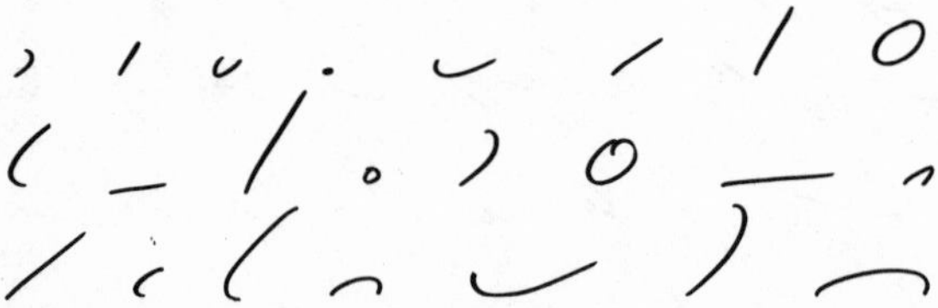

24. Ă, Ä. The large *a* circle also represents the sounds of *ă*, as in *has*, and *ä*, as in *mark*.

Ă

has, *h-a-s*
acting, *a-k-t-ing*
fast, *f-a-s-t*
had, *h-a-d*
facts, *f-a-k-t-s*
past, *p-a-s-t*
man, *m-a-n*
matters, *m-a-t-r-s*
last, *l-a-s-t*

Ä

mark, *m-a-r-k*
far, *f-a-r*
calm, *k-a-m*
parked, *p-a-r-k-t*
farms, *f-a-r-m-s*
arm, *a-r-m*
large, *l-a-r-j*
cars, *k-a-r-s*
start, *s-t-a-r-t*

25. Ĕ, Ĭ, Obscure Vowel. The tiny *e* circle also represents the sound of *ĕ*, as in *let*, the sound of *ĭ*, as in *trim*, and the obscure vowel heard in *her, church*.

Ĕ

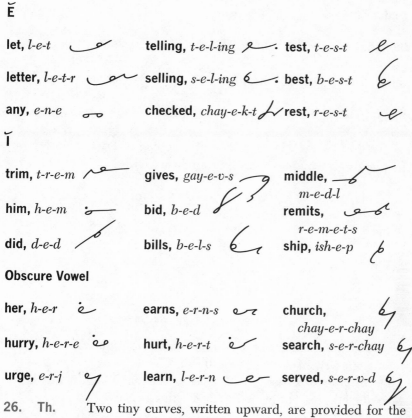

let, *l-e-t* **telling,** *t-e-l-ing* **test,** *t-e-s-t*

letter, *l-e-t-r* **selling,** *s-e-l-ing* **best,** *b-e-s-t*

any, *e-n-e* **checked,** *chay-e-k-t* **rest,** *r-e-s-t*

Ĭ

trim, *t-r-e-m* **gives,** *gay-e-v-s* **middle,** *m-e-d-l*

him, *h-e-m* **bid,** *b-e-d* **remits,** *r-e-m-e-t-s*

did, *d-e-d* **bills,** *b-e-l-s* **ship,** *ish-e-p*

Obscure Vowel

her, *h-e-r* **earns,** *e-r-n-s* **church,** *chay-e-r-chay*

hurry, *h-e-r-e* **hurt,** *h-e-r-t* **search,** *s-e-r-chay*

urge, *e-r-j* **learn,** *l-e-r-n* **served,** *s-e-r-v-d*

26. Th. Two tiny curves, written upward, are provided for the sounds of *th*. These curves are called "ith."

At this time you need not try to decide which *th* stroke to use in any given word; this will become clear to you as your study of shorthand progresses.

Over Th **Under Th**

Over Th

these, *ith-e-s* **then,** *ith-e-n* **bath,** *b-a-ith*

thick, *ith-e-k* **theme,** *ith-e-m* **teeth,** *t-e-ith*

Under Th

though, *ith-o* **both,** *b-o-ith* **cloth,** *k-l-o-ith*

throw, *ith-r-o* **health,** *h-e-l-ith* **clothes,** *k-l-o-ith-s*

three, *ith-r-e* **earth,** *e-r-ith* **thorough,** *ith-e-r-o*

27. Brief Forms. Here is another group of brief forms for very frequently used business words. Learn them well.

is, his **can** **of**

the **you, your** **with**

that **Mrs.** **but**

Reading Practice

Your progress has been so rapid that you can already read business letters written entirely in shorthand.

28. Brief-Form Letter. This letter contains one or more illustrations of all the brief forms you studied in this lesson.

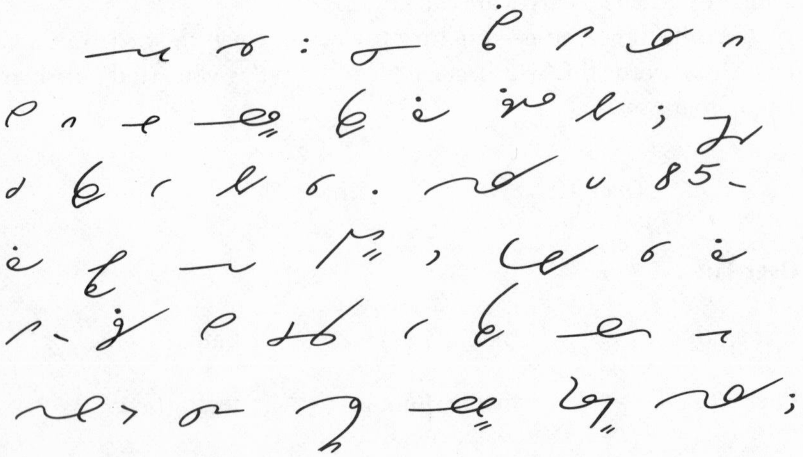

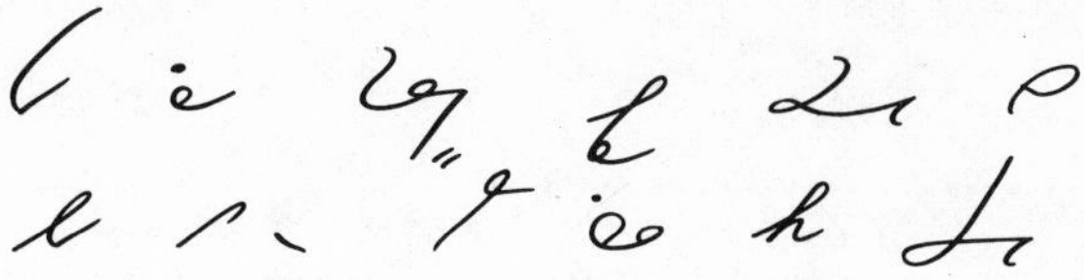
(59)

29.
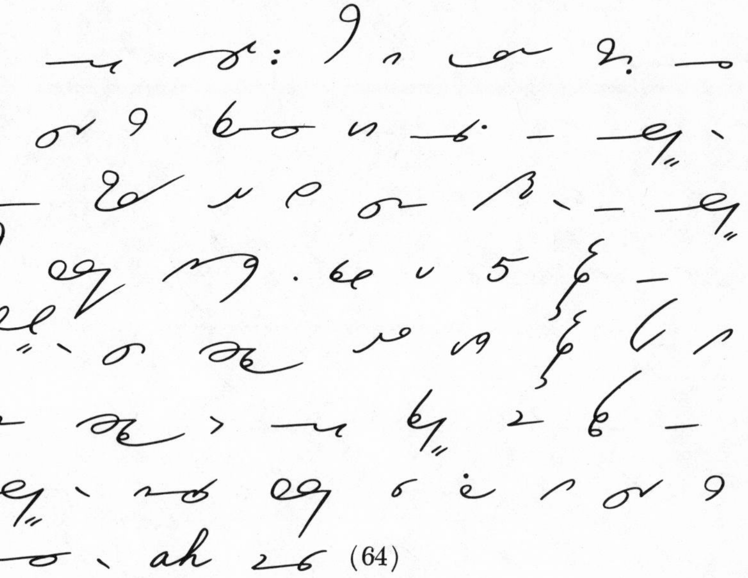
(64)

30.
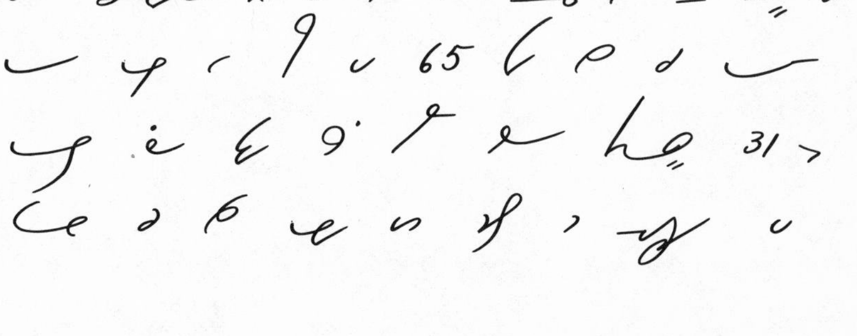

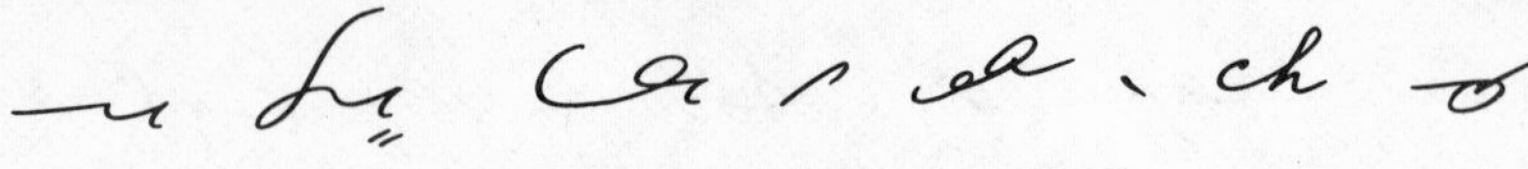
(58)

31.
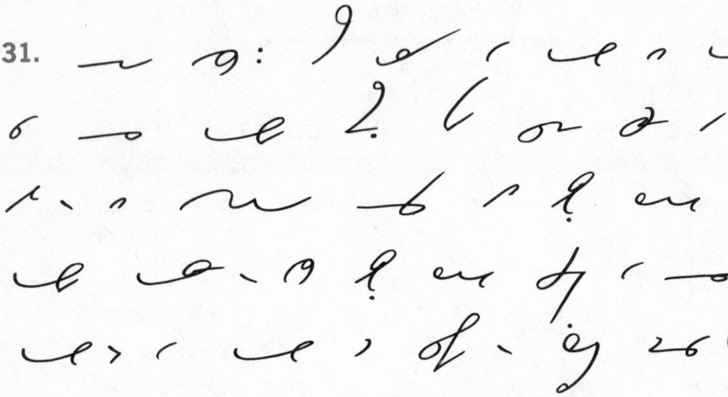
(40)

32.
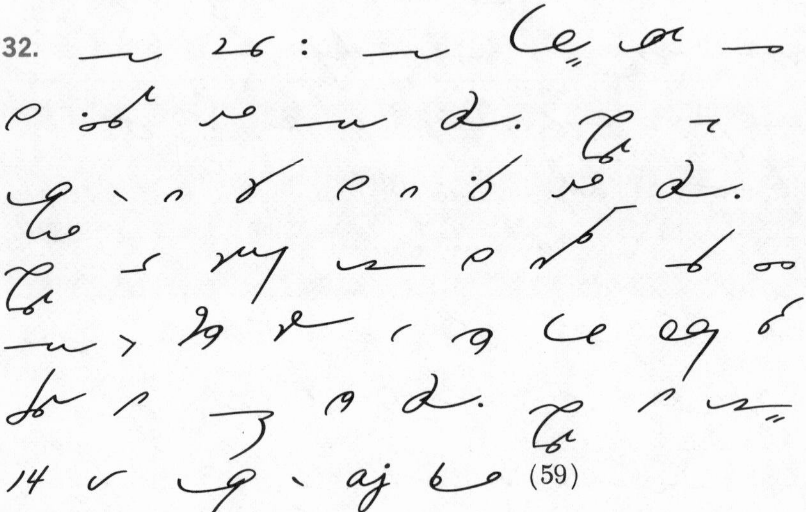
(59)

Lesson 6 RECALL

Lesson 6 contains no new strokes for you to learn. In this lesson you will find a simple explanation of the principles that govern the joining of the strokes you studied in Lessons 1 through 5, as well as a helpful Recall Chart and a Reading Practice based on the shorthand devices of Lessons 1 through 5.

Principles of Joining

33. Circles are written inside curves and outside angles.

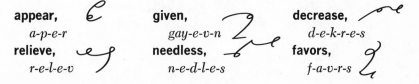

appear, *a-p-e-r* 
given, *gay-e-v-n* 
decrease, *d-e-k-r-e-s* 
relieve, *r-e-l-e-v* 
needless, *n-e-d-l-e-s* 
favors, *f-a-v-r-s* 

34. Circles are written clockwise on a straight line or between two straight strokes in the same direction.

each, *e-chay* 
aim, *a-m* 
may, *m-a* 
mean, *m-e-n* 
man, *m-a-n* 
dates, *d-a-t-s* 

35. Between two curves written in opposite directions, the circle is written on the back of the first curve.

gear, *gay-e-r* 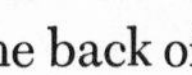
rack, *r-a-k*
paved, *p-a-v-d* 
carriage, *k-a-r-j* 
leak, *l-e-k* 
vapor, *v-a-p-r* 

36. The *o* hook is written on its side before *n, m* unless a downward character comes before the hook.

owns, *o-n-s*  **loan,** *l-o-n*  **homes,** *h-o-m-s* 

BUT

bone, *b-o-n*  **zone,** *s-o-n*  **shown,** *ish-o-n* 

37. The *oo* hook is written on its side after *n, m.*

noon, *n-oo-n* **moon,** *m-oo-n*  **moved,** *m-oo-v-d* 

38. The over *th* is used in most words; but when *th* is joined to *o, r, l,* the under *th* is used.

these, *ith-e-s*  **both,** *b-o-ith*  **threads,** *ith-r-e-d-s* 

39. Recall Chart. The following chart, which reviews all the shorthand devices you studied in Lessons 1 through 5, is divided into three parts: (1) words that illustrate the principles, (2) brief forms, (3) phrases.

Spell out each word aloud, thus: *a-k-t, act.* You need not spell the brief forms and phrases.

The chart contains 84 words and phrases. Can you read the entire chart in 9 minutes or less? If you can, you are making good progress.

WORDS

1
2
3
4
5
6

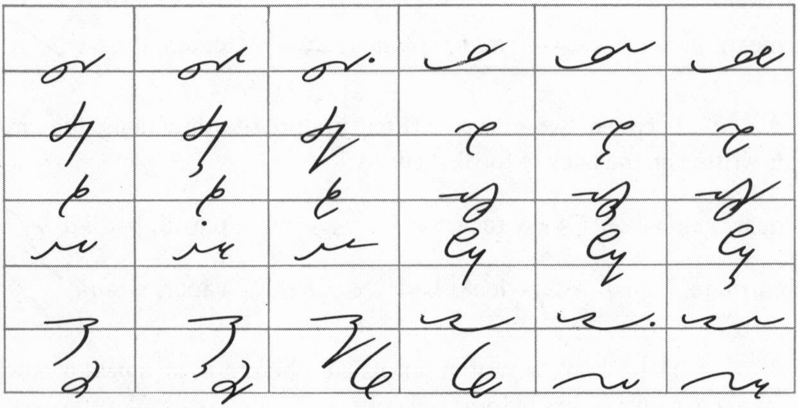

BRIEF FORMS

7
8
9

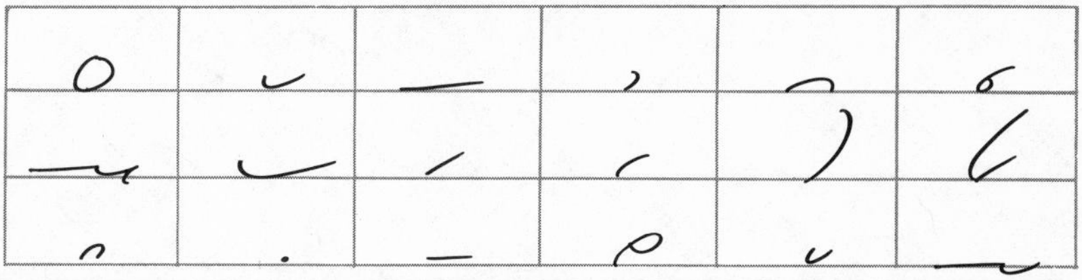

PHRASES

10
11
12
13
14

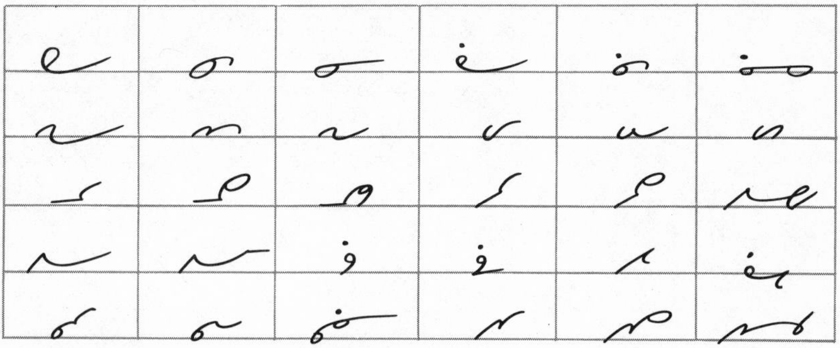

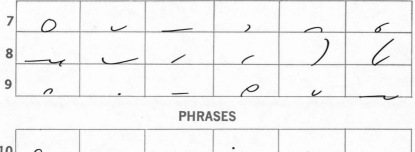

Reading Practice

40.

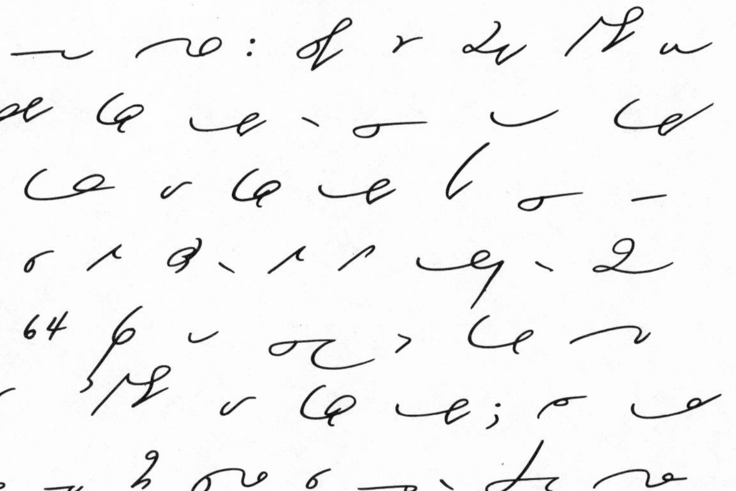

(52)

41.

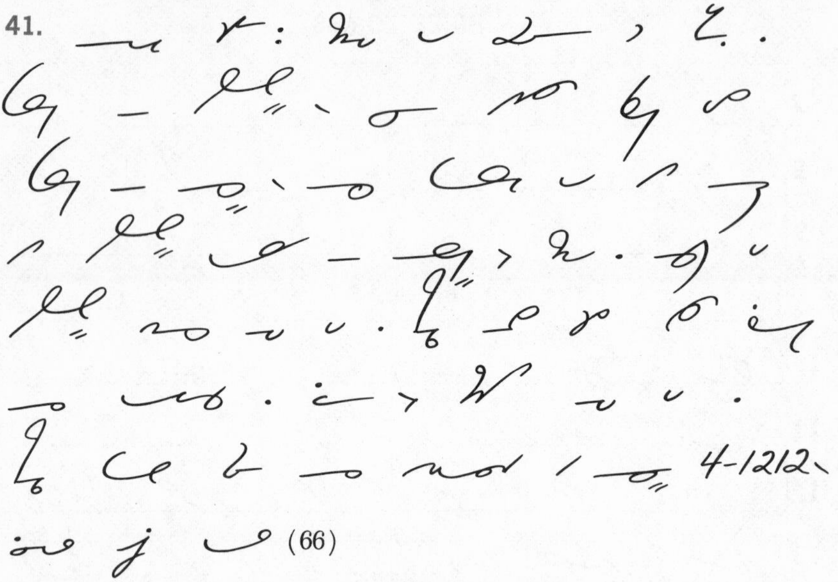

(66)

42.

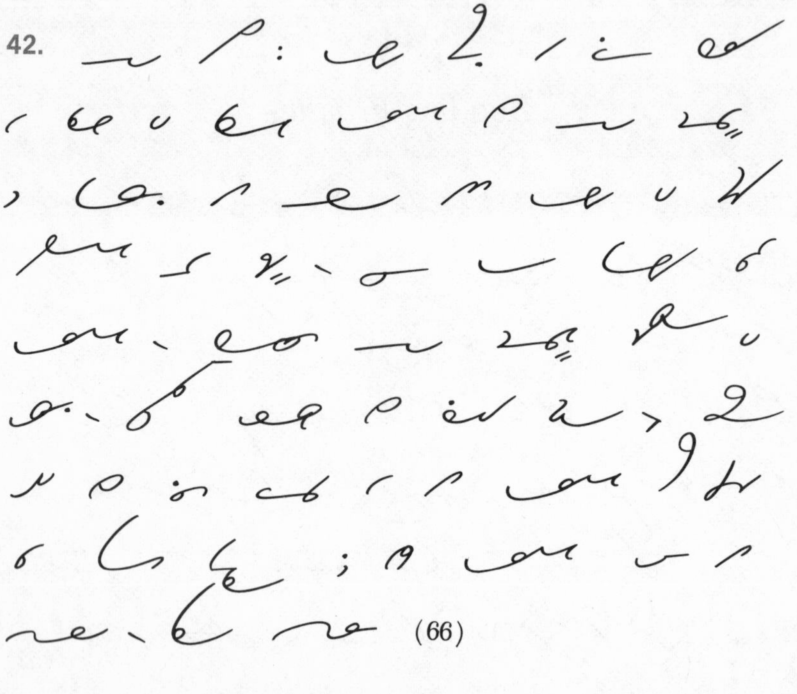

(66)

43.

(74)

44.

(61)

Shorthand in the Business Office

"Miss Phillips, please bring in your notebook. I want to dictate some letters . . ."

". . . and, John, be sure to send a copy of that report to Mr. Castle in Denver, and two copies to Ed Smith in Toledo—no, better send him three. By the way, when you send Smith's copies, include a list of our recent price changes. A copy of the report should go to Alison, too; I think he is in Miami this week. Be sure that everything goes airmail special. . . ."

"When Mrs. Cochran calls, tell her our group will meet her at the National Airport, South Terminal, at 3:30. Ask her to bring along the photographs and news releases on the Wilson project. Tell her she should plan to stay over in Wichita an extra day or two—Fred Toffi wants her to see the public relations people at Boeing. . . ."

Many times during the day secretaries and other office employees are given instructions or dictation by their bosses or supervisors, such as in the three examples cited above. Only if these employees can write shorthand rapidly can they be sure of getting the facts—all of them—down on paper. Studies show that almost half of our communicating time in the office is spent in listening to others, and much of what the business employee hears must be recorded word for word. Nearly all business employees have occasional need for a fast writing ability. For the stenographer or secretary, however, such a skill is a constant need. Shorthand is as important to her (or him) as the ability to type. Taking things down in shorthand is so much a part of her daily routine that when she is summoned by her boss—either directly, or by buzzer or telephone—she automatically picks up her notebook and pen.

Every year hundreds of thousands of people in all parts of the country learn shorthand. Most of them study shorthand because they want to become secretaries. Secretarial work is perhaps the most popular—and frequently the most important—career in the world for young women.

Chapter

2

More and more young men are learning shorthand, too. Some executives in such fields as transportation, engineering, and manufacturing hire men exclusively as secretaries or shorthand reporters. Frequently men who do not intend to become secretaries or reporters learn shorthand and find it a valuable skill in helping them to advance more rapidly in their chosen field. Thousands have found shorthand the open-sesame to administrative positions.

And speaking of business offices, the United States Government runs perhaps the largest "business office" in the world. The armed services alone need thousands of stenographers to record the many details of military activities. Many of these stenographers are civilians employed in the different branches of the armed forces. Other Government installations, in Washington and throughout the free world, employ hundreds of thousands of civilian office personnel and offer an almost unlimited choice of fields of work for the skilled shorthand writer.

Lesson 7

Principles

45. Ŏ, Aw. The small deep hook that represents *o,* as in *row,* also represents the sounds heard in *hot* and *drawing.*

Ŏ

hot		**job**		**sorry**	
top	 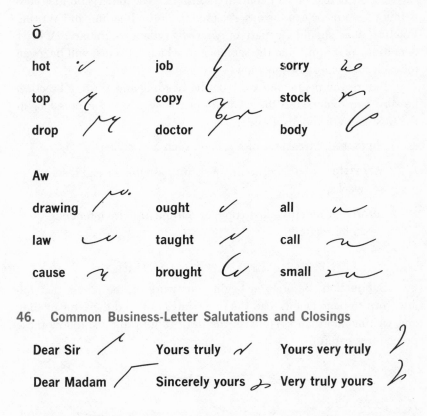	**copy**		**stock**	
drop		**doctor**		**body**	

Aw

drawing	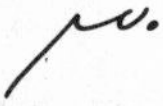	**ought**		**all**	
law		**taught**		**call**	
cause		**brought**	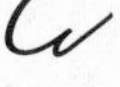	**small**	

46. Common Business-Letter Salutations and Closings

Dear Sir		**Yours truly**		**Yours very truly**	
Dear Madam		**Sincerely yours**		**Very truly yours**	

Note: While the expressions *Dear Sir, Dear Madam,* and *Yours truly* are considered too impersonal by experts in letter writing, they are still used by many businessmen. Therefore, special abbreviations are provided for them.

Building Transcription Skills

47. BUSINESS VOCABULARY BUILDER

Words are the stenographer's tools of her trade. The more words she knows and understands, the easier her task of taking dictation and transcribing will be.

To help you increase your knowledge and understanding of words, each lesson hereafter will contain a Business Vocabulary Builder consisting of words or expressions, selected from the Reading and Writing Practice, that should be part of your everyday vocabulary. A brief definition, as it applies in the sentence in which it occurs, will be given for each such word or expression.

Before you begin your work on the Reading and Writing Practice, be sure you understand the meaning of the words and expressions in the Business Vocabulary Builder.

bursar A treasurer of a school, such as a college.

semester A school term consisting, usually, of eighteen weeks.

draft A tentative first copy, or outline, usually intended to be revised.

Reading and Writing Practice

Suggestion: Before you begin your work on the letters that follow, turn to page 11 and read the procedures outlined there for reading and writing shorthand. To make the most rapid progress, follow those procedures carefully.

48.

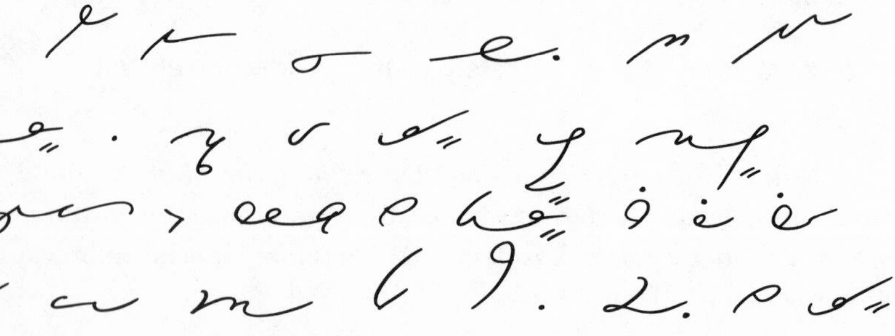

(71)

49.

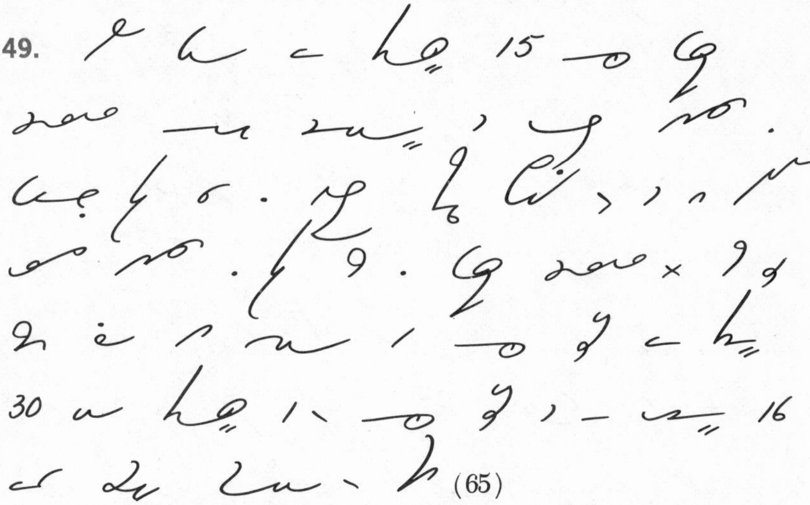

(65)

50.

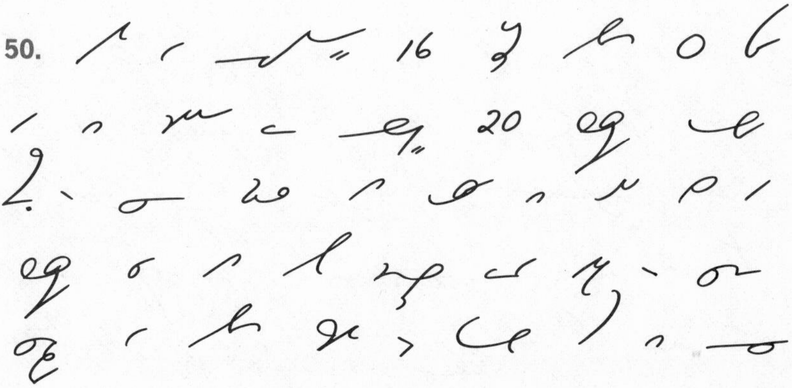

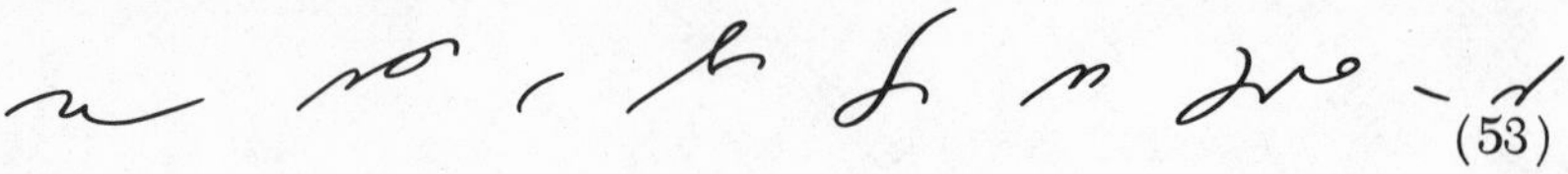

(53)

51.

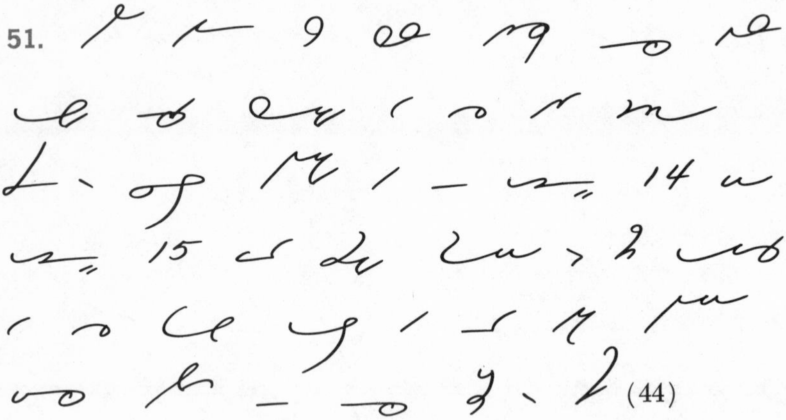

(44)

52.

(72)

Lesson 8

Principles

53. Brief Forms. Here is the third group of brief forms for frequently used words.

for		**be, by**		**their, there**	
shall		**put**		**this**	
which		**would**		**good**	

54. Word Ending -ly. The very common word ending *-ly* is expressed by the *e* circle.

briefly		**nearly**		**highly**	
only		**merely**		**totally**	
mostly	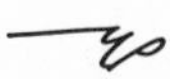	**properly**		**daily**	

Notice how the circle for *ly* in *daily* is added to the other side of the *d* after the *a* has been written.

55. Amounts and Quantities. In business you will frequently have to take dictation in which amounts and quantities are used. Here is a quick way to express them.

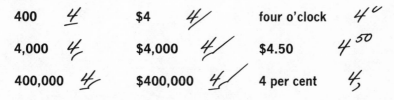

400		**$4**		**four o'clock**	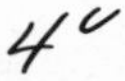
4,000		**$4,000**		**$4.50**	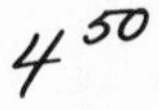
400,000		**$400,000**		**4 per cent**	

Notice that the *n* for *hundred* and the *th* for *thousand* are placed underneath the figure.

Building Transcription Skills

56. BUSINESS VOCABULARY BUILDER

earnestly Sincerely.

billing machines Machines used in the preparation of bills or invoices.

gross Twelve dozen (144).

minor *(adjective)* Of less importance. (Do not confuse with *miner*, which means "one who works in a mine.")

Reading and Writing Practice

57. Brief-Form Letter. This letter contains one or more illustrations of the brief forms in this lesson.

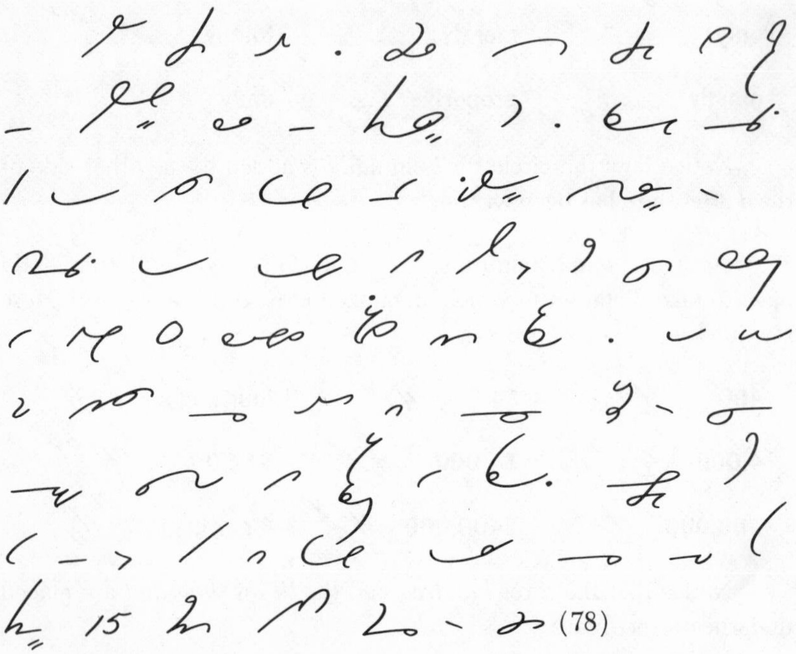

(78)

58.

(111)

59.

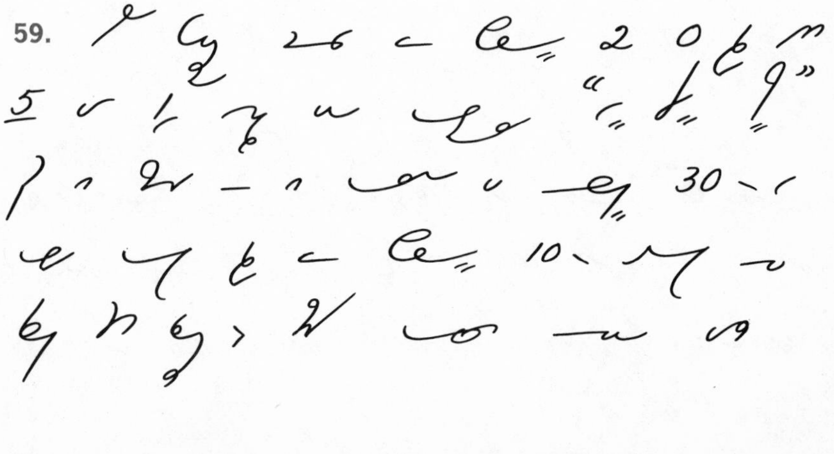

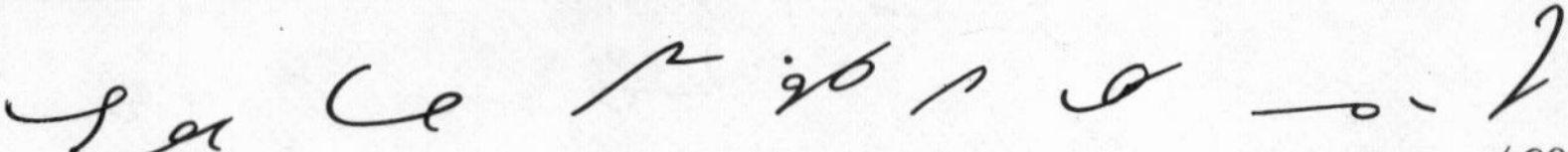

(60)

60. 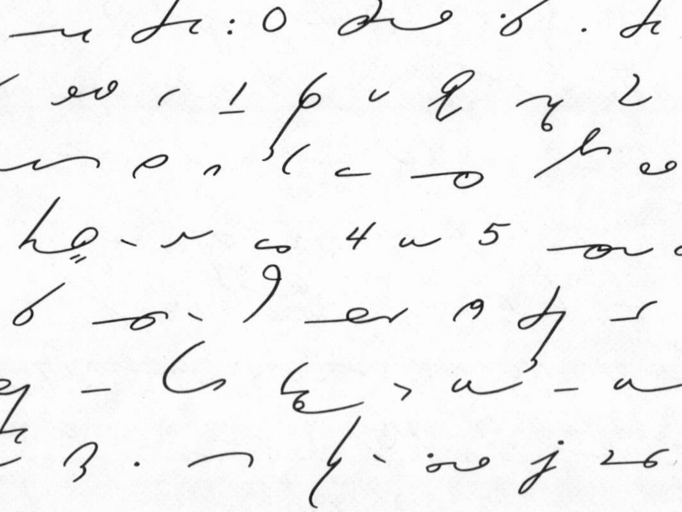

(60)

61. 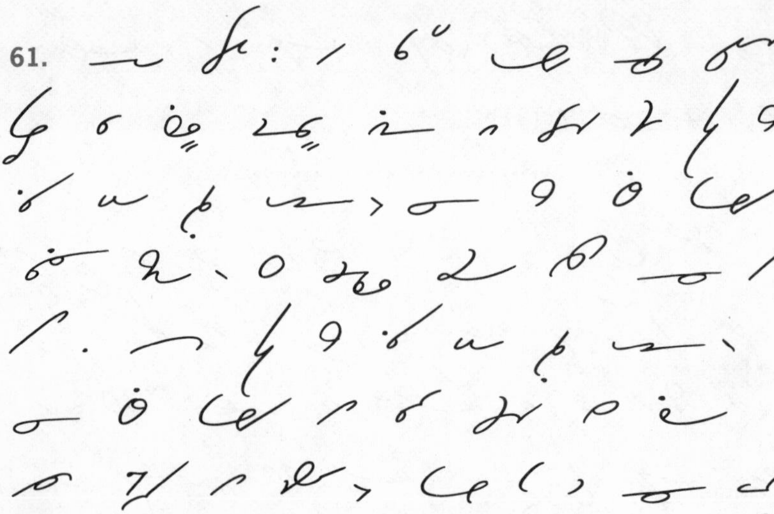

(71)

Lesson 9

Principles

62. Word Ending -tion. The word ending *-tion* (sometimes spelled *-sion, -cian,* or *-shion*) is represented by *sh.*

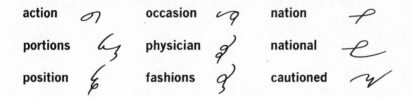

action		**occasion**		**nation**	
portions		**physician**		**national**	
position		**fashions**		**cautioned**	

63. Word Endings -cient, -ciency. The word ending *-cient* (or *-tient*) is represented by *sh-t; -ciency,* by *sh-s-e.*

patient		**efficient**		**efficiency**	

64. Word Ending -tial. The word ending *-tial* (or *-cial*) is represented by *sh.*

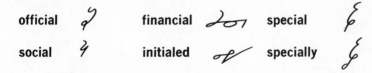

official		**financial**		**special**	
social		**initialed**		**specially**	

65. T for to in Phrases. In phrases, *to* is represented by *t* when it is followed by a downstroke.

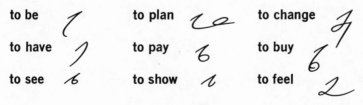

to be		**to plan**		**to change**	
to have		**to pay**		**to buy**	
to see		**to show**		**to feel**	

Building Transcription Skills

66. BUSINESS VOCABULARY BUILDER

ranch-type home A dwelling in which all the rooms are on one floor.

data Information; facts. (*Note:* The word *data* is the plural form of the word *datum.*)

financial position The worth of a company at a given time.

essential Necessary.

corporation A type of business organization that is owned by stockholders.

Reading and Writing Practice

67.

12
10
12
(82)

68.

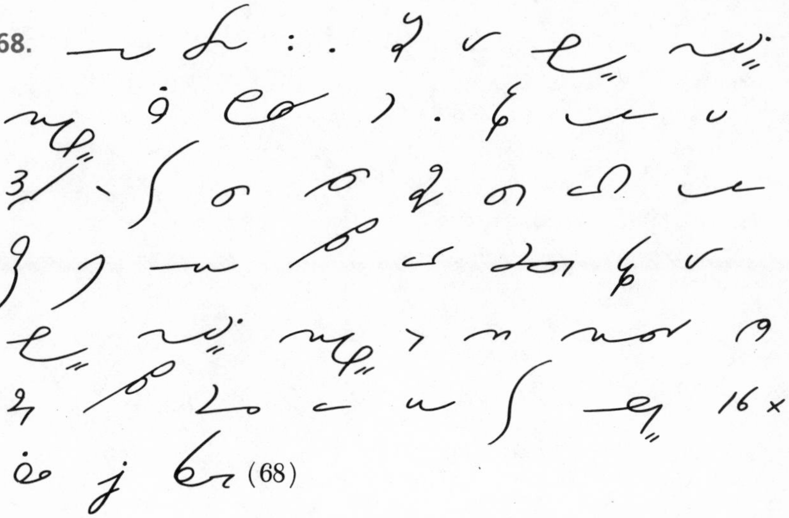

(68)

69.

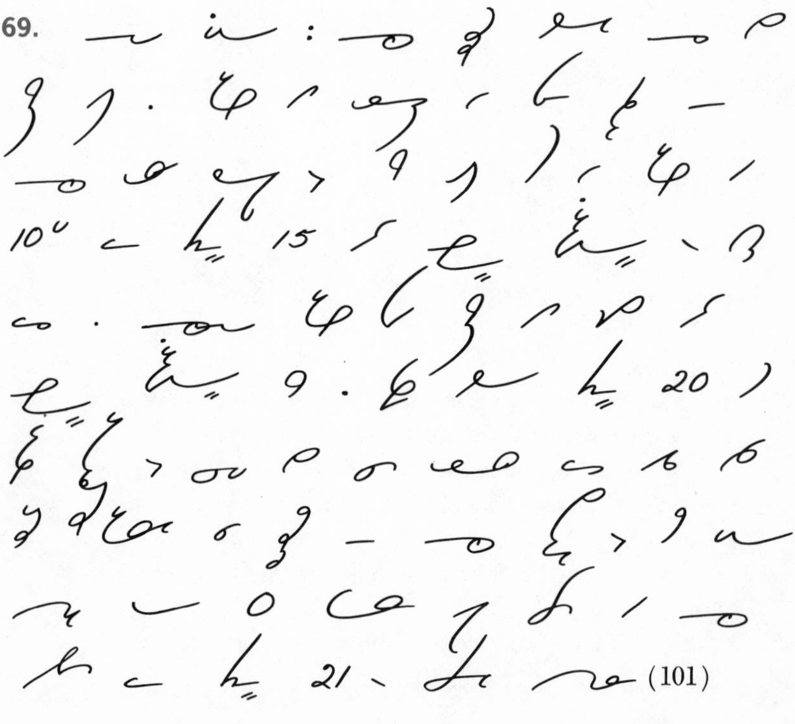

(101)

70. 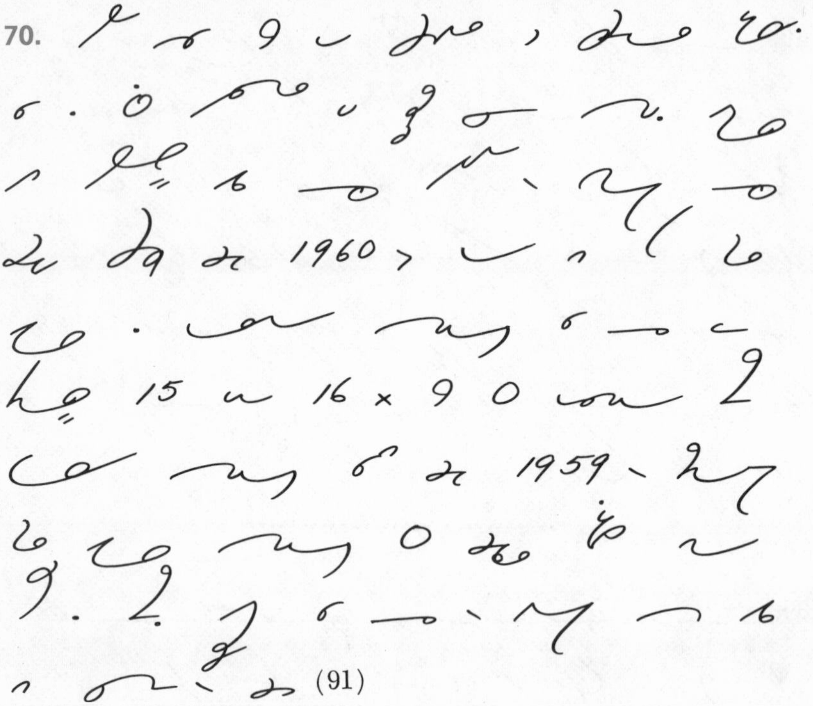 (91)

SHORTHAND READING CHECK LIST

When you read shorthand, do you –

1. Read aloud so that you know that you are concentrating on each outline that you read?

2. Spell each outline that you cannot immediately read?

3. Write the outline on a slip of paper or a card when the spelling does not give you the meaning?

4. On the following day ask your teacher or your classmates the meaning of any outlines that you could not read?

5. Reread each Reading and Writing Practice a second time?

6. Occasionally reread the suggestions for reading shorthand given on pages 10 and 11?

Lesson 10

Principles

71. Nd. The shorthand strokes for *n-d* are joined without an angle to form the *nd* blend, as in *lined.*

Nd 

Compare: **line**  **lined** 

trained 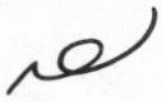 **signed**  **mind** 

strained 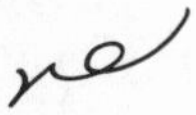 **friendly**  **find** 

planned  **kind**  **spend** 

72. Nt. The stroke for *nd* also represents *nt,* as in *sent.*

sent  **renting**  **agent** 

events  **painted**  **into** 

prevent  **parent**  **entirely** 

73. Ses. The sound of *ses,* as in *senses,* is represented by joining the two forms of *s.* The similar sounds of *sis,* as in *sister,* and *sus,* as in *versus,* are represented in the same way.

Compare: **sense**  **senses** 

face  **faces** 

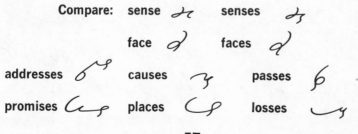

addresses  **causes**  **passes** 

promises 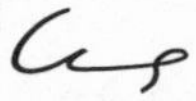 **places**  **losses** 

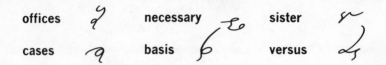

offices	**necessary**	**sister**
cases	**basis**	**versus**

Building Transcription Skills

74. BUSINESS VOCABULARY BUILDER

initial First.

premises A piece of land or real estate.

current Belonging to the present time.

Reading and Writing Practice

75.

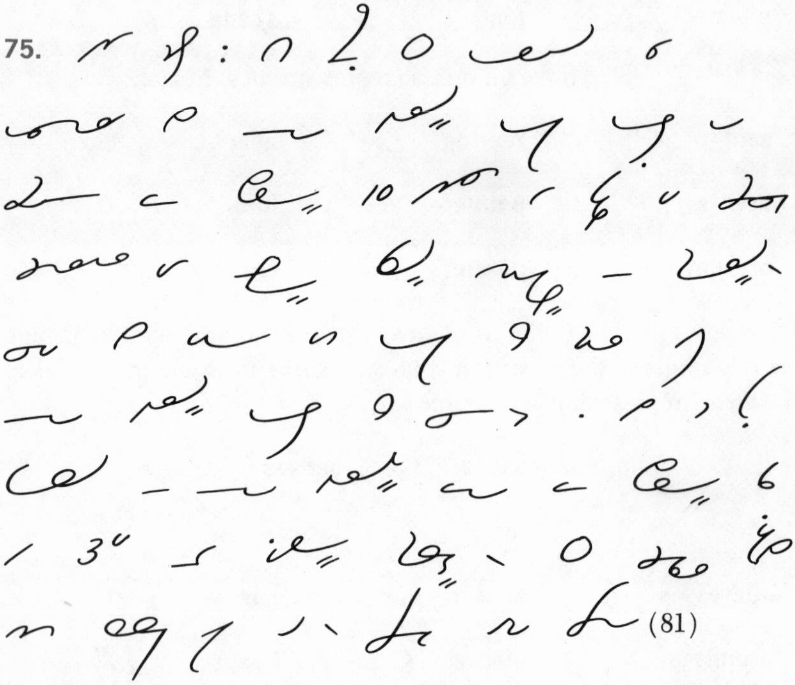

(81)

76.

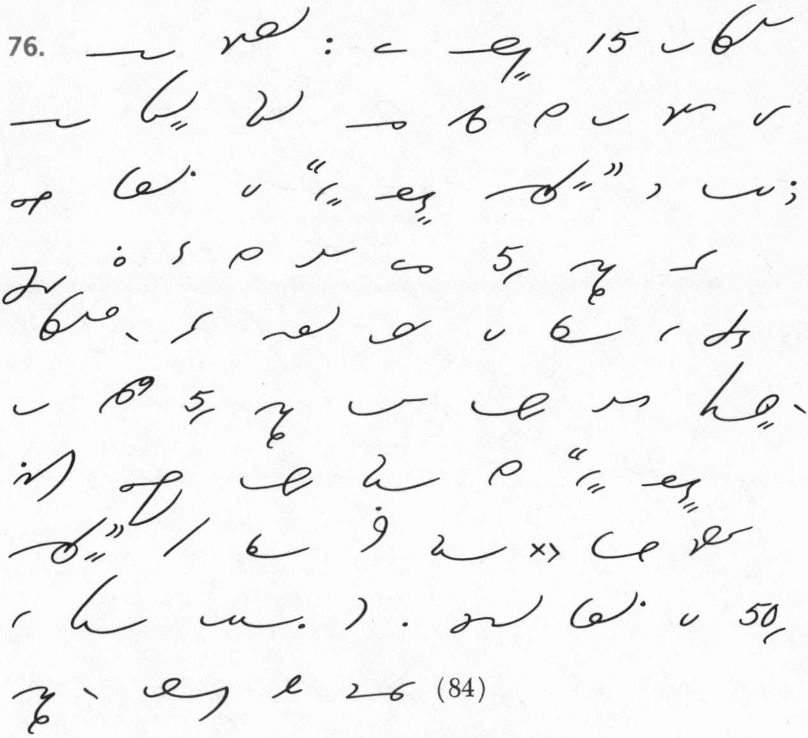

(84)

77.

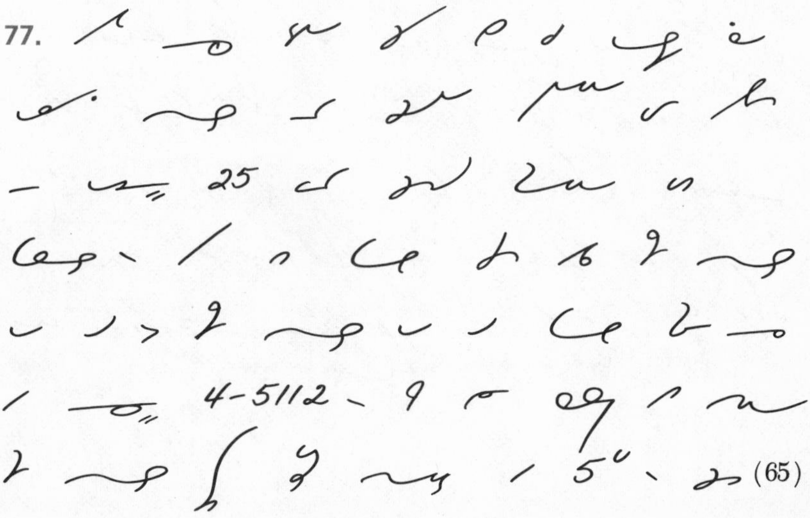

(65)

78. 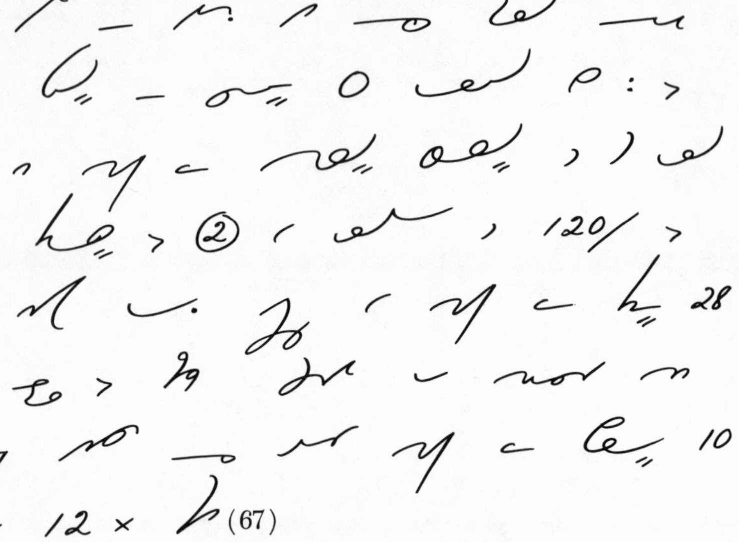
120/
28
10
12
(67)

79. 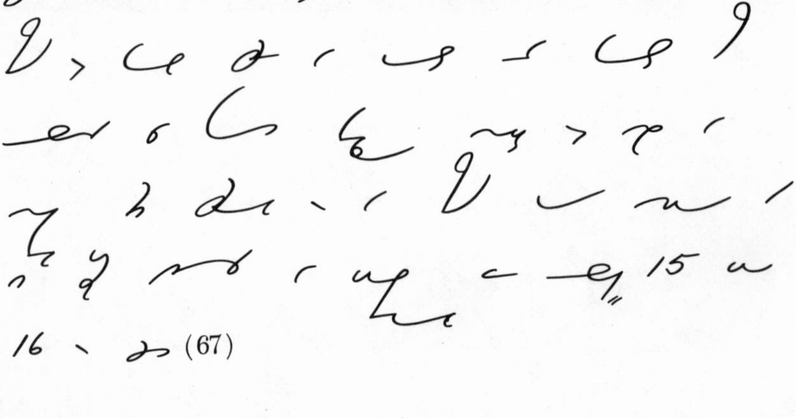
15
16
(67)

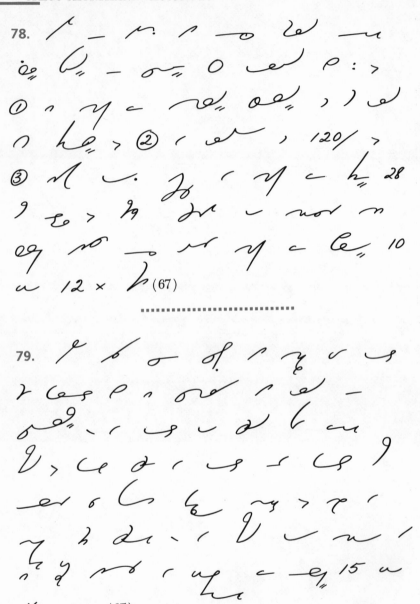

Lesson 11

Principles

80. Brief Forms

and		**was**		**should**	
them		**when**		**could**	
they		**from**		**send**	

81. Rd. The combination *rd* is represented by writing *r* with an upward turn at the finish.

Compare: **fear**  **feared** 

stored	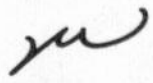	**appeared**		**heard**	
tired		**guarded**		**toward**	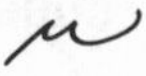
hired		**record**		**harder**	

82. Ld. The combination *ld* is represented by writing the *l* with an upward turn at the finish.

Compare: **nail**  **nailed** 

failed		**mailed**		**billed**	
old		**child**		**held**	
settled		**folded**		**told**	

83. Been in Phrases. The word *been* is represented by *b* after *have, has, had.*

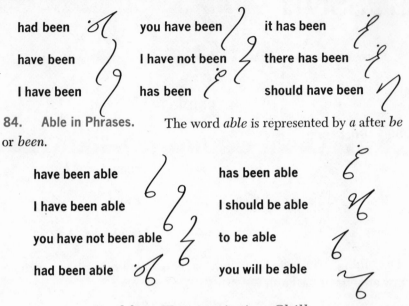

had been	**you have been**	**it has been**
have been	**I have not been**	**there has been**
I have been	**has been**	**should have been**

84. Able in Phrases. The word *able* is represented by *a* after *be* or *been.*

have been able	**has been able**
I have been able	**I should be able**
you have not been able	**to be able**
had been able	**you will be able**

Building Transcription Skills

85. BUSINESS VOCABULARY BUILDER

entitled Having rightful claim to.

record keeping The keeping of records in an office – usually bookkeeping and accounting.

air-travel card A card that enables a traveler to purchase a plane ticket on credit.

Reading and Writing Practice

86. Brief-Form Letter. The following letter contains at least one illustration of every brief form in paragraph 80.

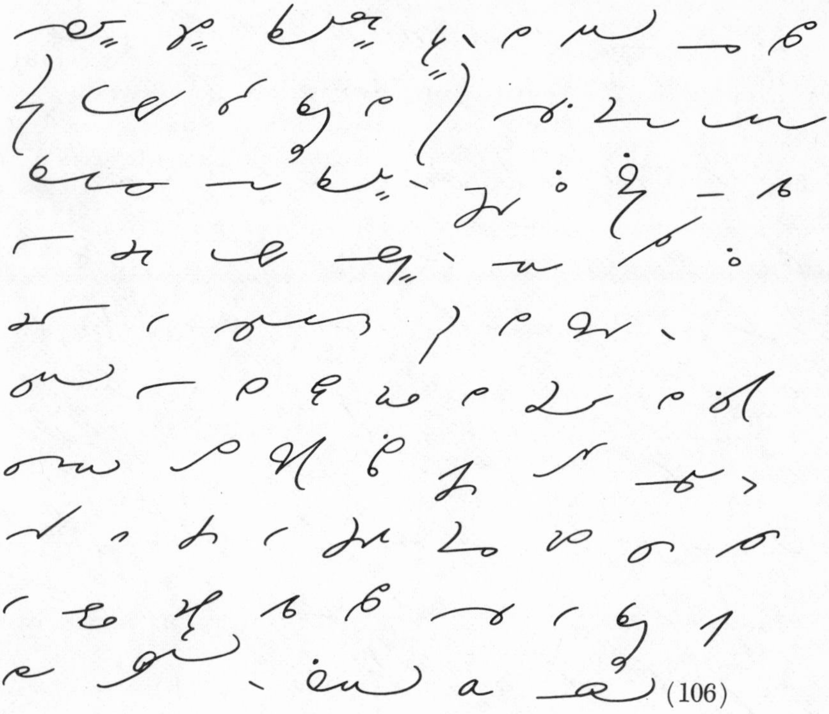

(106)

87.

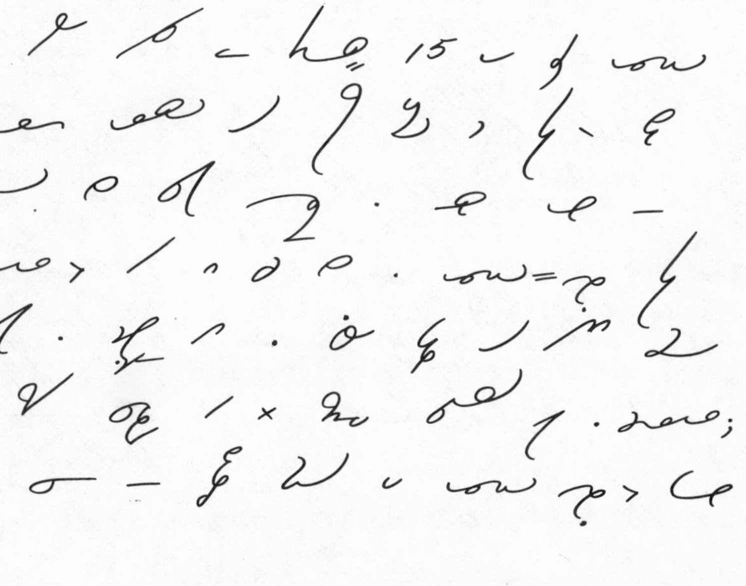

(79)

88.

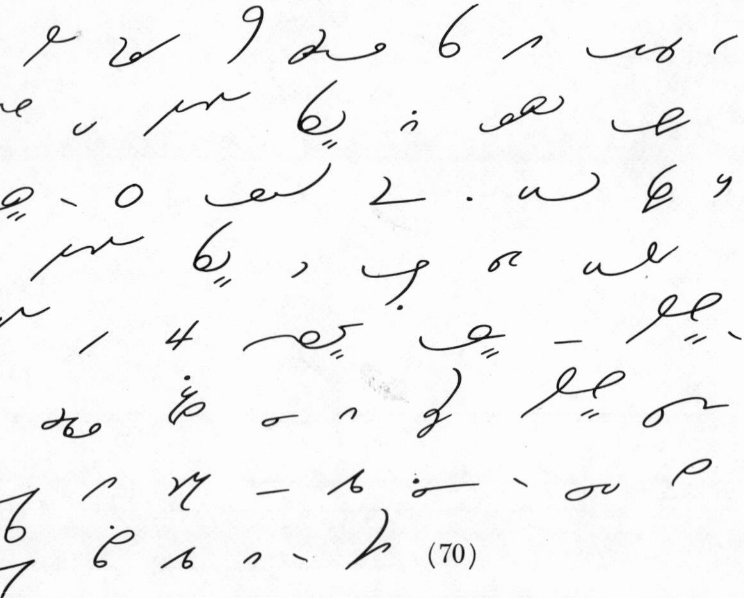

(70)

89.

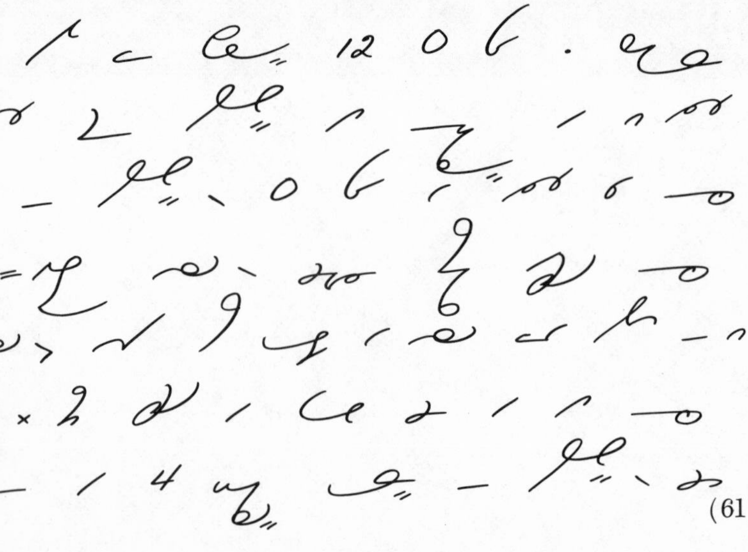

(61)

Lesson 12 RECALL

Lesson 12 is a "breather" for you; it presents no new shorthand devices for you to learn. It contains a number of principles of joining, a helpful Recall Chart, and several short letters that you should have no difficulty reading.

Principles of Joining

90. At the beginning and end of words, the comma *s* is used before and after *f, v, k, g;* the left *s,* before and after *p, b, r, l.*

safes		**globes**		**sales**	
sips		**skate**		**rags**	

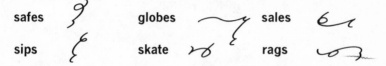

91. The comma *s* is used before *t, d, n, m, o;* the left *s* is used after those characters.

stones		**solos**		**needs**	

92. The comma *s* is used before and after *sh, ch, j.*

sashes		**reaches**		**stages**	

93. The comma *s* is used in words consisting of an *s* and a circle vowel or *s* and *th* and a circle vowel.

see		**these**		**seethe**	

94. Gregg Shorthand is equally legible whether it is written on ruled or on unruled paper; consequently, you need not worry about the exact placement of your outlines on the printed lines in your notebook. You will be able to read your outlines regardless of their placement on the printed line. The main purpose that the printed lines in your notebook serve is to keep you from wandering uphill and downhill as you write.

However, so that all outlines may be uniformly placed in the shorthand books from which you study, this general rule has been followed:

The base of the first consonant of a word is placed on the line of writing. When *s* comes before a downstroke, however, the downstroke is placed on the line of writing.

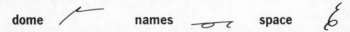

dome  **names**  **space** 

95. Recall Chart. The following chart contains all the brief forms in Chapter 2 and one or more illustrations of all the shorthand devices you have studied in Chapters 1 and 2.

Can you read the entire chart in 9 minutes or less?

BRIEF FORMS

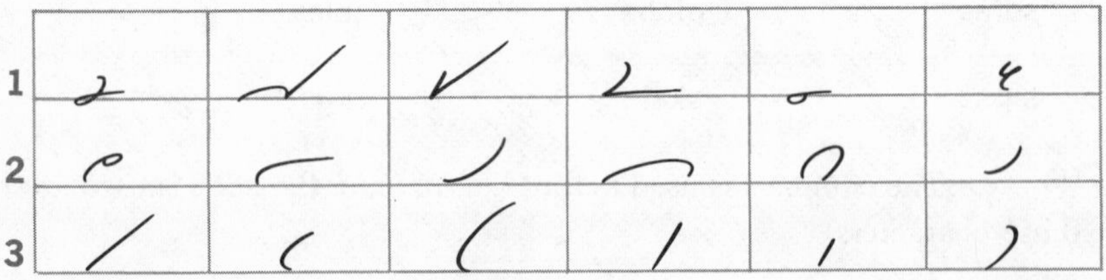

WORDS

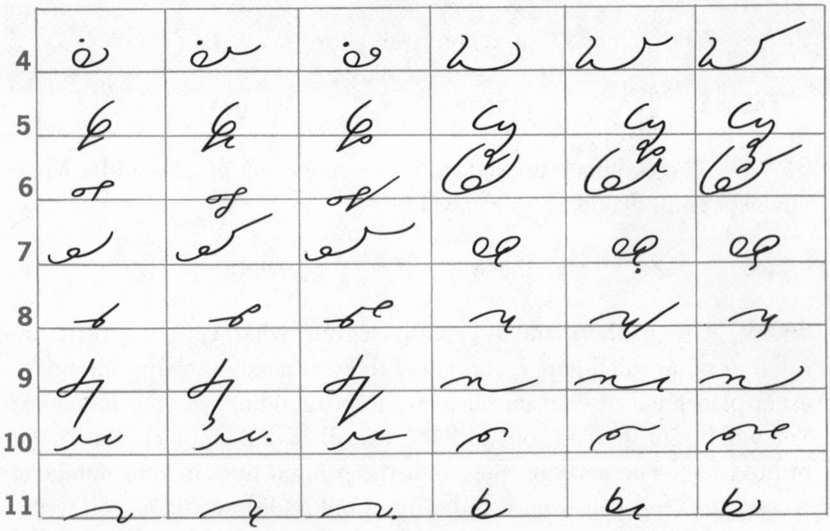

PHRASES AND AMOUNTS

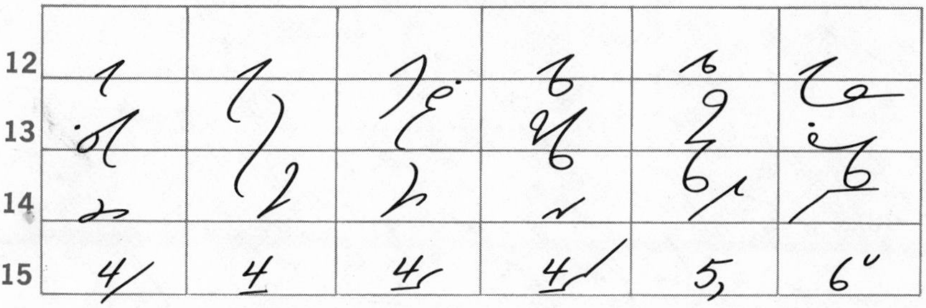

Building Transcription Skills

96. BUSINESS VOCABULARY BUILDER

parcel post A department of the post office that collects and delivers packages; a method of shipping merchandise.

pamphlet A small book, usually with a paper cover.

foreign operations A company's customers and branch offices overseas.

Reading and Writing Practice

97.

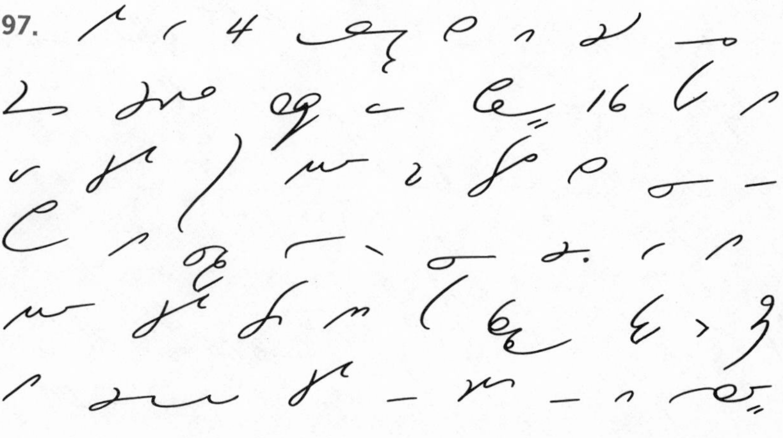

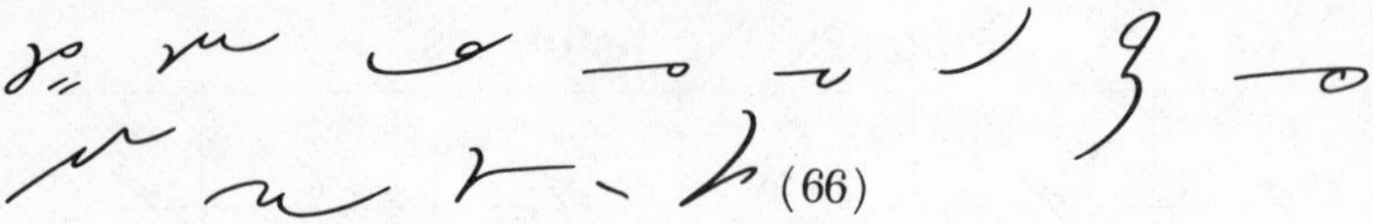

(66)

98.

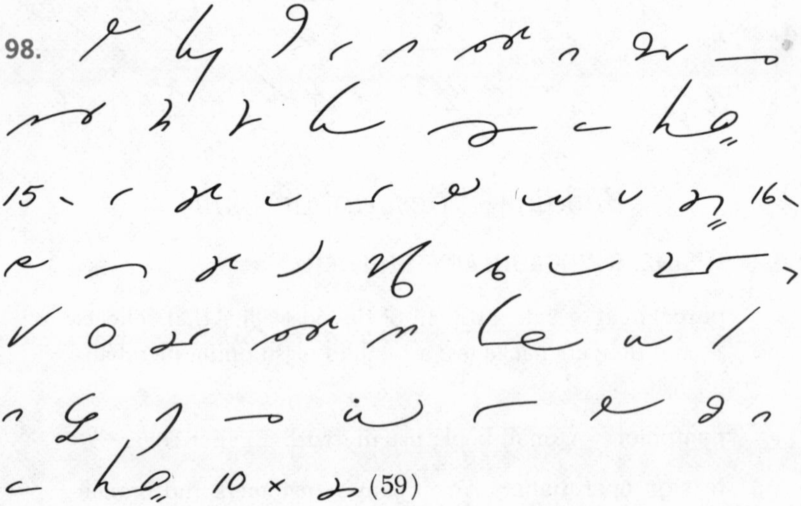

(59)

99.

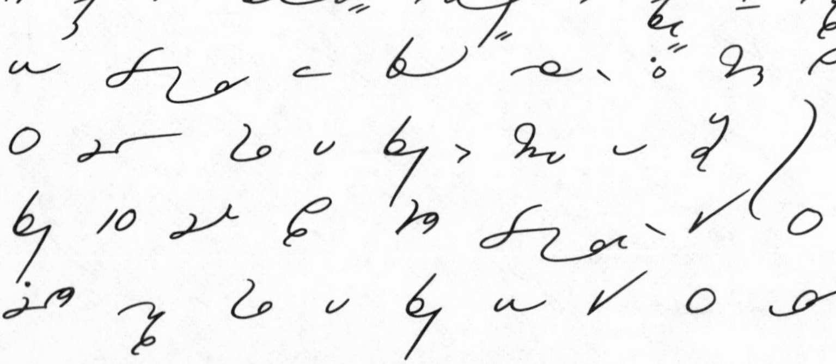

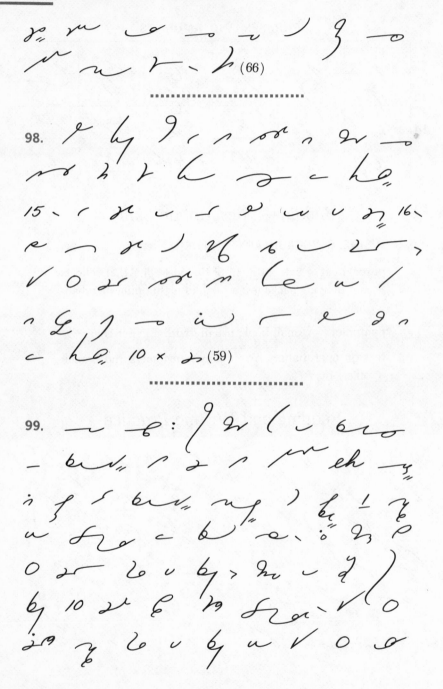

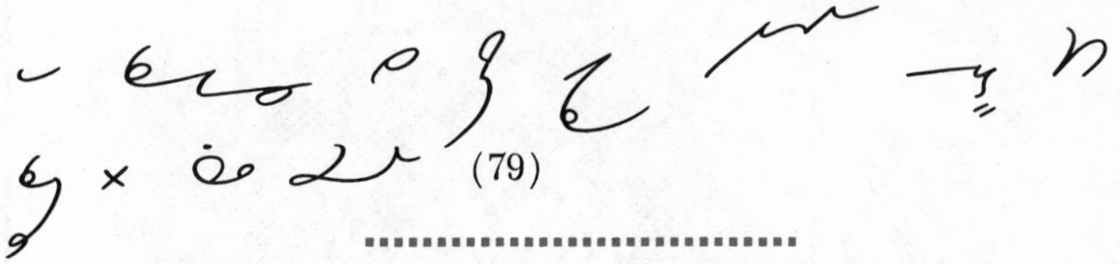

(79)

100.

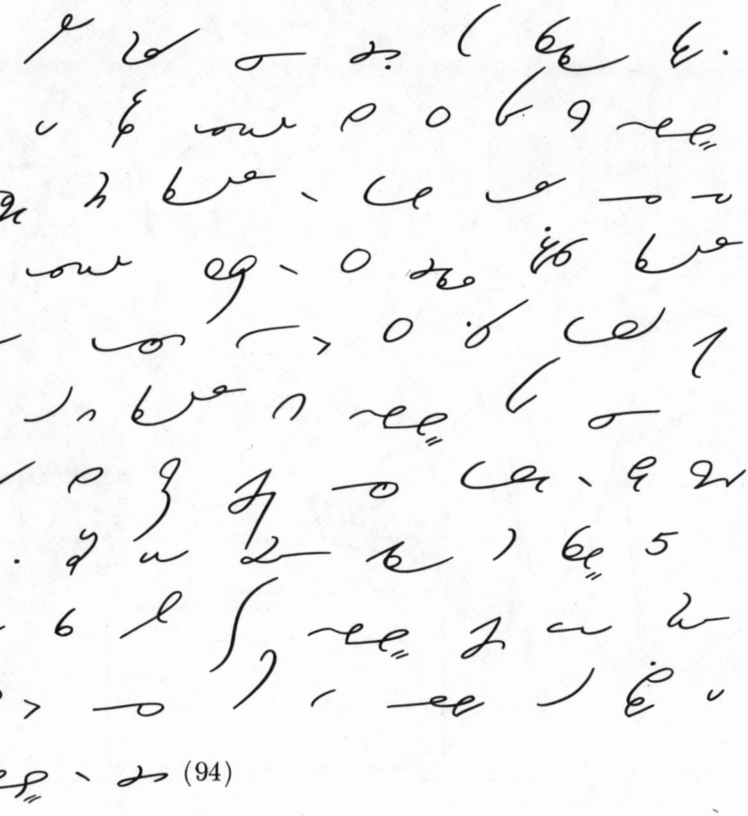

(94)

Why Be a Secretary?

Why do young people choose secretarial work as a career? If you were to ask ten different secretaries, you would be likely to get ten different answers! Their answers, though, could be "capsuled" into five primary reasons why secretaries like their jobs:

1. "The work is interesting." The secretary in a travel-agency office gave this reason. Would you find it exciting to work in an organization that makes and sells phonograph records? broadcasts radio and television programs? produces advertisements for radio, TV, magazines, and newspapers? operates an airline? These are only a few of the types of firms that need secretaries.

2. "A secretary often has dealings with important people." This was the reason given by a secretary to a lawyer. Secretaries do work for and with important people. These important people, and those with whom they come in contact, make the decisions that turn the wheels of industry, of business, of the professions, and of the arts. The secretary is brought into the "inner circle" of management where she can observe big things happening.

3. "An office is a pleasant place in which to work." Does this sound like a strange reason for choosing secretarial work? Not if you consider the fact that more of a secretary's waking hours are spent in the office than at home. The important people in an office rate the best accommodations. If the executive for whom the secretary works has a choice location, she is likely to have one, too.

4. "The salary is good." The secretary who gave this reason works in an engineering firm that manufactures electronic devices for rockets. In comparison with general office employees, the secretary receives excellent pay; often, the magic word "shorthand" makes the difference between a medium-paying job and a well-paying one!

5. "The work has variety." Most secretaries won't argue with the one who gave that reason. The secretary has dozens of opportunities for variety every day. The alert secretary will find all the variety she can possibly want—one day is never like another!

Chapter 3

Lesson 13

Principles

101. Brief Forms

glad		**very**		**soon**	
work		***thank**		**enclose**	
yesterday		**order**		**were, year**	

*In phrases, the dot is omitted from *thank*. *Thanks* is written with a disjoined left *s* in the dot position.

thank you		**thank you for**		**thanks**	

102. Ŭ, O͝O. The hook that expresses the sound of *oo,* as in *to,* also represents the sound of *ŭ,* as in *does,* and the sound of *o͝o,* as in *foot.*

Ŭ

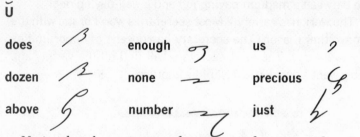

does		**enough**		**us**	
dozen		**none**		**precious**	
above		**number**	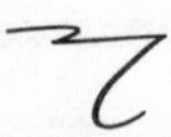	**just**	

Notice that the *oo* in *enough, none, number* is turned on its side; that *oo-s* join without an angle in *us, precious, just.*

O͝O

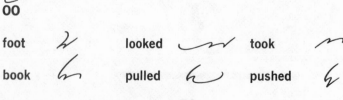

foot		**looked**		**took**	
book		**pulled**		**pushed**	

full		**stood**		**cooked**	

103. W, Sw. At the beginning of words, the sound of *w* is represented by the *oo* hook; *sw*, by *s-oo*.

we		**wash**		**sweet**	
way		**wanted**		**swim**	
wait		**wood**		**swell**	
week, weak		**wool**		**swear**	

Building Transcription Skills

104. BUSINESS VOCABULARY BUILDER

apparel Clothing; garments.

cruise A pleasure trip by boat.

booklet. A little book, usually bound in paper covers.

Reading and Writing Practice

105. Brief-Form Letter. In the following letter, all the brief forms presented in this lesson are used at least once.

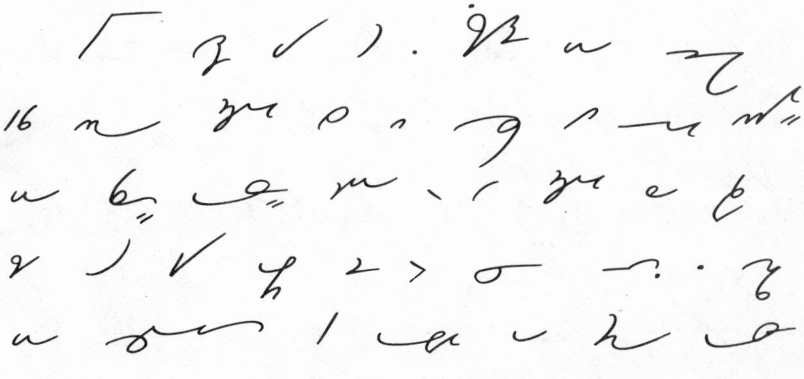

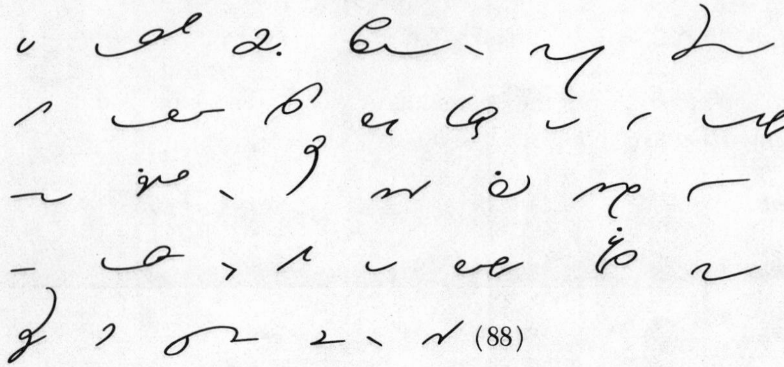

(88)

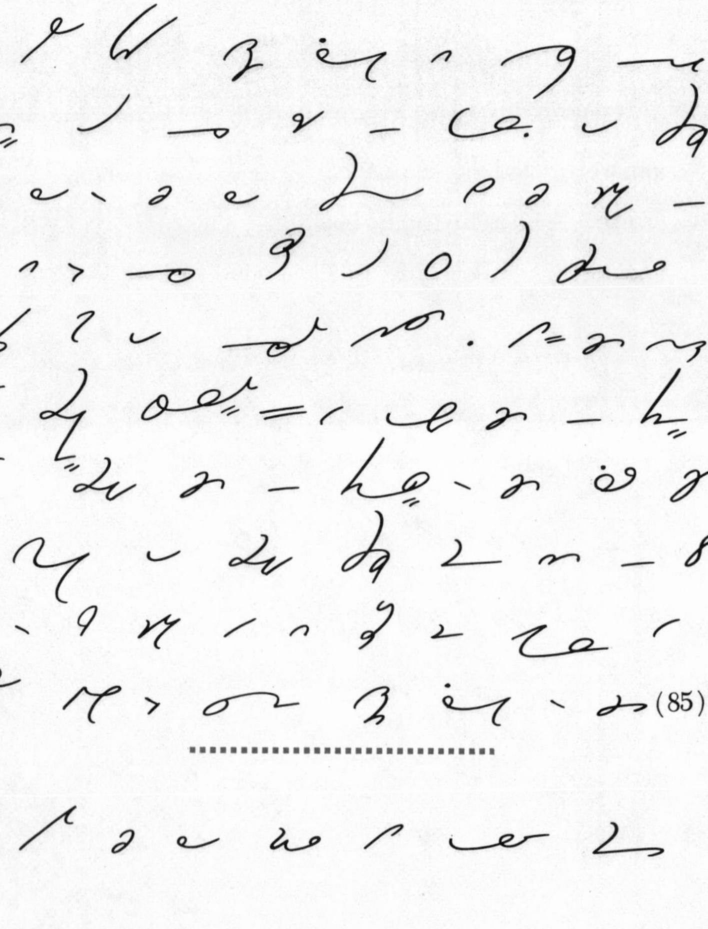

106.

(85)

107.

(95)

108. 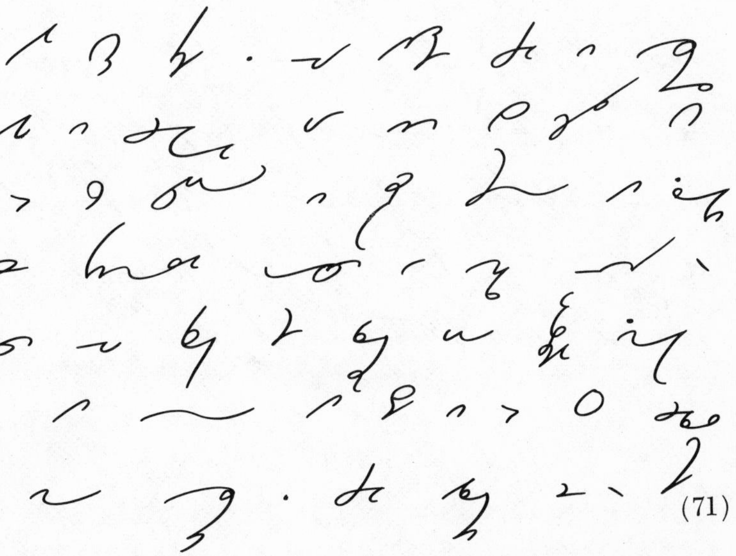

(71)

109.

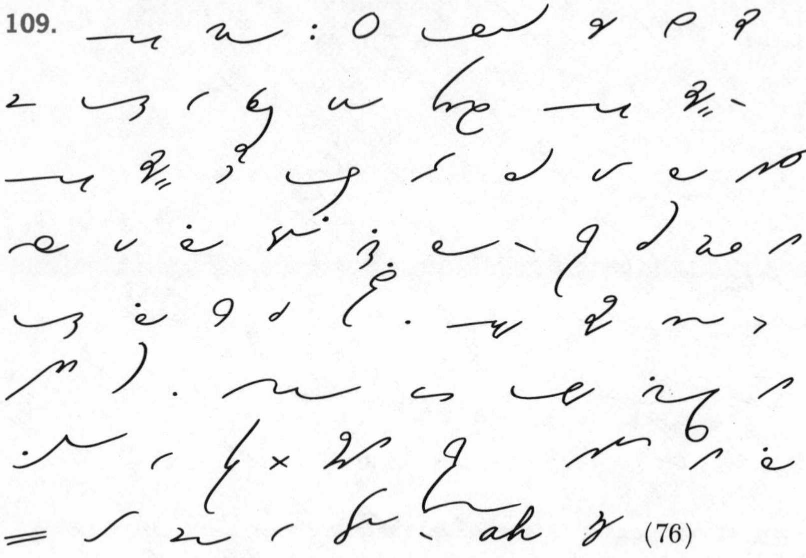

(76)

110.

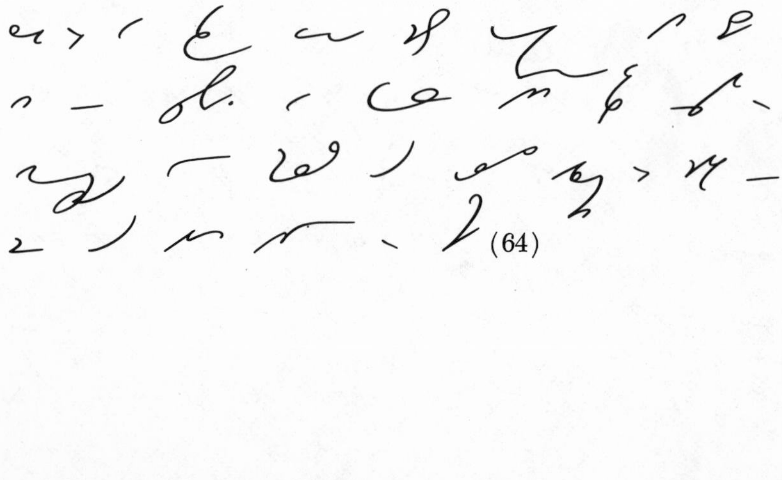

(64)

Lesson 14

Principles

111. Wh. *Wh,* as in *while,* is pronounced *hw* – the *h* is pronounced first. Therefore, in shorthand, we write the *h* first.

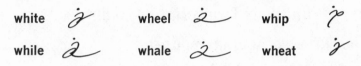

white	wheel	whip
while	whale	wheat

112. W in the Body of a Word. When the sound of *w* occurs in the body of a word, as in *quick,* it is represented by a short dash underneath the vowel following the *w* sound. The dash is inserted after the rest of the outline has been written.

quick	twice	always
quit	liquid	roadway
quite	equipped	Broadway

113. Ted. The combination *ted* is represented by joining *t* and *d* into one long upward stroke.

Ted

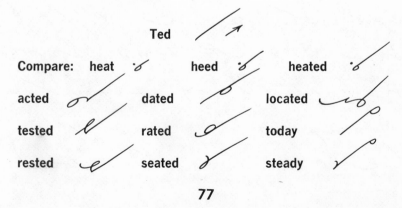

Compare: heat	heed	heated
acted	dated	located
tested	rated	today
rested	seated	steady

114. Ded, Det, Dit. The long upward stroke that represents *ted* also represents *ded, det, dit.*

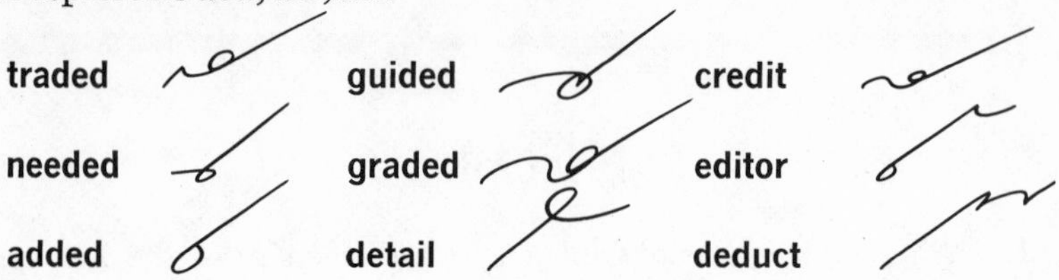
traded
guided
credit
needed
graded
editor
added
detail
deduct

Building Transcription Skills

115. BUSINESS VOCABULARY BUILDER

auditor A person who checks the accuracy of accounting and financial records.

queries Questions.

portion A part of a whole.

in vain Without any result; to no purpose.

Reading and Writing Practice

116.

4-5151

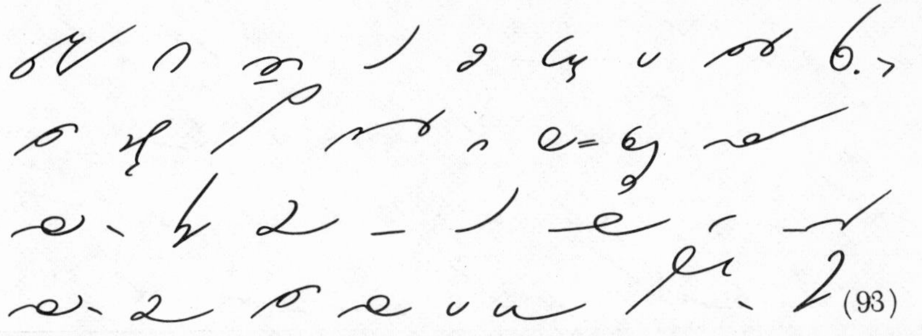
(93)

117.

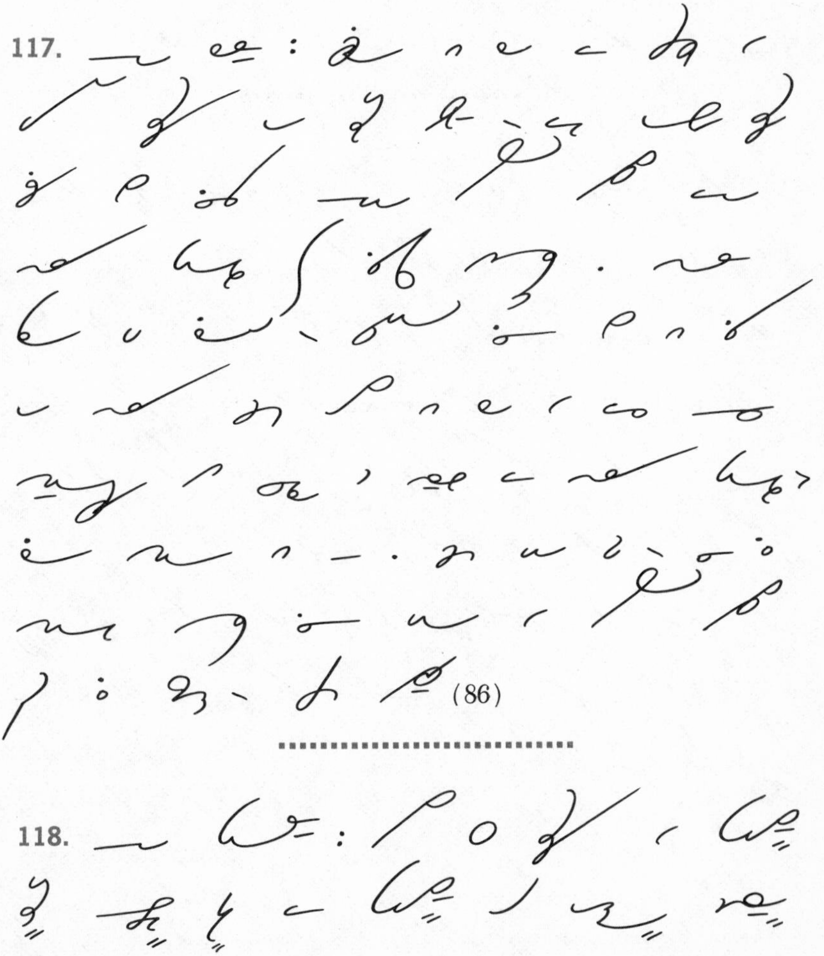
(86)

118.

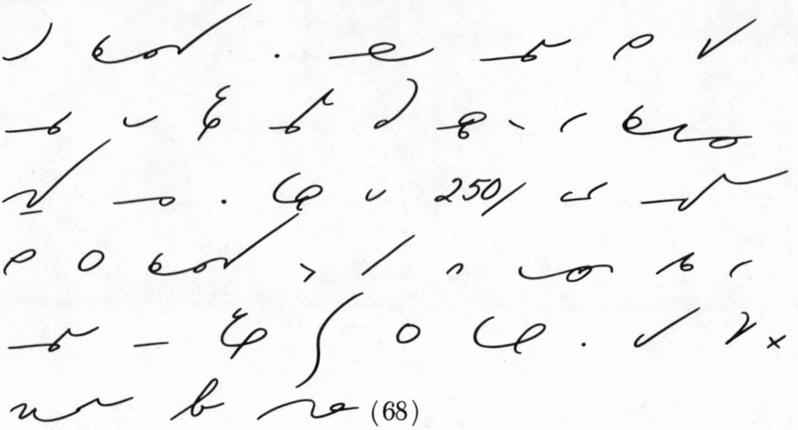

(68)

119.

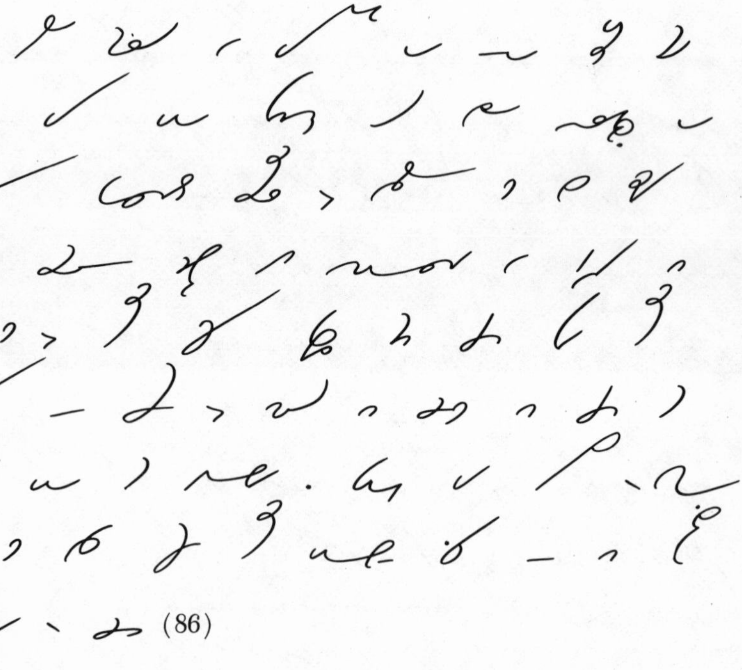

(86)

Lesson 15

Principles

120. Brief Forms

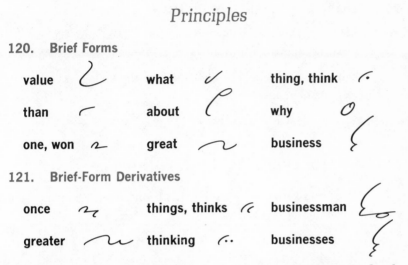

value	what	thing, think
than	about	why
one, won	great	business

121. Brief-Form Derivatives

once	things, thinks	businessman
greater	thinking	businesses

Notice that a disjoined left *s* is used to express *things, thinks;* that the plural of *business* is formed by adding another left *s*.

122. Word Ending -ble. The word ending *-ble* is represented by *b*.

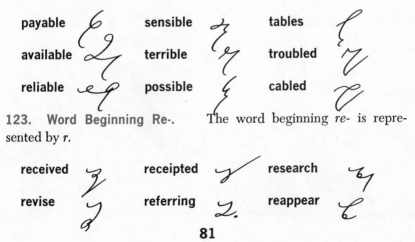

payable	sensible	tables
available	terrible	troubled
reliable	possible	cabled

123. Word Beginning Re-. The word beginning *re-* is represented by *r*.

received	receipted	research
revise	referring	reappear

repaired  **resisted**  **reopen** 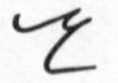

Building Transcription Skills

124. BUSINESS VOCABULARY BUILDER

asset Anything of value owned by a company, e.g., cash, equipment, furniture, etc.

receipt A written acknowledgment of the taking or receiving of goods or money.

severely Harshly, gravely.

Reading and Writing Practice

125. Brief-Form Letter. All the brief forms in this lesson are used at least once in this letter.

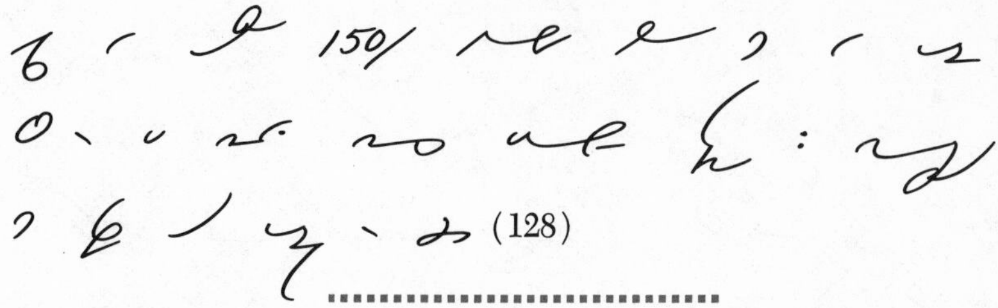

(128)

126.

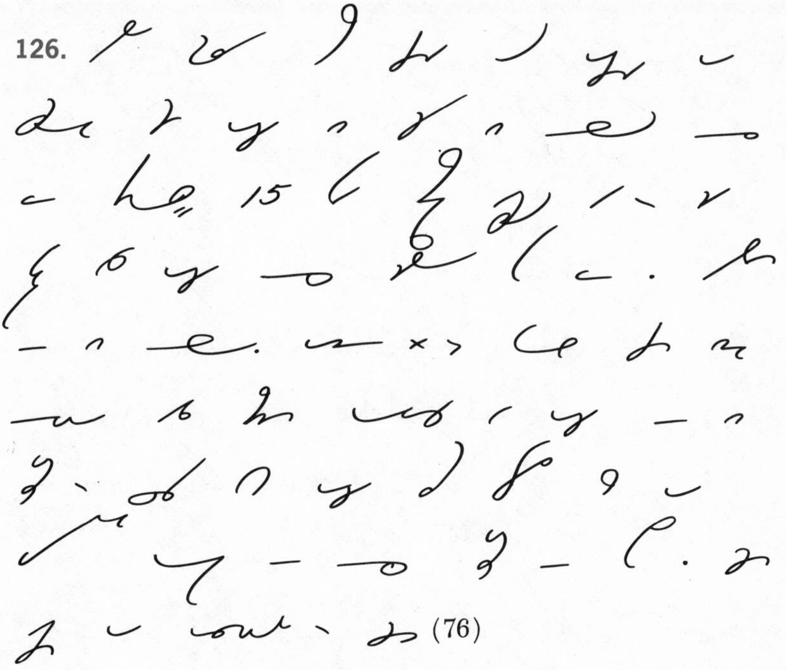

(76)

127.

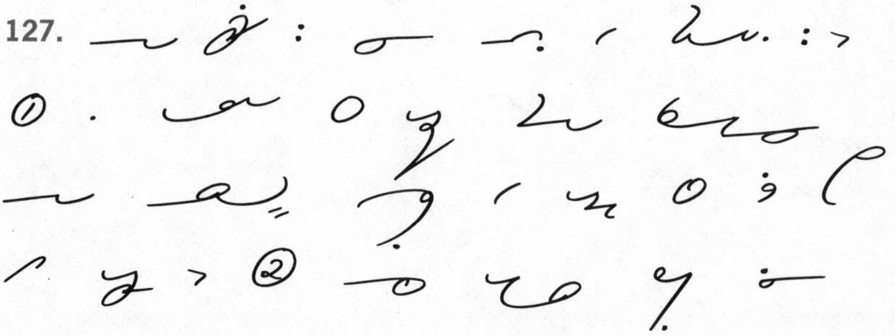

(110)

128. Chuckle

(44)

Lesson 16

Principles

129. Oi. The sound of *oi,* as in *toy,* is represented by .

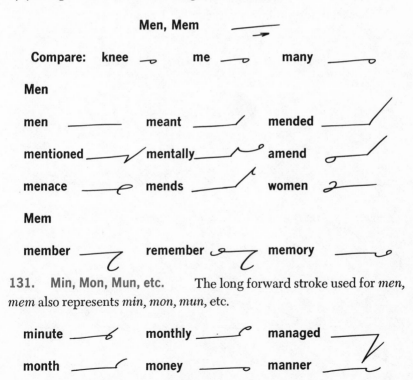

toy	**joy**	**noise**
oil	**join**	**appoint**
annoy	**voice**	**choice**

130. Men, Mem. The combinations *men, mem* are represented by joining *m* and *n* into one long forward stroke.

Men, Mem

Compare: **knee** **me** **many**

Men

men	**meant**	**mended**
mentioned	**mentally**	**amend**
menace	**mends**	**women**

Mem

member	**remember**	**memory**

131. Min, Mon, Mun, etc. The long forward stroke used for *men, mem* also represents *min, mon, mun,* etc.

minute	**monthly**	**managed**
month	**money**	**manner**

132. Word Beginning Be-. The word beginning *be* is represented by *b*.

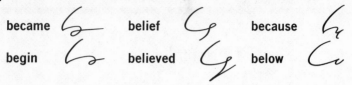

became		**belief**		**because**	
begin		**believed**		**below**	

Building Transcription Skills

133. BUSINESS VOCABULARY BUILDER

credit manager A person who is in charge of a credit department in a company or store.

treasurer An official in charge of the funds of a company or organization.

succeeding Filling a vacancy left by someone.

Reading and Writing Practice

134.

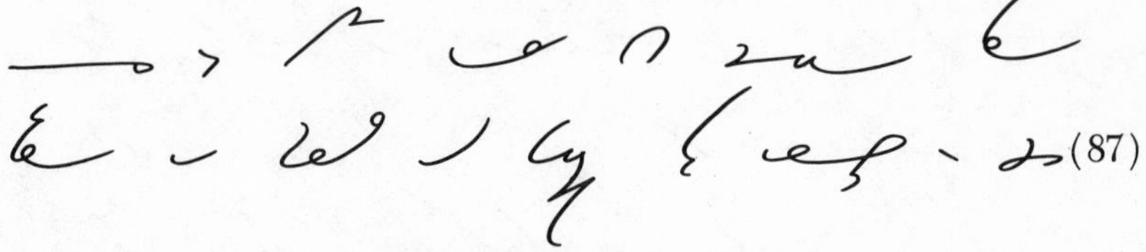

(87)

135.

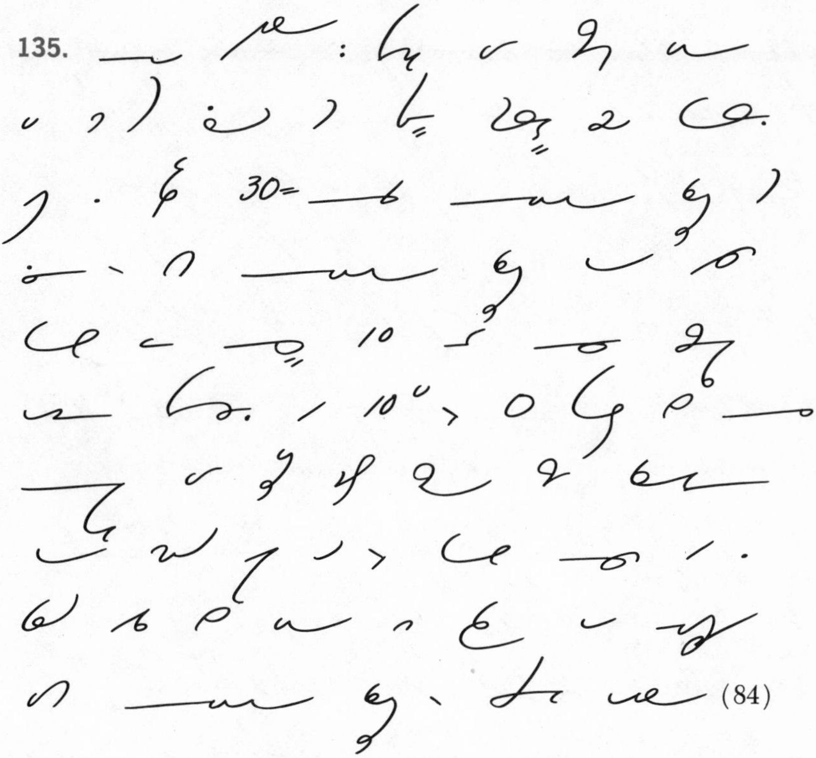

(84)

136.

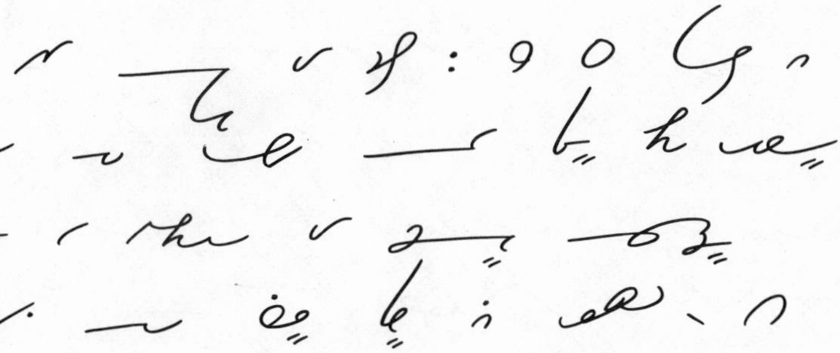

(111)

137.

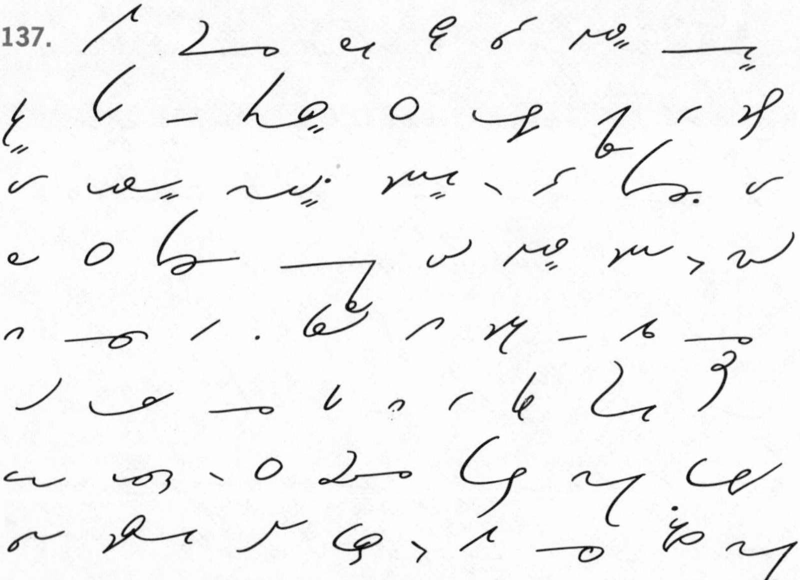

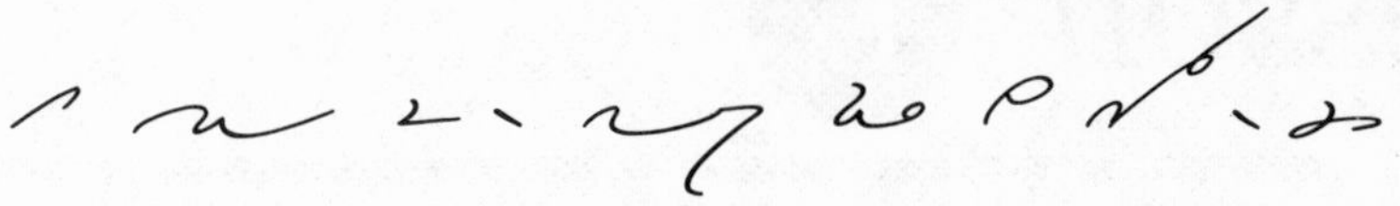 (84)

138. 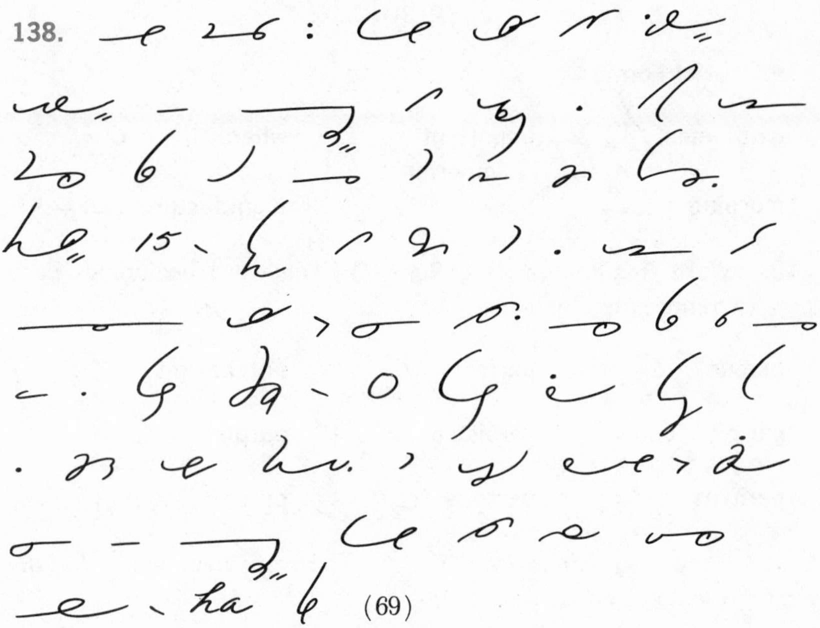 (69)

UP AND DOWN CHECK LIST

Do you always write the following strokes *upward?*

1. And  their-there 
2. It-at  would 

Do you always write the following strokes *downward?*

1. Is-his 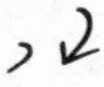 for 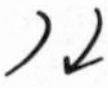 have 
2. Shall  which 

Lesson 17

Principles

139. Brief Forms

gentlemen		**important, importance**	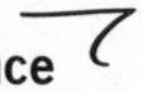	**where**	
morning		**those**		**manufacture**	

140. Word Beginnings Per-, Pur-. The word beginnings *per-*, *pur-* are represented by *pr*.

person		**perfect**		**purchasing**	
permit		**persisted**		**purple**	
perhaps		**personal**		**purse**	

141. Word Beginnings De-, Dĭ-. The word beginnings *de-*, *dĭ-* are represented by *d*.

decide		**desired**		**direct**	
delayed		**deserves**		**diploma**	
deposit		**derive**		**diplomat**	

Building Transcription Skills

142. BUSINESS VOCABULARY BUILDER

personnel records Information concerning the people who work for a company.

proceed To go ahead; to advance (do not confuse with *precede*, which means "to come before").

deprived Denied; kept from.

collection agency A firm that specializes in collecting accounts for a company such as a department store.

143. SIMILAR-WORDS DRILL

In the English language there are many groups of words that sound or look alike, but each member of the group is spelled differently and each has its own meaning.

Example: **cite** (to quote), **sight** (the ability to see), **site** (place).

There are many other groups of words that sound or look *almost* alike.

Example: **defer** (to put off), **differ** (to disagree).

The unwary or careless stenographer will sometimes select the wrong member of the group when transcribing, with the result that her transcript does not make sense.

From time to time in the lessons ahead, you will be given a similar-words exercise designed to help you select the correct word, so that when you become a stenographer you will not suffer the embarrassment of having your letters returned for correction.

Read carefully the definitions and the illustrative sentences in each similar-words exercise.

It's, its

it's The contraction of *it is.*

It's a fine day.

its (*no apostrophe*) Possessive form meaning *belonging to it.*

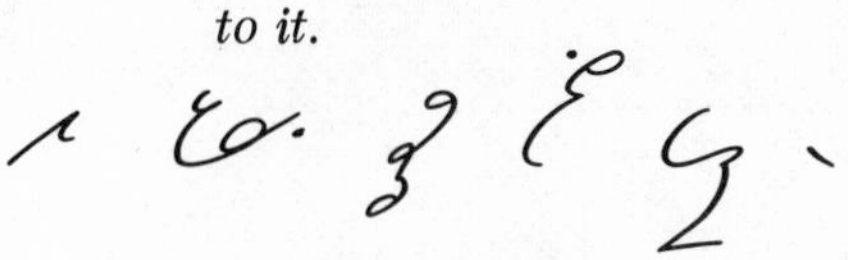

Its operating efficiency has been proven.

Reading and Writing Practice

144. Brief-Form Letter. This letter contains one or more examples of all the brief forms in this lesson.

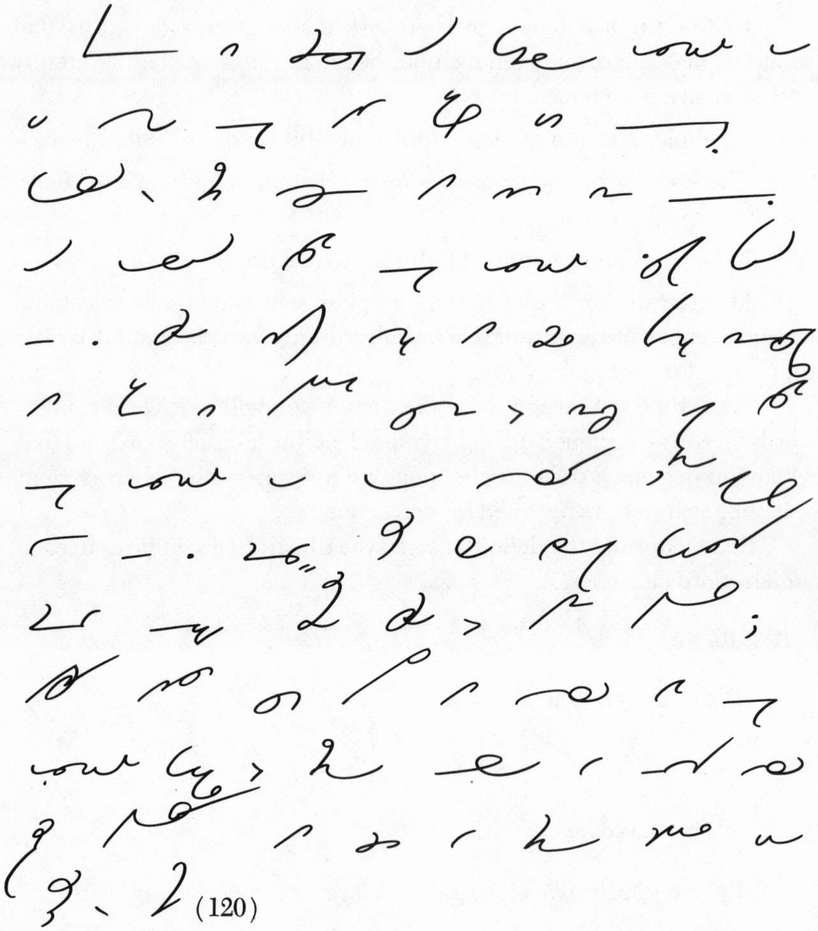

(120)

145. 

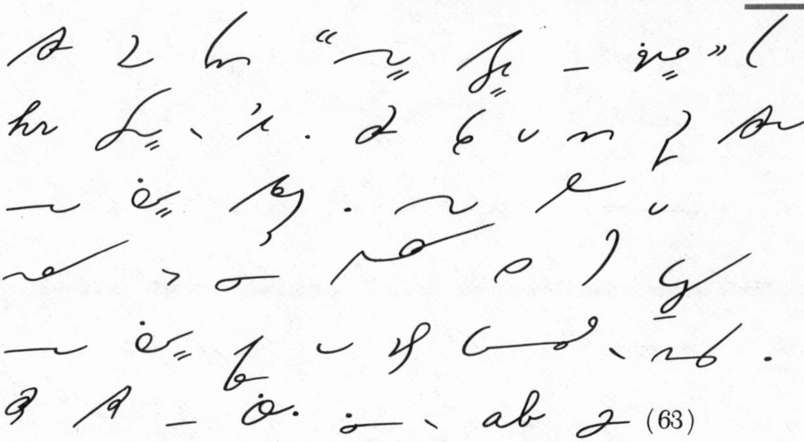

(63)

146.

(104)

147.

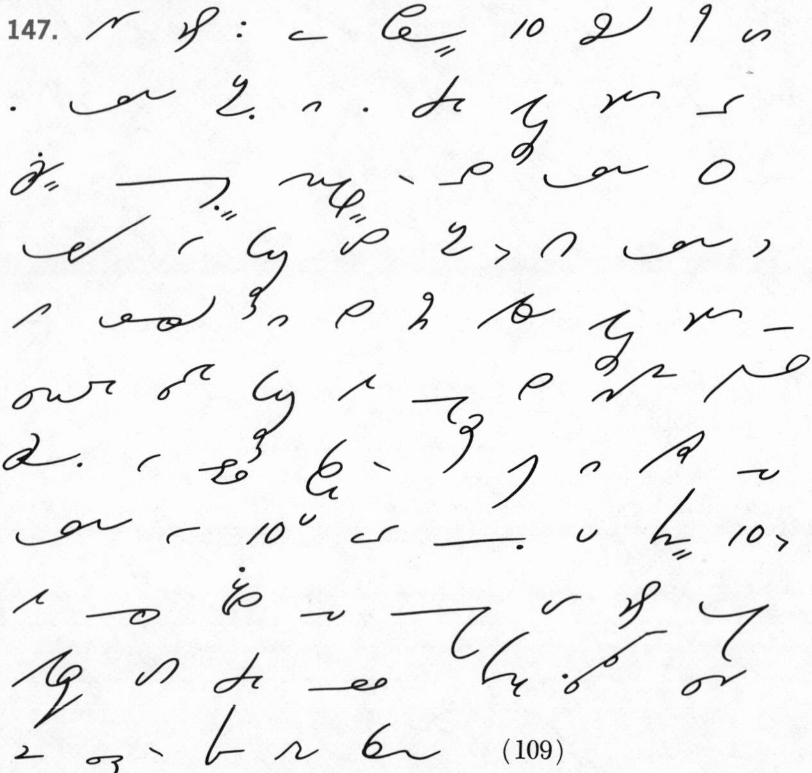

(109)

148.

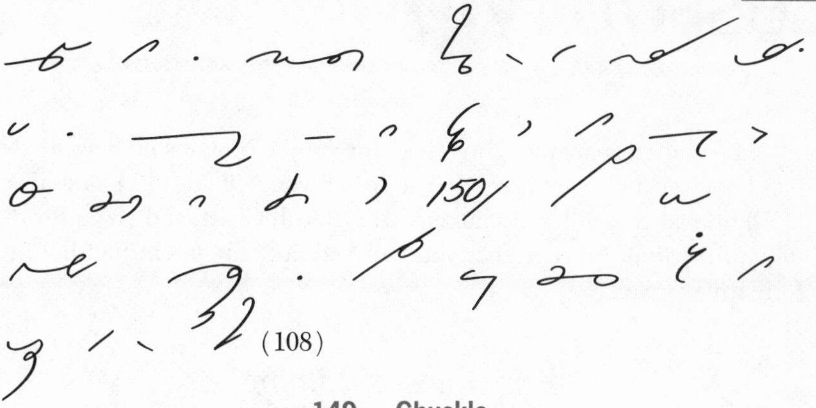

(108)

149. Chuckle

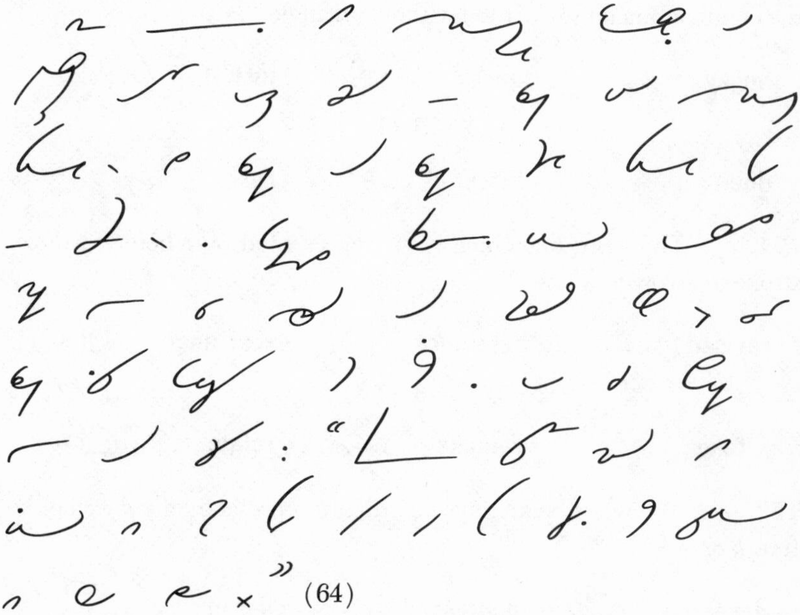

(64)

Lesson 18 RECALL

Lesson 18 is another "breather" for you; it contains no new shorthand devices for you to learn. In this lesson you will find: (1) a number of additional principles of joining, (2) a Recall Chart, and (3) a Reading and Writing Practice that you will find not only interesting but informative as well.

Principles of Joining

150. At the beginning of a word and after *k*, *g*, or a downstroke, the combination *oo-s* is written without an angle.

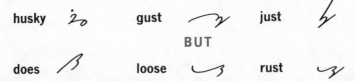

husky  **gust**  **just** 

BUT

does  **loose**  **rust** 

151. The word beginning *re-* is represented by *r* before a downstroke or a vowel.

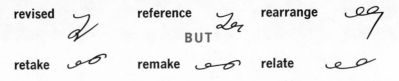

revised  **reference** 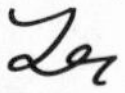 **rearrange** 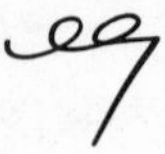

BUT

retake  **remake**  **relate** 

152. The word beginnings *de-*, *dĭ-* are represented by *d* except before *k* or *g*.

deserving  **depressed**  **derail** 

BUT

declare  **degrade**  **digress** 

153. As you have perhaps already noticed from your study of Lessons 1 through 17, the past tense of a verb is formed by adding the stroke for the sound that is heard in the past tense. In some words, the past tense will have the sound of *t,* as in *baked;* in others, it will have the sound of *d,* as in *saved.*

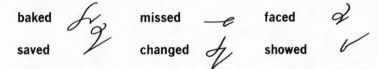

baked  **missed**  **faced** 

saved  **changed**  **showed** 

154. Recall Chart. This chart reviews all the brief forms in Chapter 3 as well as the shorthand devices you studied in Chapters 1, 2, and 3.

The chart contains 90 words and phrases. Can you read the entire chart in 8 minutes or less?

BRIEF FORMS

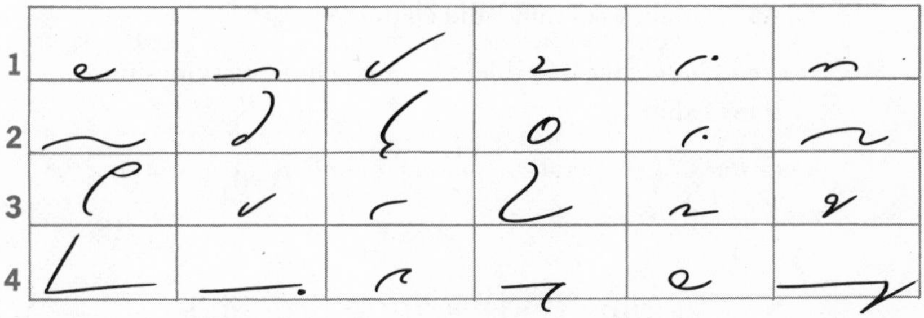

WORDS

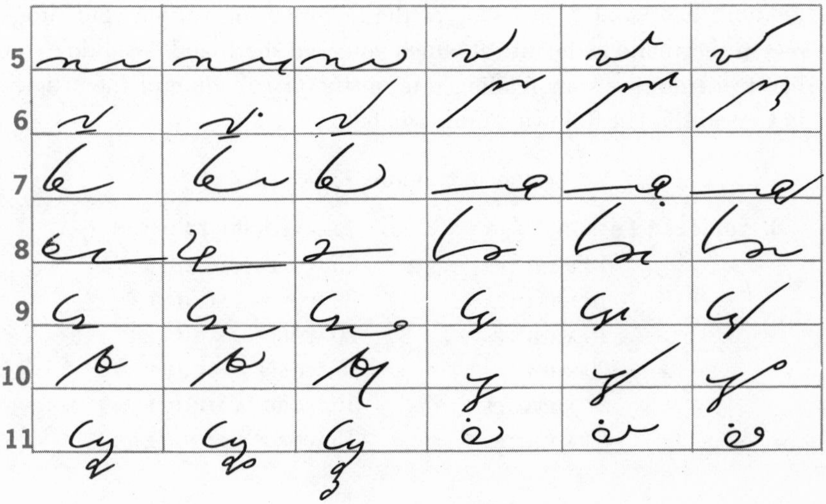

12
13

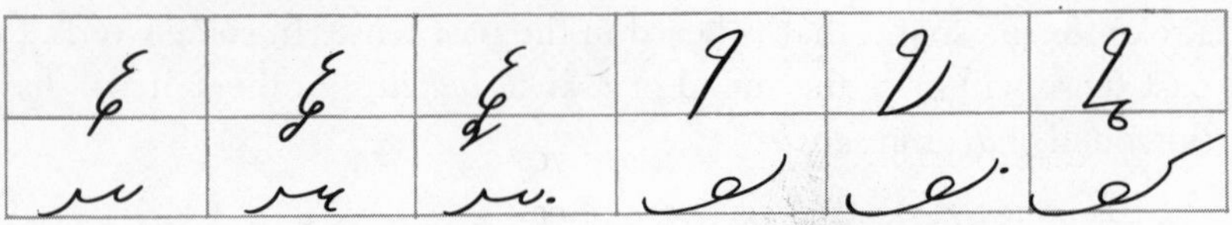

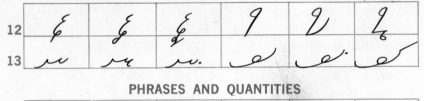

PHRASES AND QUANTITIES

14
15

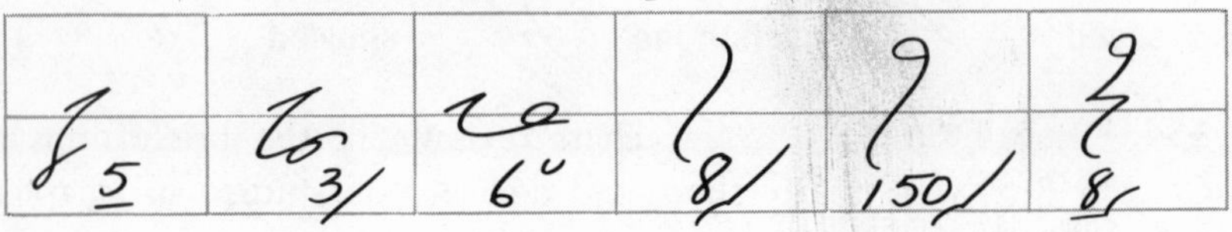

Building Transcription Skills

155. BUSINESS VOCABULARY BUILDER

traits Qualities of mind and character.

poised (*adjective*) Able to meet embarrassing situations calmly.

teamwork Co-operation among members of a working group.

Reading and Writing Practice

Reading Scoreboard. One of the factors in measuring your progress in shorthand is the rate at which you read shorthand. Wouldn't you like to determine your reading rate on the *first reading* of the articles in Lesson 18? The following table will help you.

Lesson 18 contains 353 words.

If you read Lesson 18 in	your reading rate is
14 MINUTES	25 WORDS A MINUTE
16 MINUTES	22 WORDS A MINUTE
18 MINUTES	20 WORDS A MINUTE
20 MINUTES	17 WORDS A MINUTE
22 MINUTES	16 WORDS A MINUTE
24 MINUTES	15 WORDS A MINUTE

If you can read Lesson 18 through the first time in less than 14 minutes, you are doing well indeed. If you take considerably longer than 24 minutes, here are some questions you should ask yourself:

1. Am I spelling each outline I cannot read immediately?
2. Am I jotting down on a card or slip of paper any outline that I cannot read even after spelling it?
3. Should I perhaps reread the directions for reading shorthand on page 11?

After you have determined your reading rate, make a record of it in some convenient place. You can then watch your reading rate grow as you time yourself on the Reading Scoreboards in later lessons.

156. Desirable Traits

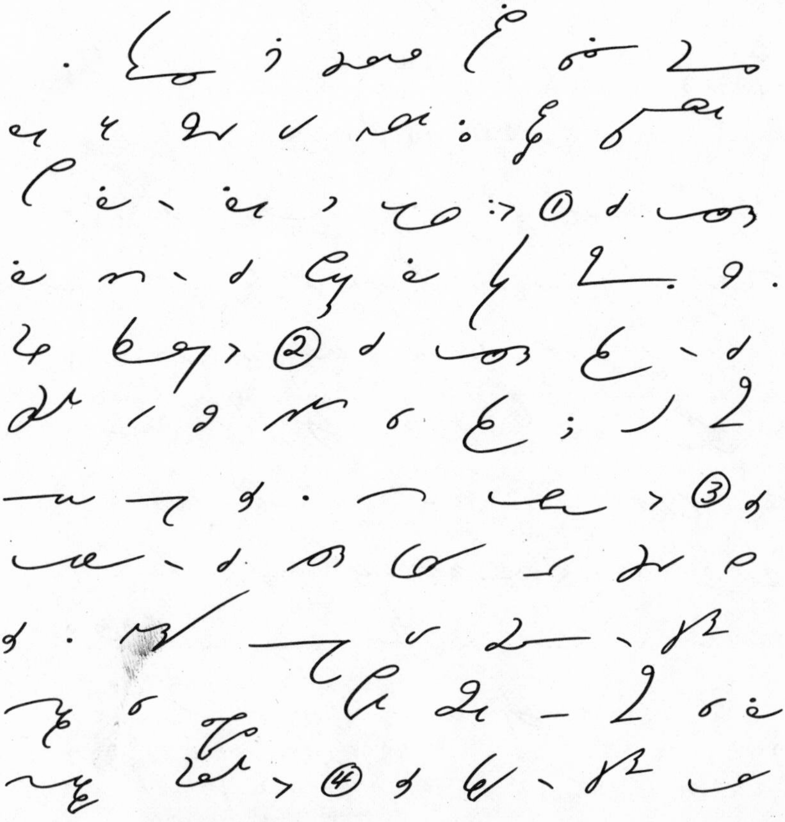

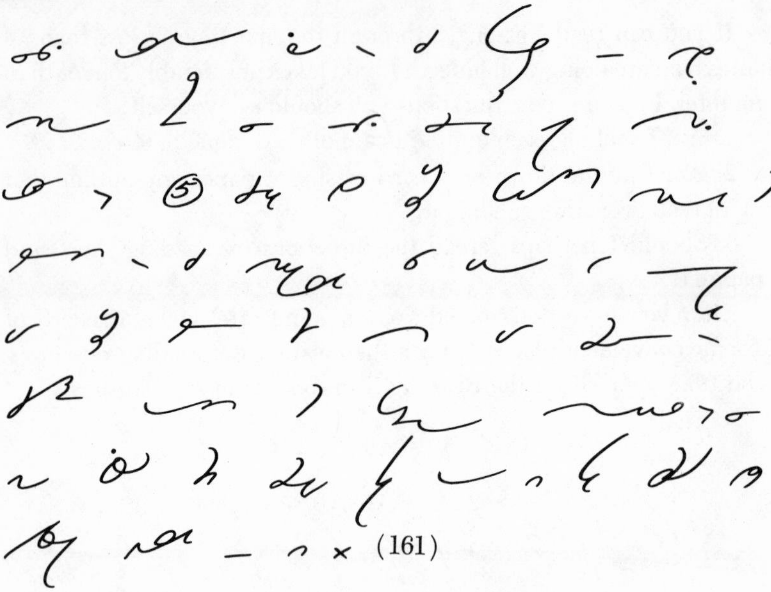

(161)

157. Good Health

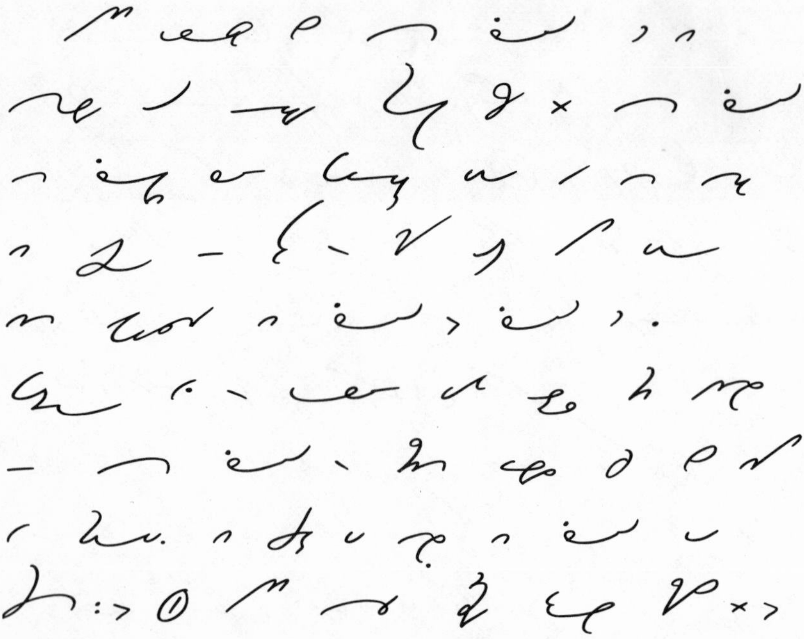

(192)

The Secretary's Day

What is a typical day like in the life of a secretary? Let's suppose you are secretary to Mr. G. O. Marsden, Sales Manager. Here is what your day might be like.

8:45 Arrive at the office. Straighten and dust Mr. Marsden's desk and other furniture. Fill water decanter. Water the plants. Check appointment calendar to be sure that his agrees with yours. You notice that he has made a 9:15 appointment with Mrs. Fuller. Get necessary papers you think he might need in talking with her.

8:55 Mr. Marsden arrives. Remind him of his 9:15 appointment and a luncheon date at 12:30 with Mr. Symond at the Belle Meade Restaurant. Ask him about arrangements for a 2:30 meeting of the Advertising Committee.

9:05 The mail arrives. Open all mail (except letters marked "Personal"); read it and place it on Mr. Marsden's desk, along with any background correspondence he may need.

9:15 The receptionist calls you to say that Mrs. Fuller has arrived. You inform Mr. Marsden and then go out to the reception office to escort Mrs. Fuller in to see Mr. Marsden.

9:35 Mr. Marsden "buzzes" you on the intercom and tells you that Mrs. Fuller is leaving and asks you to get some papers that she is to take with her. You do so, bidding Mrs. Fuller good-bye at the elevator.

9:40-10:15 1. The telephone rings several times—company executives and outsiders asking for appointments and information.
2. A messenger brings you a package of books C. O. D., and you take the money from petty cash to pay him.
3. Other executives call in person to speak to Mr. Marsden.

10:15 Mr. Marsden calls you for dictation.

11:00 You return to your desk and begin transcribing.

11:15 Mr. Marsden asks for several papers that must be obtained from the files.

11:30 You call the receptionist on the third floor to be sure that the conference room has been reserved for Mr. Marsden's 2:30 meeting.

Chapter

4

12:00 You get ready to go to lunch with another secretary who works a few blocks away. Before leaving, you again remind Mr. Marsden about his luncheon date. You tell the relief receptionist that you are leaving for lunch.

12:55 Back from lunch, you return to your transcribing.

1:15-1:40
1. You answer eight telephone calls.
2. You greet two callers who have come to see Mr. Marsden (neither has an appointment), and you persuade them to make an appointment for later in the week.
3. You duplicate the agenda for the advertising meeting and make photocopies of an advertising brochure to be discussed there.
4. You visit the conference room to see that there are enough chairs and that the room is in order; you distribute the materials for the meeting.

2:00 Mr. Marsden calls you in to dictate a short memo. He asks you to arrange to have a film and an operator in the conference room at three o'clock. You call the library for the film and Office Services to arrange for an operator.

2:25 You make sure that Mr. Marsden has all the necessary materials for the 2:30 meeting, then you return to your transcribing.

2:30-4:00 You get out two telegrams and finish transcribing Mr. Marsden's dictation. You telephone various people for information he needs for a report he is writing.

4:30 You prepare for Mr. Marsden's signature the letters that you have just typed and take them to him. After he has signed them, you get them ready for mailing.

4:45 You receive a call from a friend about going bowling this evening. You hurriedly agree, saying you'll be ready by 6:15.

5:00 You clear your desk, tell Mr. Marsden you are leaving (he is working late tonight), and then catch the first bus home.

As you think about the day's work, you are certain of only two things: (1) you did a good day's work, and (2) tomorrow will be entirely different!

Lesson 19

Principles

158. Brief Forms

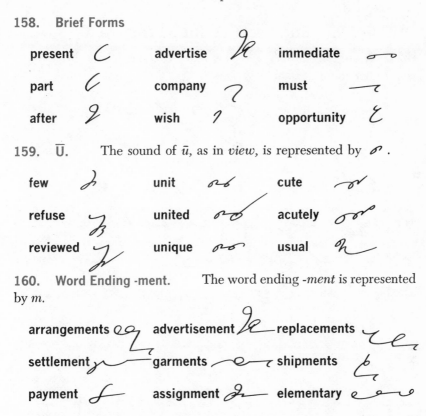

present		**advertise**		**immediate**	
part		**company**		**must**	
after		**wish**		**opportunity**	

159. Ū. The sound of *ū*, as in *view,* is represented by .

few		**unit**		**cute**	
refuse		**united**		**acutely**	
reviewed		**unique**		**usual**	

160. Word Ending -ment. The word ending *-ment* is represented by *m.*

arrangements		**advertisement**		**replacements**	
settlement		**garments**		**shipments**	
payment		**assignment**		**elementary**	

Notice that in *assignment* the *m* for *-ment* is joined to the *n* with a jog.

Building Transcription Skills

161. BUSINESS VOCABULARY BUILDER

partial Pertaining to a part only; not all.

tracer A follow-up investigation to locate a missing shipment of merchandise.

elements Conditions of weather, such as rain, snow, and lightning.

Reading and Writing Practice

162. Brief-Form Letter. This letter contains all the brief forms you studied in this lesson.

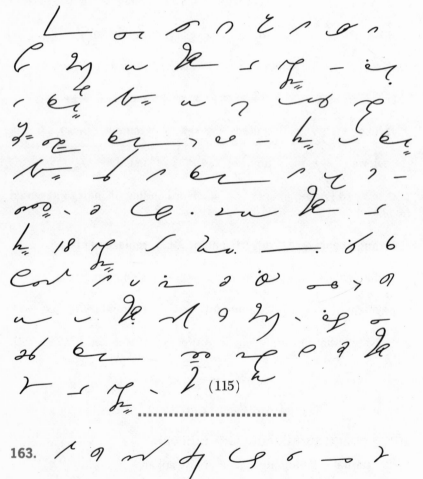

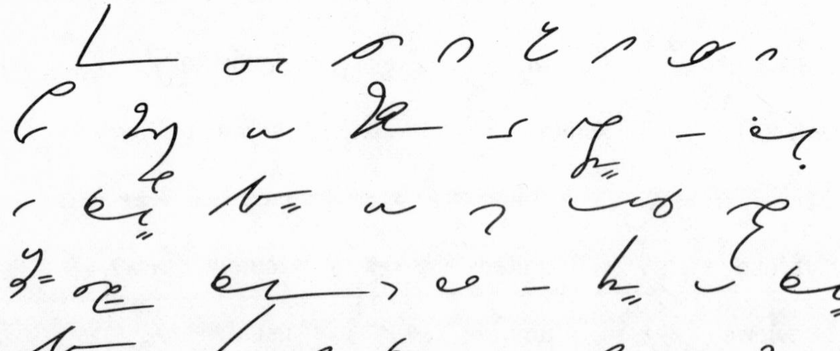

(115)

163. 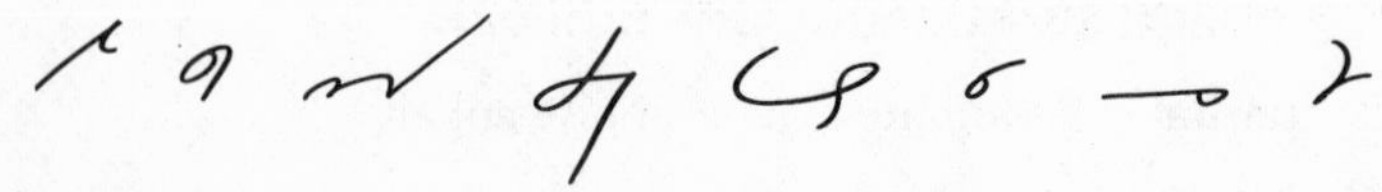

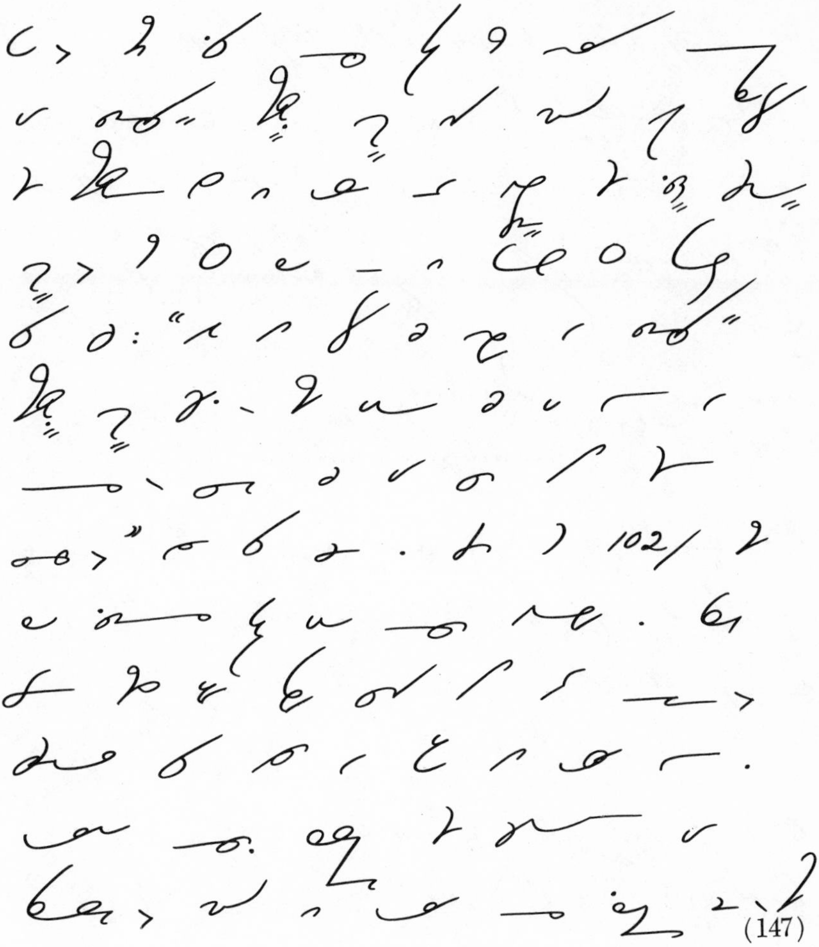

(147)

164.

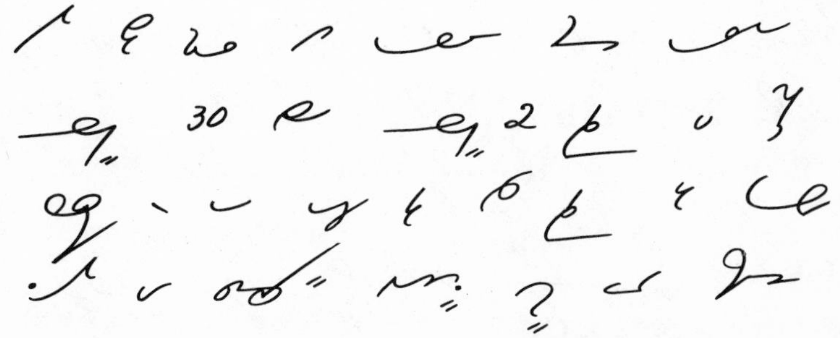

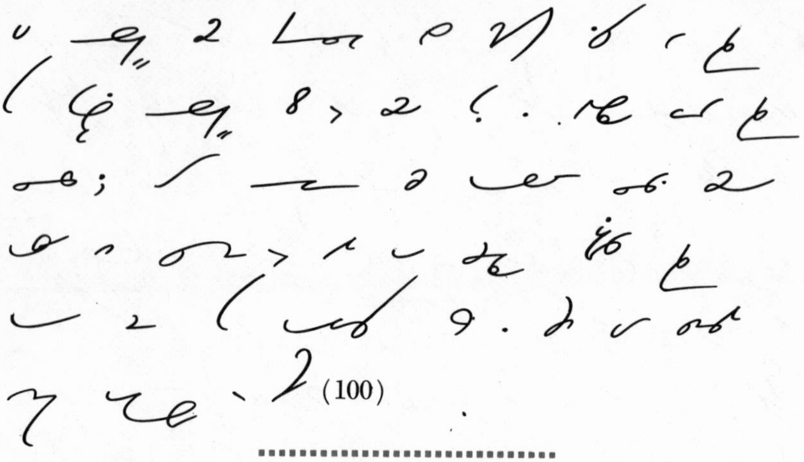
(100)

165. 
(84)

166. 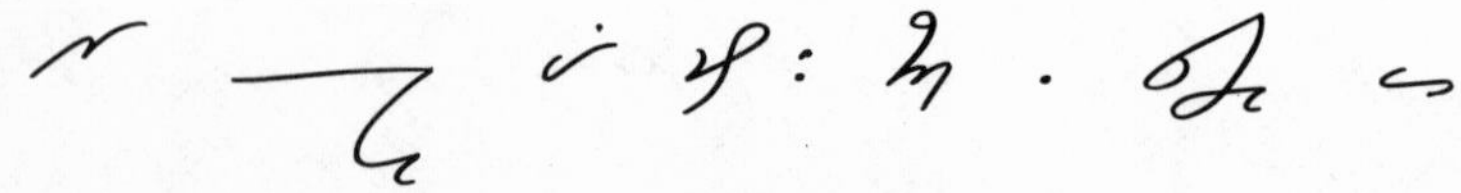

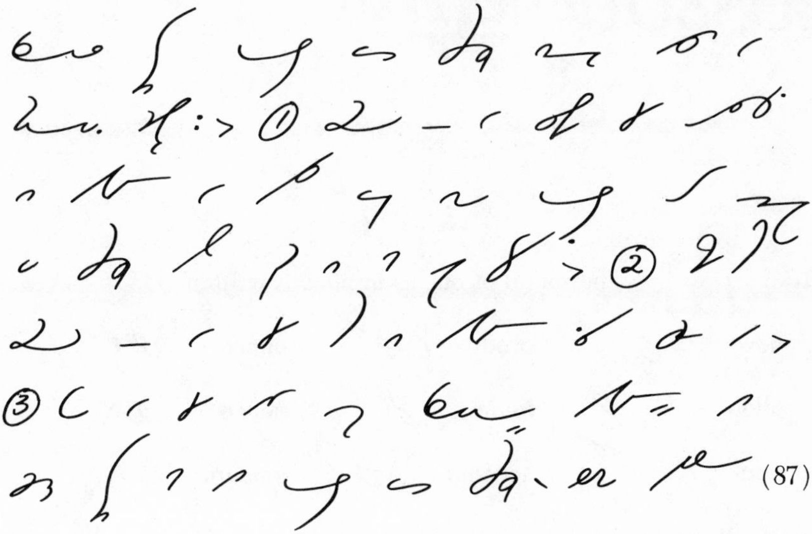

(87)

167. Chuckle

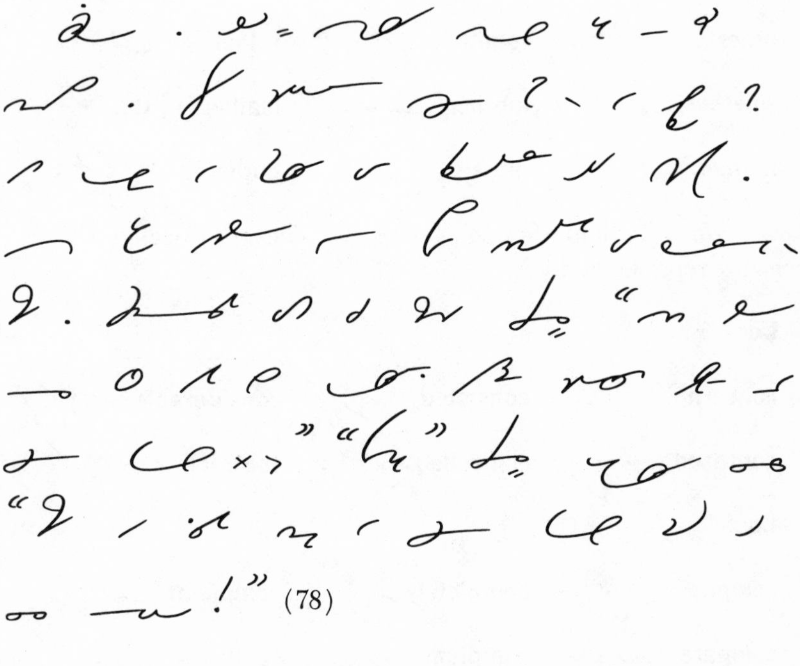

(78)

Lesson 20

Principles

168. Ow. The sound of *ow,* as in *now,* is written .

now	proud	ounce
allow	found	house
doubt	account	amount

169. Word Ending -ther. The word ending *-ther* is represented by *th.*

other	together	rather
whether	mother	leather
neither	either	bothered

170. Word Beginnings Con-, Com-. The word beginnings *con-, com-* are represented by *k.*

Con-

concern	consisted	considerable
confused	controlled	contract

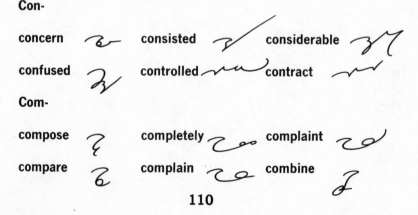

Com-

compose	completely	complaint
compare	complain	combine

171. Con-, Com- Followed by a Vowel. When *con-, com-* are followed by a vowel, these word beginnings are represented by *kn* or *km.*

connect  **connote** 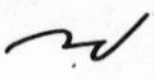 **committee** 

connection  **commerce**  **commercial** 

Building Transcription Skills

172. BUSINESS VOCABULARY BUILDER

accommodate To provide with sleeping quarters; to oblige.

confirm To verify.

decade Ten years.

competitor A company that sells goods or services similar to those of another company.

Reading and Writing Practice

173. 

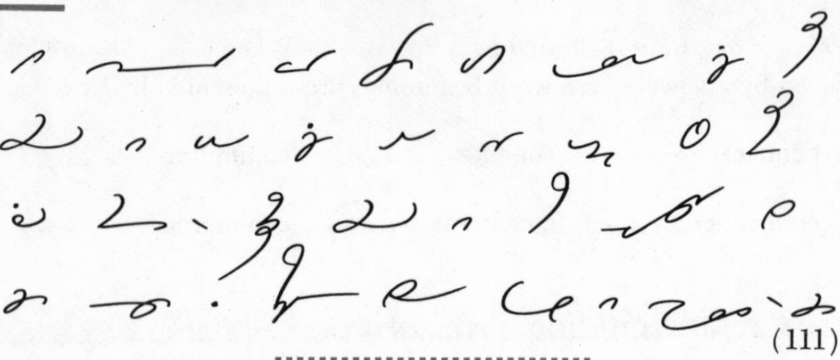

(111)

174.

18
ab

(119)

175.

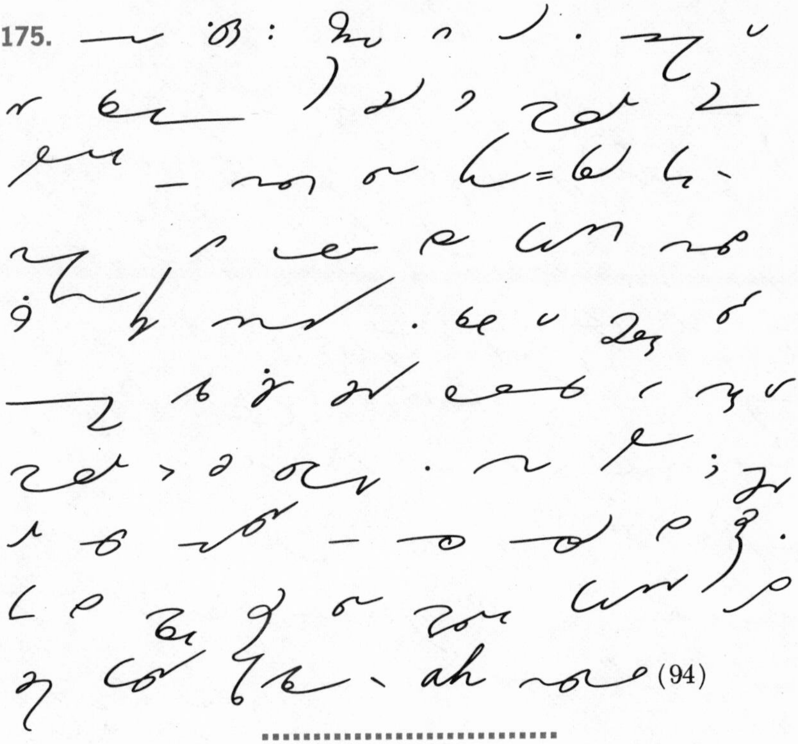

(94)

176.

(68)

177. Chuckle

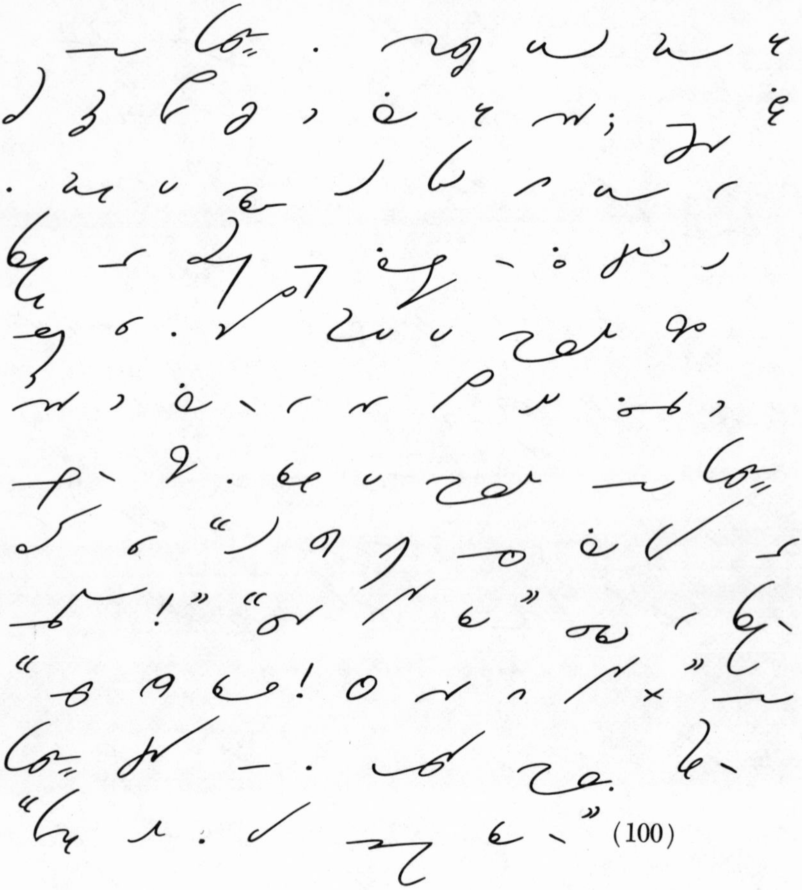

(100)

Lesson 21

Principles

178. Brief Forms

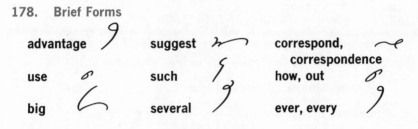

advantage	**suggest**	**correspond, correspondence**
use	**such**	**how, out**
big	**several**	**ever, every**

179. Den. By rounding off the angle between *d-n,* we obtain the fluent *den* blend.

Den

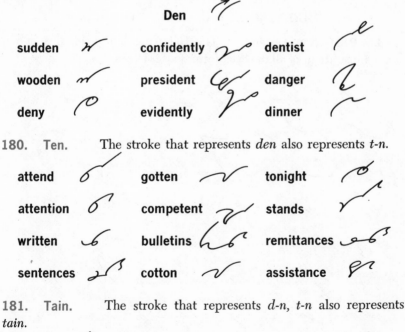

sudden	**confidently**	**dentist**
wooden	**president**	**danger**
deny	**evidently**	**dinner**

180. Ten. The stroke that represents *den* also represents *t-n.*

attend	**gotten**	**tonight**
attention	**competent**	**stands**
written	**bulletins**	**remittances**
sentences	**cotton**	**assistance**

181. Tain. The stroke that represents *d-n, t-n* also represents *tain.*

obtain	**certain**	**obtainable**

contain  **attain**  **container** 

maintain  **detain**  **certainly** 

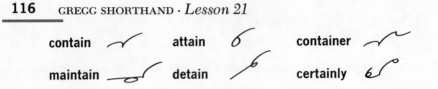

Building Transcription Skills

182. BUSINESS VOCABULARY BUILDER

unique Being the only one of its kind. (It is, therefore, incorrect to say "more unique" or "most unique.")

complimentary Presented free.

evidently Apparently.

council A governing body.

Reading and Writing Practice

183. Brief-Form Letter. The following letter contains one or more illustrations of all the brief forms in this lesson.

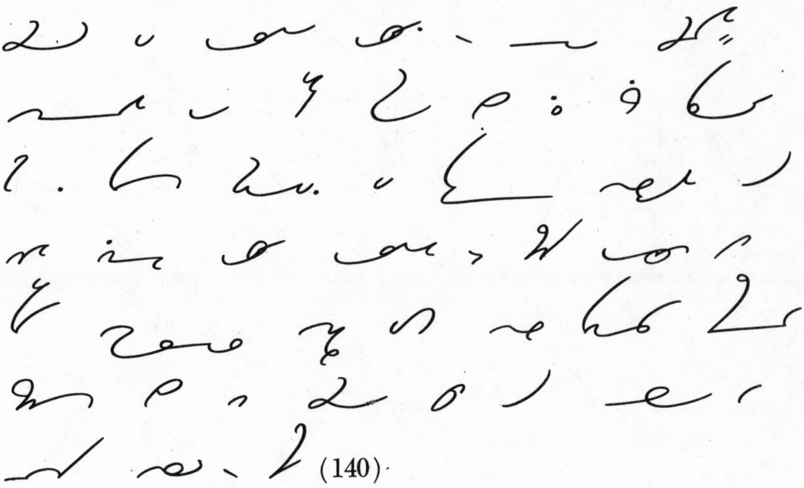

(140)

184.

(94)

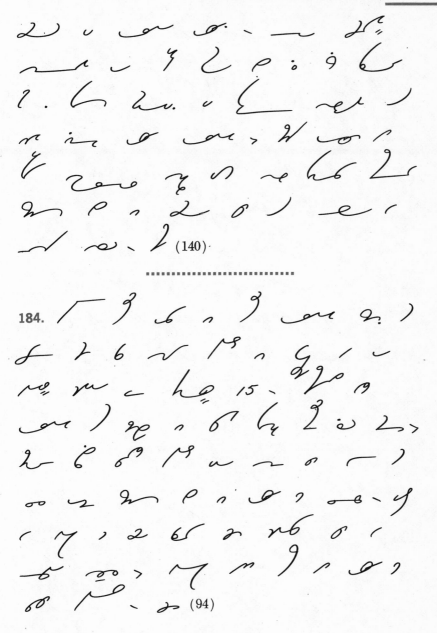

185.

(114)

186.

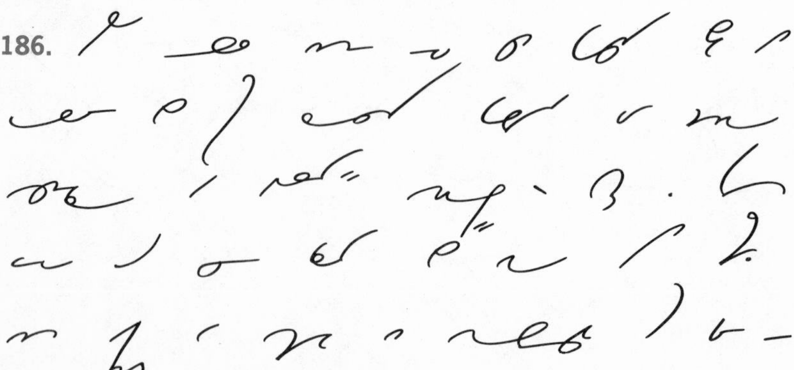

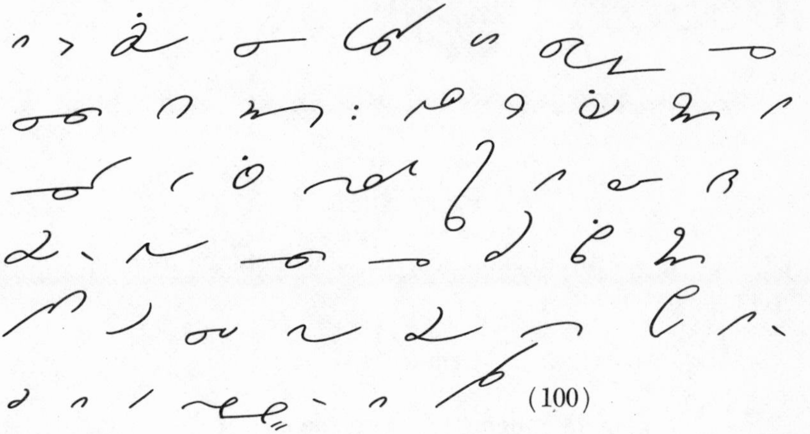

(100)

187.

(86)

Lesson 22

Principles

188. Dem. By rounding off the angle between *d-m,* we obtain the fluent *dem* blend.

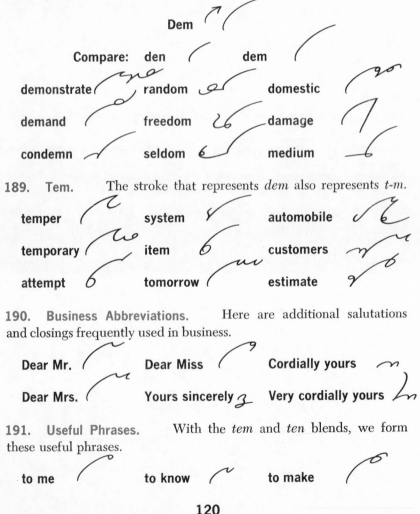

Dem

Compare: den dem

demonstrate	**random**	**domestic**
demand	**freedom**	**damage**
condemn	**seldom**	**medium**

189. Tem. The stroke that represents *dem* also represents *t-m.*

temper	**system**	**automobile**
temporary	**item**	**customers**
attempt	**tomorrow**	**estimate**

190. Business Abbreviations. Here are additional salutations and closings frequently used in business.

Dear Mr.	**Dear Miss**	**Cordially yours**
Dear Mrs.	**Yours sincerely**	**Very cordially yours**

191. Useful Phrases. With the *tem* and *ten* blends, we form these useful phrases.

to me	**to know**	**to make**

192. Days of the Week

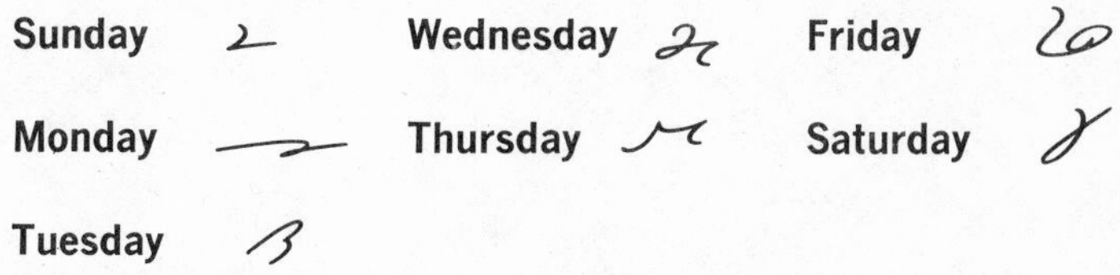
Sunday
Wednesday
Friday
Monday
Thursday
Saturday
Tuesday

193. Months of the Year. You are already familiar with the outlines for several of the months, as they are written in full.

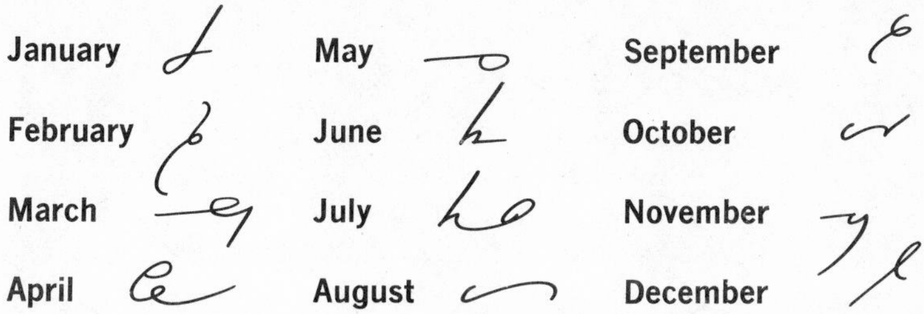
January
May
September
February
June
October
March
July
November
April
August
December

Building Transcription Skills

194. BUSINESS VOCABULARY BUILDER

justified Proved to be wise, good.

domestic market Customers in the United States.

estimates Makes an approximate calculation.

Reading and Writing Practice

195.

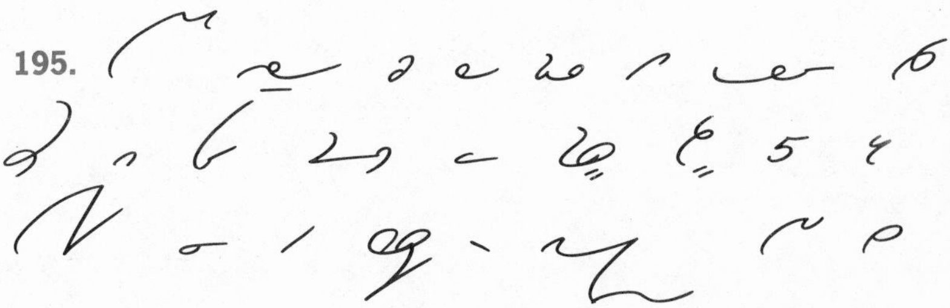

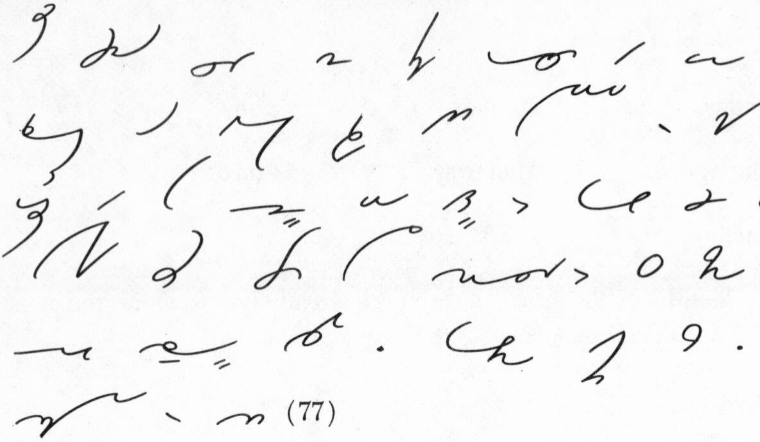

(77)

196.

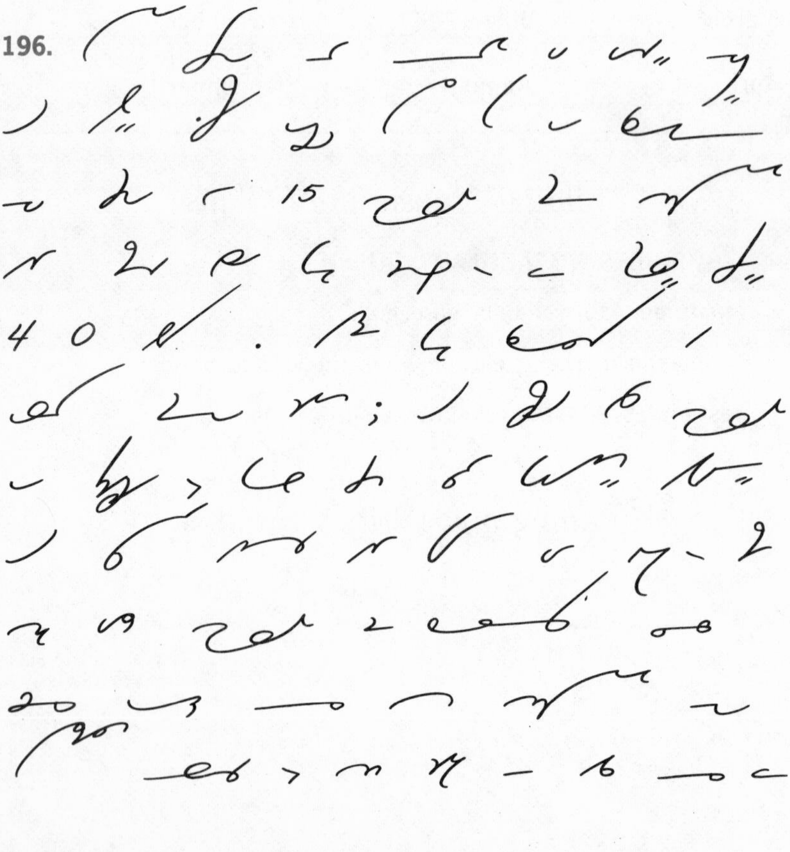

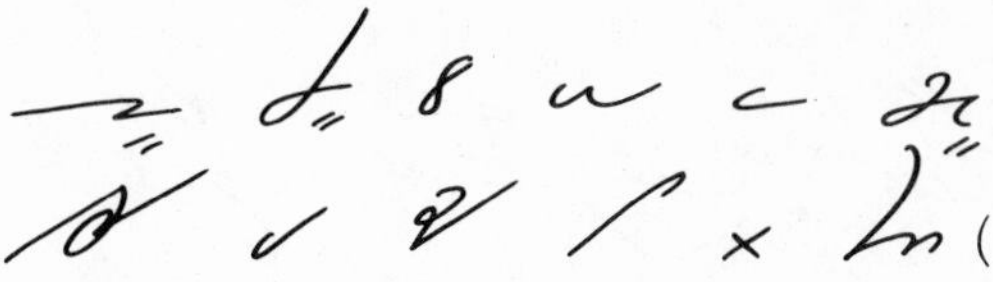 (128)

197.  (106)

198. 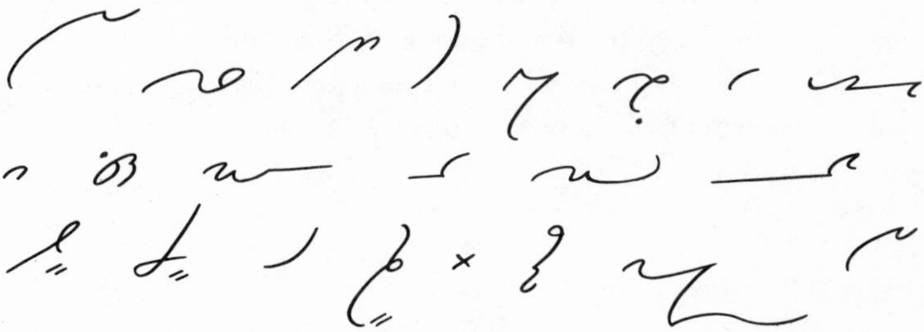

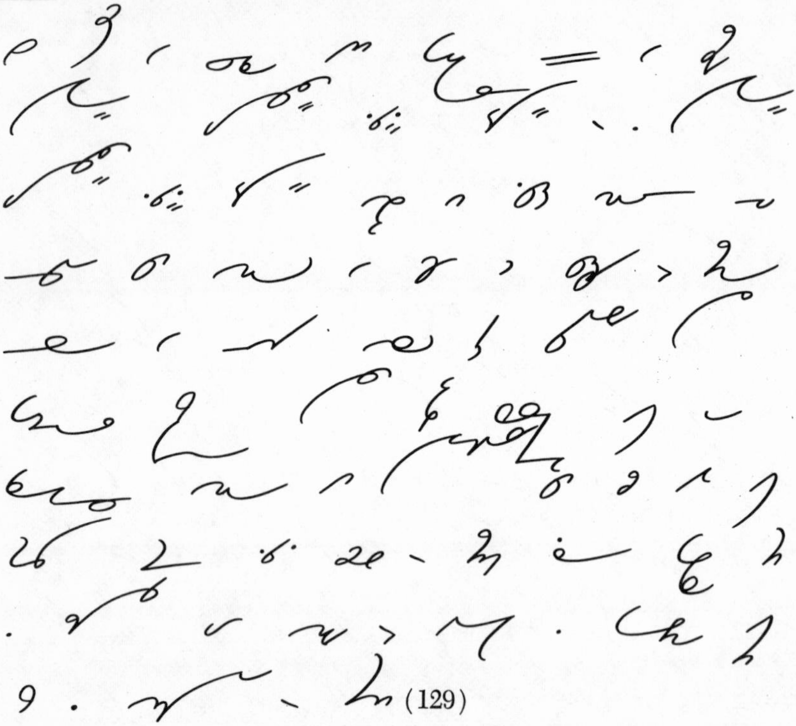

(129)

PROPORTION CHECK LIST

As a result of the shorthand writing that you have already done, no doubt you have come to realize how important it is to –

1. Make the *a* circles huge; the *e* circles tiny.

2. Make the short strokes like *n* and *t* very short; the long strokes like *men* and *ted* very long.

3. Keep the straight lines straight; the curves deep.

4. Keep the *o* and *oo* hooks deep and narrow.

The readability of your shorthand will depend to a large extent on how you observe these pointers in your everyday writing.

Lesson 23

Principles

199. Brief Forms. After this group, you have only five more to learn!

time  gone  question 

acknowledge  during  yet 

general  *over  worth 

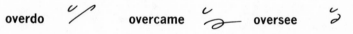

*The outline for *over* is written above the following character. It is also used as a prefix form, as in:

overdo  overcame  oversee 

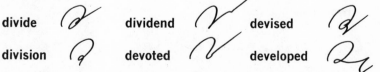

200. Def, Dif. By rounding off the angle between *d-f*, we obtain the fluent *def, dif* blend.

Def, Dif 

definite  defeat  different 

defied  defined  differences 

201. Div, Dev. The stroke that represents *def, dif* also represents *div* and *dev*.

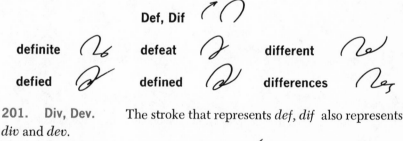

divide  dividend  devised 

division  devoted  developed 

202. Ū represented by OO. The *oo* hook is often used to represent the sound of *ū*.

new  **avenues**  **continued** 

issue  **suits** 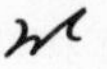 **induce** 

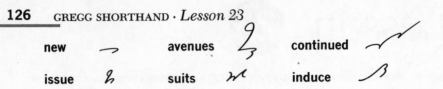

Building Transcription Skills

203. BUSINESS VOCABULARY BUILDER

sales volume The amount of sales made to customers.

renewal An extension of a subscription.

vividly Clearly; sharply.

204. SIMILAR-WORDS DRILL

To, too, two

to (*preposition*) In the direction of. (*To* is also used as the sign of the infinitive.)

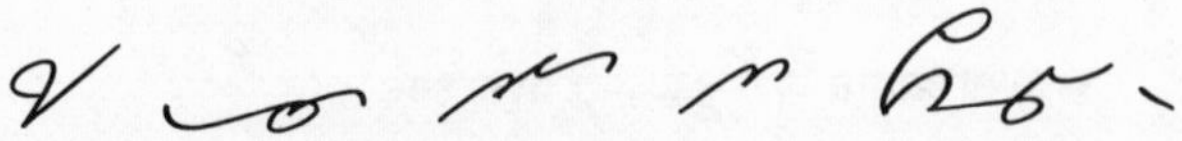

I should like to talk to you about this matter.

too Also; more than enough.

I, too, was in the Navy.

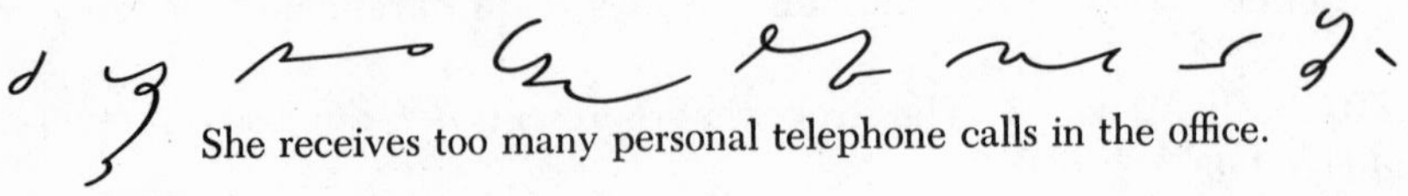

She receives too many personal telephone calls in the office.

two One plus one.

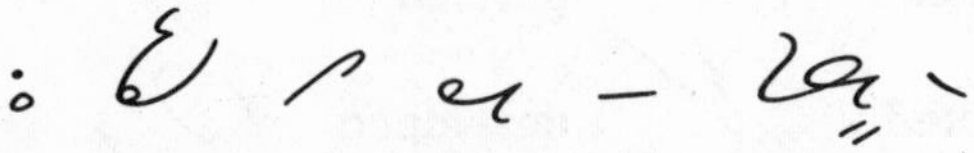

He spent two years in France.

The word in this group on which stenographers often stumble is *too*—they carelessly transcribe *to.* Don't *you* make that mistake.

Reading and Writing Practice

205. Brief-Form Letter. The following letter contains one or more illustrations of all the brief forms you studied in this lesson.

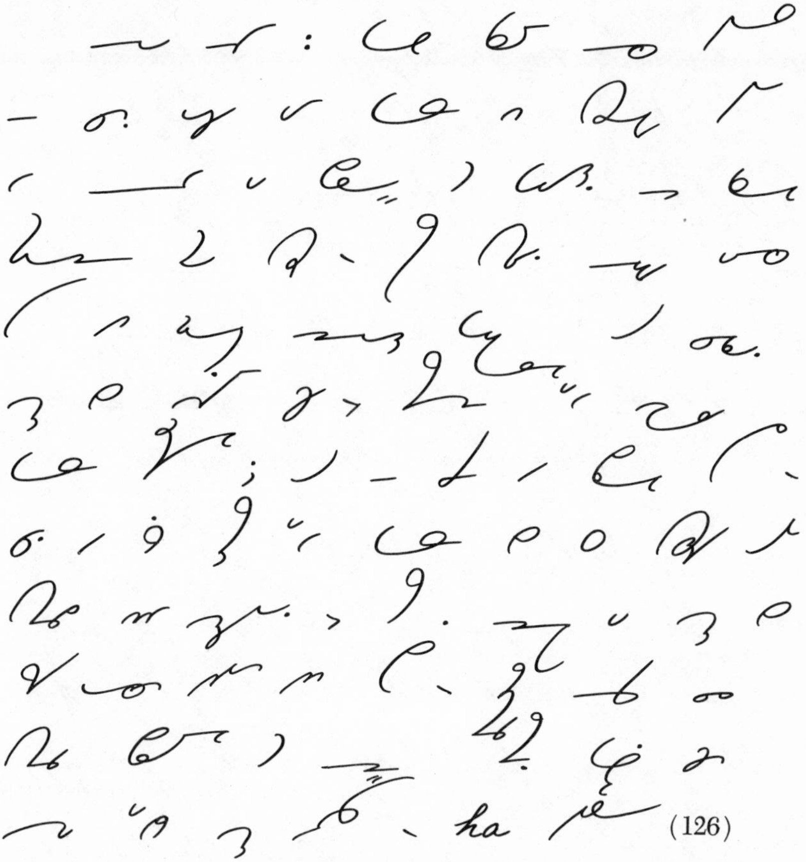

(126)

206.

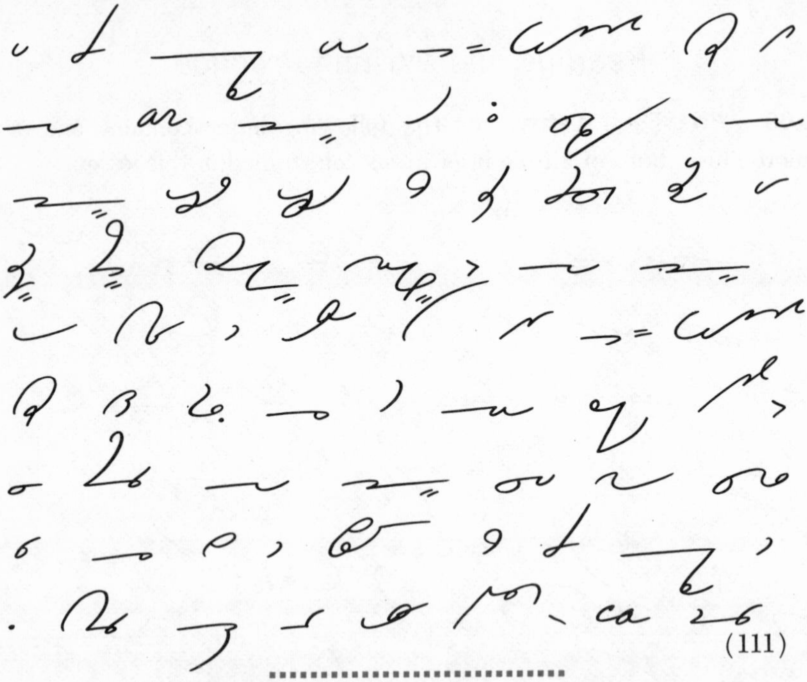

(111)

207.

(84)

208. Chuckle

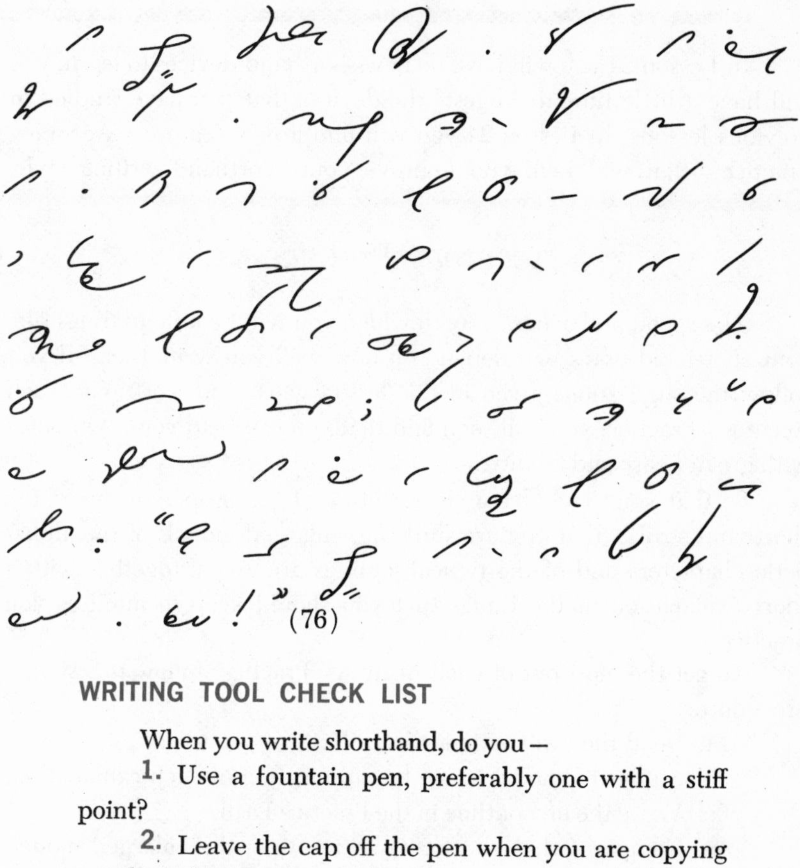
(76)

WRITING TOOL CHECK LIST

When you write shorthand, do you –

1. Use a fountain pen, preferably one with a stiff point?

2. Leave the cap off the pen when you are copying or taking dictation?

3. Place the cap back on the pen firmly when you are not actually writing so that the ink will not clot on the point?

4. Fill your pen before you come to class each day so that you will not run out of ink in the middle of a dictation?

5. Carry a pencil "just in case"?

6. Date each day's dictation at the bottom of your notebook page, just as the stenographer does in the office?

Lesson 24 RECALL

In Lesson 24 you will have no new shorthand devices to learn; you will have a little time to "digest" the devices that you have studied in previous lessons. In Lesson 24 you will find a new feature – Accuracy Practice – that will help you improve your shorthand writing style.

Accuracy Practice

The speed and accuracy with which you will be able to transcribe your shorthand notes will depend on how well you write them. If you follow the suggestions given in this lesson when you work with each Accuracy Practice, you will soon find that you can read your own notes with greater ease and facility.

So that you may have a clear picture of the proper shapes of the shorthand strokes that you are studying, enlarged models of the alphabetic characters and of the typical joinings are given, together with a short explanation of the things that you should keep in mind as you practice.

To get the most out of each Accuracy Practice, follow this simple procedure:

a. Read the explanations carefully.

b. Study the model to see the application of each explanation.

c. Write the first outline in the Practice Drill.

d. Compare what you have written with the enlarged model.

e. Write three or four more copies of the outline, trying to improve your outline with each writing.

f. Repeat this procedure with the remaining outlines in the Practice Drill.

209. **R** **L** **K** **G**

To write these strokes accurately:

a. Start and finish each one on the same level of writing.

b. Make the *beginning* of the curve in *r* and *l* deep. Make the *end* of the curve in *k* and *g* deep.

c. Make the *l* and *g* considerably longer than *r* and *k*.

Practice Drill

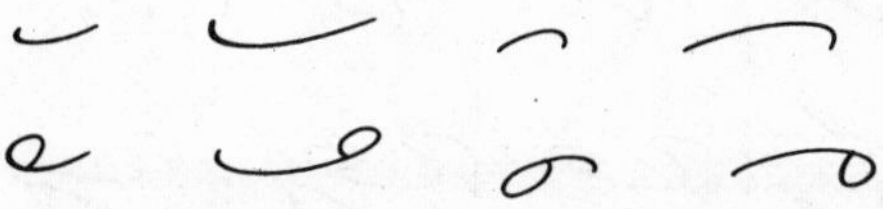

Are-our-hour; will-well; can, good.
Air, lay, ache, gay.

210. **Kr** **Rk** **Gl**

To write these combinations accurately:

a. Make the curves rather flat.

b. Make the combinations *kr* and *rk* somewhat shorter than the combined length of *r* and *k* when written by themselves.

c. Make the combination *gl* somewhat shorter than the combined length of *g* and *l* when written by themselves.

Practice Drill

Cream, crate, maker, mark, dark.
Gleam, glean, glare, eagle.

211. Recall Chart. This chart contains all the brief forms in Chapter 4 and one or more illustrations of all the shorthand devices you have studied in Chapters 1 through 4.

The chart contains 84 words. Can you read the entire chart in 7 minutes or less?

WORDS

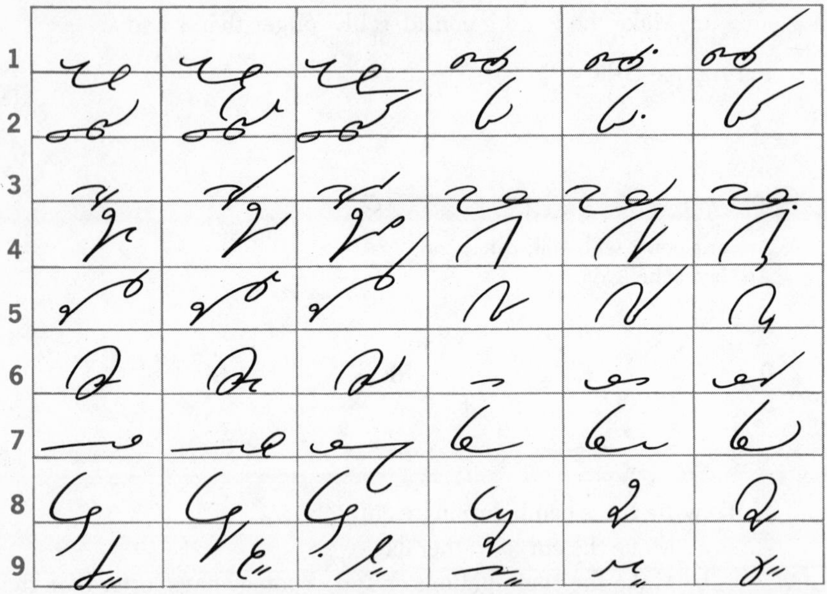
1
2
3
4
5
6
7
8
9

BRIEF FORMS AND PHRASES

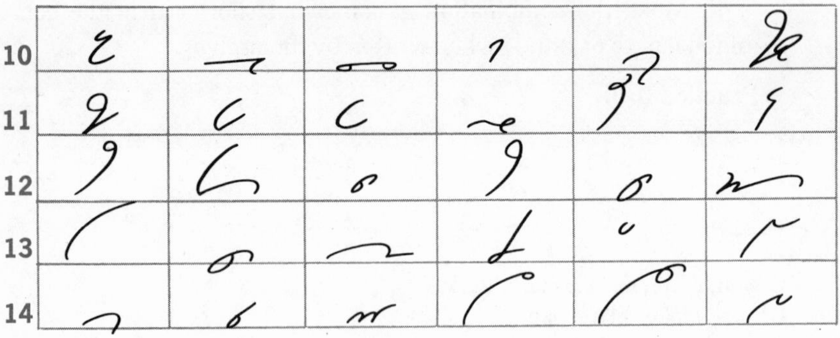
10
11
12
13
14

Building Transcription Skills

212. BUSINESS VOCABULARY BUILDER

participation Act of taking active part in anything.

comprehend To understand.

skim To read quickly without concern for details.

legible Can be read easily.

Reading and Writing Practice

213. Check Your Study Habits

(272)

214. Chuckle

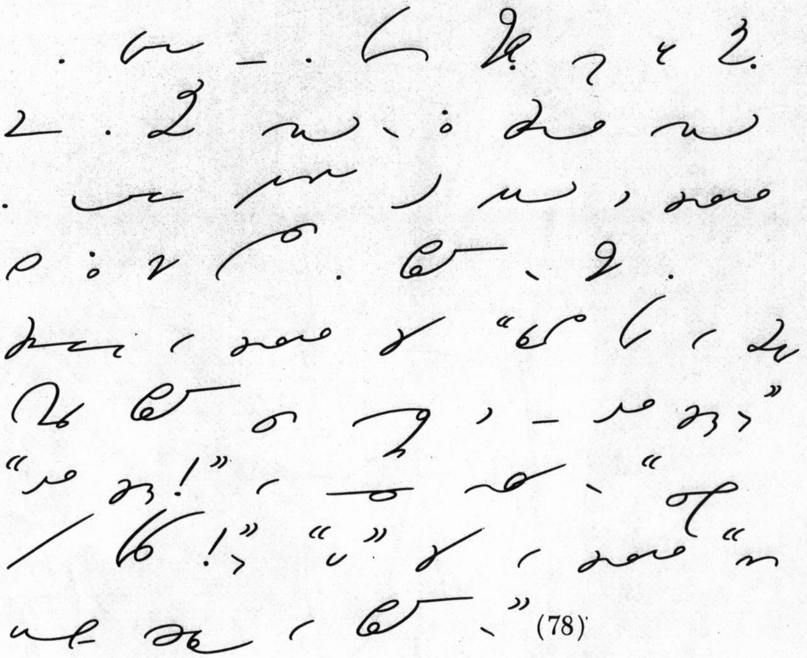
(78)

The Secretary Takes Dictation

The number one requirement of a secretary is the ability to take dictation at a rate that enables her to keep up with the dictator comfortably and to transcribe it quickly and correctly. The major part of almost every executive's job is communications. Each day he must write many letters, memoranda, and reports. This is where the secretary really earns the right to her title. An efficient secretary saves her boss's time; she supplies the "hand" while he supplies the ideas —an effective combination! She quickly learns his dictating habits so that they work together as a team.

Some dictators think fast and know exactly what they want to say, and their secretaries must constantly use every ounce of skill to keep pace with them. Others think in spurts; that is, there will often be long pauses between thoughts. Then, when an idea has been framed in their minds, they are off at a fast clip for several minutes. Then, for a moment or so — nothing. Still other dictators are more deliberate. They think slowly, especially on difficult letters, and may change their minds many times during the dictation of a letter. Even so, their secretaries must be prepared for sudden bursts of speed when their ideas jell and they know what they want to say. No two executives dictate alike, and the secretary must be prepared for all types.

The good secretary has a reserve speed for any emergency. Even though a dictator's rate may be fairly low on the average, that "average" can be disastrous. Did you ever hear about the man who almost drowned in a river that averaged only six inches deep? Well, most of the river bed consisted only of sand; but there were several holes that were twelve feet deep, and it was in one of these that he almost met his sad fate!

Therefore, beware of averages. Build your skill so that you don't "drown in a cloudburst of dictation." It's good insurance to have more speed than the dictator's average.

Chapter 5

Lesson 25

Principles

215. Brief Forms

difficult	satisfy, satisfactory	state
envelope	success	*under
progress	next	request

*The outline for *under* is written above the following shorthand character. It is also used as a prefix form, as in:

underneath	understudy	undertake
undergo	underpay	underground

216. Cities and States. In your work as a stenographer and secretary, you will frequently have occasion to write geographical expressions. Here are a few important cities and states.

Cities

New York	Boston	Los Angeles
Chicago	Philadelphia	St. Louis

States

Michigan	Massachusetts	Missouri
Illinois	Pennsylvania	California

217. Useful Business Phrases. The following phrases are used so frequently in business that special forms have been provided for them. Study these phrases as you would study brief forms.

of course		**to do**		**let us**	
as soon as		**I hope**		**to us**	
as soon as possible		**we hope**		**your order**	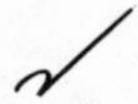

Building Transcription Skills

218. BUSINESS VOCABULARY BUILDER

Manila envelope An envelope made of a strong brown paper.

traveler A salesman, representative.

progress Advancement to an objective.

Reading and Writing Practice

219. Brief-Form Letter. The following letter contains one or more illustrations of all the brief forms you studied in this lesson.

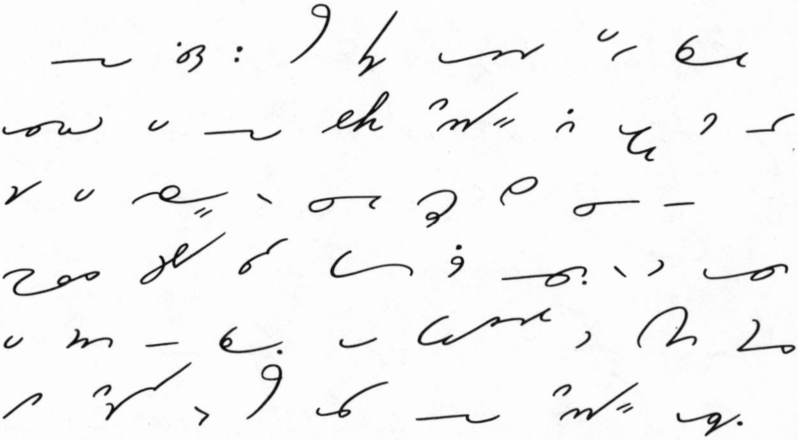

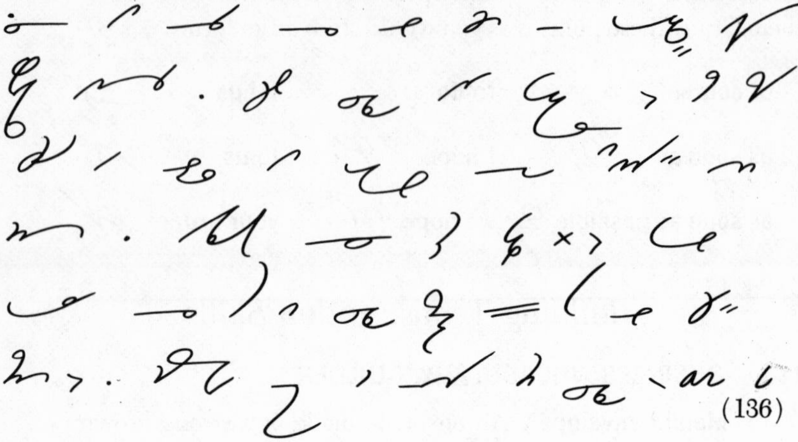

(136)

220.

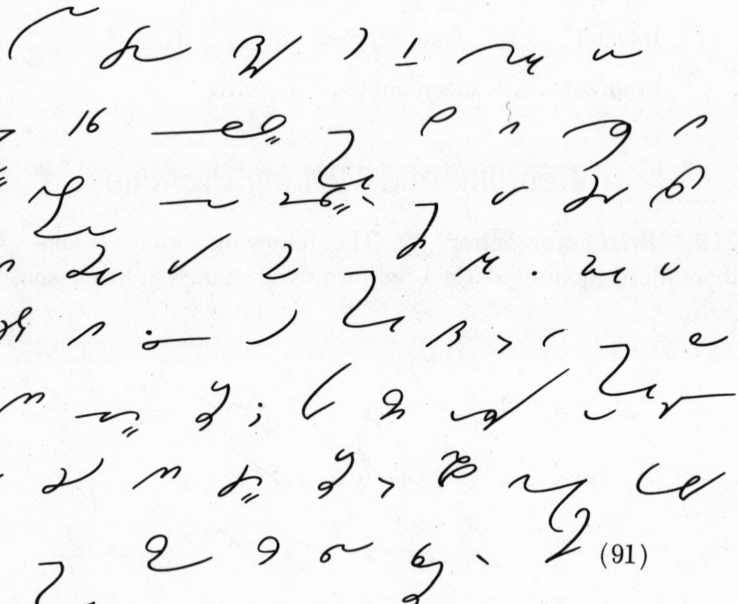
16
26

(91)

221.

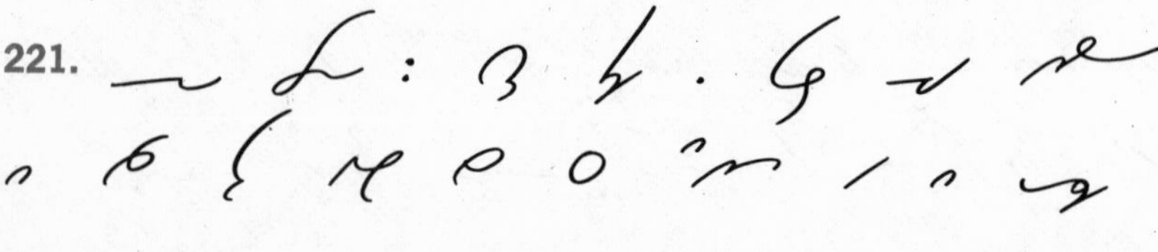

(123)

....

222.

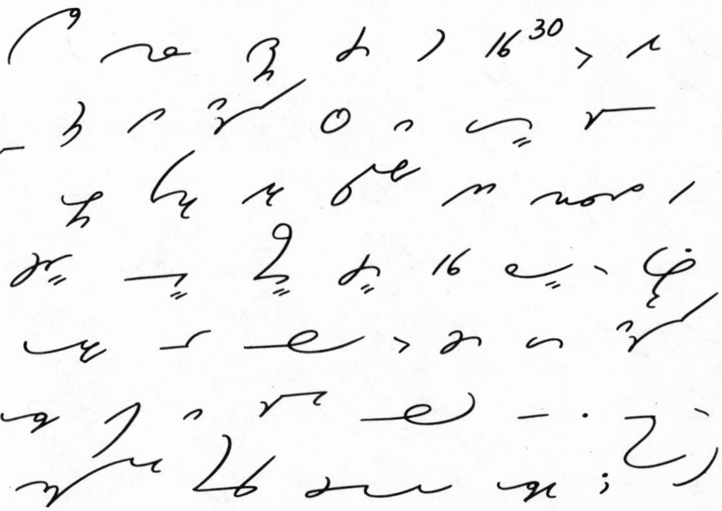

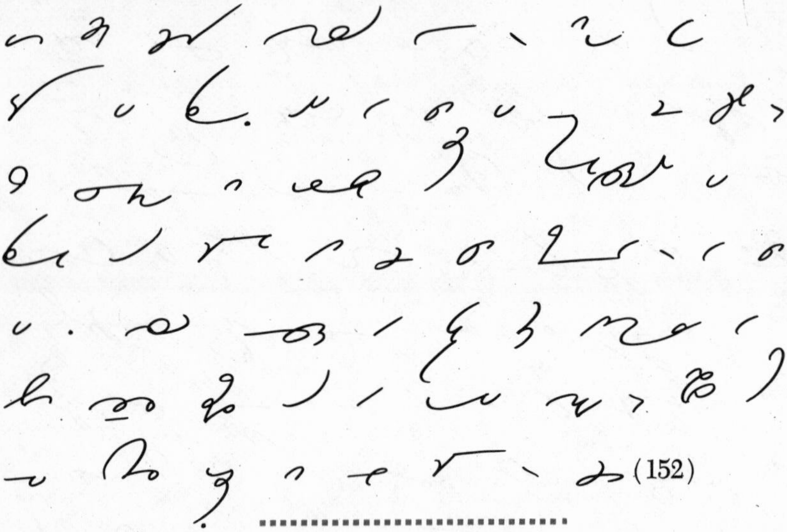

(152)

223.

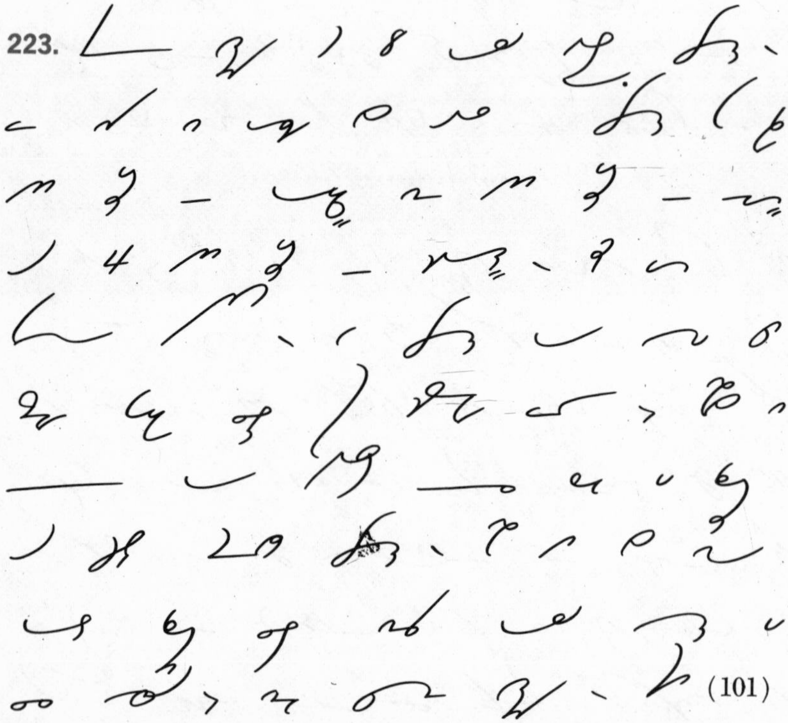

(101)

Lesson 26

Principles

224. Long Ī and a Following Vowel. Any vowel following long *ī* is represented by a small circle within the large circle.

Compare: **line**  **lion** 

trial		**prior**		**appliances**	
science		**quietly**		**reliant**	

225. Ĭa, Ēa. The sounds of *ĭa*, as in *piano*, and *ēa*, as in *create*, are represented by a large circle with a dot placed within it.

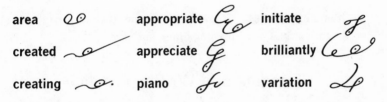

area		**appropriate**		**initiate**	
created		**appreciate**		**brilliantly**	
creating		**piano**		**variation**	

226. Word Beginnings In-, Un-, En-. The word beginnings *in-*, *un-*, *en-* are represented by *n* before a consonant.

In-

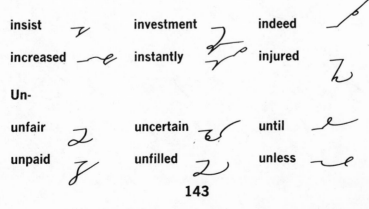

insist		**investment**		**indeed**	
increased		**instantly**		**injured**	

Un-

unfair		**uncertain**		**until**	
unpaid		**unfilled**		**unless**	

En-

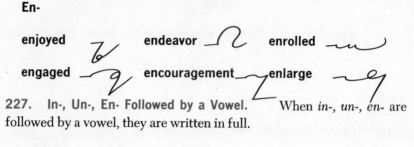

enjoyed **endeavor** **enrolled**

engaged **encouragement** **enlarge**

227. In-, Un-, En- Followed by a Vowel. When *in-*, *un-*, *en-* are followed by a vowel, they are written in full.

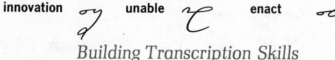

innovation **unable** **enact**

Building Transcription Skills

228. BUSINESS VOCABULARY BUILDER

endeavor To try.

associates (*noun*) Fellow workers.

home appliances Items for the home, such as refrigerators, stoves, washing machines, and dryers.

Reading and Writing Practice

229.

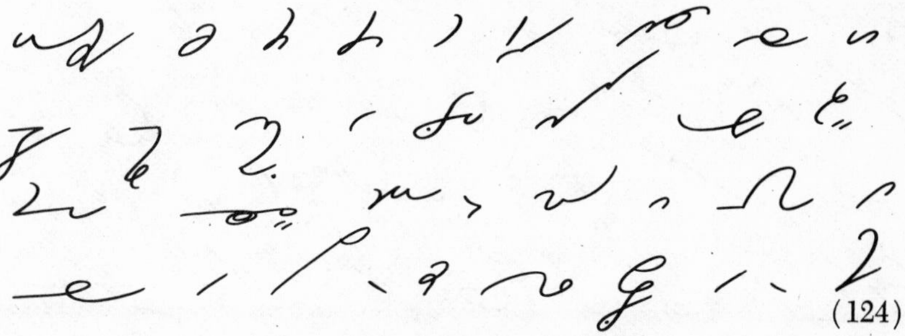

(124)

230.

(136)

231.

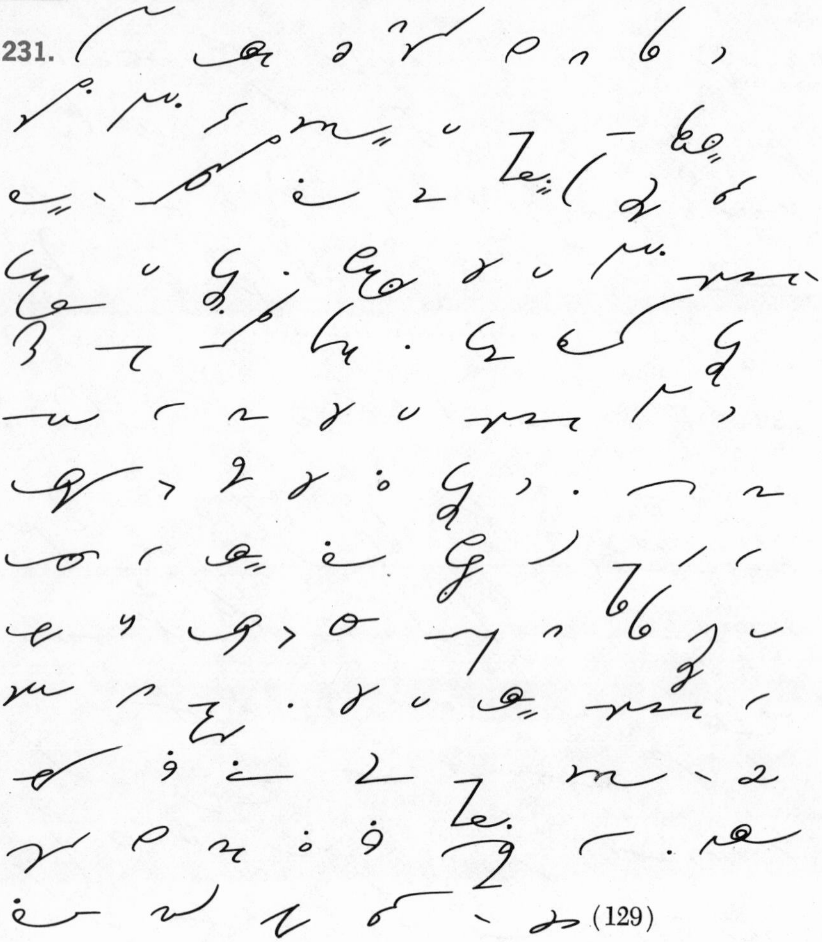

(129)

232.

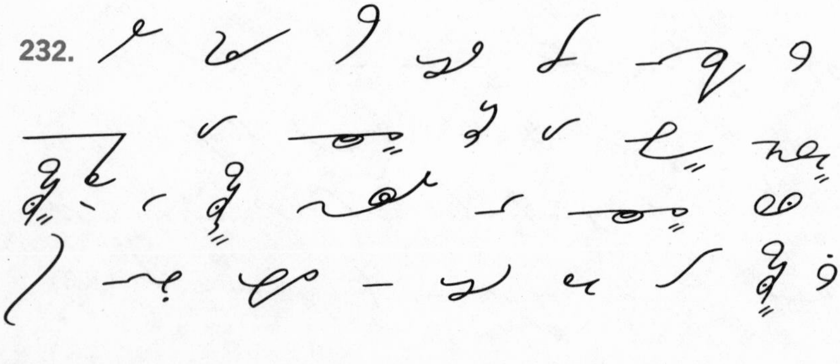

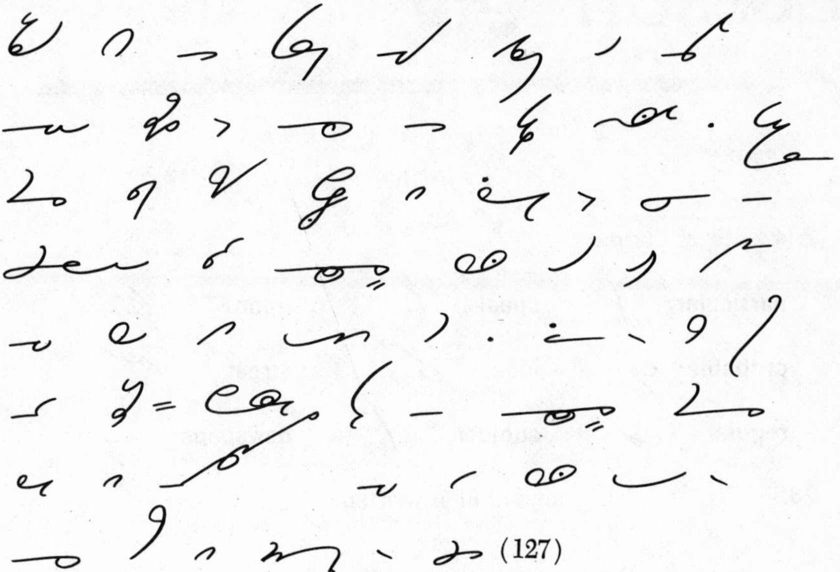

(127)

233. Chuckle

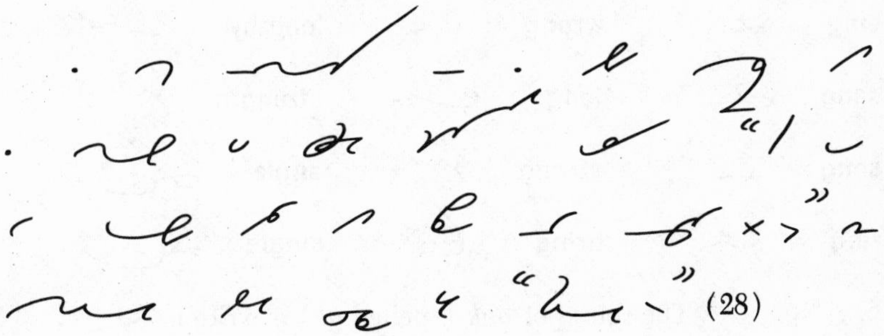

(28)

Lesson 27

Principles

234. Brief Forms

particular	speak	upon
probable	idea	street
regular	subject	newspaper

235. Ng. The sound of *ng* is written .

Compare: seen sing

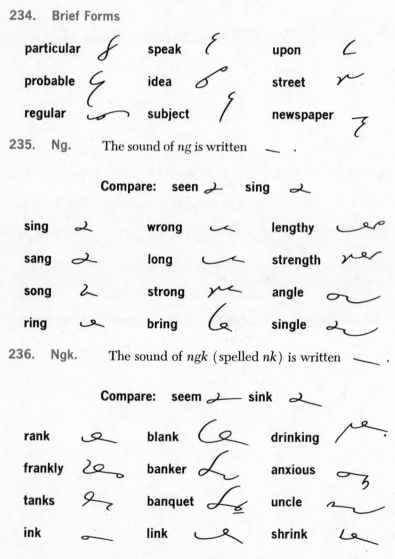

sing	wrong	lengthy
sang	long	strength
song	strong	angle
ring	bring	single

236. Ngk. The sound of *ngk* (spelled *nk*) is written .

Compare: seem sink

rank	blank	drinking
frankly	banker	anxious
tanks	banquet	uncle
ink	link	shrink

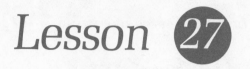

237. Omission of Vowel Preceding -tion. When *t, d, n,* or *m* is followed by *-ition, -ation,* the circle is omitted.

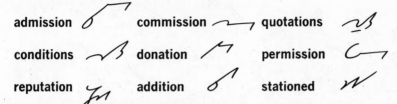

admission  **commission**  **quotations** 

conditions  **donation** 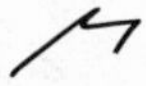 **permission** 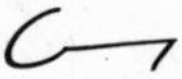

reputation  **addition**  **stationed** 

Building Transcription Skills

238. BUSINESS VOCABULARY BUILDER

render To give.

in the vicinity Near.

beyond reproach Cannot be criticized.

Reading and Writing Practice

239. Brief-Form Letter. This letter contains one or more illustrations of all the brief forms you studied in this lesson.

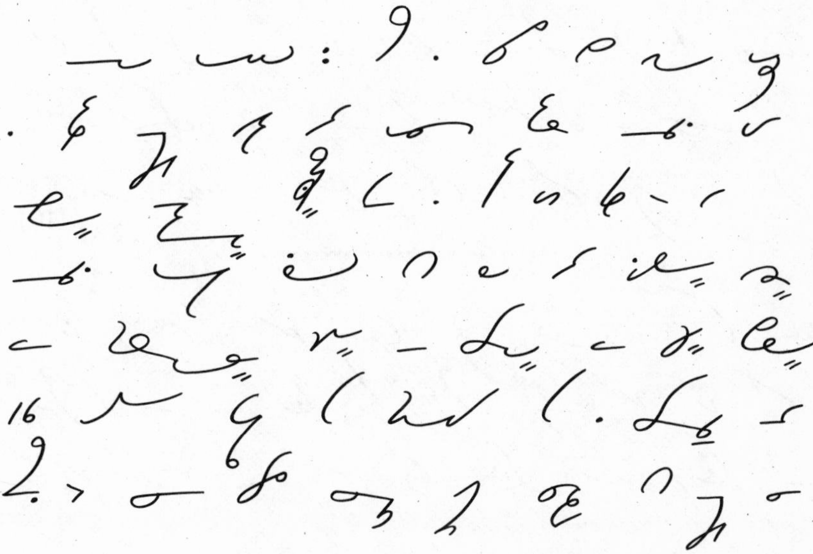

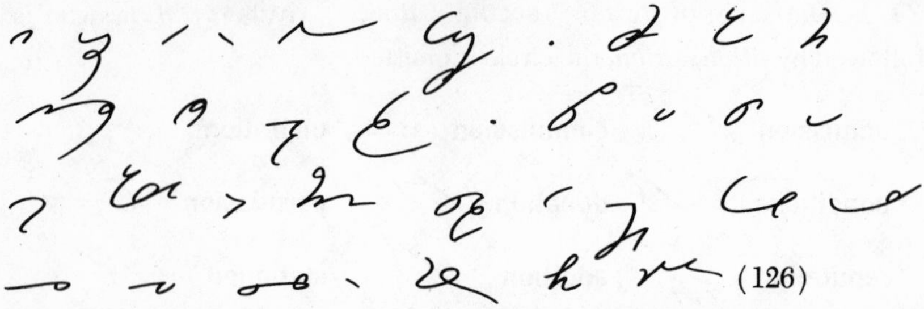

(126)

240.

(110)

241.

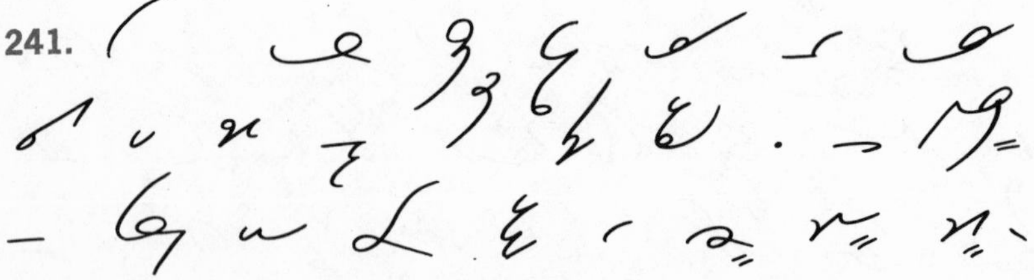

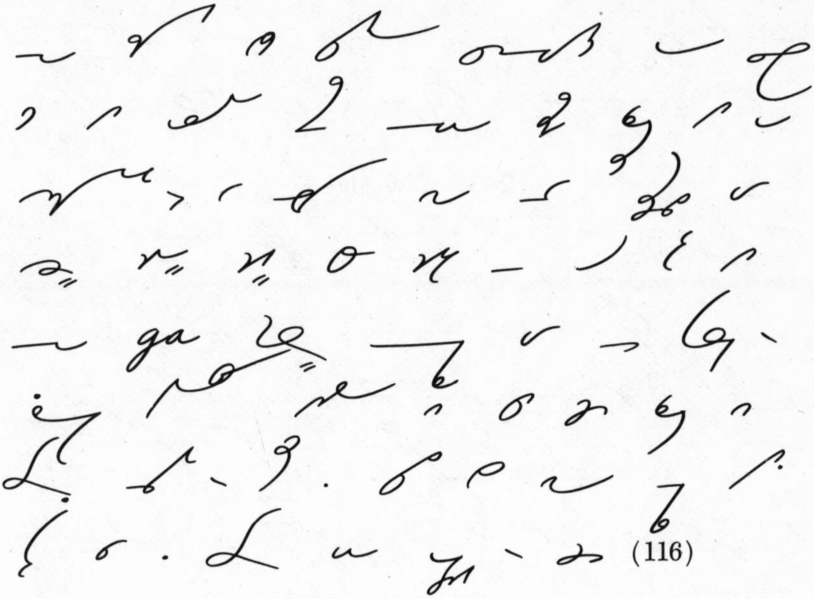

(116)

242.

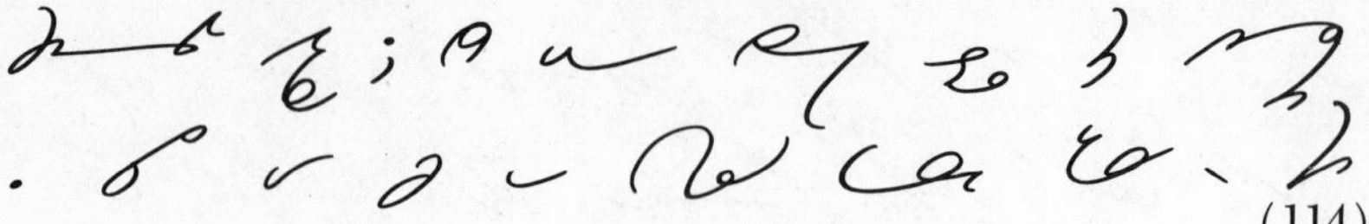

(114)

243. Chuckle

(86)

Lesson 28

Principles

244. Ah, Aw. A dot is used for *a* in words that begin with *ah* and *aw.*

ahead		**await**		**awoke**	
away		**awake**		**aware**	

245. Y. Before *o* and *oo, y* is expressed by the small circle, as *y* is pronounced *e. Ye* is expressed by a small loop; *ya,* by a large loop.

yawn		**yellow**		**yard**	
youth		**yielded**		**yarn**	

246. X. The letter *x* is usually represented by an *s* written with a slight backward slant.

Compare: **miss**  **mix** 

fees  **fix** 

box		**relax**		**tax**	
boxes		**relaxes**		**taxes**	

247. Omission of Short Ŭ. In the body of a word, short *ŭ* is omitted before *n, m,* or a straight downstroke.

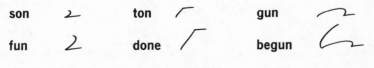

Before N

son		**ton**		**gun**	
fun		**done**		**begun**	

Before M

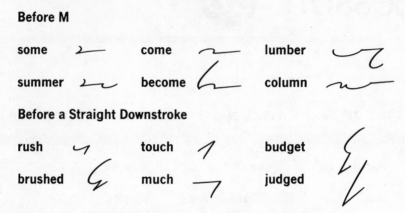

some | **come** | **lumber**

summer | **become** | **column**

Before a Straight Downstroke

rush | **touch** | **budget**

brushed | **much** | **judged**

Building Transcription Skills

248. BUSINESS VOCABULARY BUILDER

bachelor's degree The first, or lowest, academic degree offered by a college or university.

flexible Not firm; capable of being bent.

proprietor An owner.

Reading and Writing Practice

249.

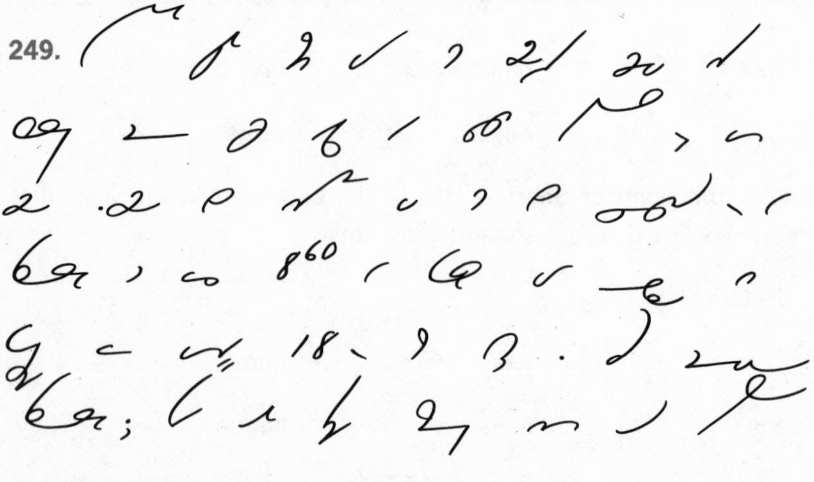

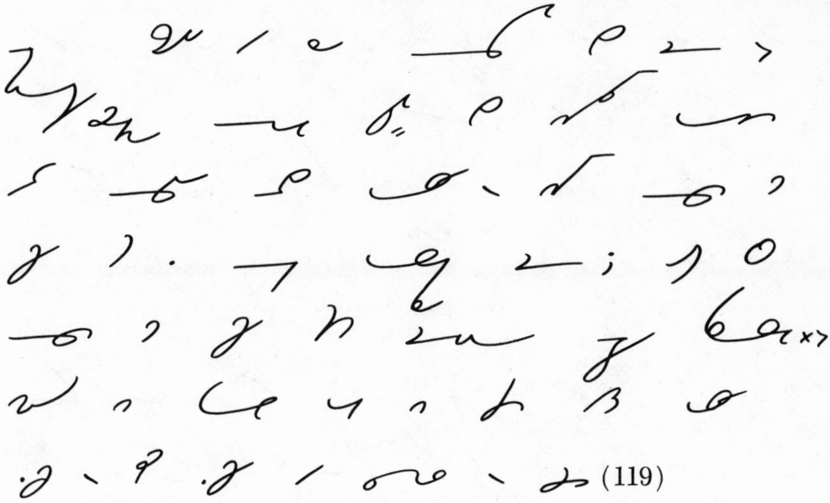

(119)

250.

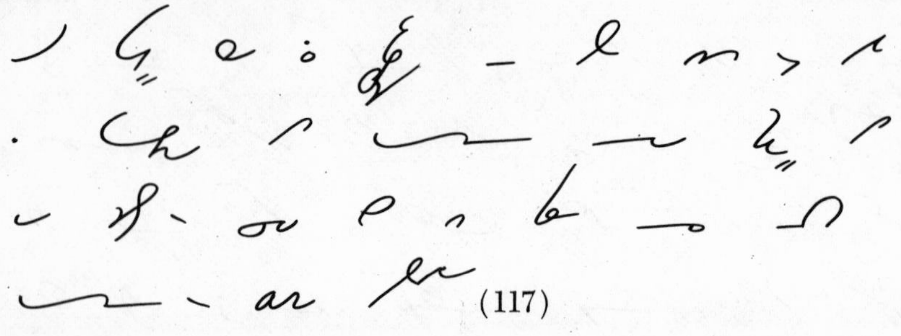

(117)

251.

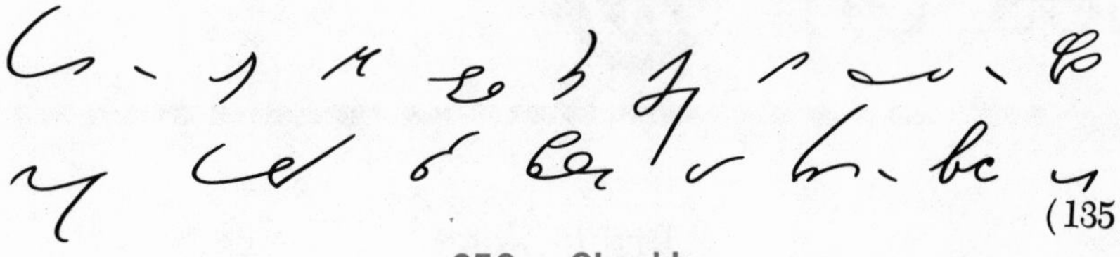

(135)

252. Chuckle

50-50

(84)

Lesson 29

Principles

253. Brief Forms

purpose **circular** **public**

regard **responsible** **publish, publication**

opinion **organize** **ordinary**

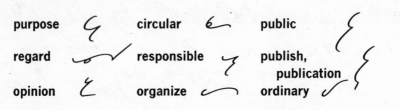

254. Word Beginning Ex-. The word beginning *ex-* is represented by *e-s.*

expense **expert** **extra**

expected **explained** **executive**

expresses **extend** **excuse**

expire **example** **examine**

255. Md, Mt. By rounding off the angle between *m-d,* we obtain the fluent *md* blend. The same stroke also represents *mt.*

Md, Mt

Compare: **seem** **seemed**

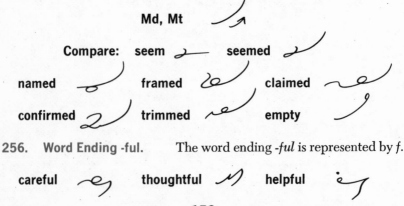

named **framed** **claimed**

confirmed **trimmed** **empty**

256. Word Ending -ful. The word ending *-ful* is represented by *f.*

careful **thoughtful** **helpful**

gratefully  **useful**  **helpfully** 

hopeful  **beautiful**  **helpfulness** 

Building Transcription Skills

257. BUSINESS VOCABULARY BUILDER

editing Preparing for publication.

overwhelmed Overpowered; crushed.

major Main; chief.

258. SIMILAR-WORDS DRILL

Addition, edition

addition Anything added.

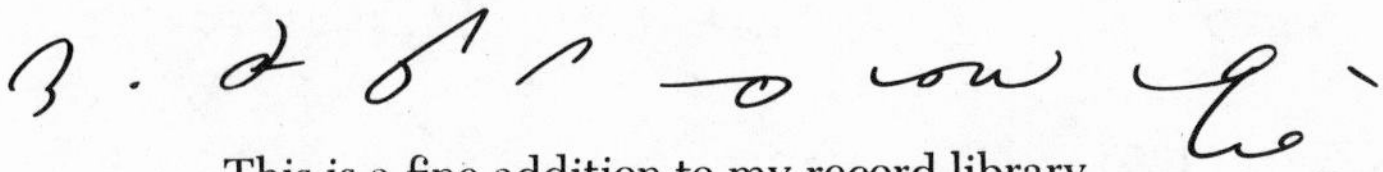

This is a fine addition to my record library.

edition All the copies of a book printed at one time.

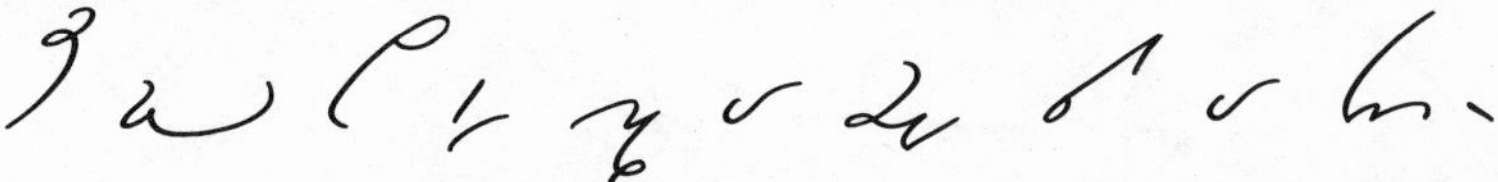

We have sold about 1,000 copies of the first edition of the book.

Reading and Writing Practice

259. Brief-Form Letter. This letter contains one or more illustrations of all the brief forms presented in this lesson.

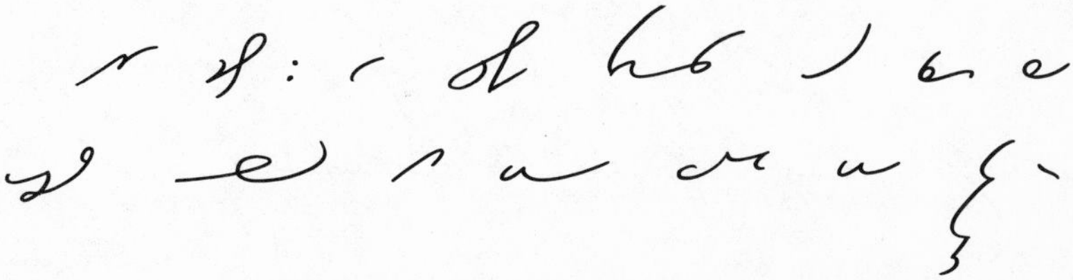

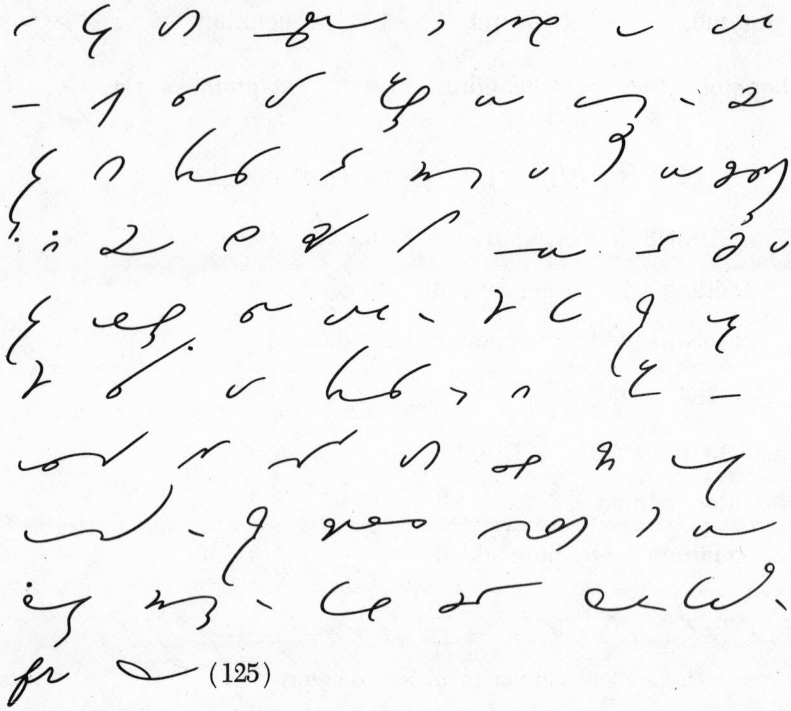

(125)

260.

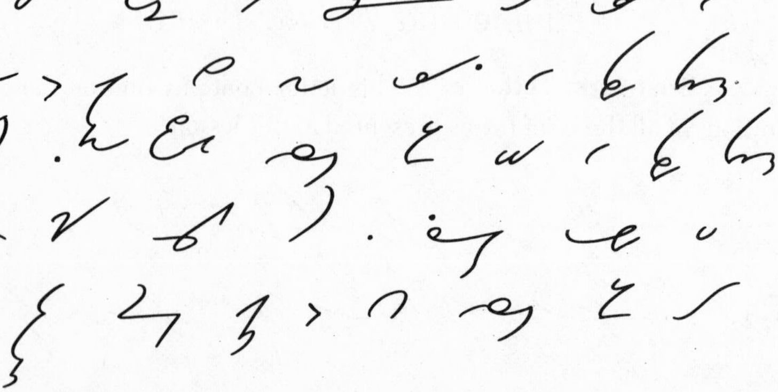

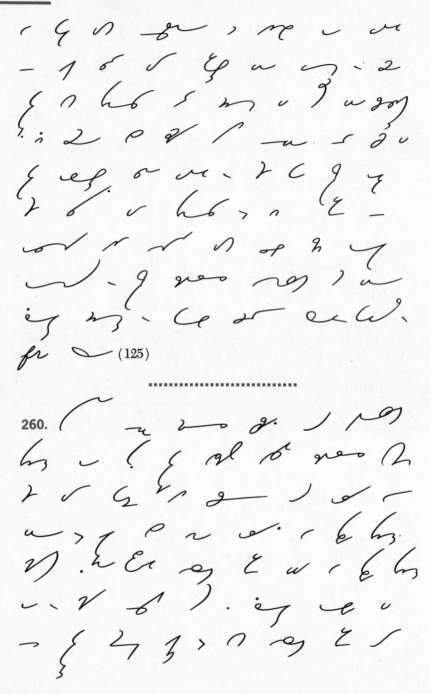

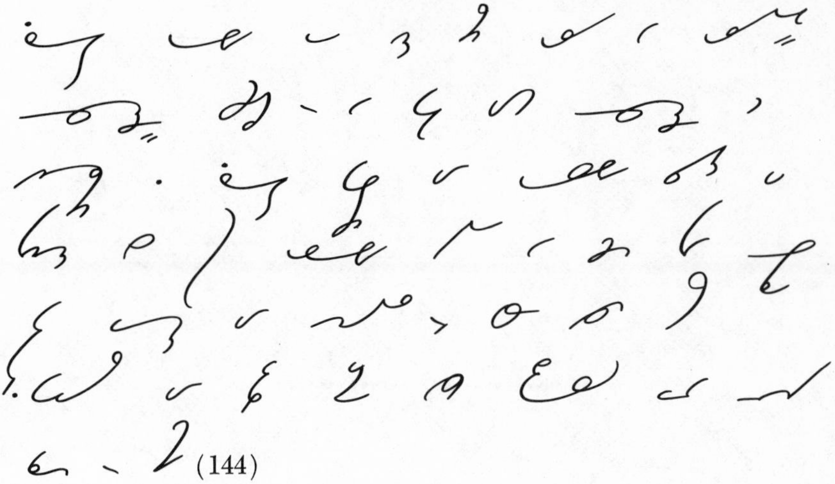

(144)

261.

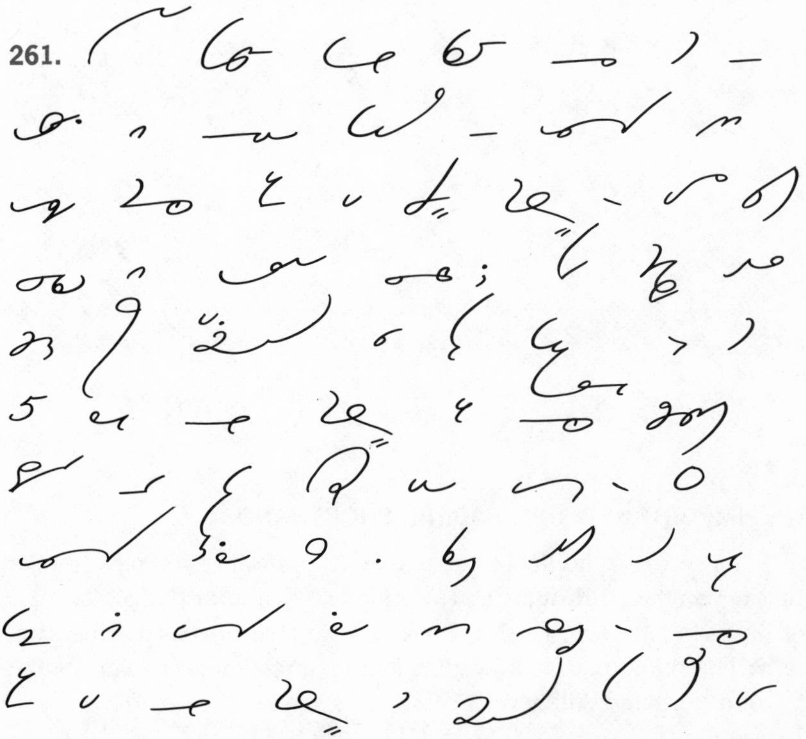

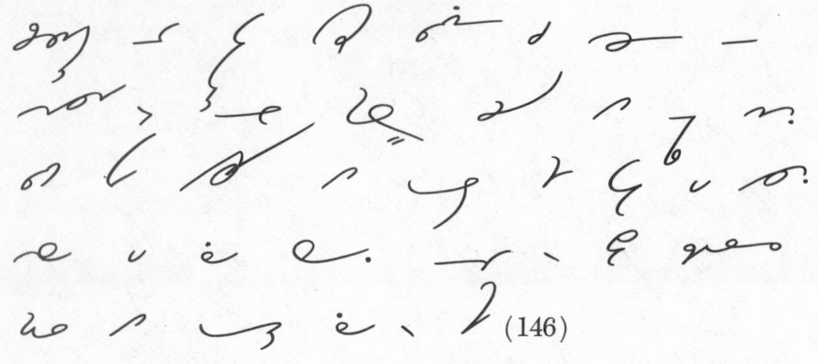

(146)

262.

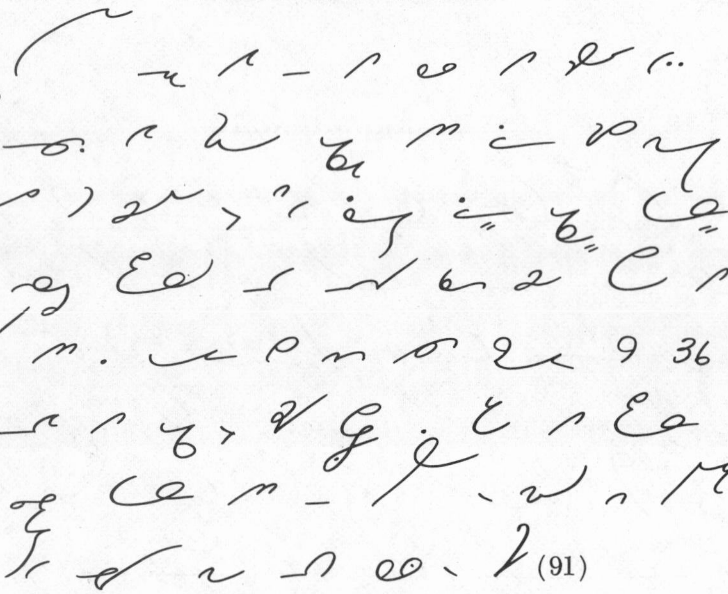

(91)

THE IMPORTANCE OF READING SHORTHAND

As you have no doubt noticed, each lesson that you have studied thus far contains a Reading and Writing Practice consisting of a number of business letters or articles. Have you stopped to consider the many important things that each Reading and Writing Practice is contributing to your shorthand skill development?

To begin with, each Reading and Writing Practice is helping you to fix in your mind the shorthand devices that are presented in the lesson. For example, in this lesson one of the devices you studied is the word beginning *ex-*. In the Reading and Writing Practice of this lesson, there are fourteen words in which *ex-* is used.

Even with the practice you have received on *ex-* in this lesson, however, it is safe to say that you will not have mastered that word beginning. But don't worry; you will meet *ex-* in the Reading and Writing Practice of every lesson hereafter.

The same is true of all the other shorthand devices that you will study. You will meet them again and again in the lessons that follow, so that you will eventually master them.

In addition to helping you fix the shorthand devices in your mind, each Reading and Writing Practice reviews many times the brief forms and phrases that you have previously studied. Each Reading and Writing Practice is helping you to stock your mind with joinings of shorthand characters and with the shapes of individual characters, so that, when you eventually take new dictation, your mind will quickly be able to form an outline for any word that is dictated.

The efficient stenographer is the one who can read shorthand easily and rapidly. To become a rapid shorthand reader, read all the shorthand you can. Remember, too, that the more shorthand you read, the more rapid shorthand *writer* you will become.

Lesson 30 RECALL

After studying the new shorthand devices in Lessons 25 through 29, you have earned another breathing spell! Therefore, you will find no new shorthand strokes or principles in Lesson 30.

In this lesson you will find an Accuracy Practice devoted to the curved strokes of Gregg Shorthand, a Recall Chart, and a Reading and Writing Practice that offers you some interesting suggestions on how to be a good conversationalist.

Accuracy Practice

To get the most benefit from this Accuracy Practice, be sure to follow the procedures suggested on page 130.

263. 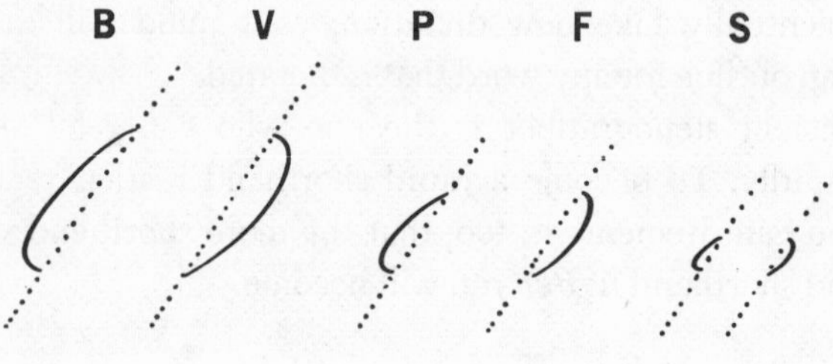
B
V
P
F
S

To write these strokes accurately:

a. Give them approximately the slant indicated by the dotted lines.

b. Make the curve deep at the beginning of *v, f,* comma *s;* make the curve deep at the end of *b, p,* left *s.*

Practice Drill

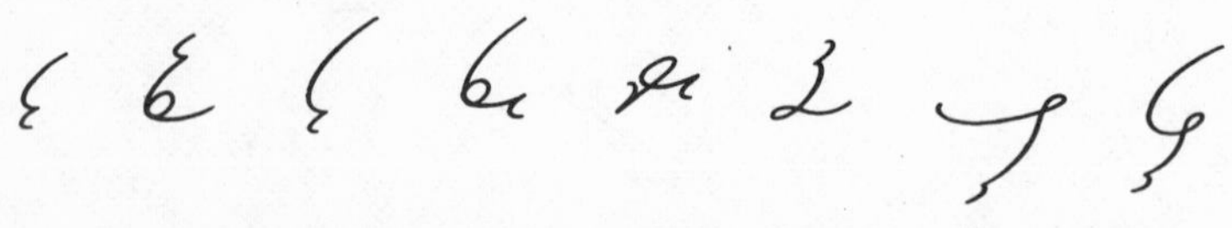

Puts, spare, business, bears, stairs, sphere, leaves, briefs.

264. **Pr** **Pl** **Br** **Bl**

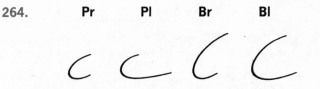

To write these combinations accurately:

a. Write each without a pause between the first and second letter of each combination.

b. Watch your proportions carefully.

Practice Drill

Press, pray, prim, plan, plate, place.
Brim, brief, bread, blame, blast.

265. **Fr** **Fl**

To write these combinations accurately:

a. Write them with one sweep of the pen, with no stop between the *f* and the *r* or *l*.

Practice Drill

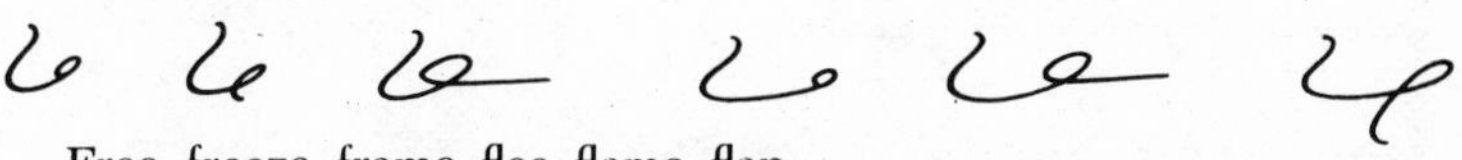

Free, freeze, frame, flee, flame, flap.

266. Recall Chart. This chart contains all the brief forms in Chapter 5 and one or more illustrations of the word-building principles you studied in Chapters 1 through 5.

As you read through the words in this chart, be sure to spell each word that you cannot read immediately.

Can you read the 84 words in the chart in 6 minutes or less?

BRIEF FORMS

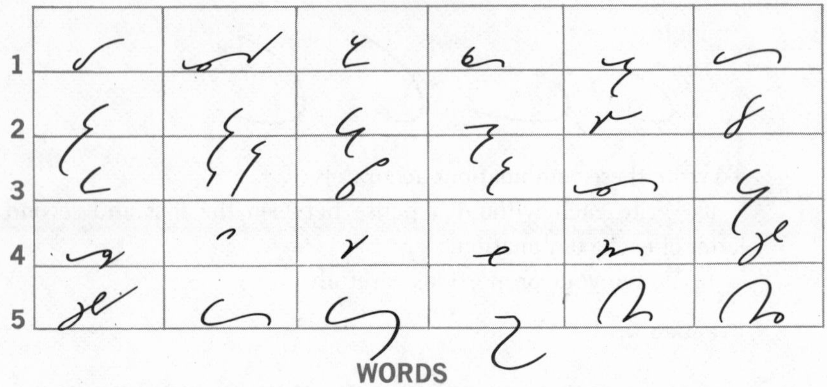
1
2
3
4
5

WORDS

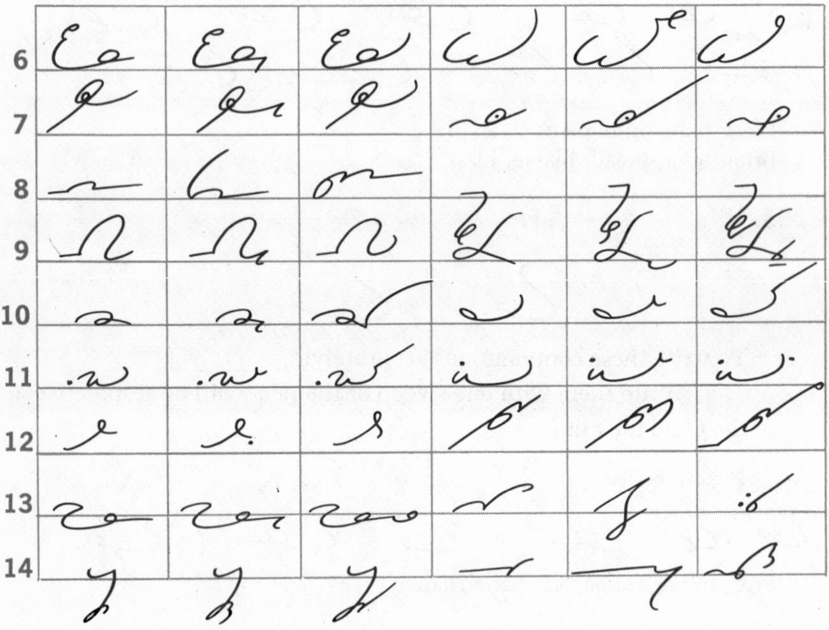
6
7
8
9
10
11
12
13
14

Building Transcription Skills

267. BUSINESS VOCABULARY BUILDER

digresses Gets off the main subject.

trite Worn out; old.

minute (pronounced *mĭ·nūt′*) Very small; of little importance.

Reading and Writing Practice

Reading Scoreboard. The previous Reading Scoreboard appeared in Lesson 18. If you have been studying each Reading and Writing Practice faithfully, no doubt there has been an increase in your reading speed. Let us measure that increase on the *first reading* of the material in Lesson 30. The following table will help you:

Lesson 30 contains 378 words.

If you read Lesson 30 in	your reading rate is
12 MINUTES	31 WORDS A MINUTE
14 MINUTES	27 WORDS A MINUTE
16 MINUTES	24 WORDS A MINUTE
18 MINUTES	21 WORDS A MINUTE
20 MINUTES	19 WORDS A MINUTE
22 MINUTES	17 WORDS A MINUTE
24 MINUTES	15 WORDS A MINUTE

If you can read Lesson 30 in 12 minutes or less, you are doing well. If you take considerably longer than 24 minutes, perhaps you should review your homework procedures. For example, are you:

1. Practicing in a quiet place at home?
2. Practicing without the radio or television set on?
3. Spelling aloud any words that you cannot read immediately?

268. Conversation Check List

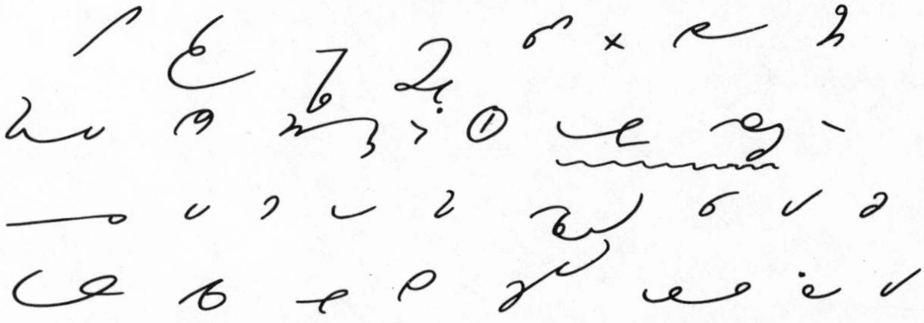

(378)

English—The Secretary's "Secret Weapon"

If you are one of those who think that "English is a bore — who needs it?" then think again. The truth is that every secretary needs a solid footing in English grammar. The executive for whom you will work will doubtless know what he wants to say; but he may not know the correct spelling, punctuation, and grammatical construction — that is, how to say it. He may have a college degree in engineering, accounting, history, or chemistry; but somewhere along the line he missed the opportunity to learn the finer points of grammar. This is where you come in. The executive's request of the secretary, "Fix the letter so that it 'reads' right," is not rare. And he really means it.

Many employers are highly expert in the English language. They may dictate every punctuation mark and spell every unusual word. If you get one of these for a boss, your job of transcribing will be greatly simplified.

Then there is the dictator who thinks he knows grammar, but doesn't, and will expect you to transcribe everything just as it was dictated whether it is really right or not. Of course, in this case there is nothing for you to do but to follow his wishes — he takes the responsibility.

But if your boss says, "You know English and I don't, so you fix this letter," then you must know. It is your responsibility. Badly constructed letters can cost your company a sale or can result in the loss of good will.

No matter how rapidly you can type or can write shorthand, these skills are greatly weakened if you cannot produce a finished transcript that is grammatically perfect. The top-notch secretary must be a real expert in business English. The surer she is of the accepted rules of English, the more secure her job and the better her chances for advancement.

Don't let anyone mislead you about the importance of grammar. It's the secretary's "secret weapon."

Chapter

6

Lesson 31

Principles

269. Brief Forms

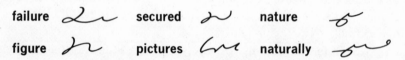

merchant  **never**  **short** 

merchandise  **experience**  **quantity** 

recognize  **between**  **situation** 

270. Word Ending -ure. The word ending *-ure* is represented by *r*.

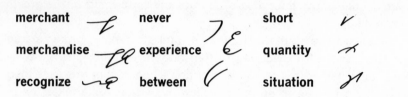

failure  **secured**  **nature** 

figure  **pictures**  **naturally** 

271. Word Ending -ual. The word ending *-ual* is represented by *l*.

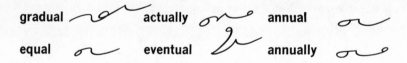

gradual  **actually** 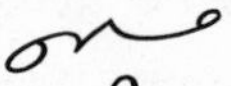 **annual** 

equal  **eventual**  **annually** 

Building Transcription Skills

272. PUNCTUATION PRACTICE

The first impression you get of the letter on page 173 is a good one. The letter is positioned properly; the margins are even; the date, inside address, closing, etc., are all in their proper places. If you read the letter casually, you find it makes good sense and apparently represents what the dictator said.

But if you read it carefully, you will quickly realize that the letter

The NELSON HARDWARE Company

TOWER PARKWAY / NEW HAVEN 4, CONNECTICUT

March 12, 196-

Mr. Frank S. Brown
Taylor Lamp Corporation
449 Terrace Avenue
St. Louis 8, Missouri

Dear Mr. Brown,

May we ask a favor of you? The regular credit agencys do not have your financial statement, and we assume that is a matter of policy on your part. In view of the friendly relationship between your fine firm and our's however would you please co-operate with us? One of our regular forms is enclosed for complesion on your part.

We fully realize that submiting a finantial statement is one of personal privilege, although we are glad to say that most customers co-operate with us.

As you already know we want to work with you on the best basis suited to your needs: and, of course, you will find us helpful and genuinely interested in serving you promply and efficiently.

Your co-operation by promptly returning the completed form will be very much apreciated.

Cordially your.

John R. Smith
Credit Manager

JRS:BA
Enc.

Can you find all the errors in this letter?

will never be signed; in fact, the dictator will no doubt have something to say to the stenographer who transcribed the letter. Why? It contains several misspelled words, as well as a number of errors in punctuation.

If you are to succeed as a stenographer or secretary, your letters must not only be an accurate transcript of what the dictator said, but they must also be correctly punctuated and free of spelling errors. A stenographer or secretary who consistently turns in transcripts with errors in spelling and punctuation will not be welcome long in a business office!

To make sure that you will be able to spell and punctuate accurately when you have completed your shorthand course, you will, from this point on, give special attention to these factors in each Reading and Writing Practice.

In the lessons ahead you will review nine of the most common uses of the comma. Each time one of these uses occurs in the Reading and Writing Practice, the comma will be encircled in the shorthand, thus calling it forcefully to your attention.

On the left side of the shorthand pages, you will find a number of words selected from the Reading and Writing Practice for special spelling study; they are words that stenographers and secretaries often misspell. Each word is correctly syllabicated.

Practice Suggestions

If you follow these simple suggestions in your homework practice hereafter, your ability to spell and to punctuate should improve noticeably.

1. Read carefully the explanation of each comma usage (for example, the explanation of the parenthetical comma on page 175) to be sure that you understand it. You will encounter many illustrations of each comma usage in the Reading and Writing Practice exercises so that eventually you will acquire the knack of applying it correctly.

2. Continue to read and copy each Reading and Writing Practice as you have always done. However, add these three important steps:

   a. Each time you see an encircled comma, note the reason for its use, which is indicated directly above the encircled comma.

   b. As you copy the Reading and Writing Practice, insert the

commas in your shorthand notes, encircling them as in the textbook.

c. When spelling words appear at the left of the shorthand pages in the textbook, spell them, aloud if possible, pausing slightly after each syllable. Spelling aloud helps to impress the correct spelling more firmly on your mind.

, parenthetical

In order to make his meaning clearer, a writer sometimes inserts a comment or an explanation that could be omitted without changing the meaning of the sentence. These added comments and explanations are called *parenthetical* and are separated from the rest of the sentence by commas.

If the parenthetical word or expression occurs at the beginning or end of a sentence, only one comma is needed.

I feel, therefore, that we should change our plans.
Don't you think, Mr. Smith, that the price is too high?
We shall send you a copy, of course.

Each time a parenthetical expression occurs in the Reading and Writing Practice, it will be indicated thus in the shorthand:

par
(,)

273. BUSINESS VOCABULARY BUILDER

revealing Bringing to light something that was not evident before.

merchandising Building sales by presenting goods to the public attractively.

accounting system The procedures and forms used for financial record keeping.

manual A handbook.

Reading and Writing Practice

274. Brief-Form Letter. All the brief forms presented in Lesson 31 are used at least once in this letter.

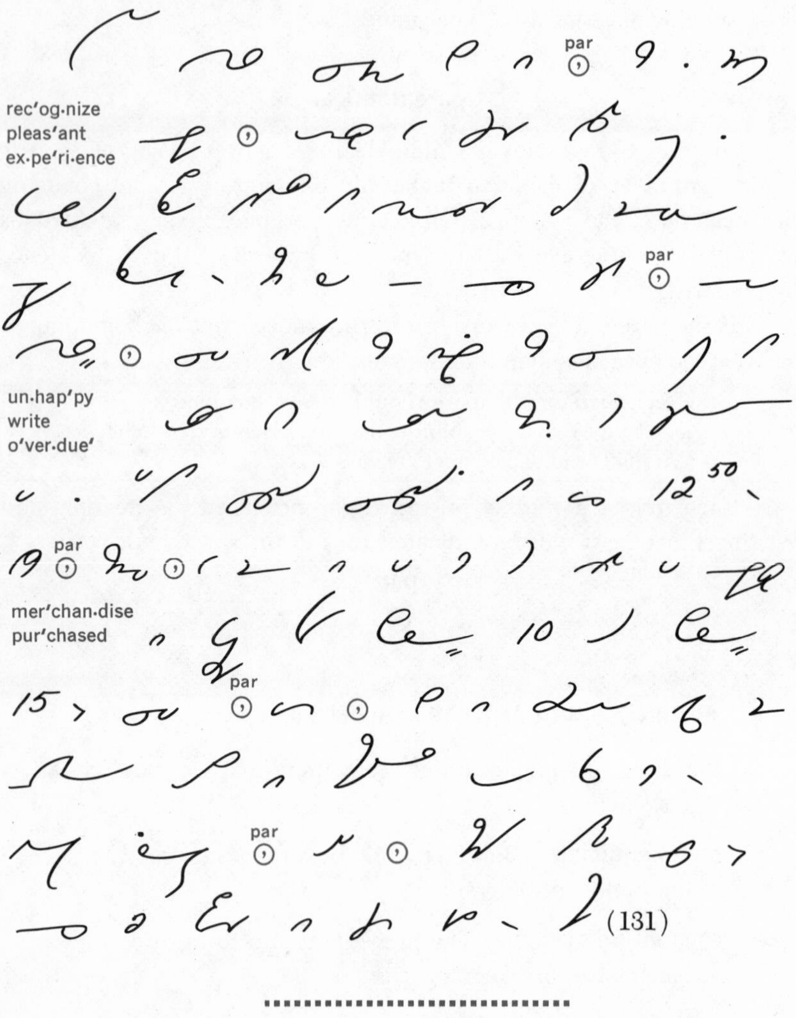

rec′og·nize
pleas′ant
ex·pe′ri·ence

un·hap′py
write
o′ver·due′

mer′chan·dise
pur′chased

(131)

275.

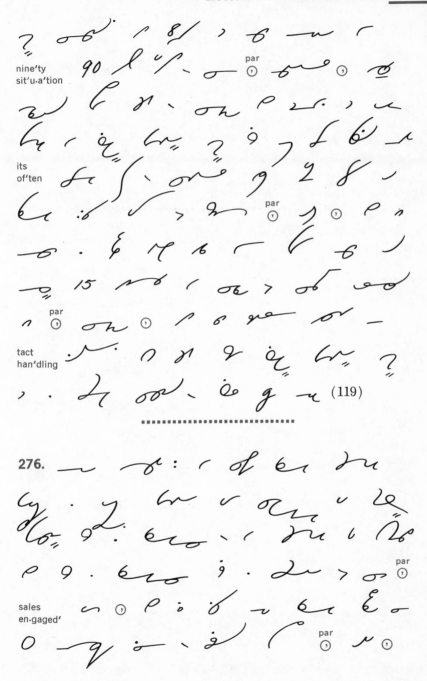

nine'ty
sit'u·a'tion

par

its
of'ten

par

par

tact
han'dling

(119)

276.

par

sales
en·gaged'

par

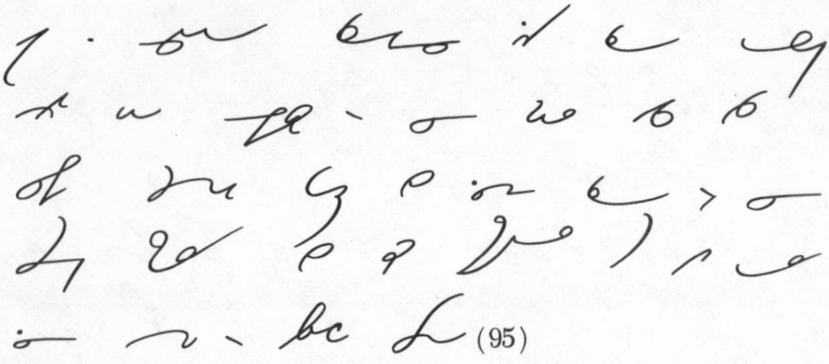

(95)

277.

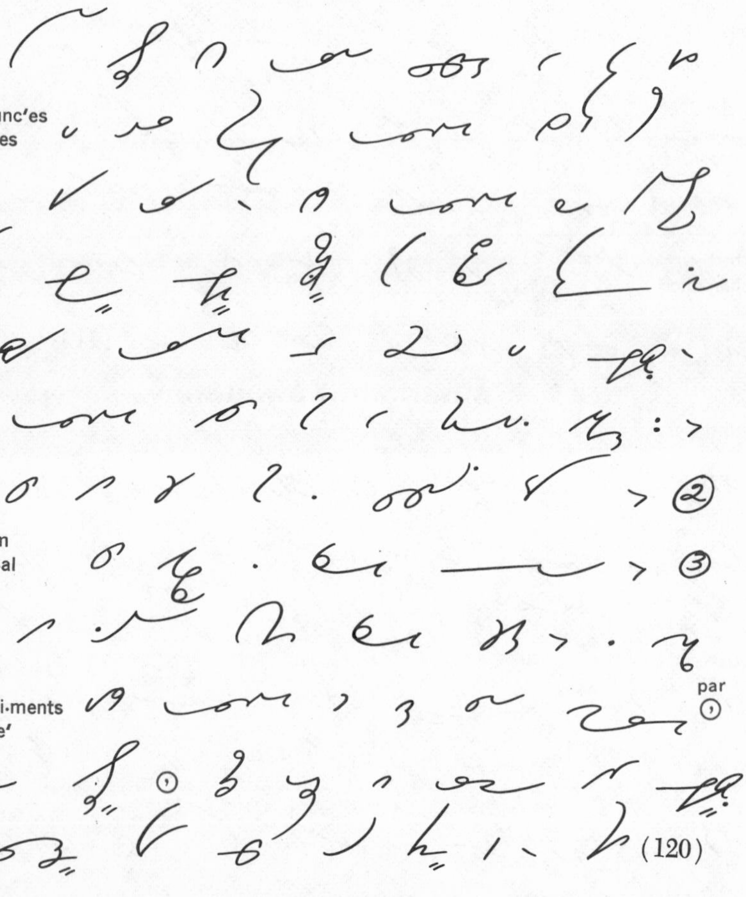

an·nounc'es
lec'tures

sys'tem
man'u·al

yours
com'pli·ments
re·ceive'

par

(120)

Lesson 32

Principles

278. Word Ending -ily. The word ending *-ily* is expressed by a narrow loop.

Compare: **steady**  **steadily** 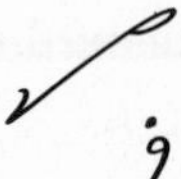

easily  **temporarily** 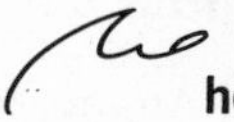 **heavily** 

readily  **family**  **hastily** 

heartily  **families**  **speedily** 

279. Word Beginning Al-. The word beginning *al-* is expressed by *o.*

also  **altogether**  **although** 

almost  **already**  **alter** 

280. Word Beginning Mis-. The word beginning *mis-* is represented by *m-s.*

mistake 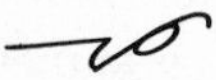 **misprint**  **misplaced** 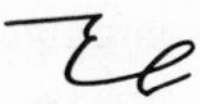

mistaken  **mislead**  **misery** 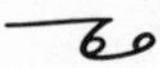

281. Word Beginnings Dis-, Des-. The word beginnings *dis-*, *des-* are expressed by *d-s.*

Dis-

discussion  **discouragement**  **distances** 

disposed  **discount**  **discover** 

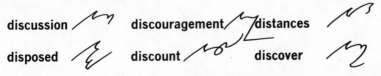

Des-

described 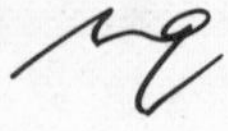 **description**  **despite** 

Building Transcription Skills

282. BUSINESS VOCABULARY BUILDER

disturbing Troubling.

in the red Showing a net loss; losing money.

misconception An incorrect idea.

283. PUNCTUATION PRACTICE

, apposition

Sometimes a writer mentions a person or thing and then, in order to make his meaning perfectly clear to the reader, says the same thing again in different words.

My neighbor, Mr. Harry Green, owns a sailboat.
The meeting will be held on Friday, April 16, at the Hotel Brown.

In many cases these constructions in apposition resemble the constructions in which the commas are used to set off parenthetical expressions. It is really immaterial whether the transcriber thinks he is using the commas to set off an appositive or to set off a parenthetical expression, for the results are identical.

An expression in apposition is set off by two commas, except at the end of a sentence, when only one comma is necessary.

Meet my neighbor, Harry Green.

Each time an expression in apposition occurs in the Reading and Writing Practice, it will be indicated thus in the shorthand:

ap

Reading and Writing Practice

284.

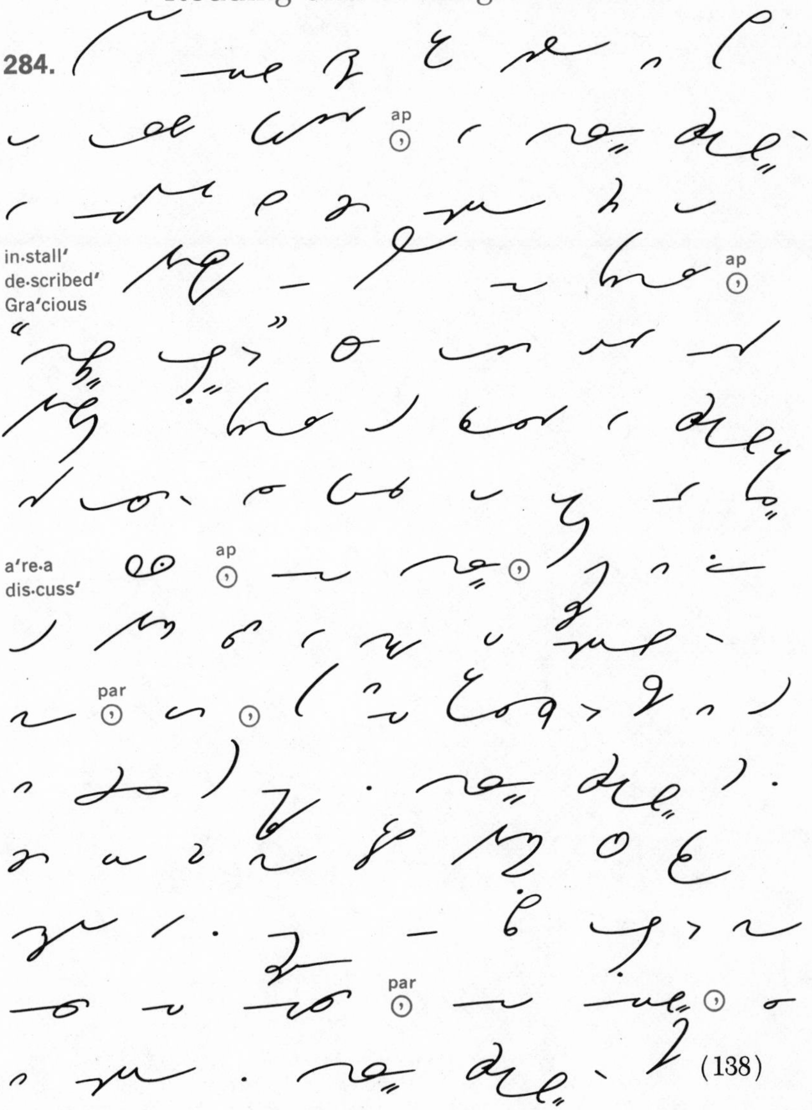
in·stall′
de·scribed′
Gra′cious
a′re·a
dis·cuss′
(138)

285.

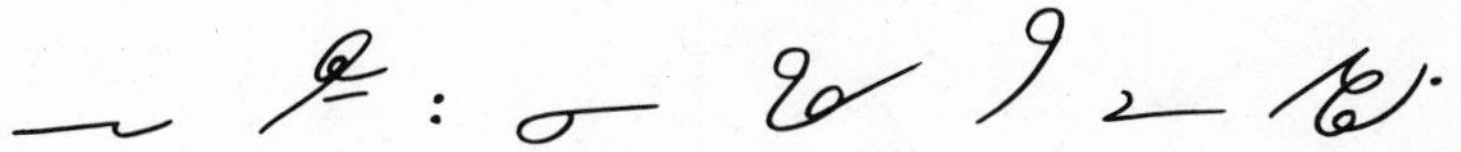

dis·turb′ing
dis′con·tin′ue

stead′i·ly
heav′i·ly
debt

mis′con·cep′tion

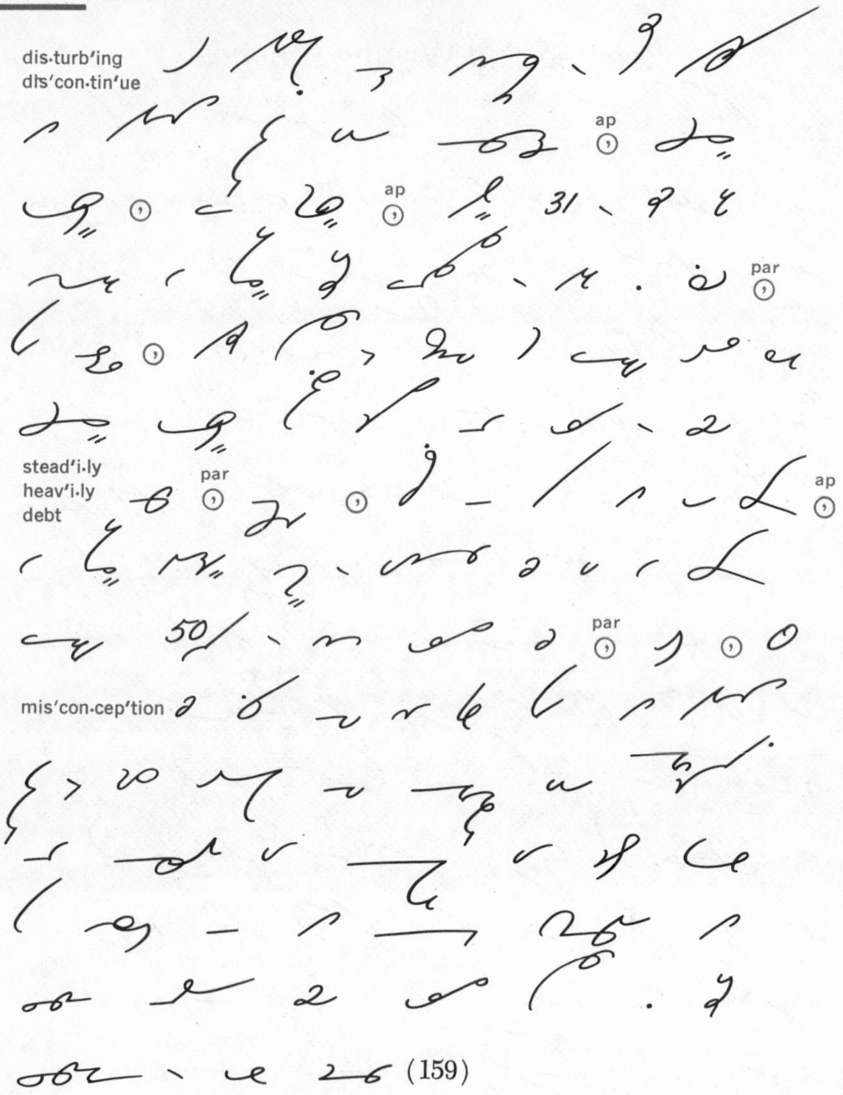

ap
ap
par
par
ap
par
31
50
16

(159)

286.

re·ceive′
dis·cour′ag·ing

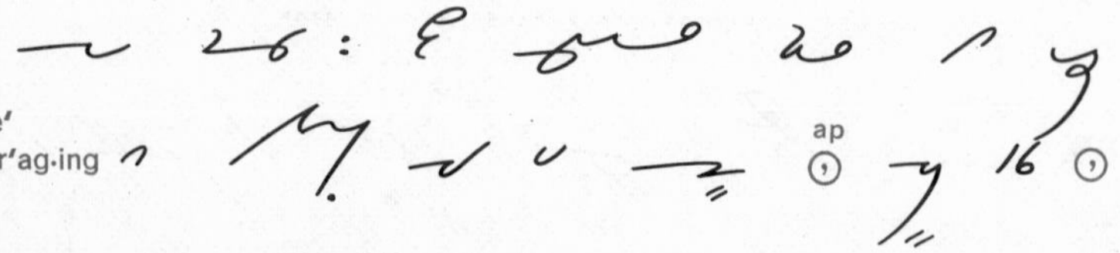

ap

dis'con·tin'u·ance
pub'li·ca'tion

tem'po·rar'i·ly
pay'roll'

ap
(105)

287.

young
mys'ter·y

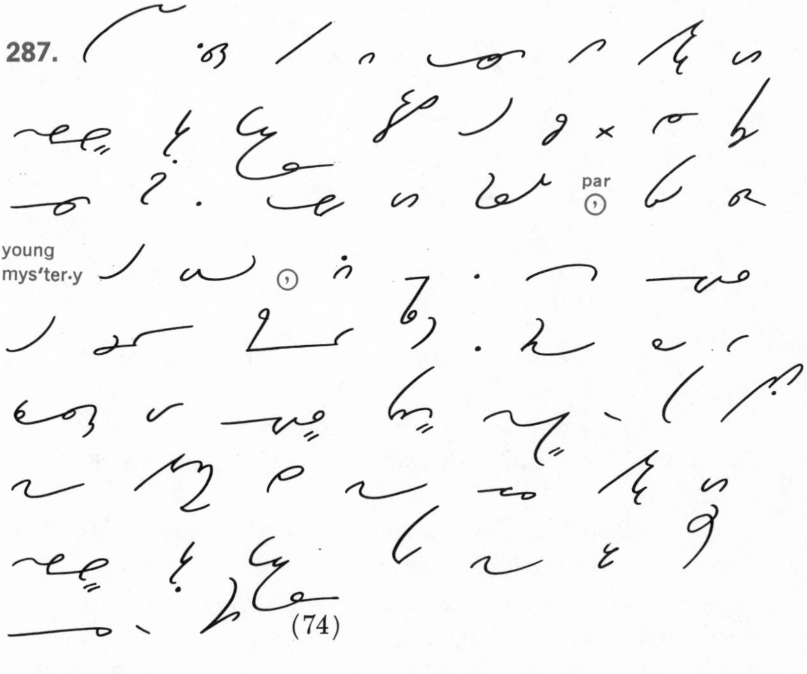
par
(74)

288. Chuckle

(82)

PERSONAL-USE CHECK LIST

Do you substitute shorthand for longhand wherever possible when you –

1. Take down your daily assignments?
2. Correspond with your friends who know shorthand?
3. Draft compositions and reports?
4. Make entries in your diary?
5. Make notes to yourself on things to do, people to see, appointments to keep, etc.?

Lesson 33

Principles

289. Brief Forms. This is the last set of brief forms you will have to learn.

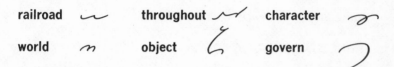

railroad throughout character

world object govern

290. Word Beginnings For-, Fore-. The word beginnings *for-*, *fore-* are represented by *f*. The *f* is joined with an angle to *r* or *l* to indicate that it represents a word beginning. The *f* is disjoined if the following character is a vowel.

forgive force forerunner

forget effort forlorn

form forth forever

informed foreclose forearm

291. Word Beginning Fur-. The word beginning *fur-* is also represented by *f*.

furnace furnish furniture

further furnished furlough

292. Ago in Phrases. In expressions of time, *ago* is represented by g.

days ago weeks ago long ago

years ago minutes ago months ago

Building Transcription Skills

293. BUSINESS VOCABULARY BUILDER

character reference One who vouches for the qualities, habits, and behavior of another.

foreman The man in charge of a gang or crew of workers.

succeeded Followed; took the place of.

294. PUNCTUATION PRACTICE

, series

When the last member of a series of three or more items is preceded by *and, or,* or *nor,* place a comma before the conjunction, as well as between the other items.

I bought a tie, a coat, and a pair of shoes.
I talked to him on July 1, on July 3, and on July 18.
Her duties consisted of receiving callers, answering the telephone, and opening the mail.

Each time a series occurs in the Reading and Writing Practice, it will be indicated thus in the shorthand:

ser

(,)

Reading and Writing Practice

295. Brief-Form Letter. The following letter contains all the brief forms presented in Lesson 33.

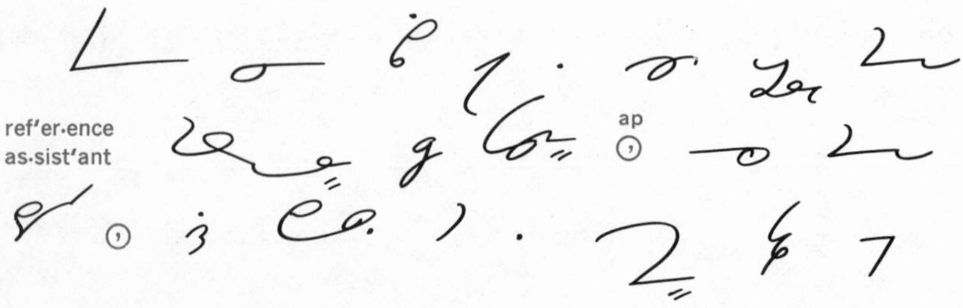
ref'er·ence
as·sist'ant
ap

dis'trict
fore'man

suc·ceed'ed
fur'nish

ser

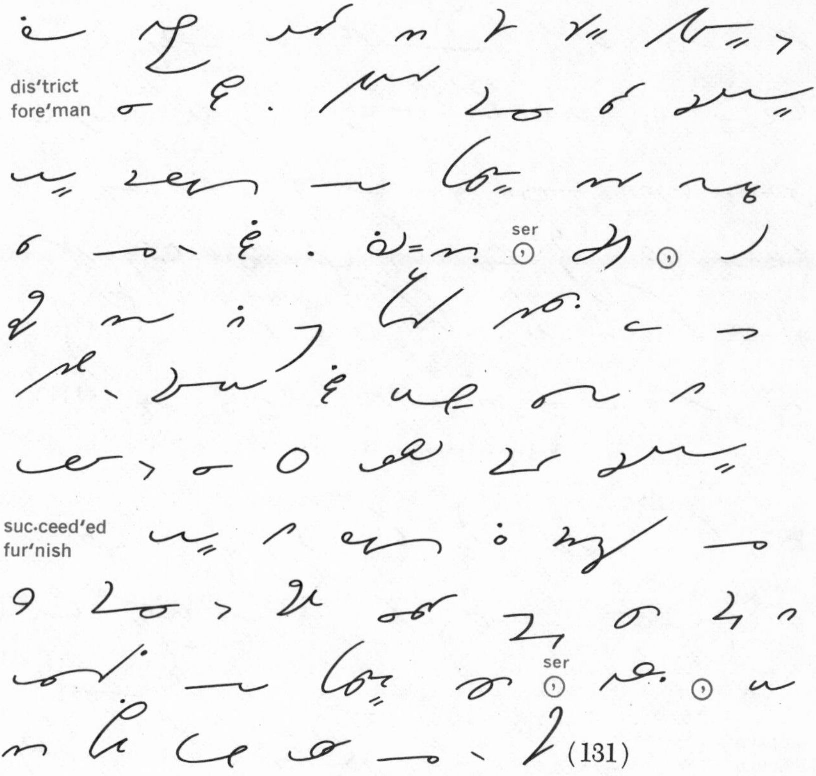

(131)

296.

its
o'ver·pay'ment

for'mal·ly
ac·cept'ed
as·sign'ment

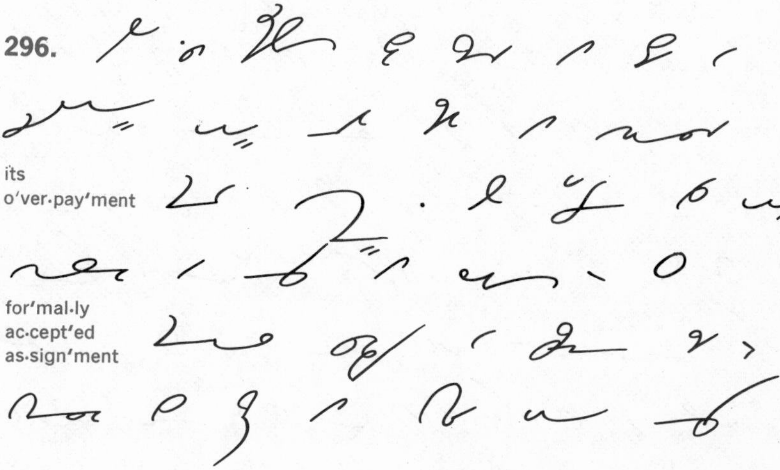

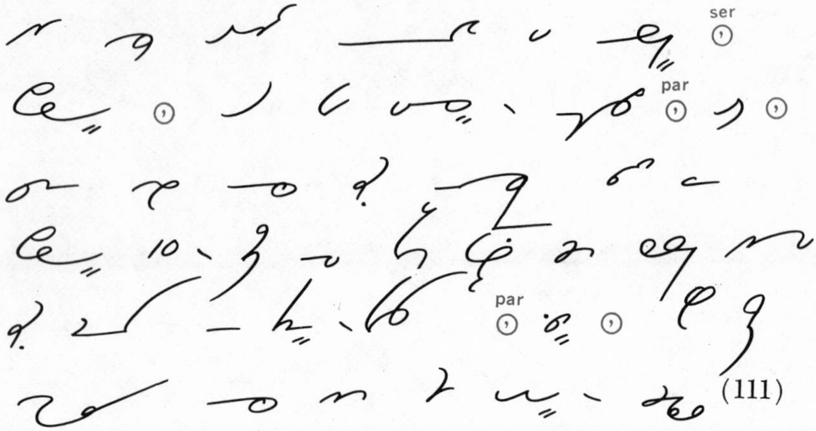

(111)

297.

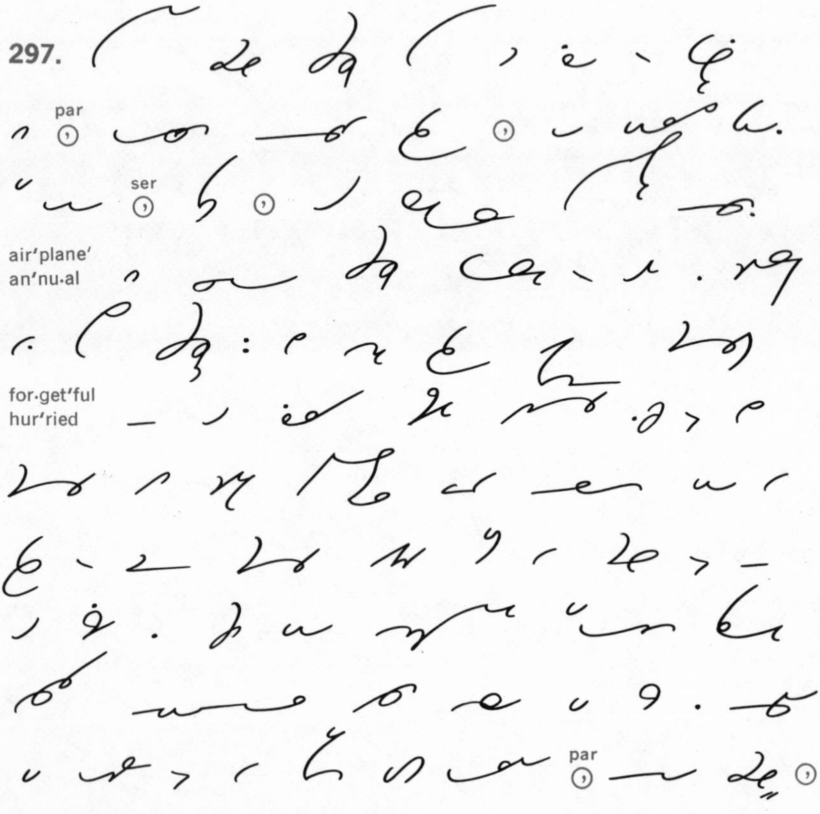

air′plane′
an′nu·al

for·get′ful
hur′ried

bal'ance
due

(146)

298.

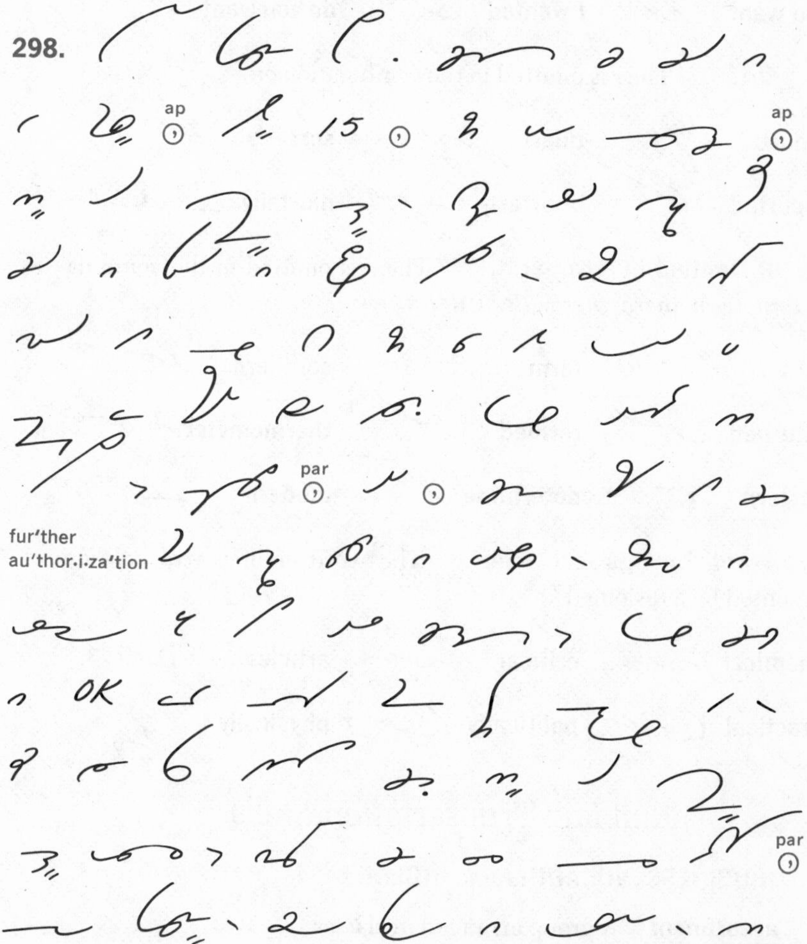
ap
ap
par
fur'ther
au'thor·i·za'tion
par

(134)

Lesson 34

Principles

299. Want in Phrases. In phrases, *want* is represented by *nt*.

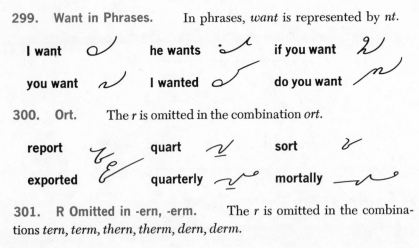

I want  **he wants**  **if you want** 

you want  **I wanted**  **do you want** 

300. Ort. The *r* is omitted in the combination *ort*.

report  **quart**  **sort** 

exported  **quarterly** 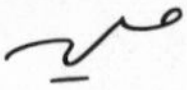 **mortally** 

301. R Omitted in -ern, -erm. The *r* is omitted in the combinations *tern, term, thern, therm, dern, derm.*

turn  **term**  **southern** 

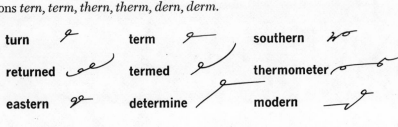

returned 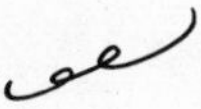 **termed**  **thermometer** 

eastern  **determine**  **modern** 

302. Word Endings -cal, -cle. The word endings *-cal, -cle* are represented by a disjoined *k*.

chemical  **critical**  **articles** 

practical  **politically**  **physically** 

Building Transcription Skills

303. BUSINESS VOCABULARY BUILDER

assortment A group arranged in classes.

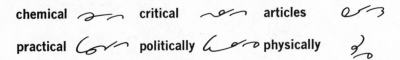

practical Useful.

liberal Generous.

distinguished Noteworthy; famous.

Reading and Writing Practice

304. Phrase Letter. This letter contains many illustrations of the word *want* in phrases, as well as a review of many other phrases that you have studied.

choose
clothes
prac'ti·cal

ad·van'tage
lib'er·al

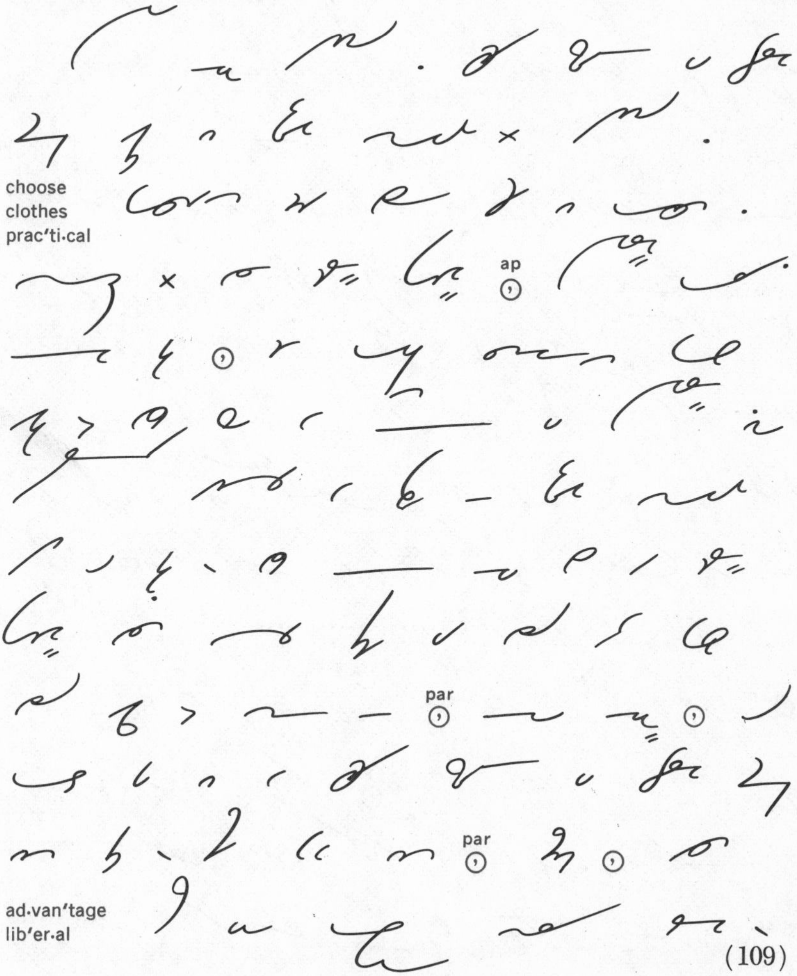
ap
par
par

(109)

305.

sight
plane
com'pa·ny's

rou·tine'
tech'ni·cal
com'pa·nies

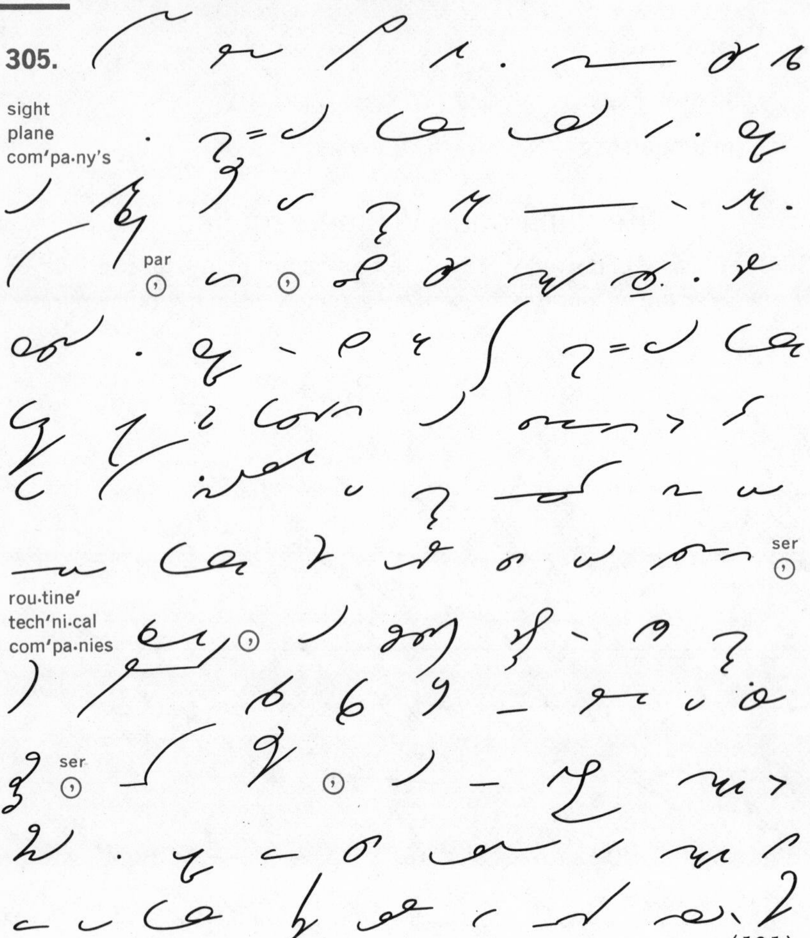
par
ser
ser

(121)

306.

per'son·al·ly

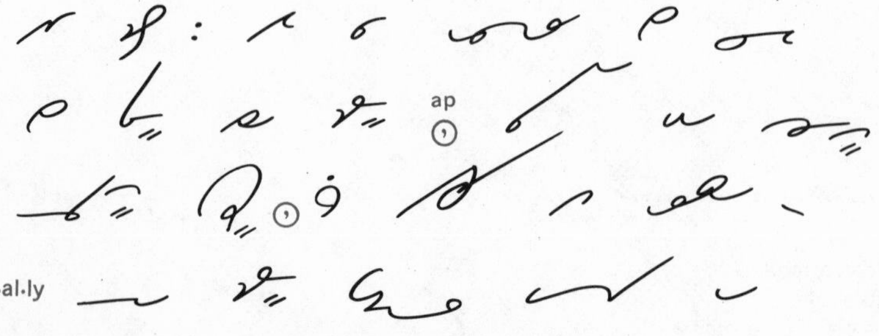
ap

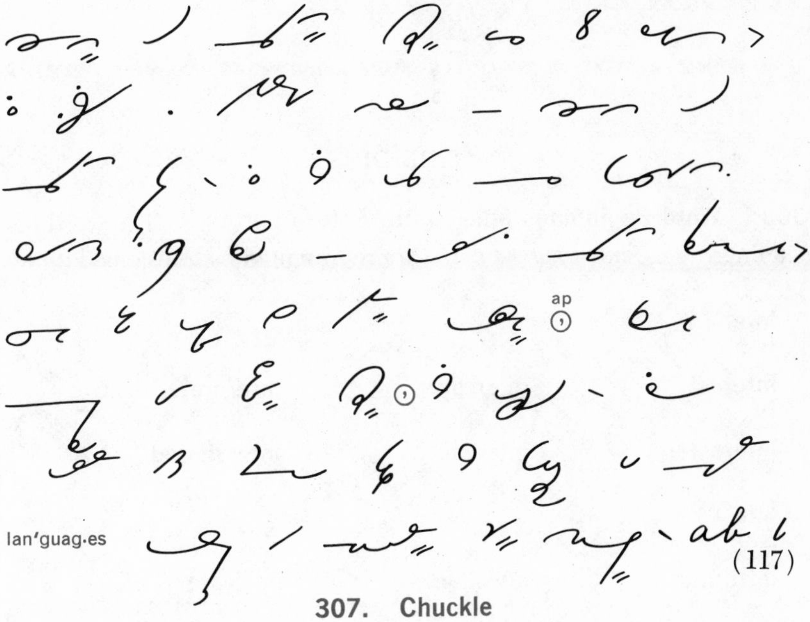
ap
lan′guag·es

(117)

307. Chuckle

(62)

Lesson 35

Principles

308. Word Beginnings Inter-, Intr-, Enter-, Entr-. The word beginnings *inter-, intr-, enter-, entr-* are represented by a disjoined *n.*

Inter-

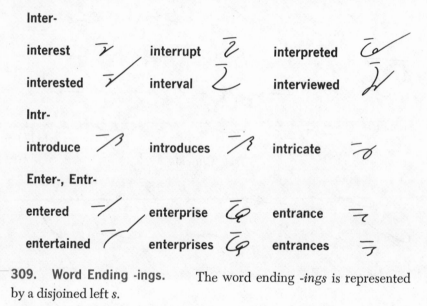

interest		**interrupt**		**interpreted**	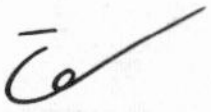
interested	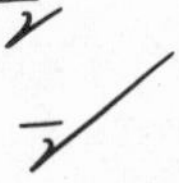	**interval**		**interviewed**	

Intr-

introduce	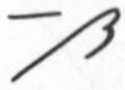	**introduces**		**intricate**	

Enter-, Entr-

entered		**enterprise**		**entrance**	
entertained		**enterprises**		**entrances**	

309. Word Ending -ings. The word ending *-ings* is represented by a disjoined left *s.*

openings		**proceedings**		**meetings**	
holdings		**clippings**		**evenings**	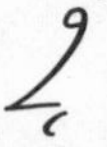

310. Omission of Words in Phrases. It is often possible to omit one or more unimportant words in a shorthand phrase. In the phrase *one of the,* for example, the word *of* is omitted; we write *one the.* When transcribing, the stenographer will insert *of,* as the phrase would make no sense without that word.

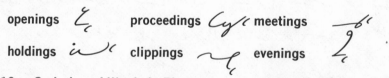

one of the	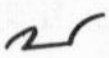	**up to date**	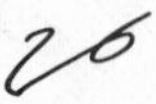

one of them  **will you please** 

many of the  **in the world** 

Building Transcription Skills

311. BUSINESS VOCABULARY BUILDER

payroll deductions Money withheld from an employee's wages for such expenses as insurance, medical care, social security, and income tax.

comptroller (pronounced *kŏn·trōl'ẽr*) The officer of a company who has the responsibility for accounting and financial operations.

interior The inside.

312. SIMILAR-WORDS DRILL

Quite, quiet

quite Completely; entirely.

He was quite pleased with the articles.

quiet Not excited; calm; free of noise.

He is a quiet person who seldom has anything to say.

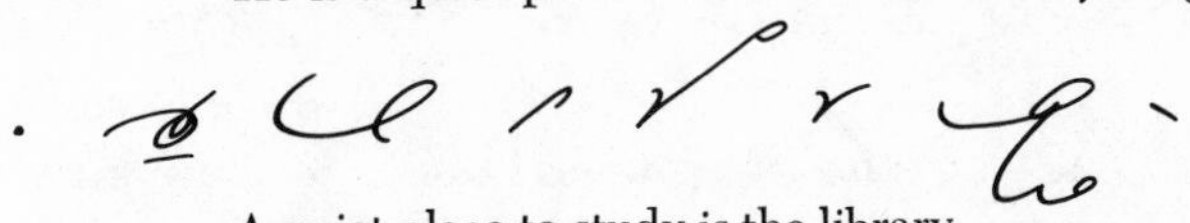

A quiet place to study is the library.

Remember that in *quiet* the *e* comes *before* the *t;* in *quite,* the *e* comes *after* the *t.* (Also, be careful of *quit,* in which there is no *e.*)

Reading and Writing Practice

313. Phrase Letter. This letter contains several illustrations of the omission of words in phrases.

of'fered
En'ter·pris'es
en·roll'ing
pur'pose
comp·trol'ler
fur'ther

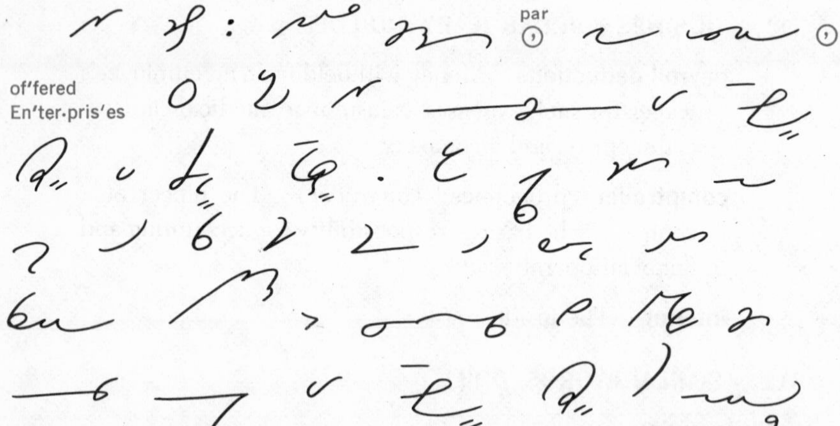

(127)

314.

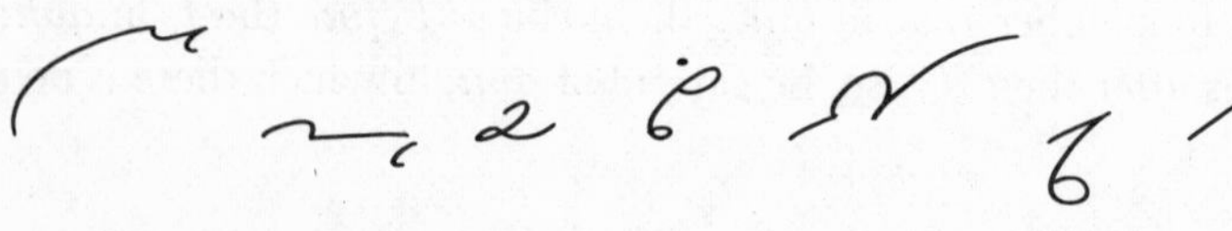

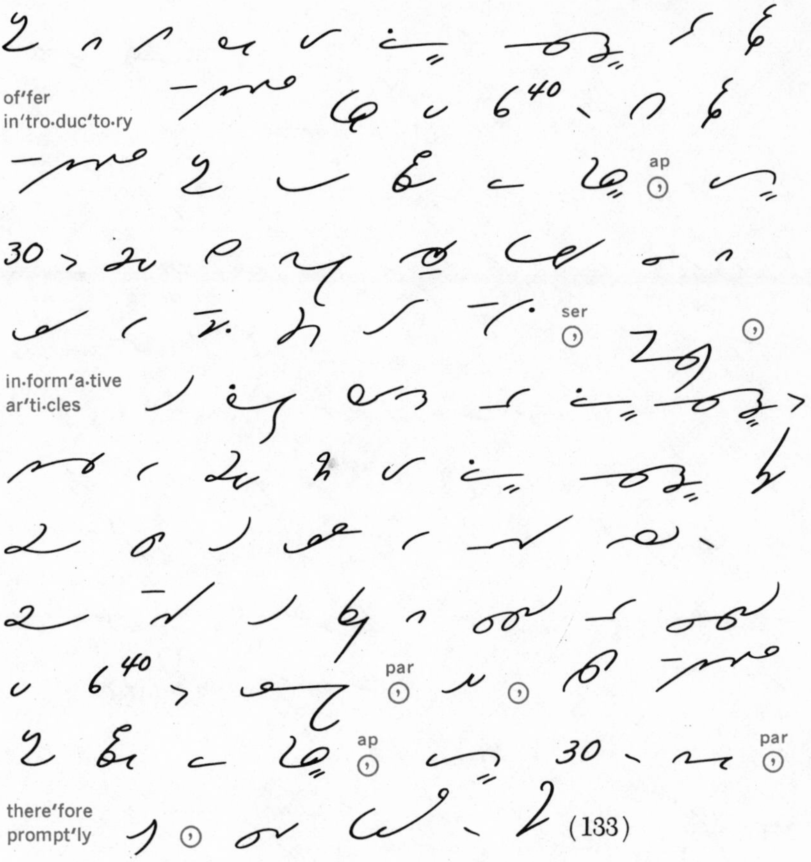

of'fer
in'tro·duc'to·ry
in·form'a·tive
ar'ti·cles
there'fore
prompt'ly

(133)

315.

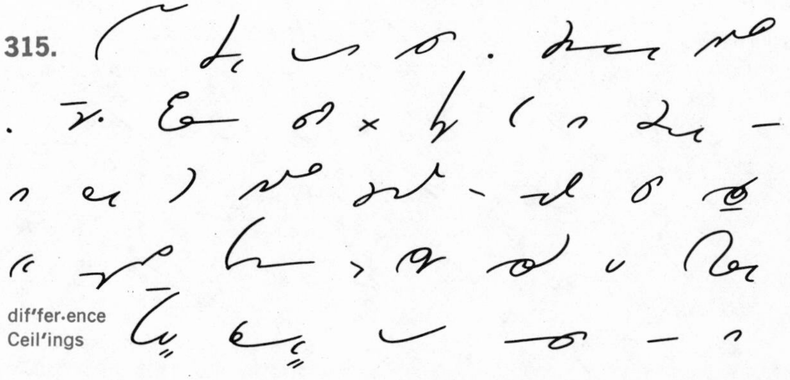

dif'fer·ence
Ceil'ings

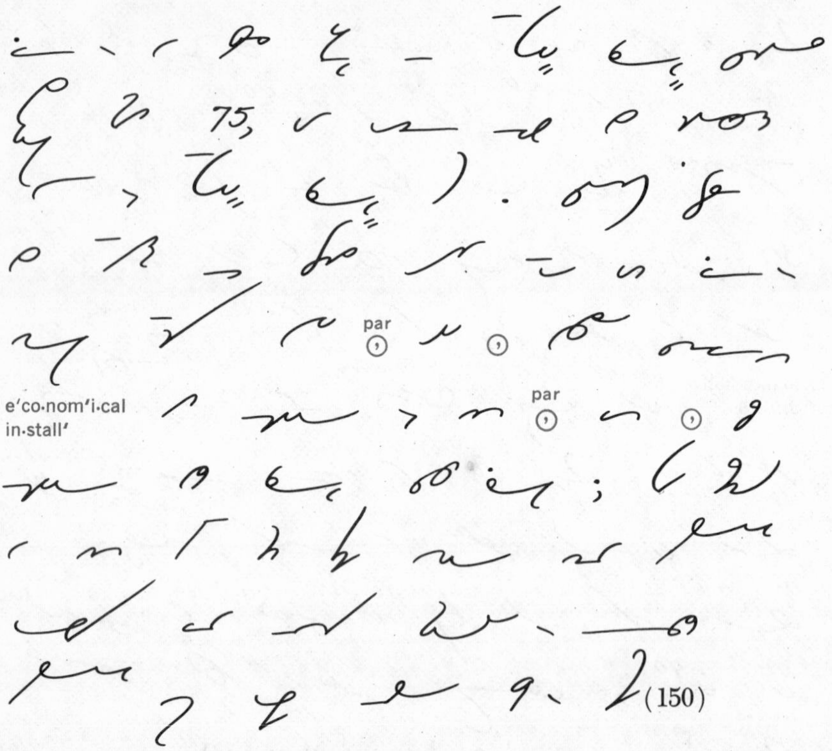

75,
par
(150)

e'co·nom'i·cal
in·stall'

316.

ap
14/
par

bul'le·tin
Fi·nan'cial

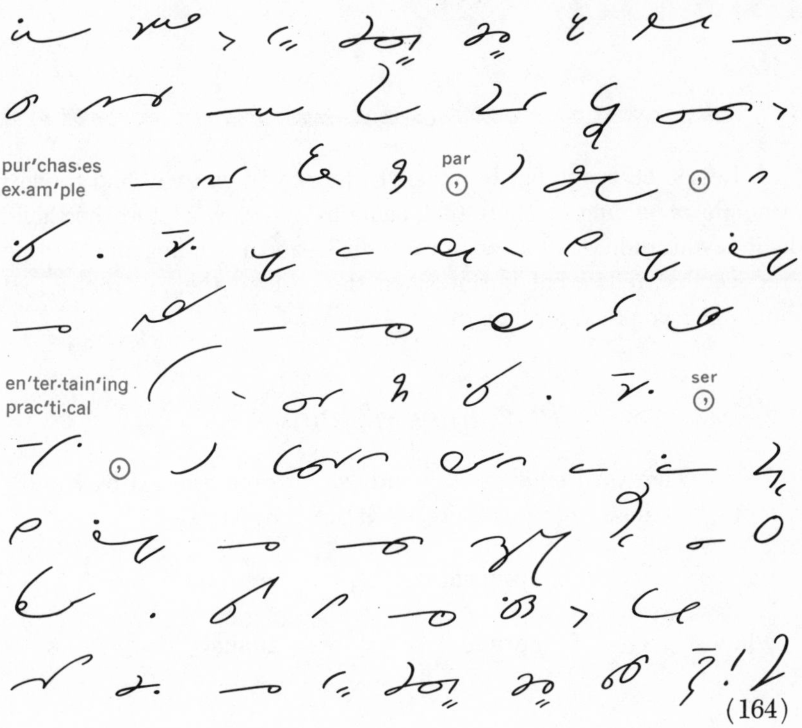
pur'chas·es
ex·am'ple
par
en'ter·tain'ing
prac'ti·cal
ser

(164)

SHORTHAND NOTEBOOK CHECK LIST

So that you can use your notebook efficiently, do you –

1. Write your name on the cover of your notebook?

2. Indicate on the cover the first and last days on which you used the notebook?

3. Place the date *at the bottom* of the first page of each day's dictation?

4. Place a rubber band around the completed pages of your notebook so that you lose no time finding the first blank page on which to start the day's dictation?

5. Draw a line through the shorthand notes that you have transcribed or read back so that you will know you are through with them?

Lesson 36 RECALL

Lesson 36 is another breather. In Lesson 36 you will find the last principle of joining, a chart that contains a review of the shorthand devices you studied in Lessons 1 through 35, and a Reading and Writing Practice that tells what businessmen think about their secretaries. It should give you food for thought!

Principles of Joining

317. The word endings *-ure* and *-ual* are represented by *r* and *l* except when those endings are preceded by a downstroke.

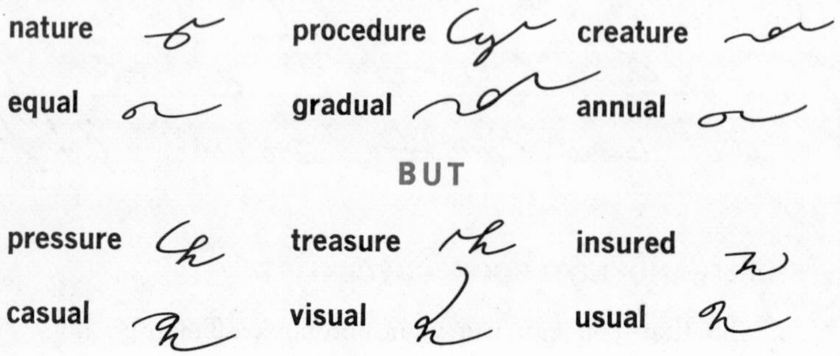

nature
procedure
creature
equal
gradual
annual
BUT
pressure
treasure
insured
casual
visual
usual

Accuracy Practice

318.

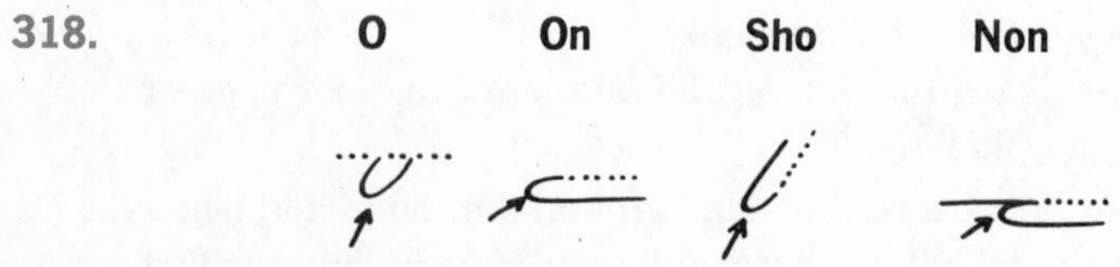

O
On
Sho
Non

To write these combinations accurately:

a. Keep the *o* hook narrow, being sure that the beginning and end are on the same level of writing, as indicated by the dotted line.

b. Keep the *o* in *on* and *sho* parallel with the consonant, as indicated by the dotted line.

c. Make the beginning of the *o* in *non* retrace the end of the first *n*.

d. Avoid a point at the curved part indicated by the arrows.

Practice Drill

Of, know, low, own, home, hot, known, moan, shown.

319. **OO** **Noo** **Noom**

To write these combinations accurately:

a. Keep the *oo* hook narrow and deep.

b. Keep the beginning and end of the hook on the same level of writing.

c. In *noo* and *noom,* keep the hook parallel with the straight line that precedes it.

d. In *noom,* retrace the beginning of the *m* on the bottom of the *oo* hook.

e. Avoid a point at the places indicated by arrows.

Practice Drill

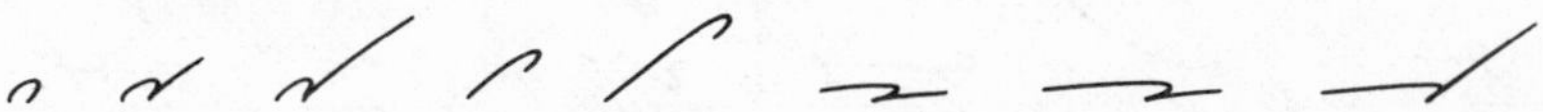

You-your, yours truly, you would, to-too-two, do, noon, moon, mood.

320. **Hard** **Hailed**

To write these combinations accurately:

a. Give the end of the *r* and of the *l* a lift upward.

b. Do not lift the end too soon, or the strokes may resemble the *nd, md* combinations.

Practice Drill

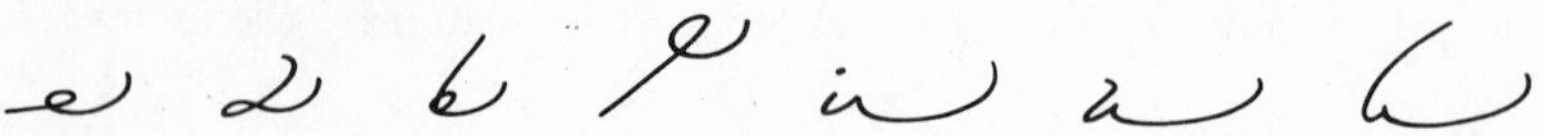

Neared, feared, cheered, dared, hold, sold, bold.

321. Recall Chart. The following chart contains a review of the shorthand devices you studied in previous lessons. It contains 78 brief forms, words, and phrases. Can you read the entire chart in 5 minutes?

BRIEF FORMS

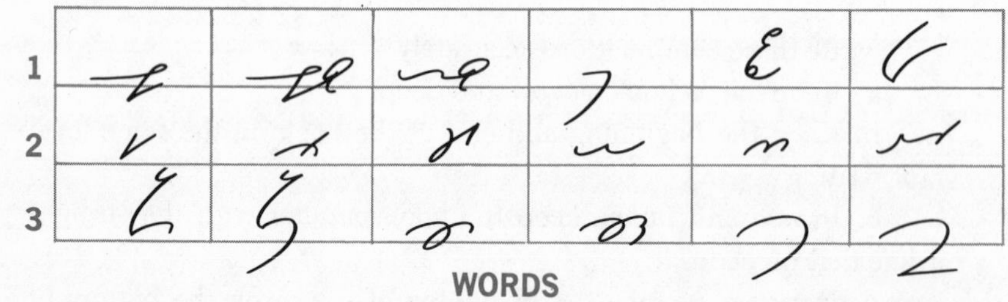
1
2
3

WORDS

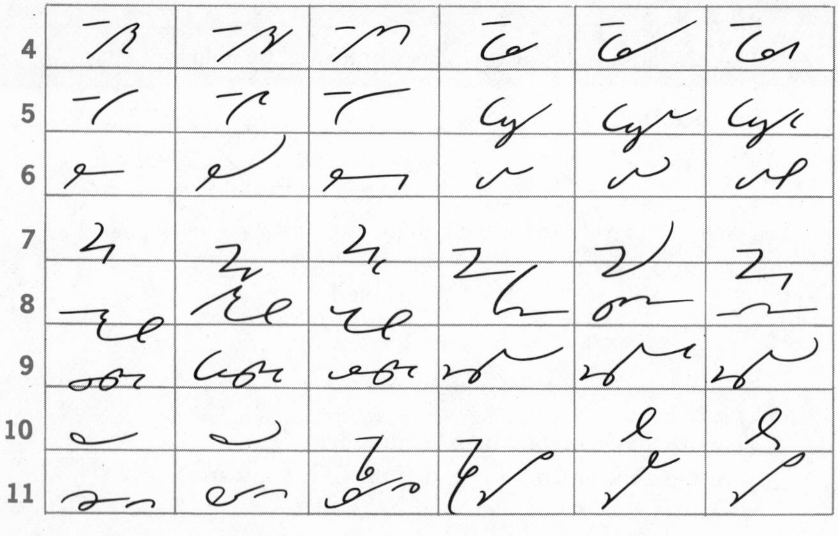
4
5
6
7
8
9
10
11

PHRASES

12
13

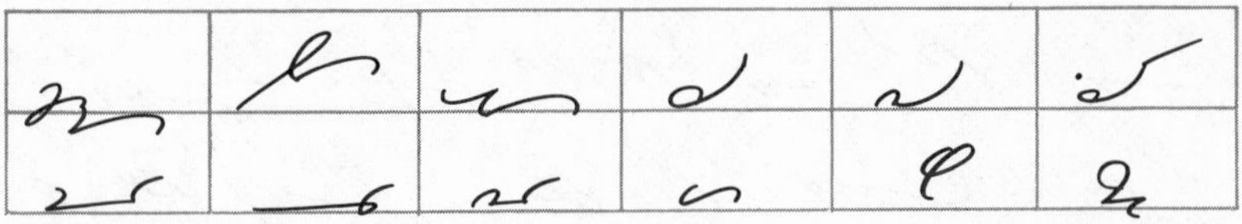

Building Transcription Skills

322. BUSINESS VOCABULARY BUILDER

comprehensive Covering a wide range.

grooming Neatness; tidiness of dress and appearance.

indispensable Absolutely necessary or essential.

Reading and Writing Practice

323. How Do You Look?

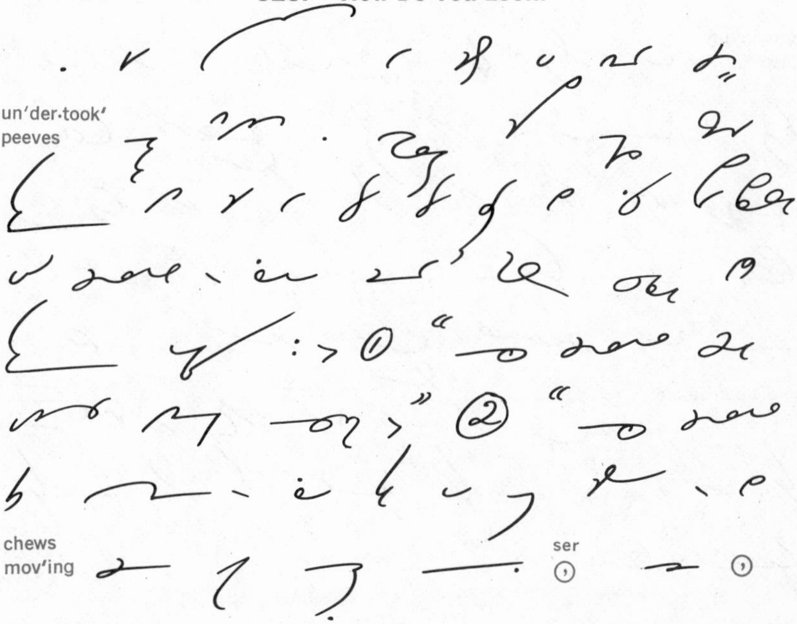

un'der·took'
peeves

chews
mov'ing

ser

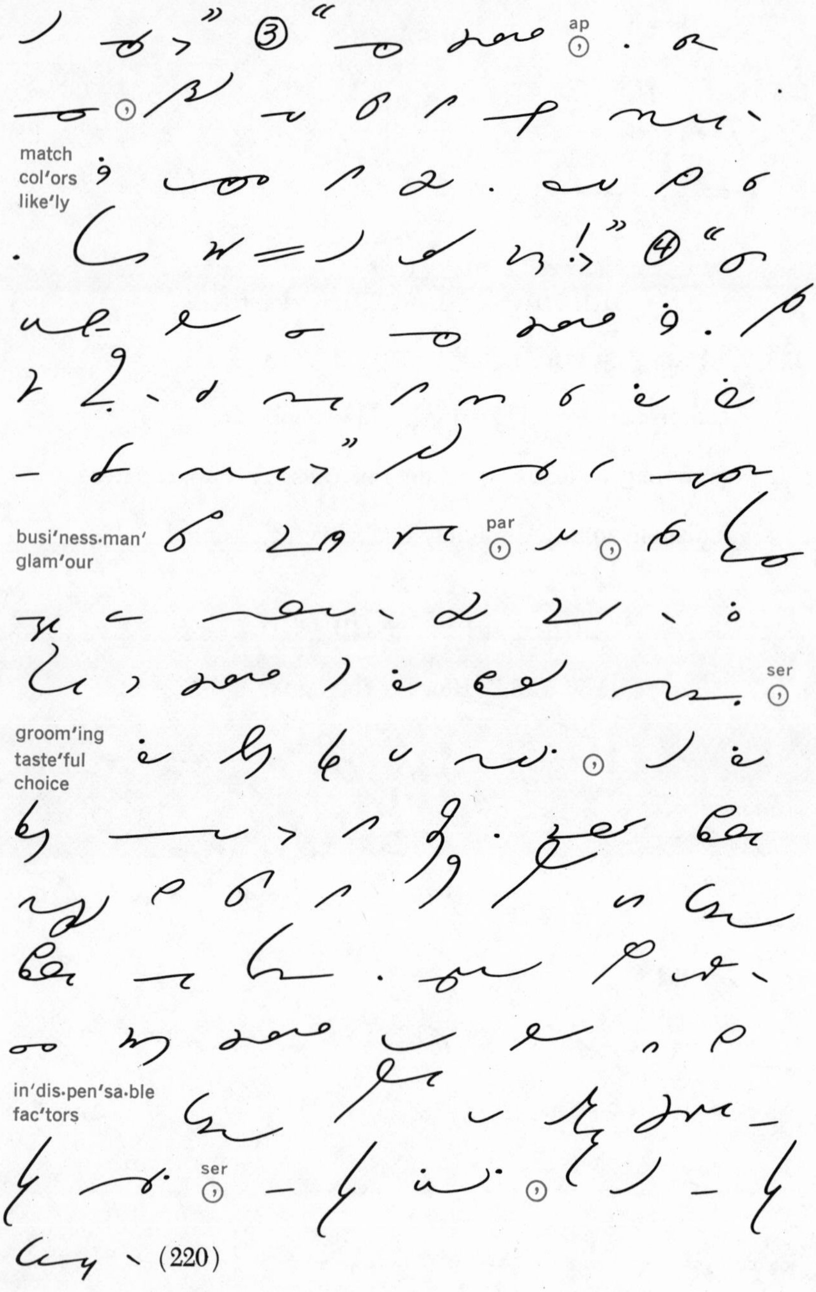

ap
match
col'ors
like'ly
busi'ness·man'
glam'our
par
ser
groom'ing
taste'ful
choice
in'dis·pen'sa·ble
fac'tors
ser

(220)

324. Courtesy

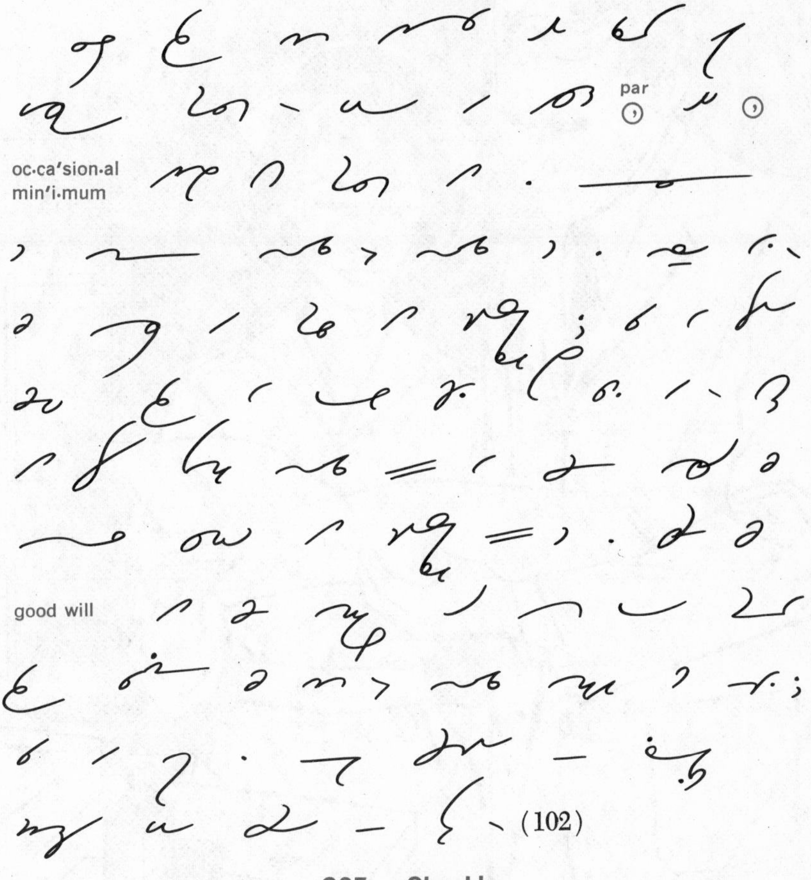
par
oc·ca'sion·al
min'i·mum
good will
(102)

325. Chuckle

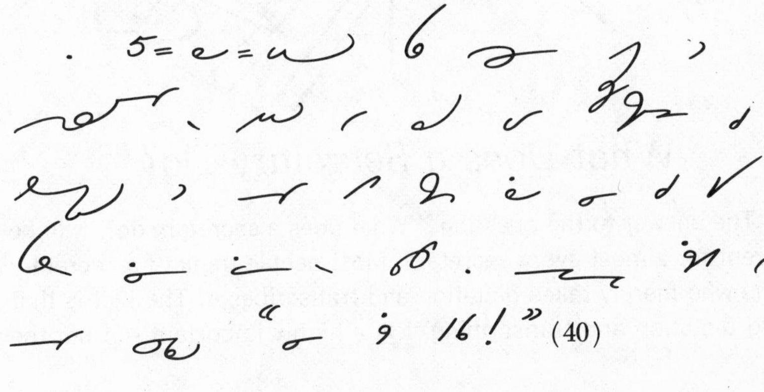
(40)

What Does a Secretary Do?

The answer to the question, "What does a secretary do?" will be different for almost every secretary. Most people think of a secretary as one who merely takes dictation and transcribes it. The fact is that taking dictation and transcribing it is a highly important—if not the most important — part of the secretary's job. But it is only one of many things that occupy her time.

The business executive thinks of the secretary as his "strong right arm." She frees him of the details of his job so that he will have time for managing people and procedures. Besides taking his dictation and transcribing it into good-looking letters, memoranda, and reports, she keeps his appointment calendar, answers his telephone, meets callers who wish to see him, files his important papers, writes letters and short reports, takes care of his mail, and arranges his business-travel accommodations. She may also do his banking, keep his income tax records — she may even shop for him and his family. Each secretary has duties connected with her job that differ in some respects from those of another secretary, depending on the kind of work her boss is engaged in and his willingness to delegate details to her.

The secretary to an accountant, to a retail store owner, or to a company treasurer is likely to need to know bookkeeping. The secretary to a lawyer must know legal forms and terminology. The secretary to a doctor may be required to know something about medical laboratory procedures and medical record keeping; she most certainly will have to know medical terminology. The secretary to a dentist may double as a technician — preparing the dental equipment for use, sterilizing instruments, assisting the dentist with X rays, keeping his records, and following up on appointments.

No two secretarial jobs are alike. Each is different, and each has its interesting facets. But there is a common thread that runs through all of them — taking dictation and transcribing it quickly and accurately.

Chapter 7

Lesson 37

Principles

326. Word Ending -ingly. The word ending *-ingly* is represented by a disjoined *e* circle.

accordingly  **increasingly**  **surprisingly** 

exceedingly  **willingly**  **knowingly** 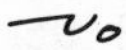

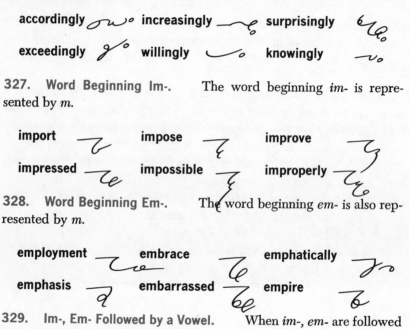

327. Word Beginning Im-. The word beginning *im-* is represented by *m*.

import  **impose** 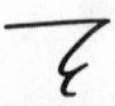 **improve** 

impressed 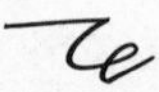 **impossible**  **improperly** 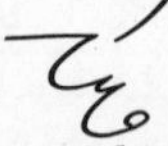

328. Word Beginning Em-. The word beginning *em-* is also represented by *m*.

employment 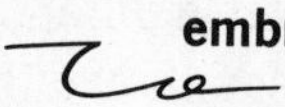 **embrace** 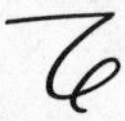 **emphatically** 

emphasis 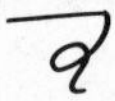 **embarrassed**  **empire** 

329. Im-, Em- Followed by a Vowel. When *im-, em-* are followed by a vowel, they are written in full.

immodest  **immoral**  **emotionally** 

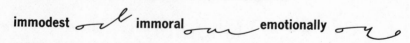

330. Omission of Minor Vowel. When two vowel sounds come together, the minor vowel may be omitted.

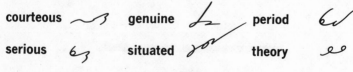

courteous  **genuine**  **period** 

serious  **situated** 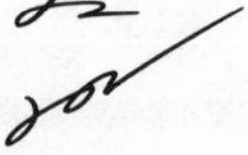 **theory** 

previously  **union**  **ideal** 

Building Transcription Skills

331. BUSINESS VOCABULARY BUILDER

progressive Characterized by continuous improvement; accepting new ideas.

quarterly Occurring four times a year.

imperative Not to be avoided; compulsory.

332. PUNCTUATION PRACTICE

, if clause

One of the most frequent errors made by the beginning transcriber is the failure to make a complete sentence. In most cases the incomplete sentence is a dependent or subordinate clause introduced by *as, when,* or *if.* The dependent or subordinate clause deceives the transcriber because it is a complete sentence except that it is introduced by a word such as *if;* therefore, it requires another clause to complete the thought.

The dependent or subordinate clause *often* signals the coming of the main clause by means of a subordinate conjunction. The commonest subordinating conjunctions are *if, as,* and *when.* Other subordinating conjunctions are *though, although, whether, unless, because, since, while, where, after, whenever, until, before,* and *now.* In this lesson you will consider clauses introduced by *if.*

A subordinate clause introduced by *if* and followed by the main clause is separated from the main clause by a comma.

> If you cannot be present, please notify me.
> If you finish before noon, you are free to go home.

Each time a subordinate clause beginning with *if* occurs in the Reading and Writing Practice, it will be indicated thus in the shorthand:

if

Reading and Writing Practice

333.

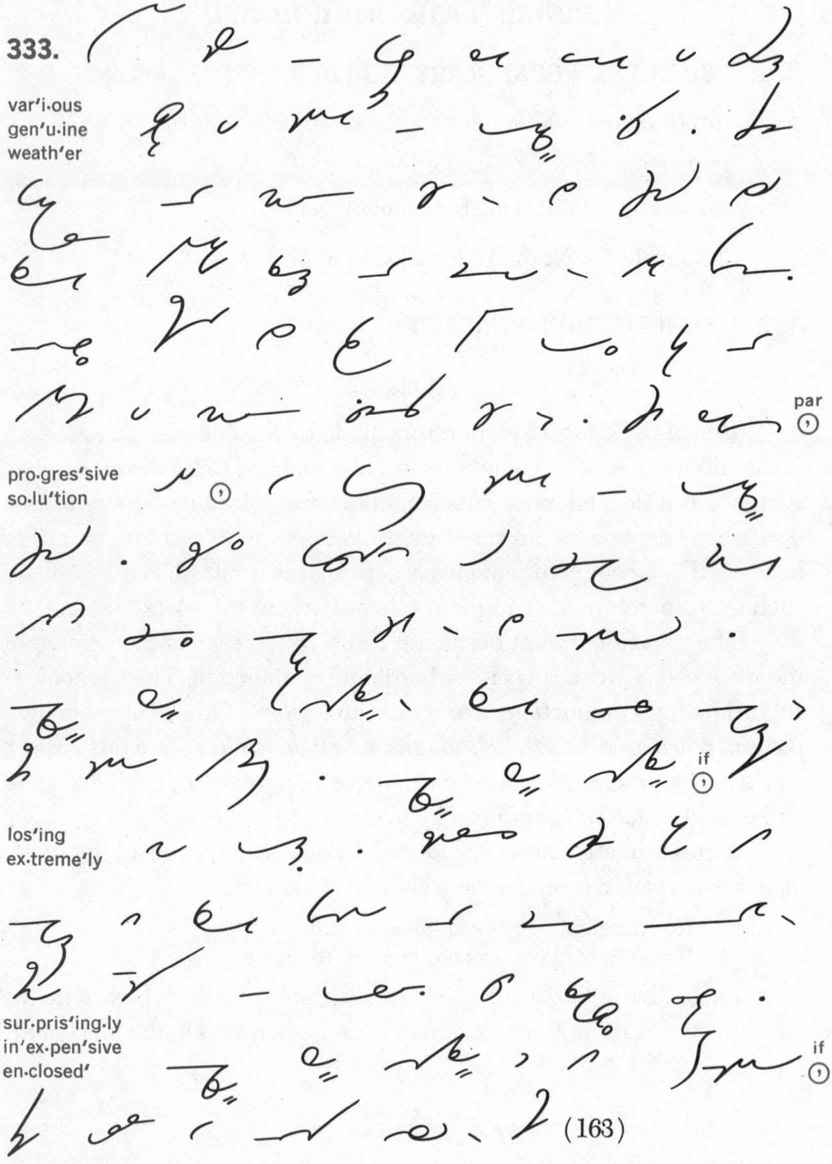
var'i·ous
gen'u·ine
weath'er
par
pro·gres'sive
so·lu'tion
if
los'ing
ex·treme'ly
sur·pris'ing·ly
in'ex·pen'sive
en·closed'
if
(163)

334.

cour'te·ous
re·ceived'
em·ploy'ees

ap
par

(116)

335.

par

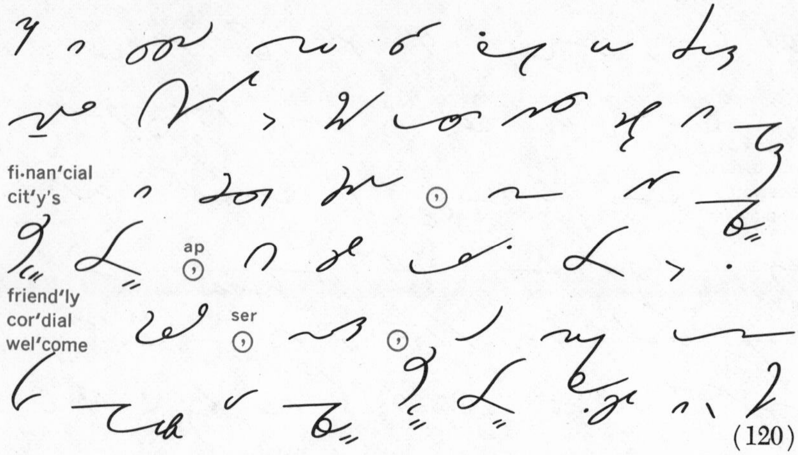

fi·nan'cial
cit'y's
friend'ly
cor'dial
wel'come

(120)

336.

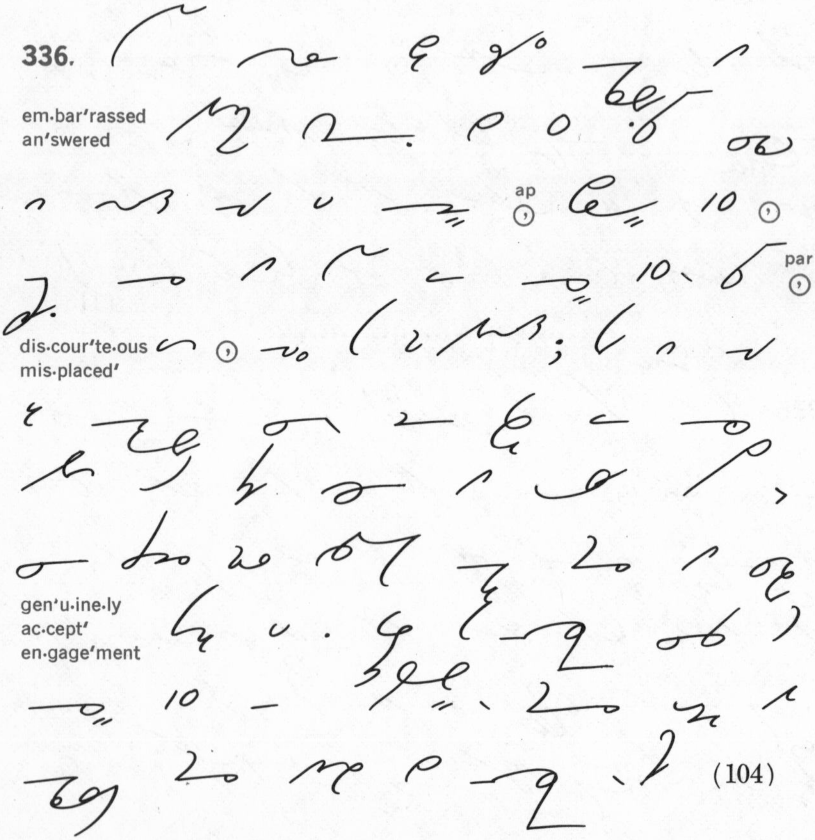

em·bar'rassed
an'swered
dis·cour'te·ous
mis·placed'
gen'u·ine·ly
ac·cept'
en·gage'ment

(104)

Lesson 38

Principles

337. Word Ending -ship. The word ending *-ship* is represented by a disjoined *sh*.

steamship  **membership**  **townships** 

friendship  **relationship**  **scholarships** 

338. Word Beginning Sub-. The word beginning *sub-* is represented by *s*.

submit  **substantial**  **sublet** 

subscribed  **subdivide**  **suburbs** 

339. Joining of Hook and Circle Vowels. When a hook and a circle vowel come together, they are written in the order in which they are pronounced.

poem  **poetry** 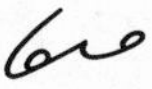 **folio** 

poet  **radio**  **snowy** 

Building Transcription Skills

340. BUSINESS VOCABULARY BUILDER

substantially To a large extent.

jeopardizing Risking the loss of.

suburbs Residential areas on the outskirts of a city.

subdivided Broken up into small sections.

341. PUNCTUATION PRACTICE

, as clause

A subordinate clause introduced by *as* and followed by the main clause is separated from the main clause by a comma.

> As I am sure you are aware, the store closes at five.
> As I told you on the telephone, I cannot preside at the meeting.

Each time a subordinate clause beginning with *as* occurs in the Reading and Writing Practice, it will be indicated thus in the shorthand:

as

Reading and Writing Practice

342.

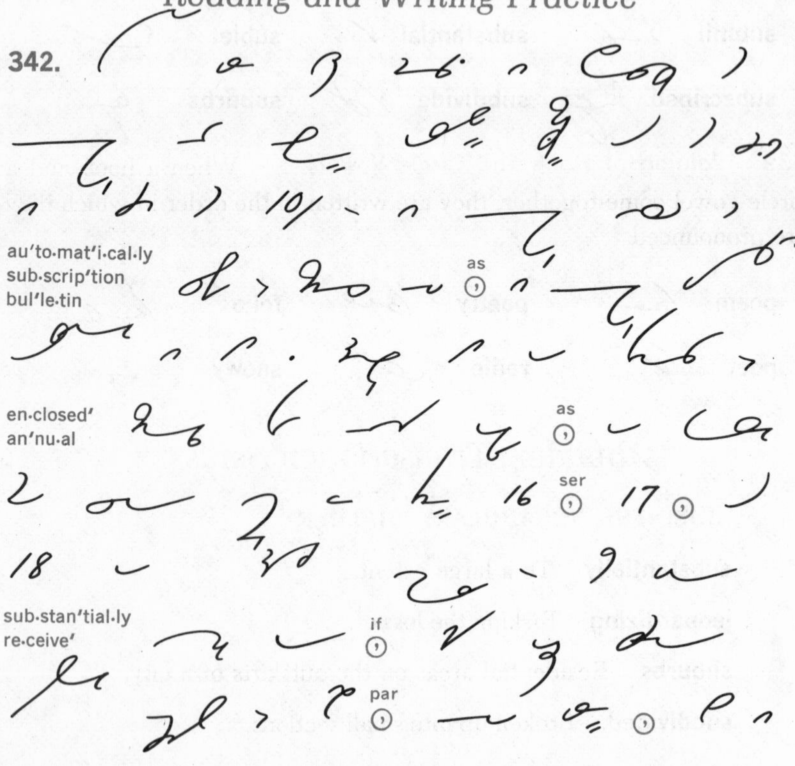
as
as
ser
if
par

au'to·mat'i·cal·ly
sub·scrip'tion
bul'le·tin

en·closed'
an'nu·al

sub·stan'tial·ly
re·ceive'

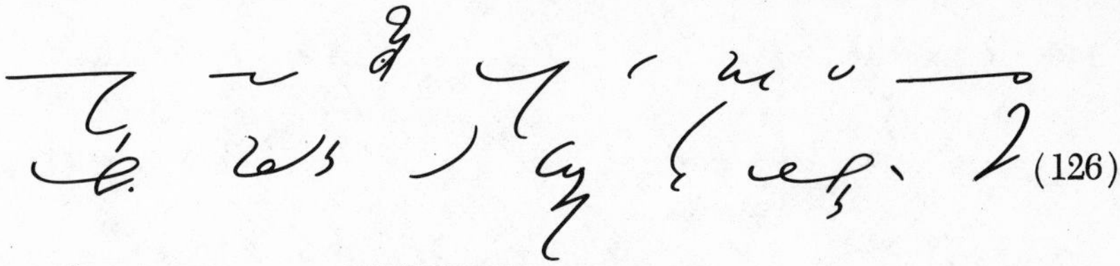

(126)

343.

schol'ar·ships
un·u'su·al

sen'iors
com·pete'

com'pe·ti'tion
sub·mit'ted

(133)

344.

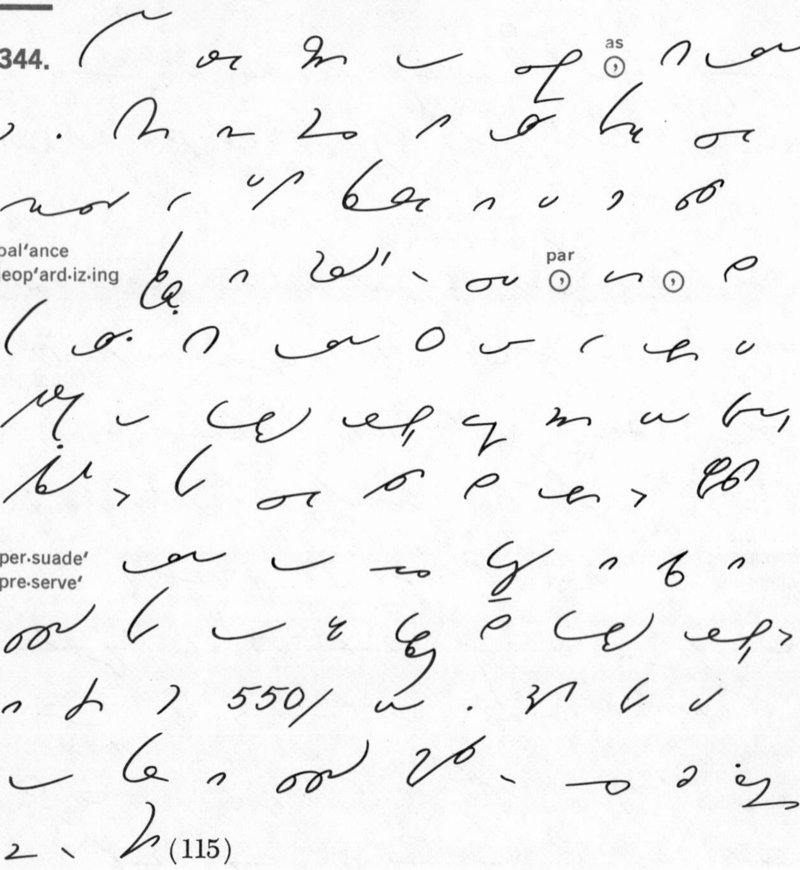

as
par

bal'ance
jeop'ard·iz·ing

per·suade'
pre·serve'

(115)

345.

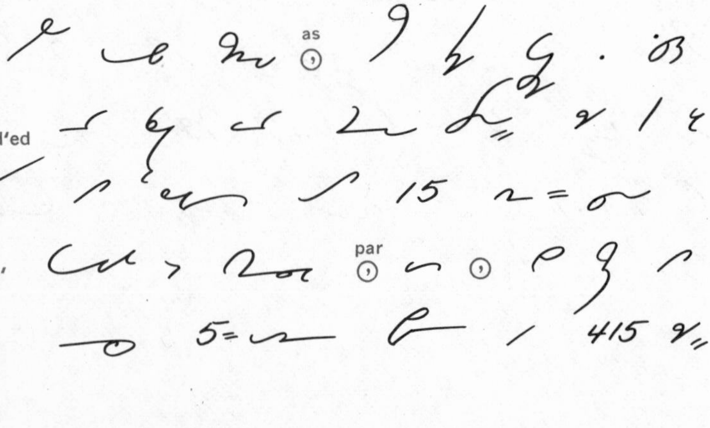

as
par
15
5
415

sub'urbs
sub'di·vid'ed

sub·lease'

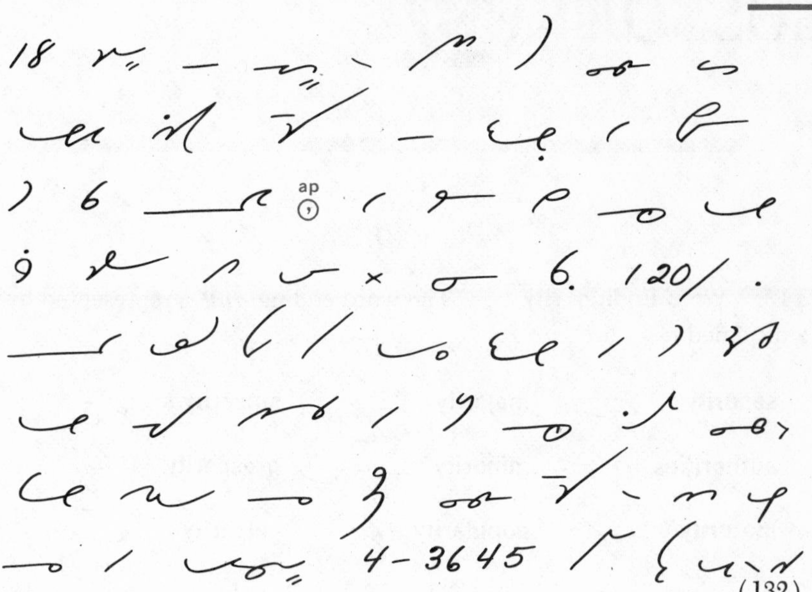

(132)

346. Chuckle

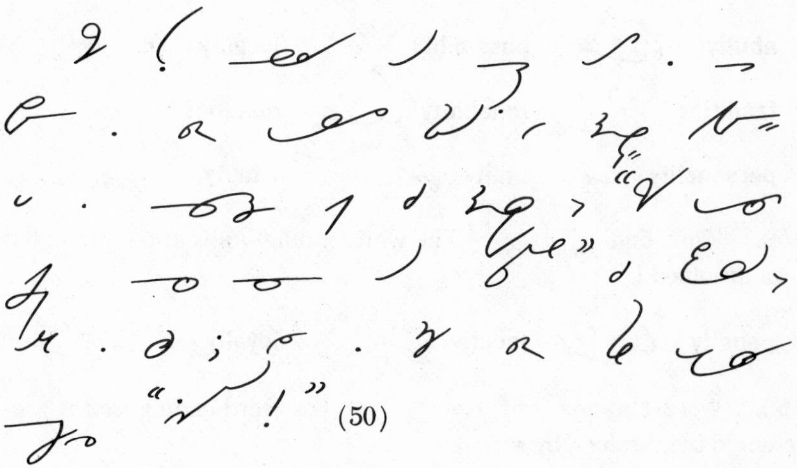

(50)

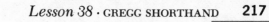

Lesson 39

Principles

347. Word Ending -rity. The word ending *-rity* is represented by a disjoined *r*.

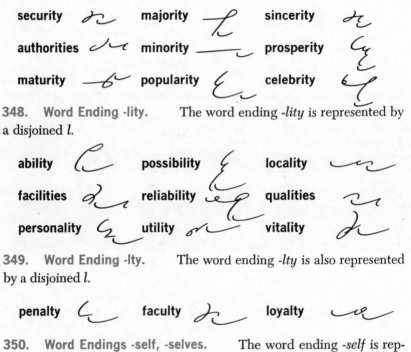

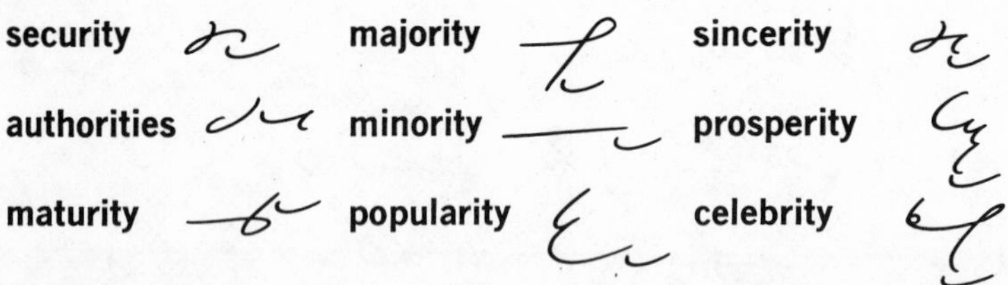
security
majority
sincerity
authorities
minority
prosperity
maturity
popularity
celebrity

348. Word Ending -lity. The word ending *-lity* is represented by a disjoined *l*.

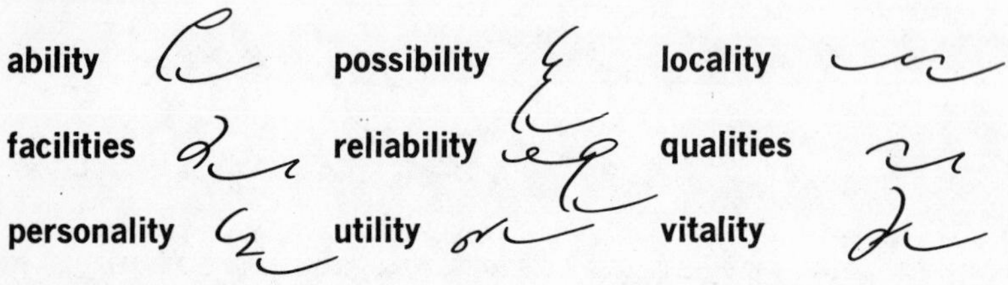
ability
possibility
locality
facilities
reliability
qualities
personality
utility
vitality

349. Word Ending -lty. The word ending *-lty* is also represented by a disjoined *l*.

penalty
faculty
loyalty

350. Word Endings -self, -selves. The word ending *-self* is represented by *s; -selves,* by *ses.*

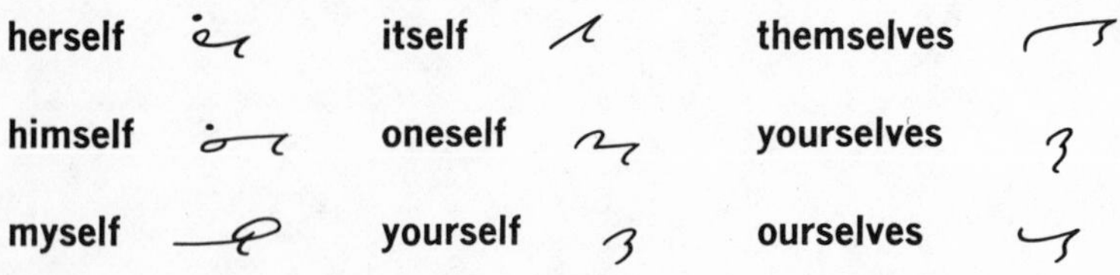
herself
itself
themselves
himself
oneself
yourselves
myself
yourself
ourselves

Building Transcription Skills

351. BUSINESS VOCABULARY BUILDER

mediocrity Quality of being ordinary.

security Freedom from anxiety or care.

prosperity Financial success.

refunded Given back.

352. PUNCTUATION PRACTICE

, when clause

A subordinate clause introduced by *when* and followed by the main clause is separated from the main clause by a comma.

When you finish the job, please let me know.
When John arrives, ask him to see me.

Each time a subordinate clause beginning with *when* occurs in the Reading and Writing Practice, it will be indicated thus in the shorthand:

when

Reading and Writing Practice

353.

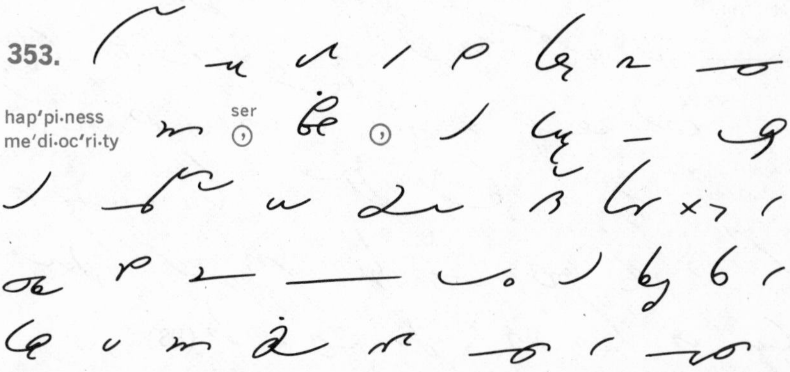
hap'pi·ness
me'di·oc'ri·ty
ser

sin·cer′i·ty
course

de·scribes′
fa·cil′i·ties

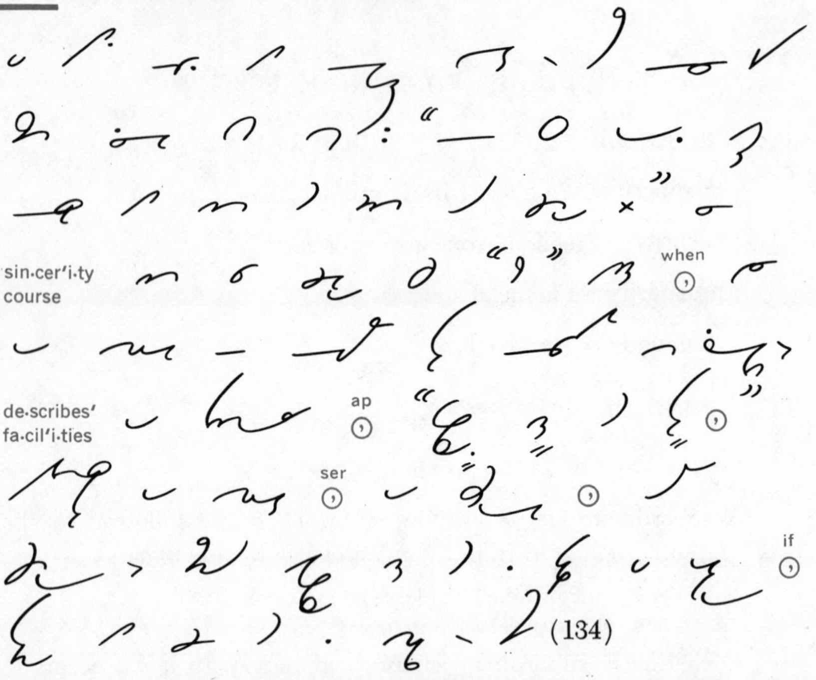
when
ap
ser
if

(134)

354.

due
in·teg′ri·ty

e·ven′tu·al·ly
sen′si·ble

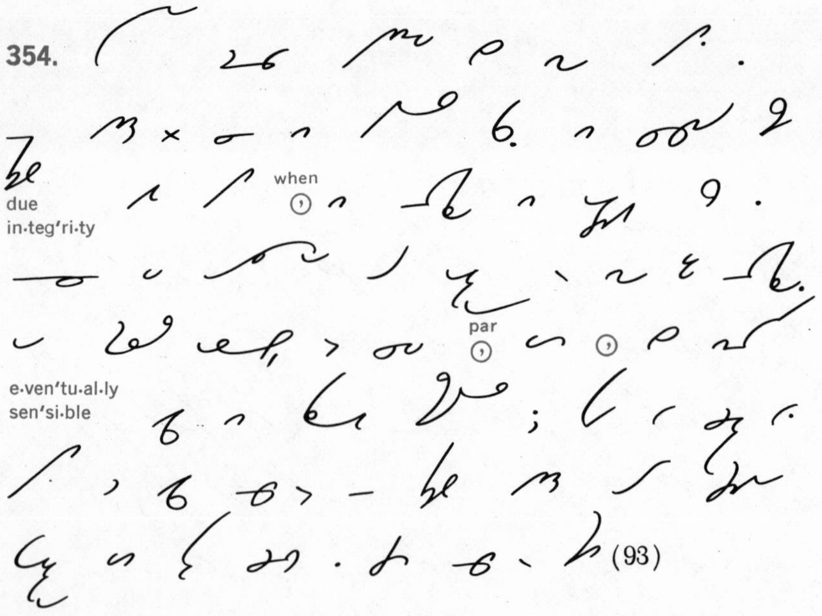
when
par

(93)

355.

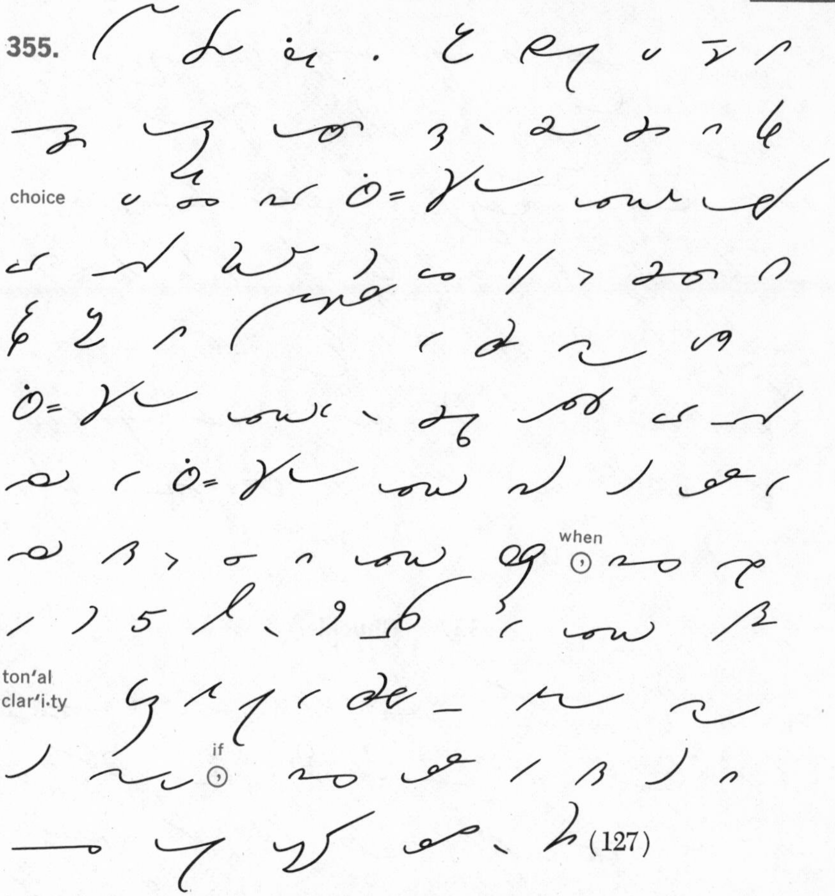

choice

when

ton'al
clar'i.ty

if

(127)

356.

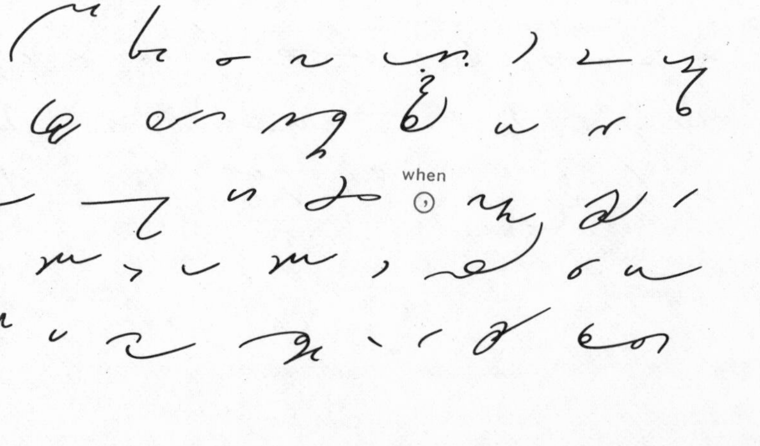

ar'ti.cle
male
fam'i.ly

when

choose
in′di·vid′u·al′i·ty
ser

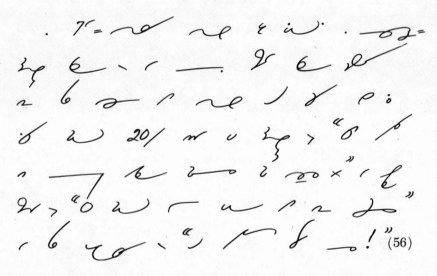

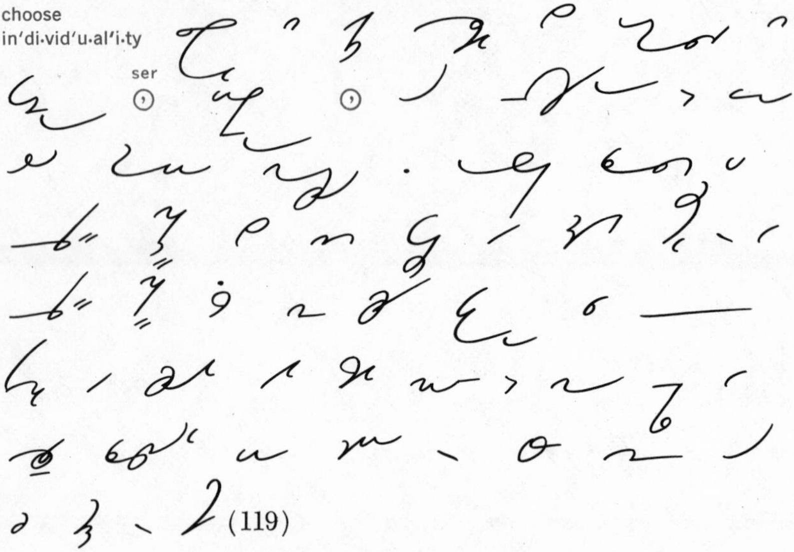

(119)

357. Chuckle

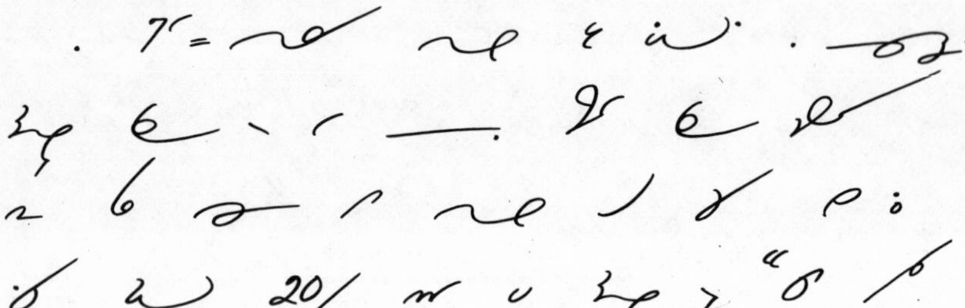

(56)

Lesson 40

Principles

358. Abbreviated Words — in Families. Many long words may be abbreviated in shorthand by dropping the endings. This device is also used in longhand, as *Jan.* for *January*. The extent to which you use this device will depend on your familiarity with the words and with the subject matter of the dictation. When in doubt, write it out! The ending of a word is not dropped when a special shorthand word-ending form has been provided, such as *-lity*.

Notice how many of the words written with this abbreviating device fall naturally into families of similar endings.

-tribute

tribute		**contribute**		**distribute**	
attribute		**contributed**		**distributor**	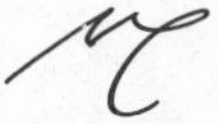

-quent

consequent		**subsequent**		**frequent**	
consequently		**subsequently**		**eloquent**	

-quire

require	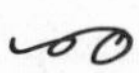	**inquires**		**inquiry**	
requirement		**inquired**		**esquire**	

-titute

substitute		**institute**		**constitution**	

-titude

aptitude  **gratitude**  **latitude** 

Building Transcription Skills

359. BUSINESS VOCABULARY BUILDER

consequently Therefore.

subsequently Later.

delinquent Behind in payment.

distributor An agent for marketing goods.

aptitude tests Tests that help to determine a person's suitability for a given line of work.

360. PUNCTUATION PRACTICE

, introductory

A comma is used to separate the subordinate clause from a following main clause. You have already studied the application of this rule to subordinate clauses introduced by *if, as,* and *when.* Here are additional examples:

While I understand the statement, I do not agree with it.
Although it was only three o'clock, he closed the office.
Before you let out your next advertising contract, give us an opportunity to discuss it with you.

A comma is also used after introductory words or phrases such as *furthermore, on the contrary,* and *for instance.*

Furthermore, you made a mistake in grammar.
On the contrary, you are at fault.
For your convenience in sending me the information I need, I am enclosing a stamped envelope.

Each time a subordinate (or introductory) word, phrase, or clause other than one beginning with *if*, *as*, or *when* occurs in the Reading and Writing Practice, it will be indicated thus in the shorthand:

intro

⦾

Note: If the subordinate clause or other introductory expression follows the main clause, the comma is usually not necessary.

> I am enclosing a stamped envelope for your convenience in sending me the information I need.

Reading and Writing Practice

361.

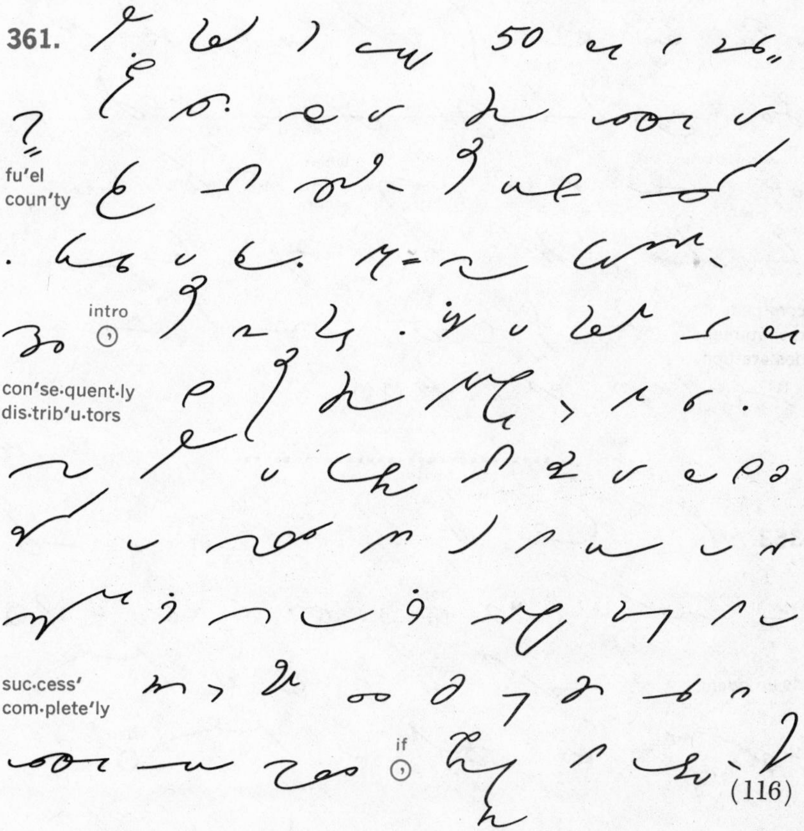
fu'el
coun'ty
intro
con'se·quent·ly
dis·trib'u·tors
suc·cess'
com·plete'ly
if
(116)

362.

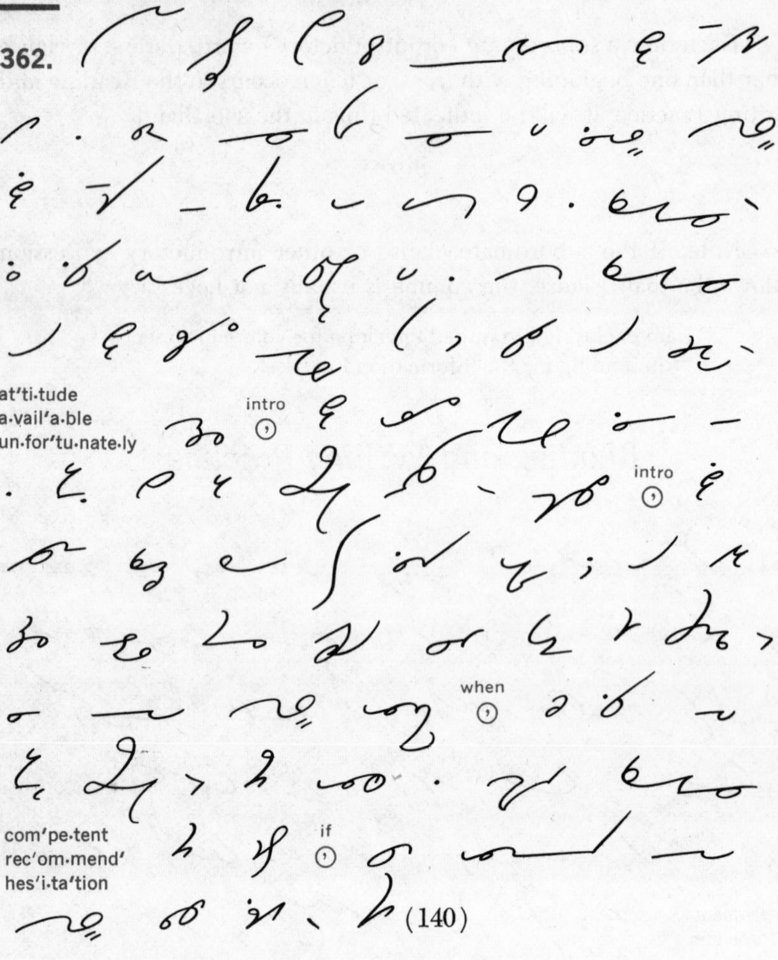

at′ti·tude
a·vail′a·ble
un·for′tu·nate·ly

com′pe·tent
rec′om·mend′
hes′i·ta′tion

(140)

363.

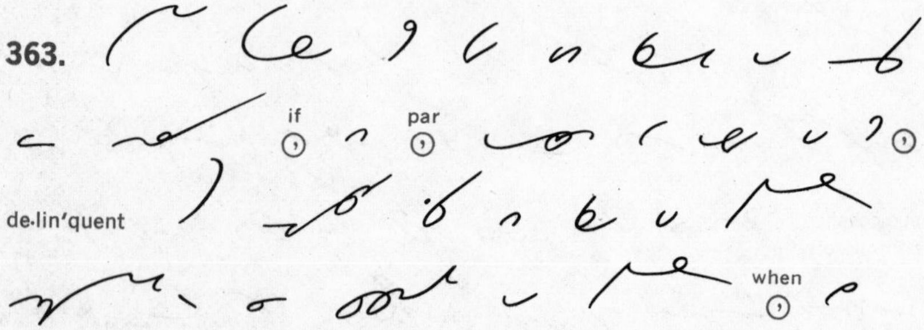

de·lin′quent

ap·pre′ci·ate
sat′is·fac′tion
pur′pose

intro
par
intro
par
(107)

364.

re·ceive′
in·quir′ies
ap′ti·tude
wheth′er
prac′ti·cal
sub·mit′ted

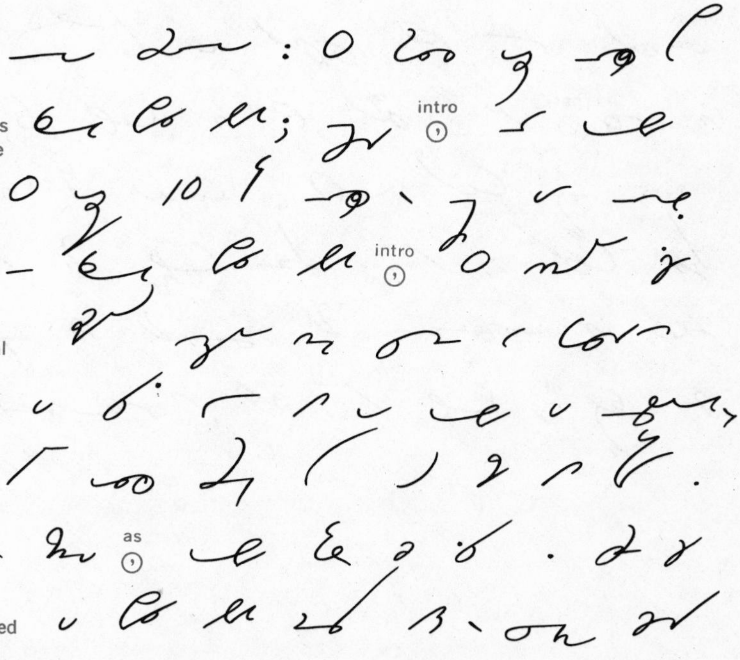
intro
intro
as

re'con·sid'er
whole

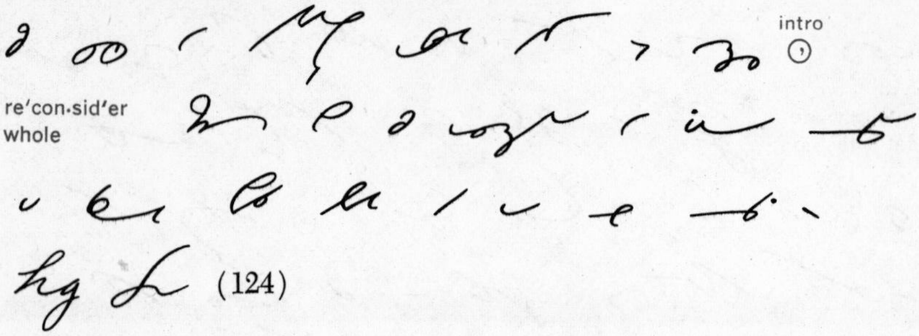
intro
(124)

365.

too

in'voic·es

intro
par
if
(101)

Lesson 41

Principles

366. Abbreviated Words — Not in Families. The ending may be omitted from some long words even though they do not fall into a family.

convenient, convenience  **equivalent**  **privilege** 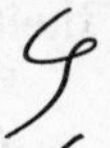

memorandum  **reluctant, reluctance**  **privileges** 

alphabet  **philosophy**  **privileged** 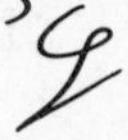

367. Word Beginning Trans-. The word beginning *trans-* is expressed by a disjoined *t*.

transact  **transported**  **transplant** 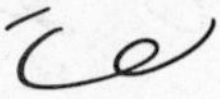

translate  **transferred**  **transcriber** 

368. Word Ending -ification. The word ending *-ification* is represented by a disjoined *f*.

classification  **notification**  **specifications** 

justification  **modification**  **qualifications** 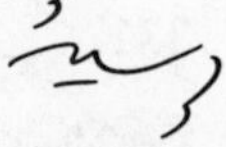

Building Transcription Skills

369. BUSINESS VOCABULARY BUILDER

specifications A written description giving details of construction.

transmitted Sent; turned over to.

significant Important.

reluctant Unwilling.

facility Ease.

transcript A written or typewritten copy, as of shorthand notes.

370. SIMILAR-WORDS DRILL

Their, there

their Belonging to them.

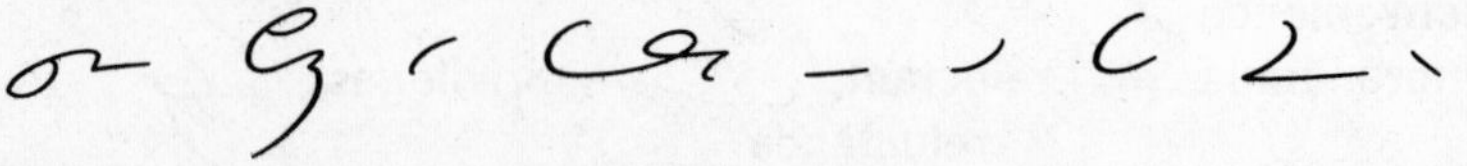

I cannot approve the plans in their present form.

there In or to that place.

I went there at his request.

(Also watch out for *they're*, the contraction of *they are*.)

Reading and Writing Practice

371.

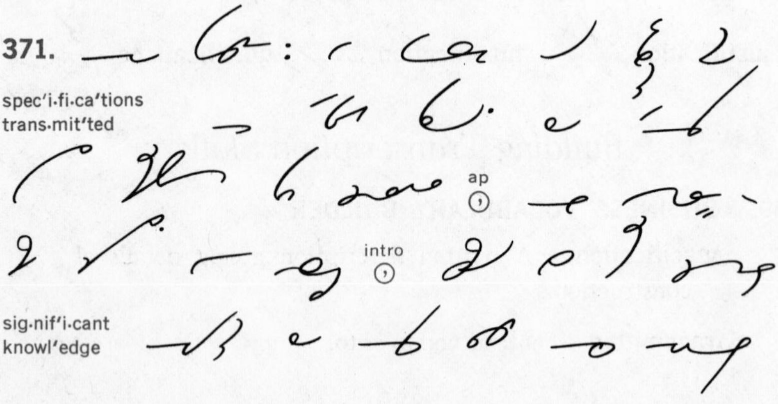
ap
intro

spec'i·fi·ca'tions
trans·mit'ted

sig·nif'i·cant
knowl'edge

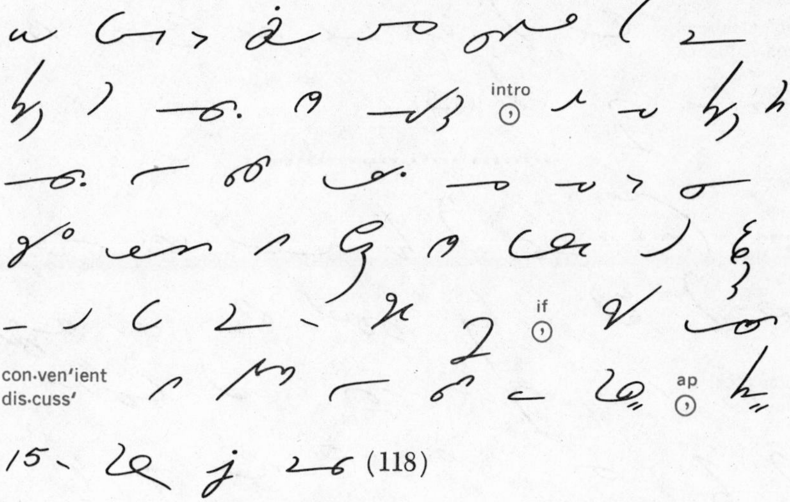
intro
if
con·ven'ient
dis·cuss'
ap
15
(118)

372.

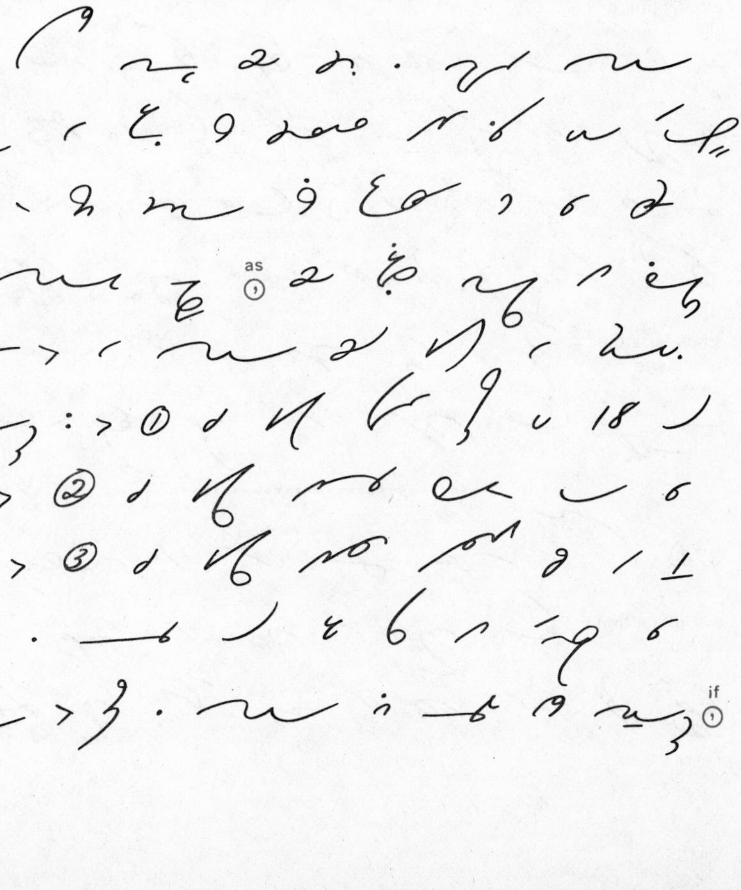
past
as
1
18
25
2
3
if

ap′pli·ca′tion
con·ven′ience

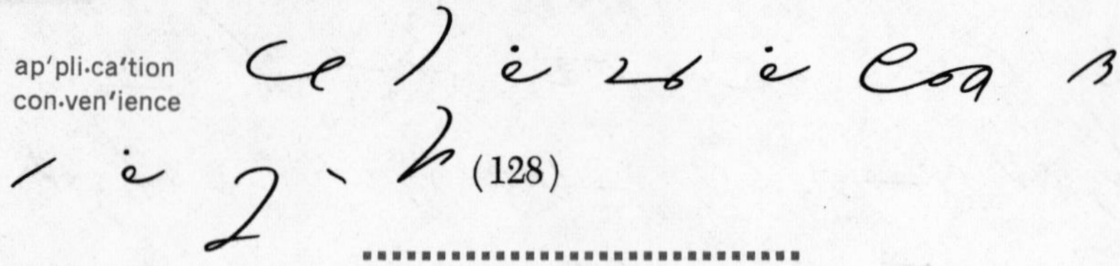

(128)

373.

prac′ti·cal
buy

shop′ping
at′mos·phere

trans·fer′a·ble
priv′i·lege

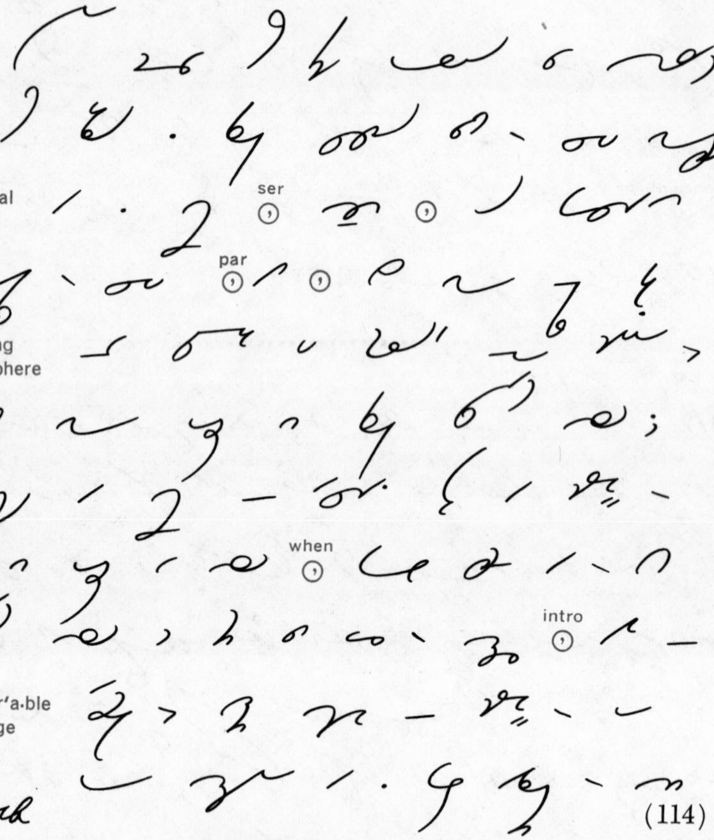
ser
par
when
intro

(114)

374.

clar′i·fi·ca′tion
ver′sus

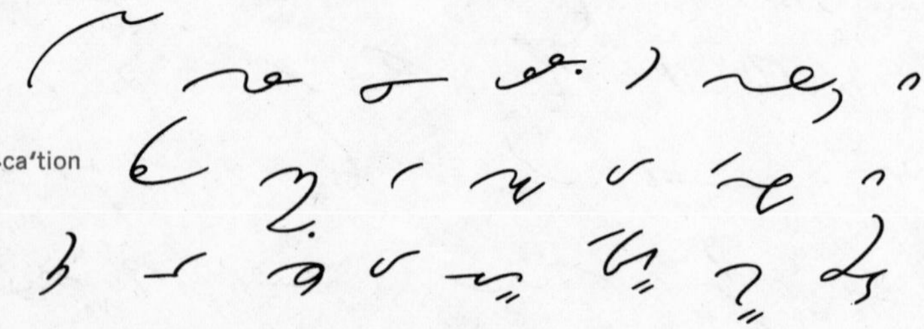

Trans'con·ti·nen'tal
in'di·cate

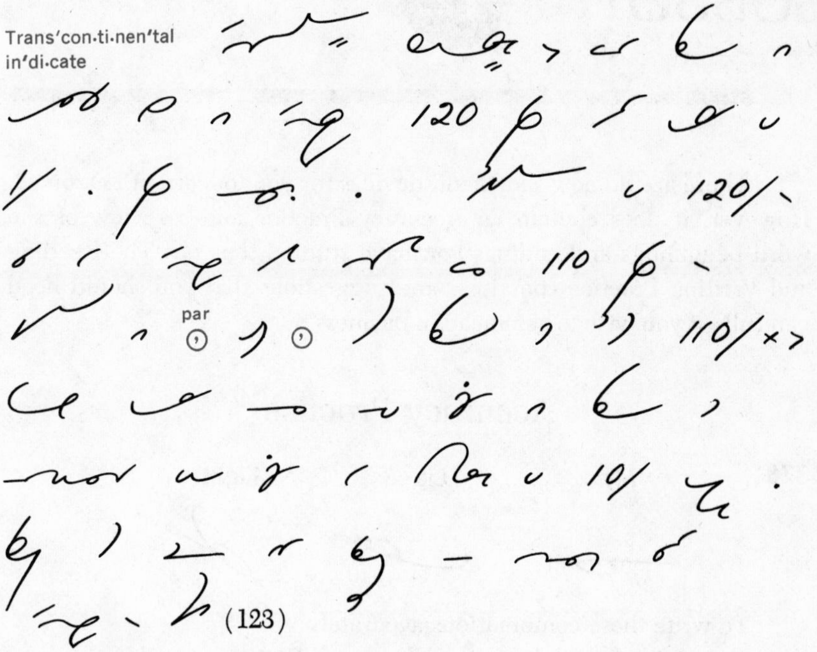

par

(123)

375. Chuckle

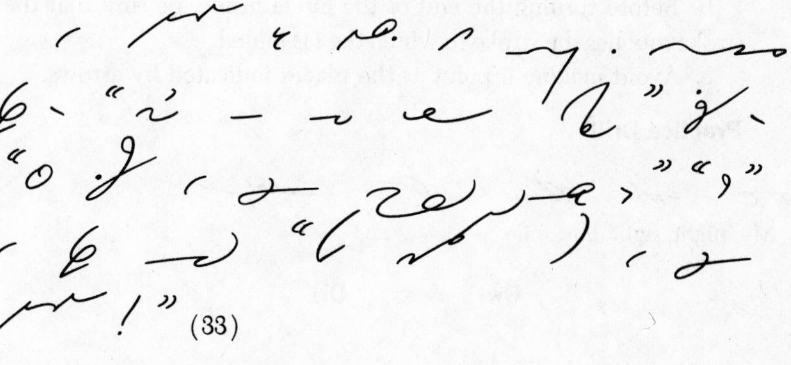

(33)

Lesson 42 RECALL

There are no new shorthand devices for you to learn in Lesson 42. However, it does contain an Accuracy Practice and a review of the word beginnings and endings you have studied thus far. The Reading and Writing Practice contains some suggestions that you should heed carefully if you wish to get ahead in business.

Accuracy Practice

376. **My** **Lie** **Fight**

To write these combinations accurately:

a. Join the circle in the same way that you would join an *a* circle, but turn the end inside the circle.

b. Before turning the end of the circle inside, be sure that the stroke touches the stroke to which the *i* is joined.

c. Avoid making a point at the places indicated by arrows.

Practice Drill

My, night, sight, line, mile.

377. **Ow** **Oi**

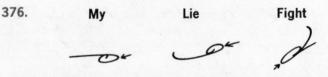

To write these combinations accurately:

a. Keep the hooks deep and narrow.

b. Place the circles outside the hooks as indicated by the dotted lines.

Practice Drill

How-out, now, doubt, scout, toy, soil, annoy.

378. **Th** **Nt, Nd** **Mt, Md**

To write these combinations accurately:

a. Slant the strokes as indicated by the dotted lines.
b. Start these strokes to the right and upward.

Practice Drill

There are, and will, empty, health, lined, ashamed.

Compare:

Hint, heard; tamed, detailed.

379. Recall Chart. There are 84 word beginnings and endings in the following chart. Can you read them in 5 minutes?

WORD BEGINNINGS AND ENDINGS

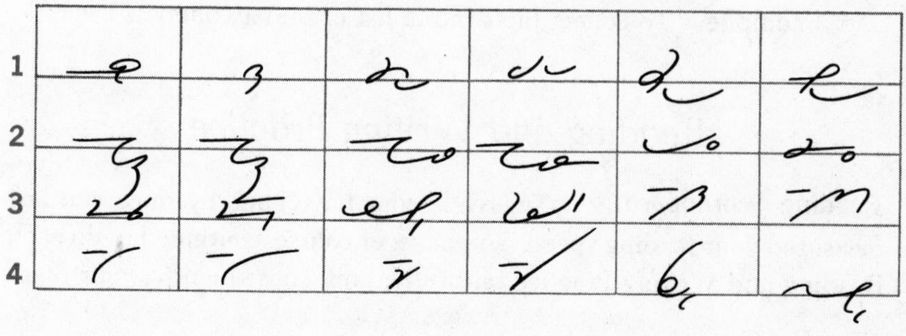

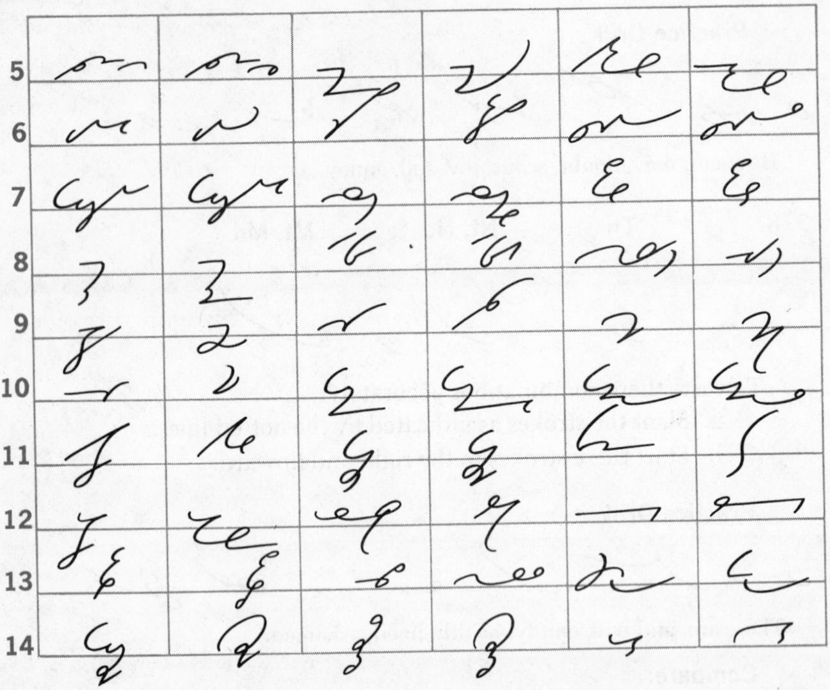
5
6
7
8
9
10
11
12
13
14

Building Transcription Skills

380. BUSINESS VOCABULARY BUILDER

encounter To meet.

vaguely In an unclear manner; uncertainly.

compile To collect facts into a list or into a volume.

Reading and Writing Practice

Reading Scoreboard. Twelve lessons have gone by since you last measured your reading speed. You have, of course, continued to do each Reading and Writing Practice faithfully; and, consequently, your reading speed will reflect this faithfulness! The following table will help you measure your reading speed on the *first reading* of Lesson 42.

Lesson 42 contains 350 words.

If you read Lesson 42 in	your reading rate is
10 MINUTES	35 WORDS A MINUTE
12 MINUTES	29 WORDS A MINUTE
14 MINUTES	25 WORDS A MINUTE
16 MINUTES	22 WORDS A MINUTE
18 MINUTES	19 WORDS A MINUTE
20 MINUTES	17 WORDS A MINUTE

If you can read Lesson 42 through the first time in less than 10 minutes, you are doing well. If you take considerably longer than 20 minutes, perhaps you should:

1. Pay closer attention in class while the shorthand devices are being presented to you.

2. Spend less time trying to decipher outlines that you cannot read.

3. Review, occasionally, all the brief forms you have studied through the chart on the inside back cover.

381. How Is Your Vocabulary?

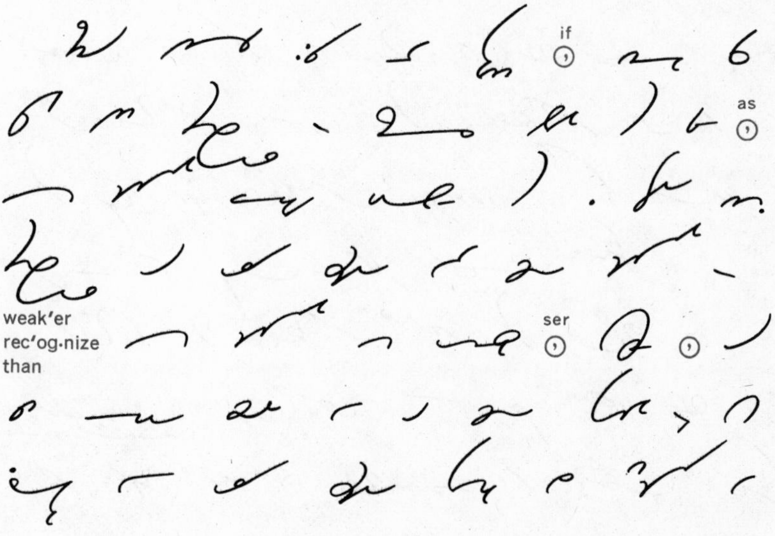
if
as
weak'er
rec'og·nize
than
ser

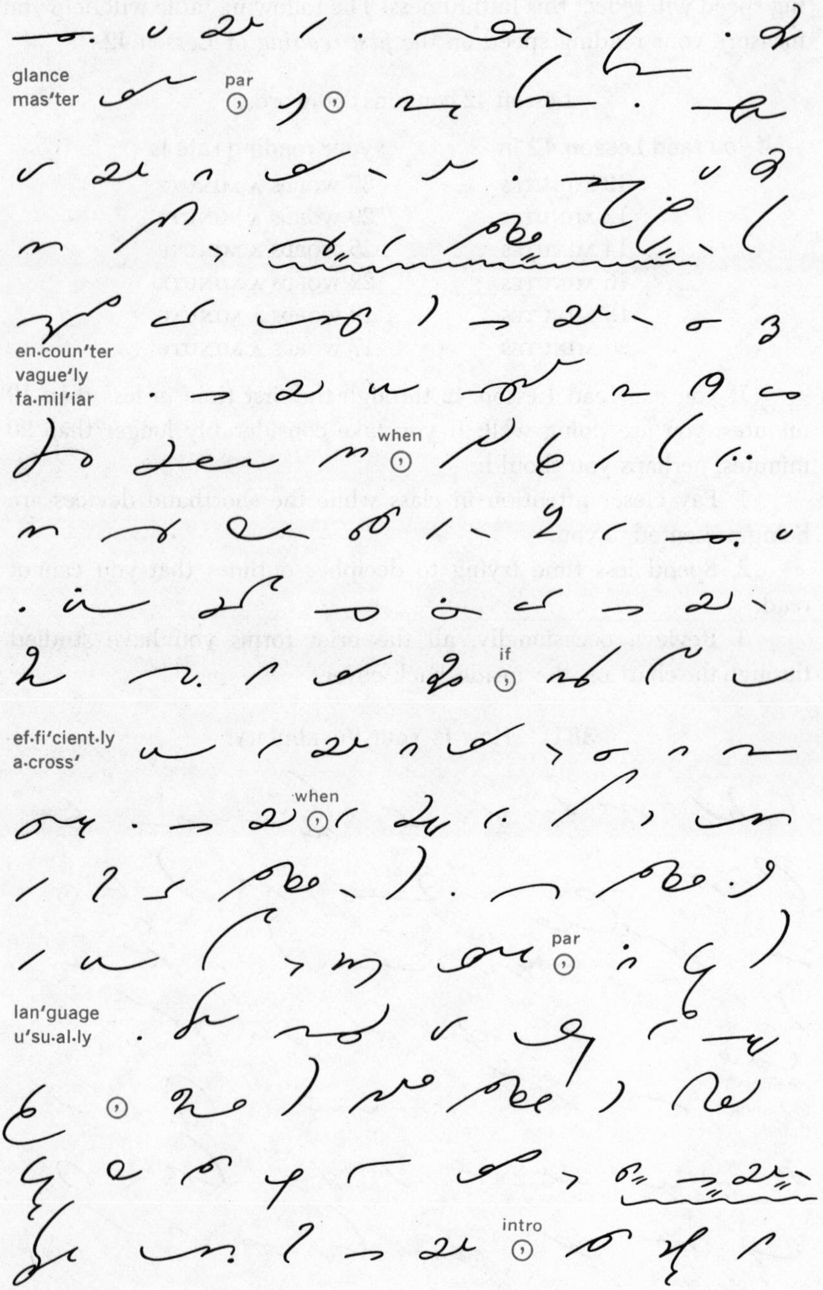
glance
mas′ter
par
en·coun′ter
vague′ly
fa·mil′iar
when
if
ef·fi′cient·ly
a·cross′
when
par
lan′guage
u′su·al·ly
intro

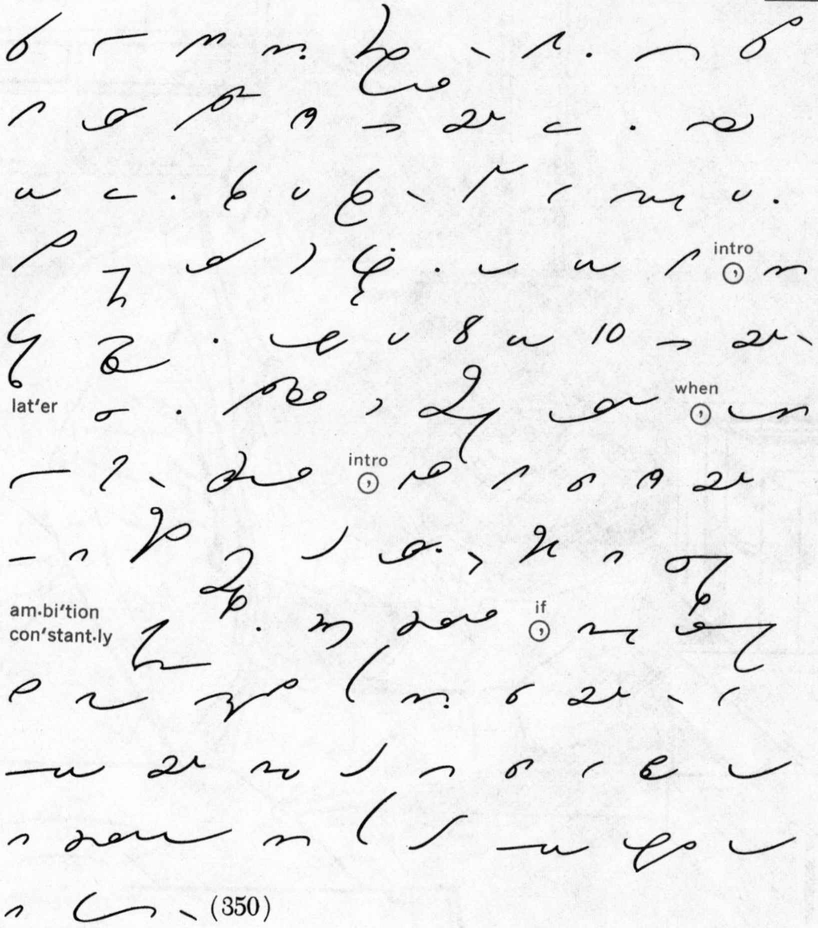
intro
lat'er
when
intro
am·bi'tion
con'stant·ly
if
(350)

The Secretary Communicates

What is communication? In the office, communication refers to anything having to do with the written or spoken word. Most of what the secretary does in the office is concerned with communications in one form or another.

In the first place, she talks in person or by phone to many people outside the company for which she works — friends of her boss, customers, business executives, sales representatives, messengers, and various visitors. She talks with many people inside the company — her boss, other executives, secretaries, department heads, accountants, repairmen, receptionists, and janitors. She talks informally in groups and more formally in meetings. Oral communication goes on constantly — much of it highly important, some of it trivial. All of it, however, requires skill. Skill in "handling" people by means of the spoken word is vital to harmonious relations both inside and outside the company. The secretary's boss depends on her to say the right thing at the right time, because what she says and how she says it reflects on him.

The secretary needs skill in written communications, too. She must know how to write letters — letters asking for information, letters answering requests for information, and thank-you letters for favors received. She needs to know how to write interoffice memos—memos about meetings, about changes in procedures, or about routine matters of company business. She may write telegrams, minutes of meetings, and messages of various kinds.

The extent to which the secretary is given responsibility for written communications depends entirely on her own initiative and the willingness of her boss to delegate these details to her. In all cases, however, her shorthand comes in very handy. Shorthand is an ideal instrument for composing written communications of all kinds. It helps the writer to think through what he is going to say before he types it — he can revise to his heart's content without sacrificing too much time and energy. Form the habit now of using your shorthand for thinking through all your written work. It will stand you in good stead later.

Chapter 8

Lesson 43

Principles

382. Word Ending -ulate. The word ending *-ulate* is represented by a disjoined *oo* hook.

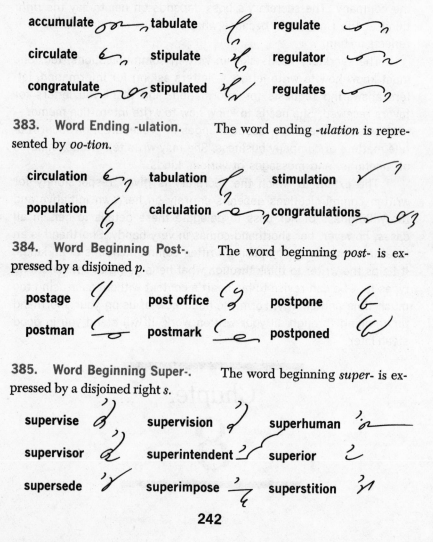

accumulate	tabulate	regulate
circulate	stipulate	regulator
congratulate	stipulated	regulates

383. Word Ending -ulation. The word ending *-ulation* is represented by *oo-tion.*

circulation	tabulation	stimulation
population	calculation	congratulations

384. Word Beginning Post-. The word beginning *post-* is expressed by a disjoined *p.*

postage	post office	postpone
postman	postmark	postponed

385. Word Beginning Super-. The word beginning *super-* is expressed by a disjoined right *s.*

supervise	supervision	superhuman
supervisor	superintendent	superior
supersede	superimpose	superstition

Building Transcription Skills

386. BUSINESS VOCABULARY BUILDER

circulation The total number of copies of a publication distributed each issue.

expenditures Moneys paid out.

calculations Figurings; computations.

387. PUNCTUATION PRACTICE

, conjunction

A comma is used to separate two independent clauses that are joined by one of the following conjunctions: *and, but, or, for, nor.*

An independent clause (sometimes called a main or a principal clause) is one that has a subject and predicate and that could stand alone as a complete sentence.

> The unit is one of the most dependable on the market, and it is economical to operate.

The first independent clause is:

> The unit is one of the most dependable on the market

and the second is:

> it is economical to operate

Both clauses could stand as separate sentences, with a period after each. Because the thoughts of the two clauses are closely related, however, the clauses were joined to form one sentence. Because the two independent clauses are connected by the co-ordinating conjunction *and,* a comma is used between them, before the conjunction.

Each time this use of the comma occurs in the Reading and Writing Practice, it will be indicated thus in the shorthand:

conj

Reading and Writing Practice

388.

be·lieve'
post·pone'
as·sist'ant
con'fi·dent
su·pe'ri·or

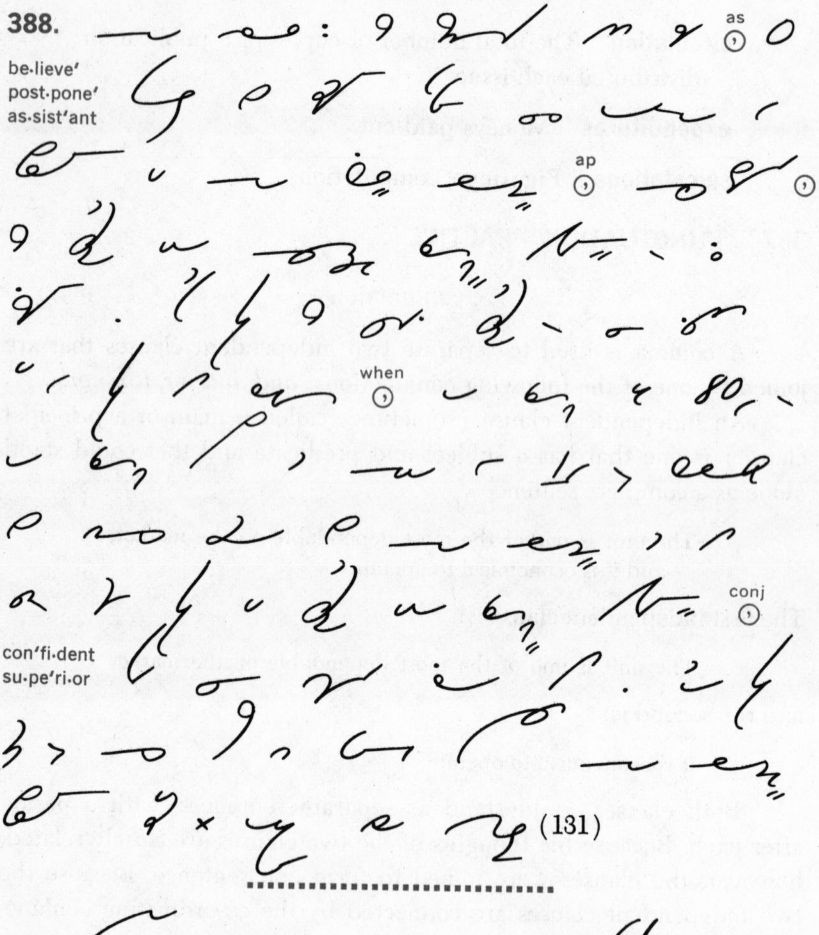
as
ap
when
conj
(131)

389.

cir'cu·lars
mail

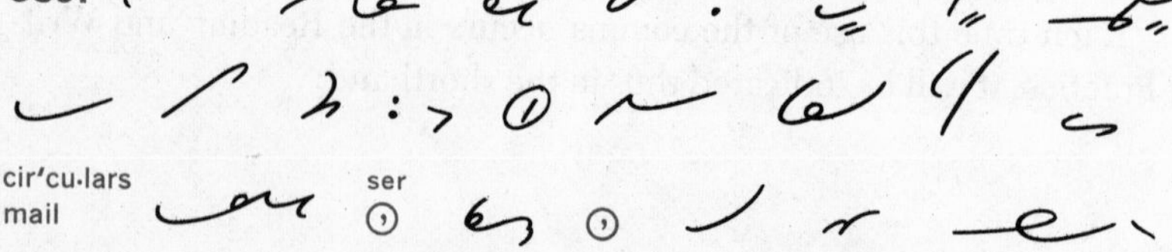
ser

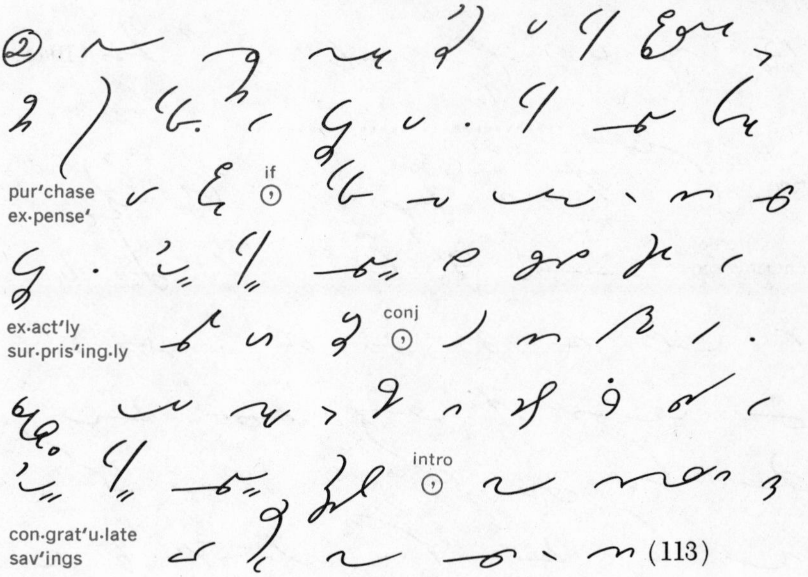

pur'chase
ex·pense'

ex·act'ly
sur·pris'ing·ly

con·grat'u·late
sav'ings

(113)

390.

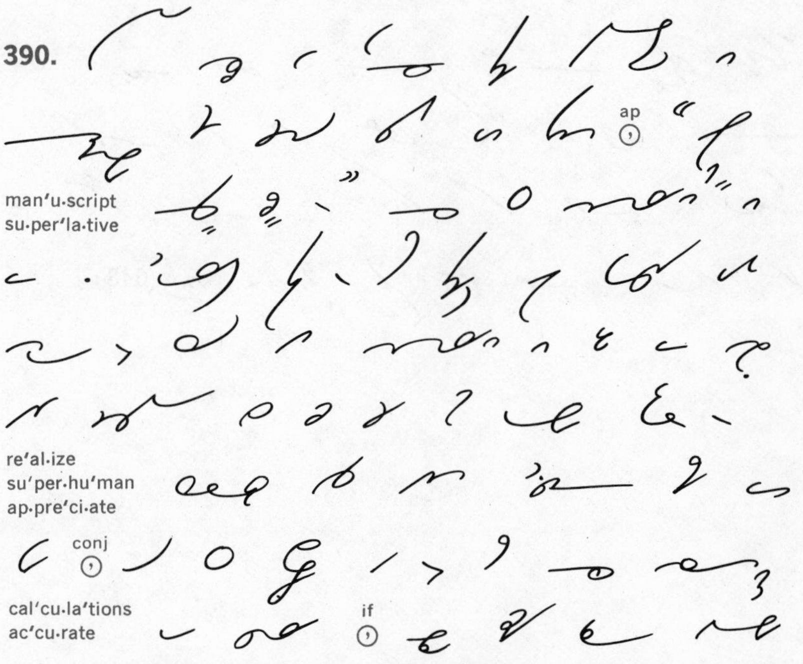

man'u·script
su·per'la·tive

re'al·ize
su'per·hu'man
ap·pre'ci·ate

cal'cu·la'tions
ac'cu·rate

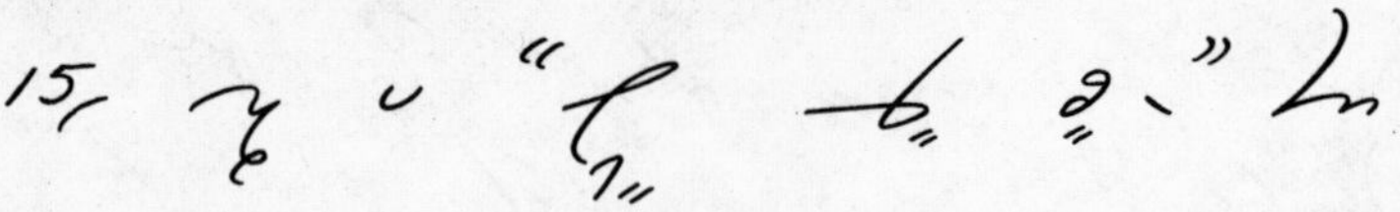

(104)

391.

sub·scrip'tion
Su'per·vi'sor's

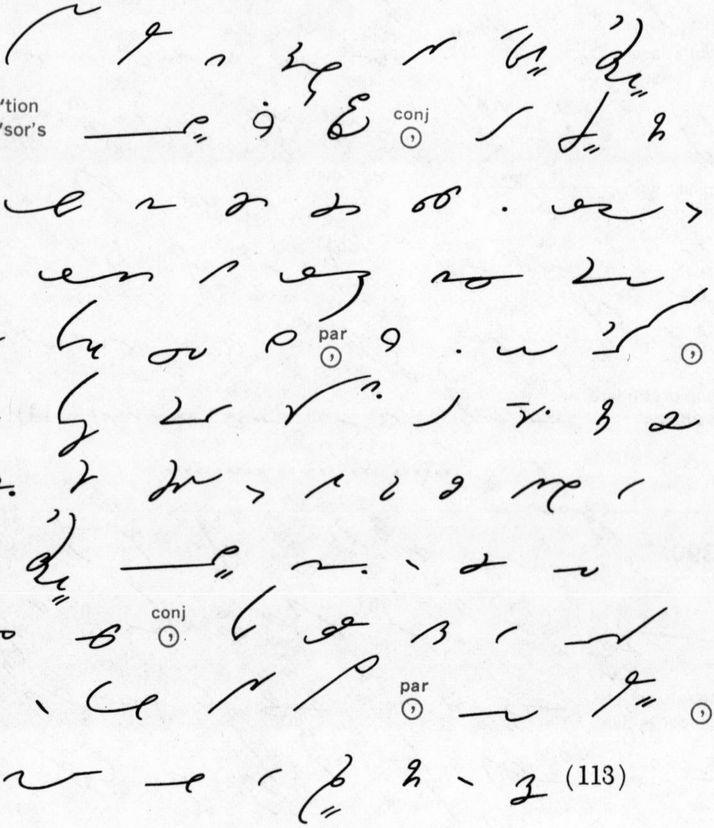
conj
par
conj
par

(113)

Lesson 44

Principles

392. Word Ending -sume. The word ending *-sume* is represented by *s-m*.

resume  **assume**  **consumer** 

consume  **presume**  **consumed** 

393. Word Ending -sumption. The word ending *-sumption* is represented by *s-m-tion*.

resumption  **consumption**  **presumption** 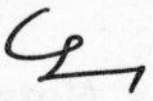

394. Word Beginning Self-. The word beginning *self-* is represented by a disjoined left *s*.

self-confident  **self-reliant**  **selfishness** 

self-made  **self-defense**  **selfishly** 

395. Word Beginning Circum-. The word beginning *circum-* is also represented by a disjoined left *s*.

circumstance  **circumstances**  **circumstantial** 

Building Transcription Skills

396. BUSINESS VOCABULARY BUILDER

manuscript Handwritten or typewritten copy prepared for publication.

submit To send in; to turn over to.

contract An agreement.

tedious Tiresome.

resumption Act of beginning again.

397. PUNCTUATION PRACTICE

, and omitted

When two or more adjectives modify the same noun, they are separated by commas.

He was a quiet, efficient worker.

However, the comma is not used if the first adjective modifies the combined idea of the second adjective plus the noun.

She wore a beautiful green dress.

Note: You can quickly determine whether to insert a comma between two consecutive adjectives by mentally placing *and* between them. If the sentence makes good sense with *and* inserted between the adjectives, then the comma is used. For example, the first illustration would make good sense if it read:

He was a quiet and efficient worker.

Each time this use of the comma occurs in the Reading and Writing Practice, it will be indicated thus in the shorthand:

and o

Reading and Writing Practice

398.

man'u·script
en·ti'tled

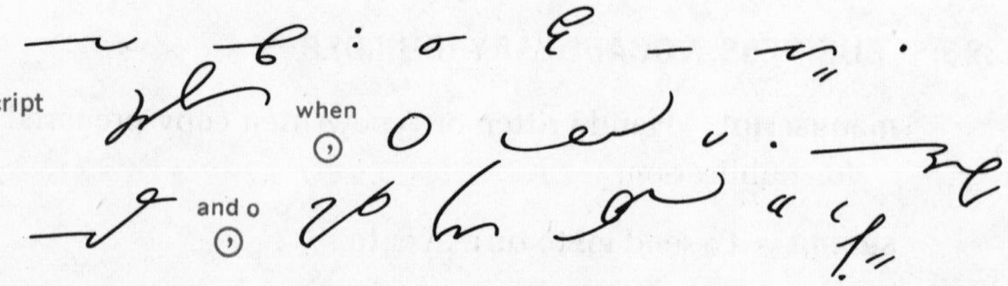
when
and o

intro
par

wheth'er
au'thor's

(148)

399.

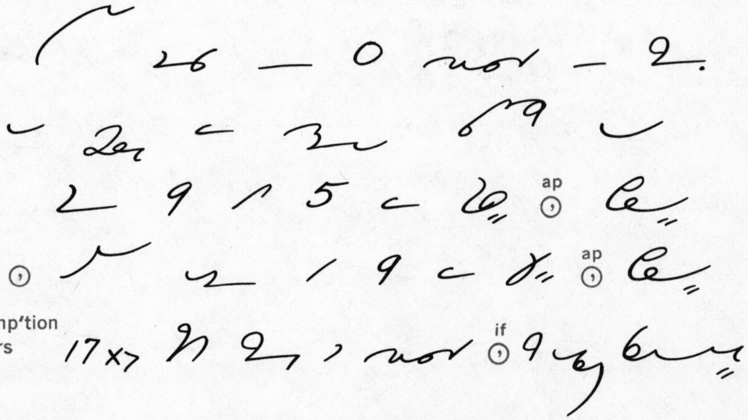
ap
ap
if

as·sump'tion
Par'lors

ser

intro

prof'it·a·ble

and o

and o

con·ven'ience

(96)

400.

if

as·sume'

o'ver·come'

fright

as

te'di·ous

course

and o

if

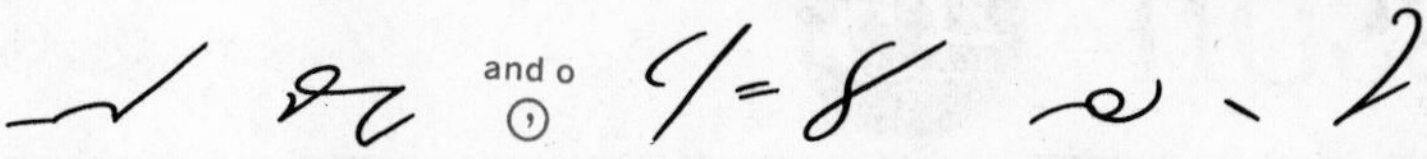
and o

(124)

401.

re·sumed'
cit'ies
in'ter·rup'tion
be·yond'
re·sump'tion
sched'ules

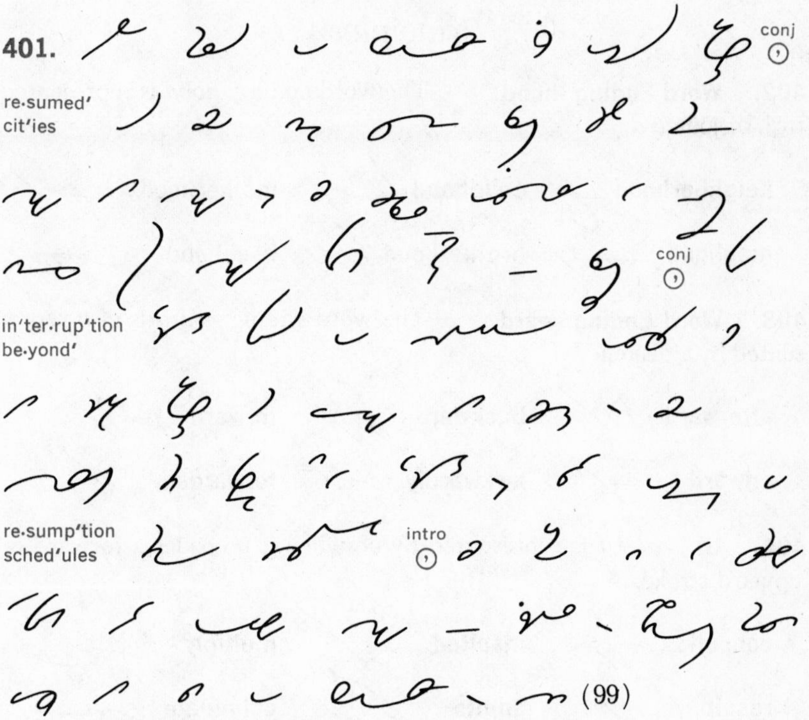
conj
conj
intro

(99)

SPELLING AND PUNCTUATION CHECK LIST

Are you careful to punctuate and spell correctly when –

1. You write your compositions in English?

2. Prepare your reports for your social studies classes?

3. Correspond with friends to whom you must write in longhand?

In short, are you making correct spelling and punctuation a habit in all the longhand writing or typing that you do?

Lesson 45

Principles

402. Word Ending -hood. The word ending *-hood* is represented by a disjoined *d.*

neighborhood **childhood** **motherhood**
manhood **brotherhood** **likelihood**

403. Word Ending -ward. The word ending *-ward* is also represented by a disjoined *d.*

afterward **backward** **forward**
onward **awkwardly** **forwarded**

404. Ul. *Ul* is represented by *oo* when it precedes a forward or upward stroke.

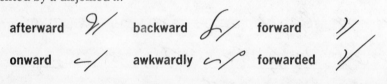

consult **insulted** **multiply**
result **adults** **culminate**

405. Quantities and Amounts. Here are a few more helpful abbreviations for quantities and amounts.

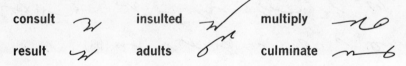

$500 **5,000,000,000** **several hundred**
5,000,000 **a dollar** **4 pounds**
$5,000,000 **a million** **8 feet**

Notice that the *m* for *million* is written beside the figure, as a positive distinction from *hundred,* in which the *n* is written underneath the figure.

Building Transcription Skills

406. BUSINESS VOCABULARY BUILDER

attorneys Lawyers.

attribute (*verb*) To assign as the reason or cause of.

depositors Those who have money on deposit in a bank.

dividends Profits of a corporation that are shared with stockholders.

407. SPELLING FAMILIES

An effective device to improve your ability to spell is to study words in related groups, or spelling families, in which all the words contain the same spelling problem; for example, words in which silent *e* is dropped before *ing.*

To get the most benefit from these spelling families, practice them in this way:

1. Spell each word aloud, pausing slightly after each syllable.
2. Write the word once in longhand, spelling it aloud as you write it.

You will find several of the words in each spelling family used in the Reading and Writing Practice.

Words in Which Silent E Is Dropped Before -ing

a·chiev'ing	**guid'ing**	**re·ceiv'ing**
de·sir'ing	**hous'ing**	**sav'ing**
ex·am'in·ing	**in·creas'ing**	**typ'ing**
forc'ing	**man'ag·ing**	**us'ing**

Reading and Writing Practice

408.

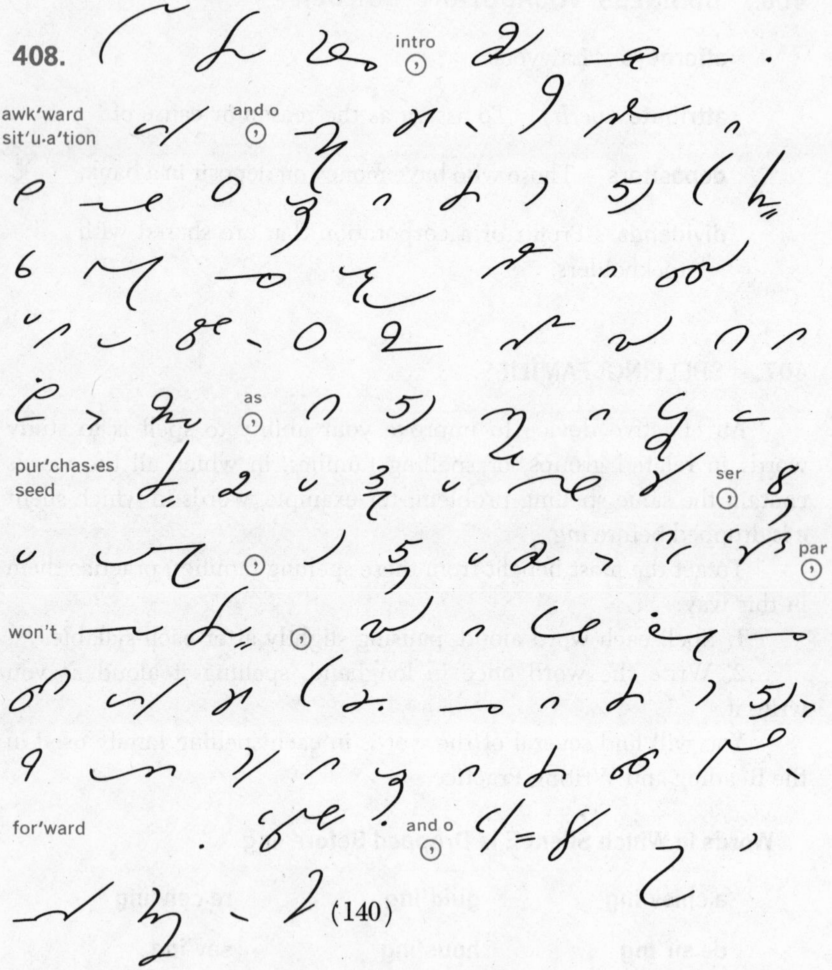
intro
awk'ward
sit'u·a'tion
and o
as
pur'chas·es
seed
ser
par
won't
for'ward
and o
(140)

409.

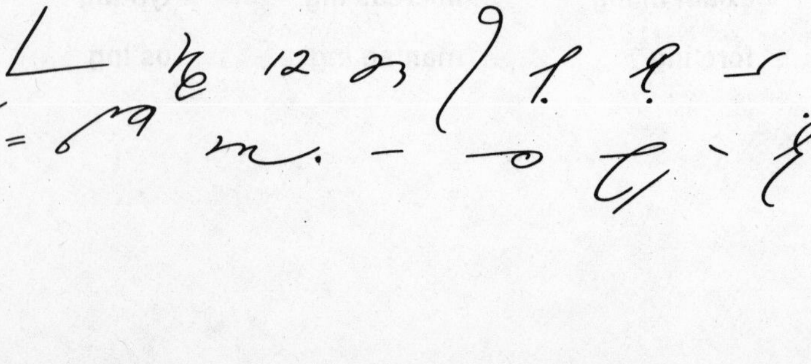

re·ward'ing
ex·pe'ri·ence
text'book'
ex·am'in·ing

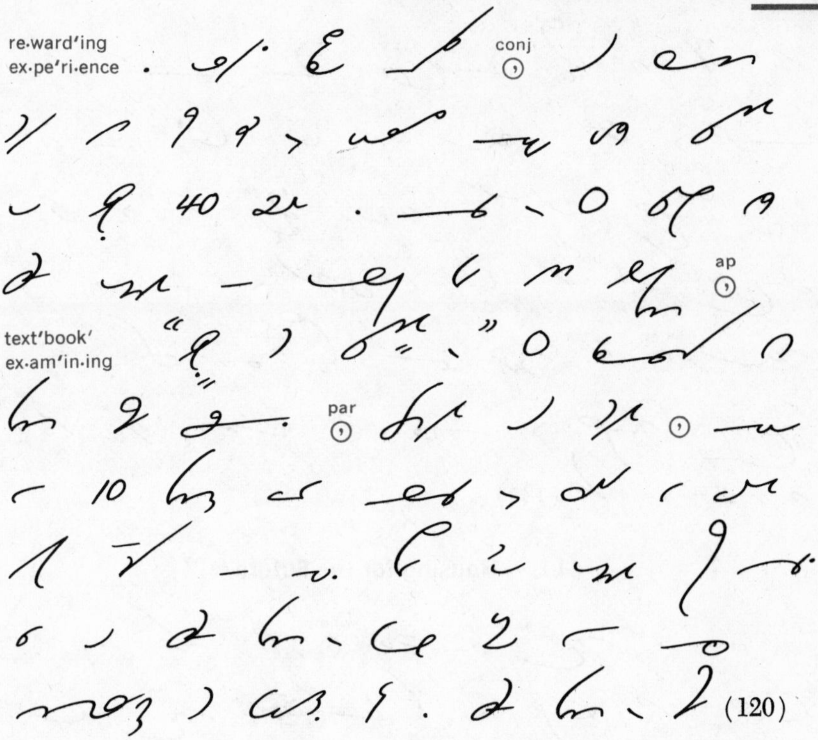
conj
ap
par

(120)

410.

re·ceived'
div'i·dends

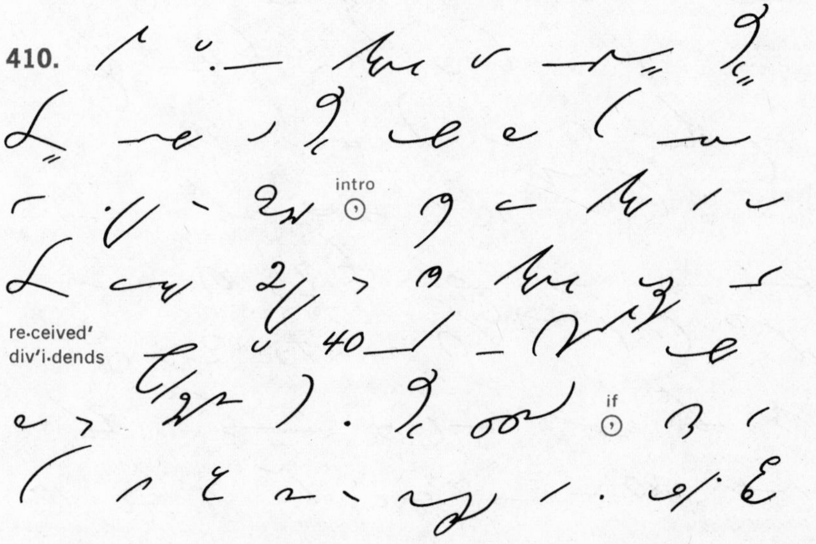
intro
if

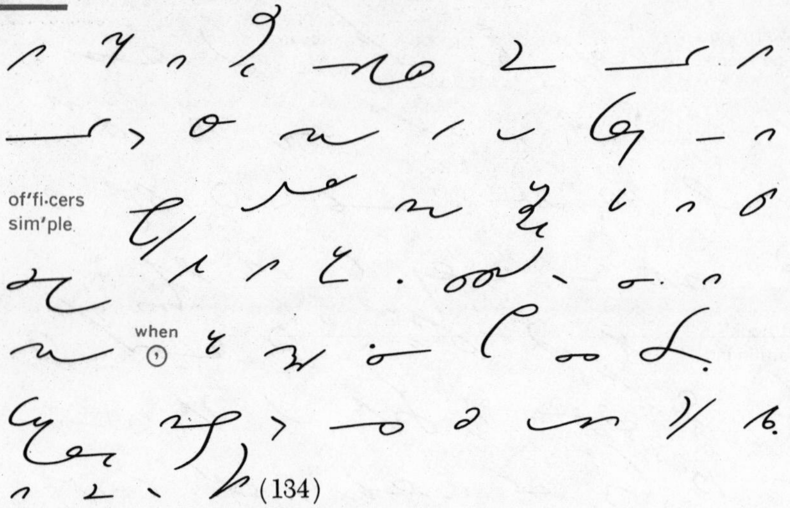

of'fi·cers
sim'ple
when

(134)

411. Housing for the Future

when
when
a·chieve'
par'ent·hood
born
de·mol'ished
when
intro

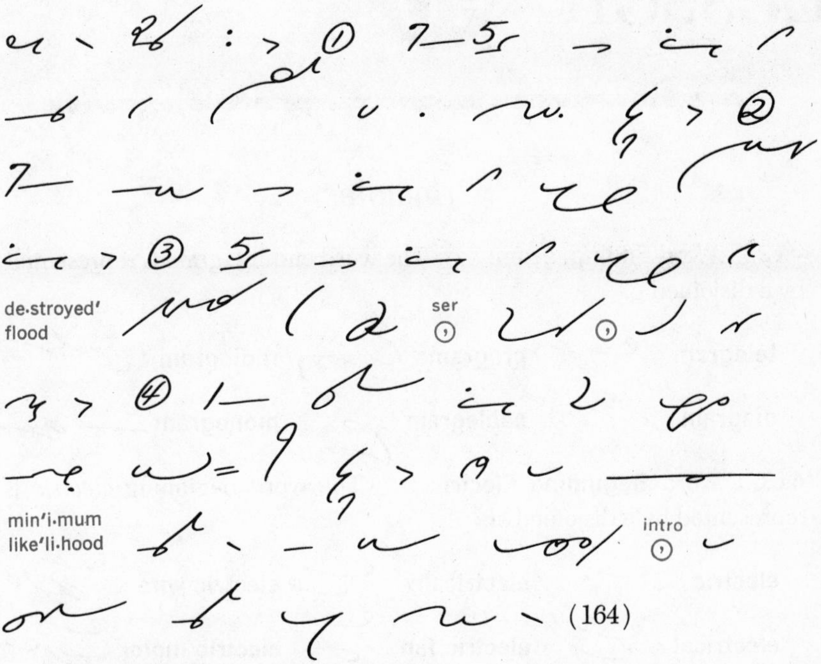
de·stroyed'
flood
ser
min'i·mum
like'li·hood
intro
(164)

HOMEWORK CHECK LIST

When you do your homework assignment each day –

1. Do you study the Business Vocabulary Builder and the other transcription helps in the lesson before you start your work on the Reading and Writing Practice?

2. Do you read aloud each Reading and Writing Practice before copying it?

3. Do you spell each shorthand outline that you cannot immediately read? Remember, nothing builds shorthand speed more rapidly than the regular reading and writing of shorthand.

4. Do you note carefully the reason for the use of each comma that is encircled in the Reading and Writing Practice?

5. Do you spell aloud all the words given in the margins of the shorthand in the Reading and Writing Practice?

Lesson 46

Principles

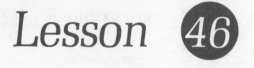

412. Word Ending -gram. The word ending *-gram* is represented by a disjoined *g*.

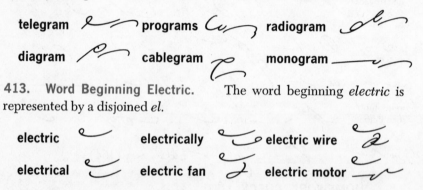

telegram  **programs** 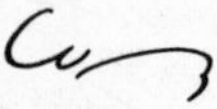 **radiogram** 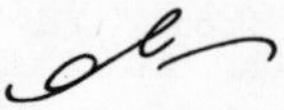

diagram  **cablegram**  **monogram** 

413. Word Beginning Electric. The word beginning *electric* is represented by a disjoined *el*.

electric  **electrically**  **electric wire** 

electrical  **electric fan**  **electric motor** 

414. Word Beginning Electr-. The word beginning *electr-* is also represented by a disjoined *el*.

electronic  **electrotype**  **electroplate** 

415. Compounds. Most compound words are formed by simply joining the outlines for the words that make up the compound. In some words, however, it is desirable to modify the outline for one of the words in order to obtain a facile joining.

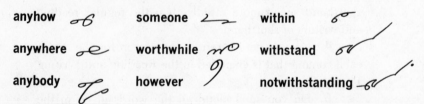

anyhow  **someone**  **within** 

anywhere 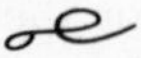 **worthwhile**  **withstand** 

anybody  **however**  **notwithstanding** 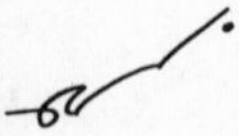

416. Intersection. Intersection, or the writing of one character through another, is sometimes useful for special phrases. You should not, however, attempt to memorize lists of such phrases; you should devise such phrases only when the constant repetition of certain phrases in your dictation makes it clearly worthwhile to form special outlines.

a.m.  **vice versa** 

p.m.  **Chamber of Commerce** 

Building Transcription Skills

417. BUSINESS VOCABULARY BUILDER

alerted Warned to be ready; made aware; placed in readiness to act.

tenant An occupant.

menacing Threatening.

418. SIMILAR-WORDS DRILL

Brought, bought

brought The past tense and past participle of *bring*.

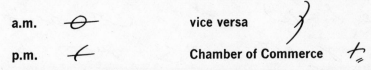

John brought the book back after having read it.

bought Purchased.

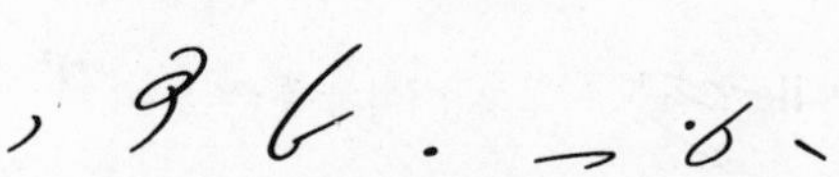

His wife bought a new hat.

Reading and Writing Practice

419.

when
ser
intro
as
par
intro
and o
(139)

e·lec'tri·cal
su'per·vi'sors

not'with·stand'ing
sac'ri·fice

breaks
trans·mis'sion

e·lec'tric'i·ty
brought

grate'ful
pa'tience

420.

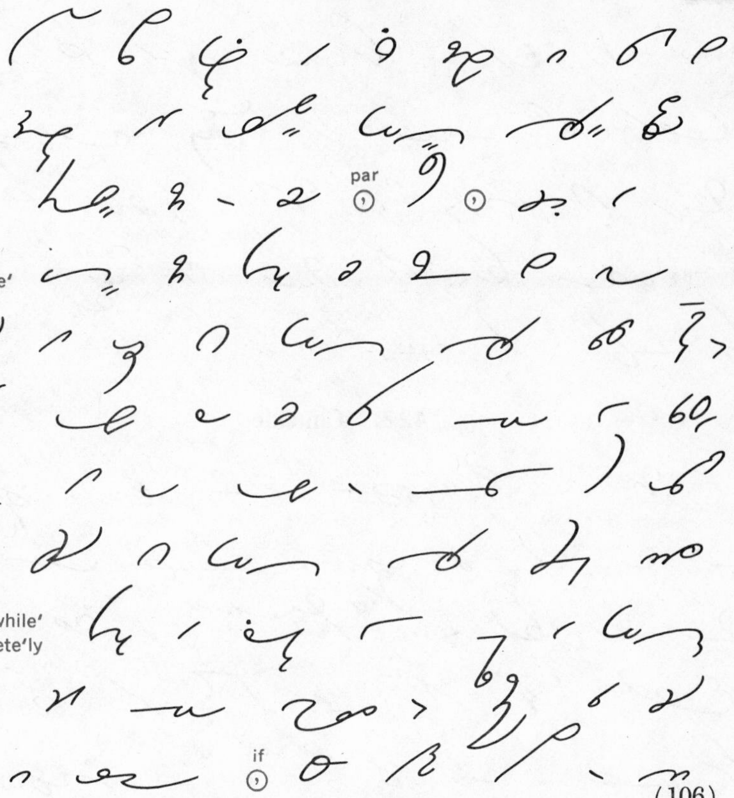
par
if

Guide
re·ceive'

worth'while'
com·plete'ly

(106)

421.

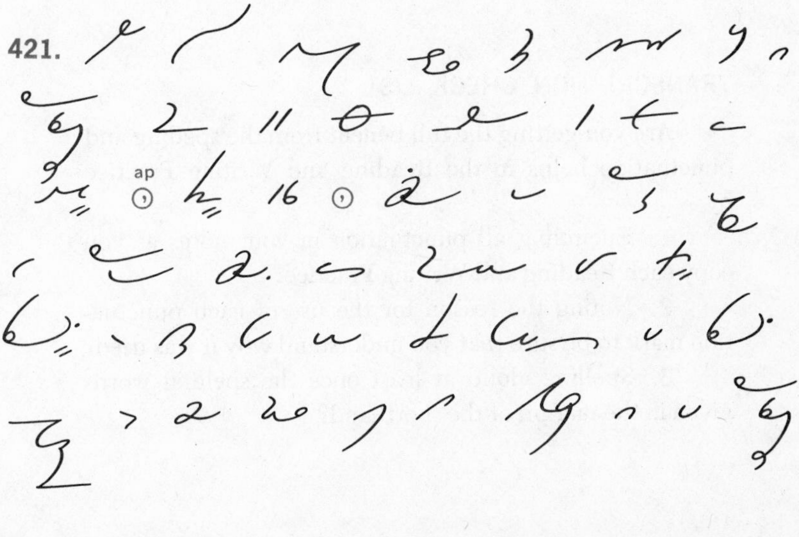
ap

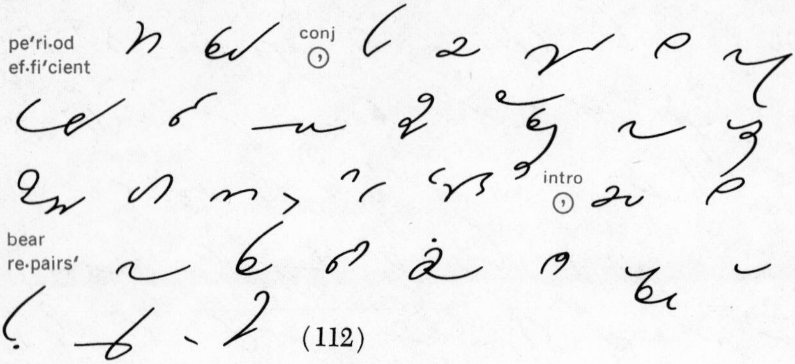
pe'ri·od
ef·fi'cient
conj
intro
bear
re·pairs'

(112)

422. Chuckle

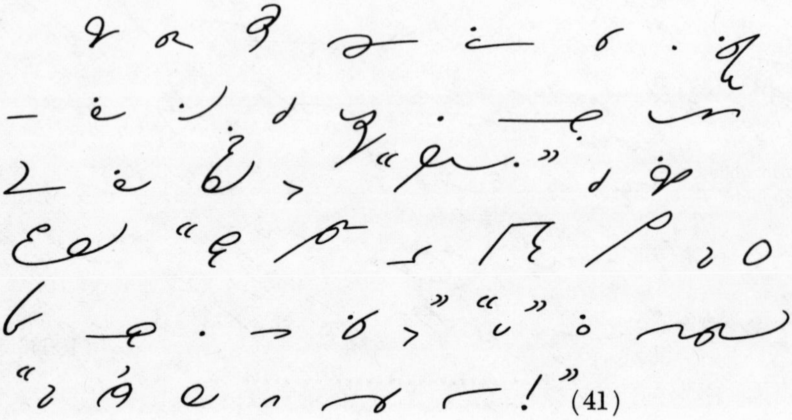

(41)

TRANSCRIPTION CHECK LIST

Are you getting the full benefit from the spelling and punctuation helps in the Reading and Writing Practice by—

1. Encircling all punctuation in your notes as you copy each Reading and Writing Practice?

2. Noting the reason for the use of each punctuation mark to be sure that you understand why it was used?

3. Spelling aloud at least once the spelling words given in the margin of the shorthand?

Lesson 47

Principles

423. Geographical Expressions. In geographical expressions, *-burg* is represented by *b*; *-ingham*, by a disjoined *m*; *-ington*, by a disjoined *ten* blend; *-ville*, by *v*.

-burg

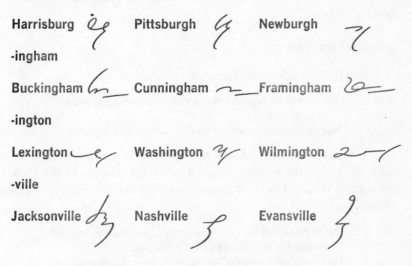

Harrisburg  **Pittsburgh**  **Newburgh** 

-ingham

Buckingham 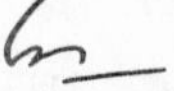 **Cunningham**  **Framingham** 

-ington

Lexington  **Washington**  **Wilmington** 

-ville

Jacksonville 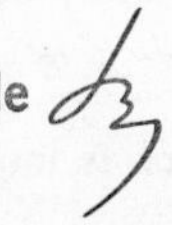 **Nashville**  **Evansville** 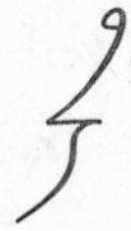

Building Transcription Skills

424. BUSINESS VOCABULARY BUILDER

complicated Hard to solve.

utmost The most possible.

enviable Desirable.

maintenance Upkeep.

425. GRAMMAR CHECKUP

Most businessmen have a good command of the English language. Some rarely make an error in grammar. There are times, though, when even the best dictators will perhaps use a plural verb with a singular noun or use the objective case when they should have used the nominative. They usually know better; but in concentrating intently on expressing a thought or idea, they occasionally suffer a grammatical lapse.

It will be your job, as a stenographer or secretary, to catch these occasional errors in grammar and to correct them when you transcribe.

From time to time in the lessons ahead, you will be given an opportunity to brush up on some of the rules of grammar that are frequently violated.

Subject and Verb

A verb must agree with its subject in number.

> Our *representative is* looking forward to the pleasure of serving you.
> Your canceled *checks are* mailed to you each month.

The inclusion of a phrase such as *in addition to, as well as,* or *along with* after the subject does not affect the number of the verb. If the subject is singular, use a singular verb; if the subject is plural, use a plural verb.

> Our *representative,* as well as our managers, *is* looking forward to the pleasure of serving you.
> Your canceled *checks,* along with your statement, *are* mailed to you each month.

Reading and Writing Practice

426.

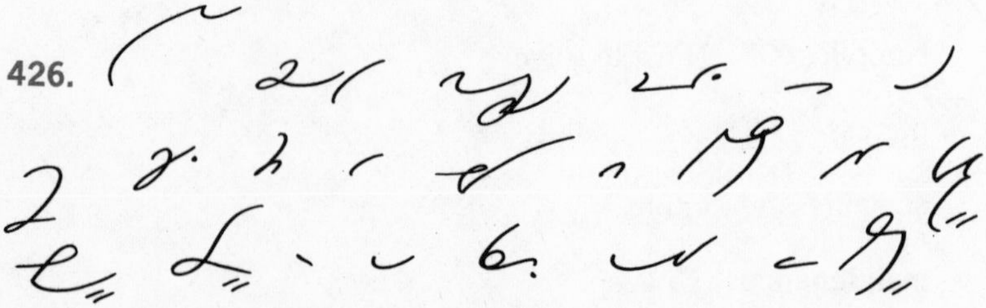

com·plete′ly
re·paved′
com′pli·cat′ed
cus′tom·ers
serv′ice
Pitts′burgh's

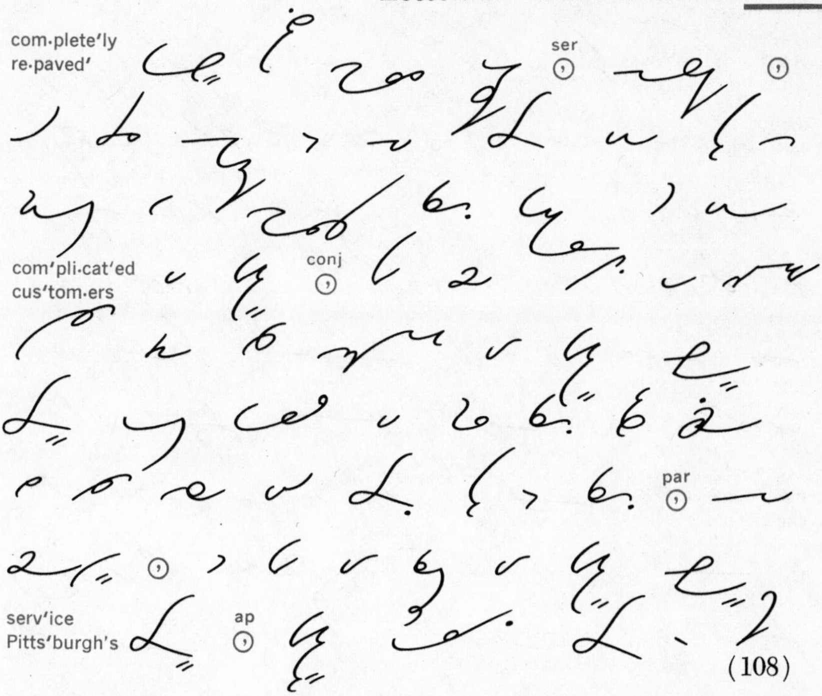
ser
conj
par
ap

(108)

427.

ar·range′ments
mov′ing
stor′age
en′vi·a·ble

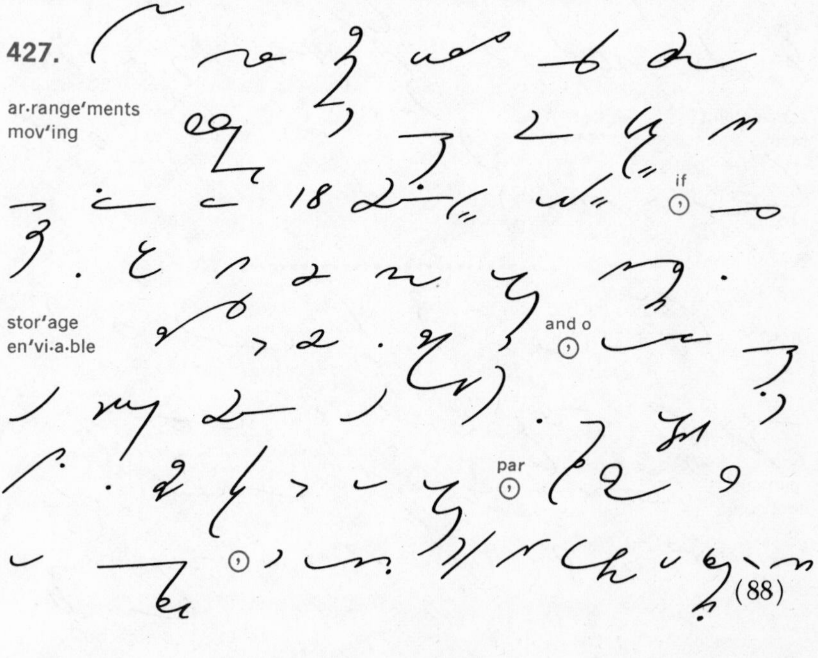
if
and o
par

(88)

428.

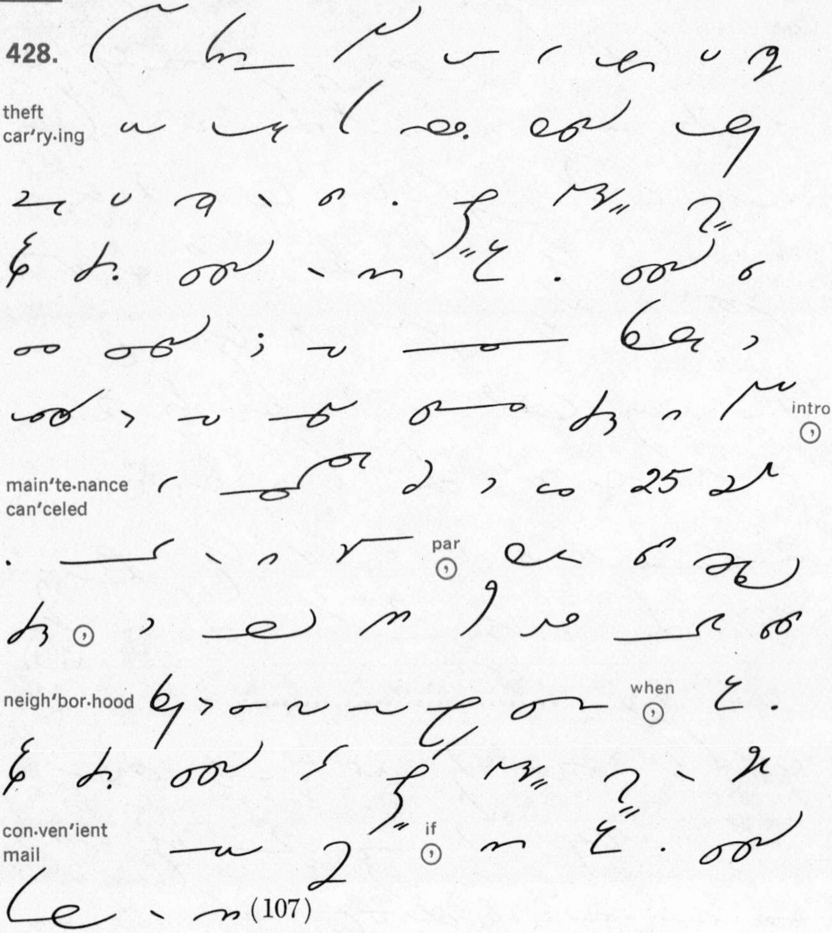
theft
car'ry·ing
intro
main'te·nance
can'celed
25
par
neigh'bor·hood
when
con·ven'ient
mail
if
(107)

429.

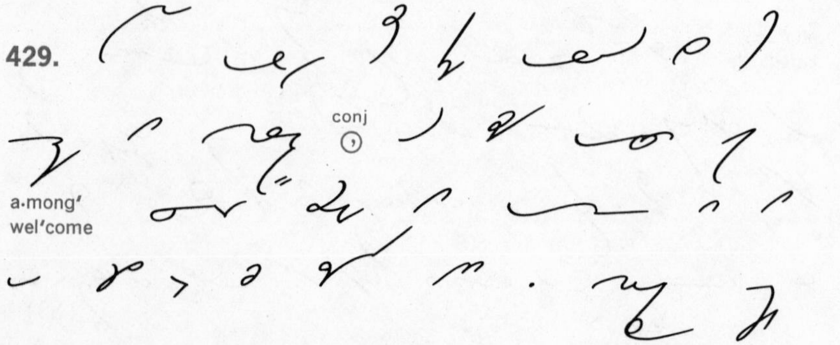
conj
a·mong'
wel'come

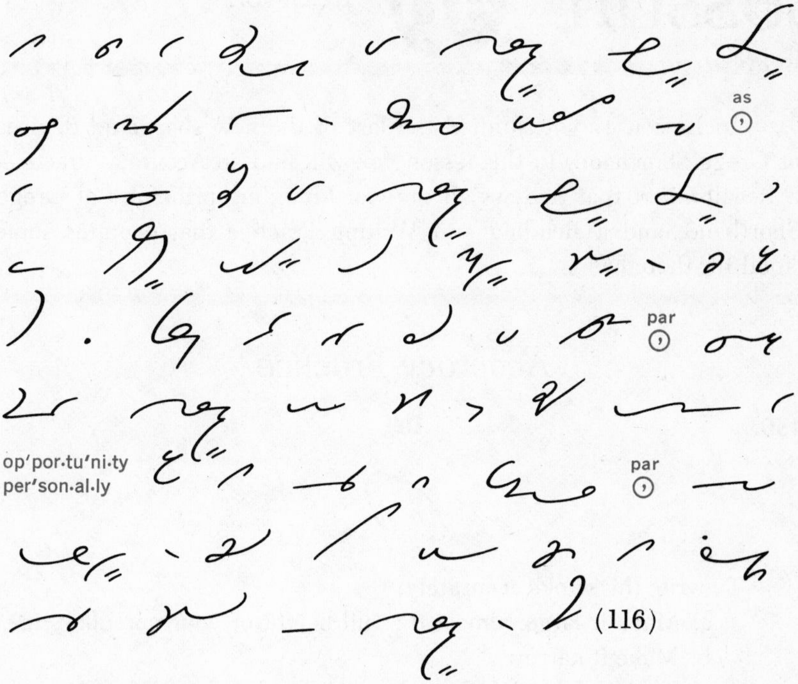
as
par
op'por·tu'ni·ty
per'son·al·ly
par
(116)

BRIEF-FORM CHECK LIST

Are you making good use of the brief-form chart that appears on the inside back cover of your textbook? Remember, the brief forms represent many of the commonest words in the language; and the better you know them, the more rapid progress you will make in developing your shorthand speed. Are you—

1. Spending a few minutes reading from the charts each day?

2. Timing yourself and trying to cut a few seconds off your reading time with each reading?

3. Reading the brief forms in a different order each time—from left to right, from right to left, from top to bottom, from bottom to top?

Lesson 48 RECALL

In Lesson 47 you studied the last of the new shorthand devices of Gregg Shorthand. In this lesson you will find an Accuracy Practice, a Recall Chart that reviews all the word-building principles of Gregg Shorthand, and a Reading and Writing Practice that contains some "food for thought."

Accuracy Practice

430. **Def**

To write this stroke accurately:

a. Make it large, almost the full height of your notebook line.

b. Make it narrow.

c. Start and finish the strokes on the same level of writing, as indicated by the dotted lines.

Practice Drill

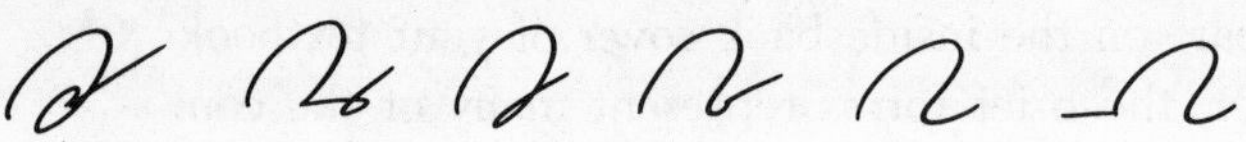

Divide, definite, defeat, devote, differ, endeavor.

431. **Th** **Ten** **Tem**

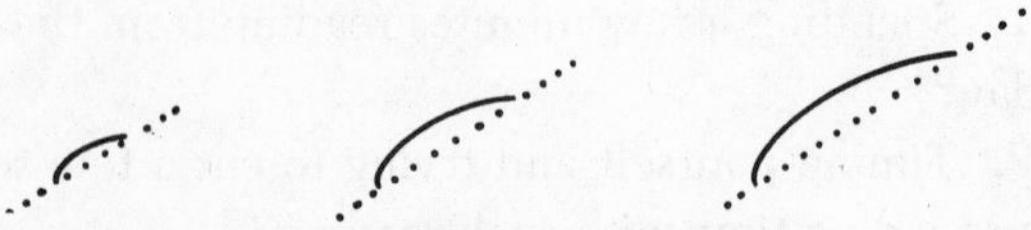

To write these strokes accurately:

a. Slant the strokes as indicated by the dotted lines.

b. Make the beginning of the curves deep.

c. Make the *tem* large, about the full height of the line; the *th* small; the *ten* about half the size of the *tem*.

Practice Drill

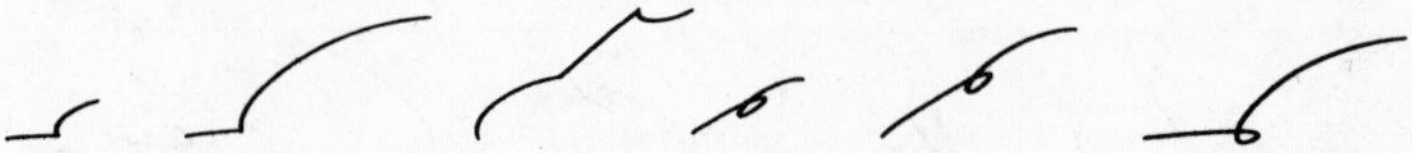

In the, in time, tender, teeth, detain, medium.

432. Recall Chart. This chart contains one or more illustrations of every word-building and phrasing principle of Gregg Shorthand.

WORDS

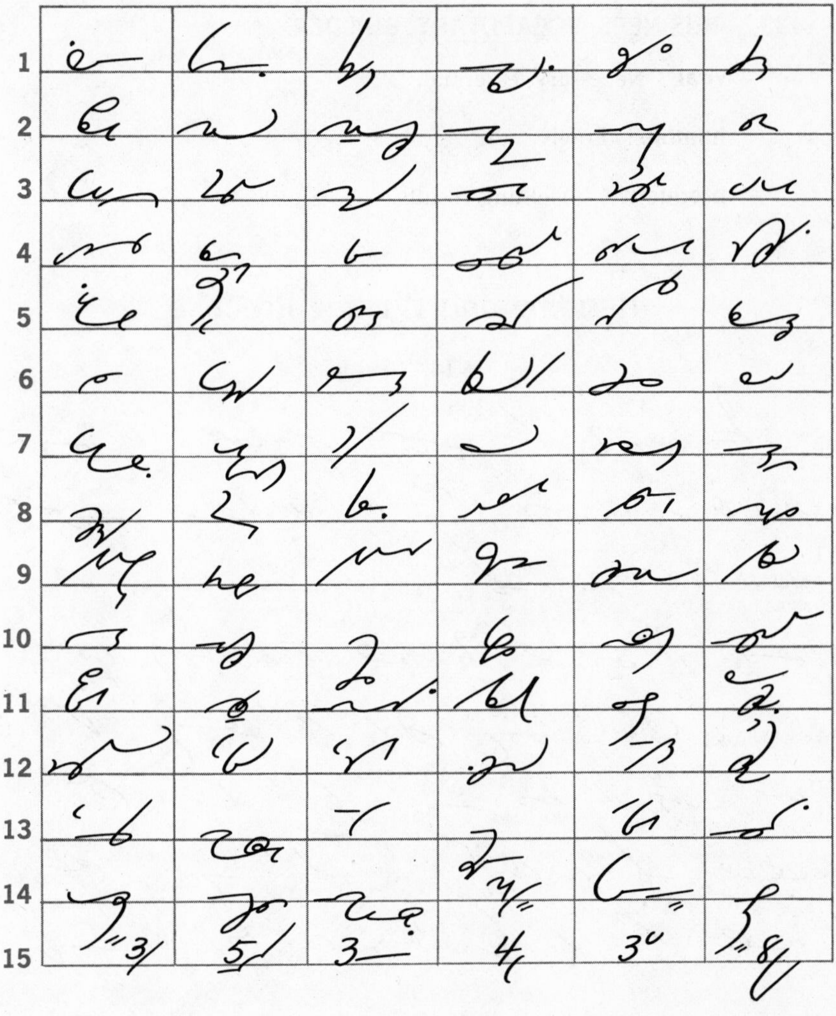
1
2
3
4
5
6
7
8
9
10
11
12
13
14
15

PHRASES

16
17

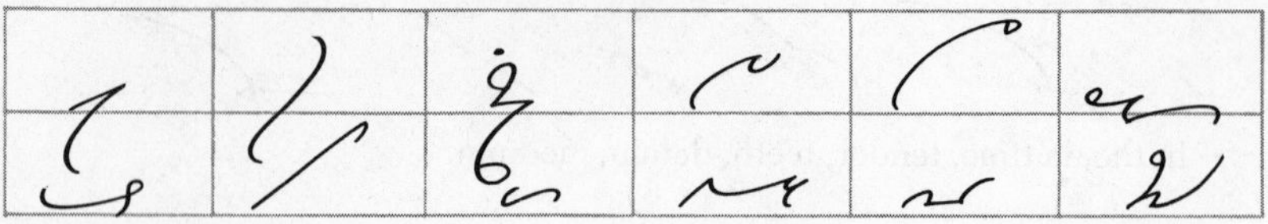

Building Transcription Skills

433. BUSINESS VOCABULARY BUILDER

vital Necessary; essential.

humble Lowly.

productive Yielding results.

Reading and Writing Practice

434. Pride

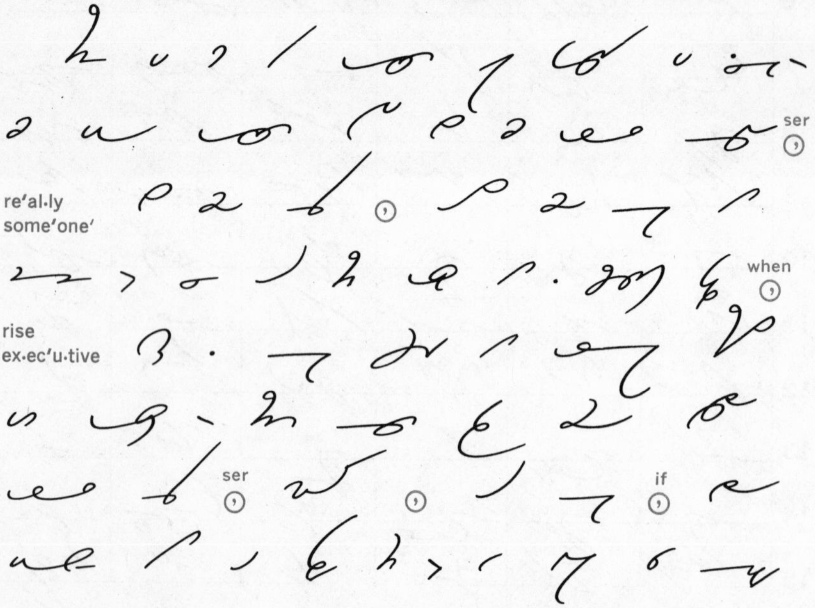
ser
re'al·ly
some'one'
when
rise
ex·ec'u·tive
ser
if

their
sat'is·fac'to·ri·ly
ex·am'ple
fac'to·ry
stand'still'
em·ploy'ee
hum'ble

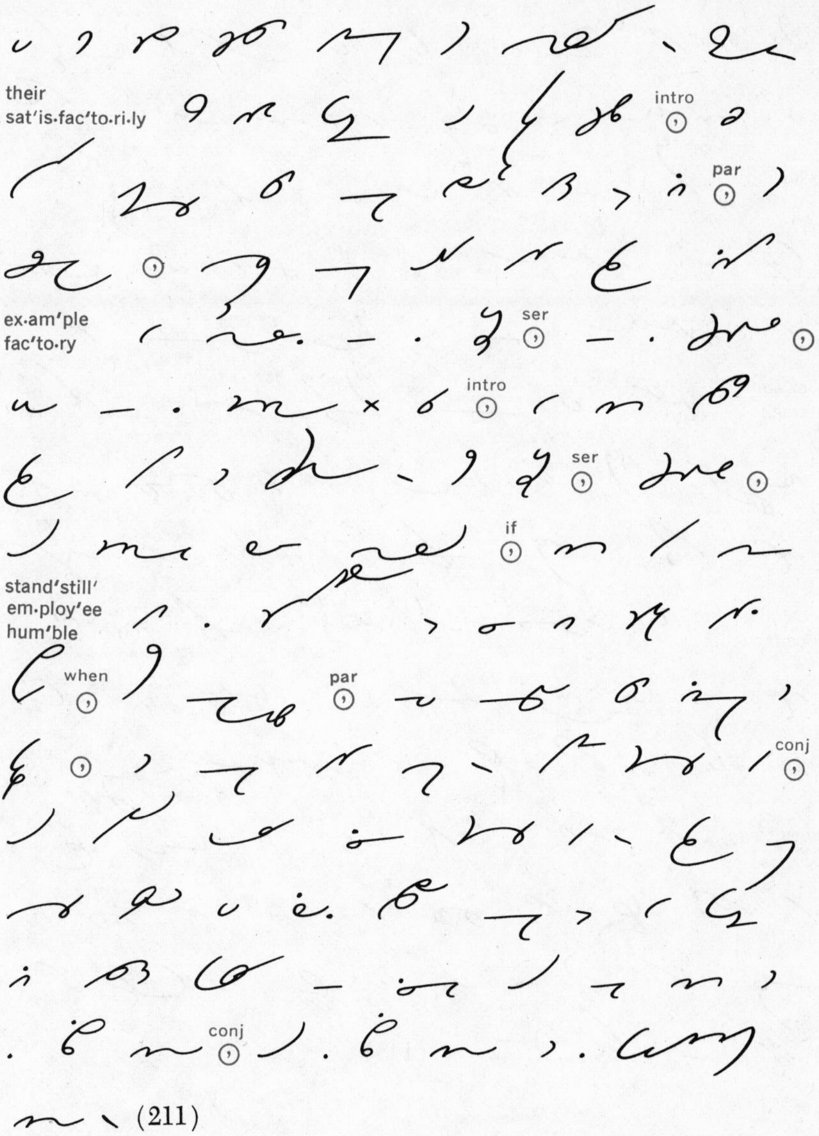

(211)

435. Self-Control

los'ing
theirs
intro
ex·am'ine
traits
if
calm'ly
per'son·al
intro
intro
con'tra·ry
(148)

REINFORCEMENT

PART 2

The Secretary "Looks It Up"

Suppose a strange word is given to you in dictation. It sounds like "ingenuous." Or was it "ingenious"? Both are perfectly good words. But which is correct? You read your notes carefully and you look up these two words in the dictionary; then you make your choice. You are right, because you make sure the word fits the meaning your notes show was intended. The smart secretary doesn't guess — she looks it up.

"I don't expect my secretary to be a 'walking encyclopedia,' " says the executive, "but I do expect her to know when she doesn't know — and to know where to look things up."

Do you know when and where to look things up? Now is the time to begin forming the habit of looking things up when you aren't sure. Even the experienced secretary turns to several reference sources during the course of a day to make absolutely sure she is right. She may use the dictionary, a grammar handbook, a company style manual for typists and stenographers, an encyclopedia, a book on filing, a letter-writing handbook, and a book on etiquette. Nothing is left to chance. To be right is important. It's the smart secretary who knows when she doesn't know.

Do you know how to address a member of the clergy? a senator? Do you know how to write an acceptance to a formal invitation? Do you know the correct salutation when writing to a company composed entirely of women? Which is correct: "Whom are you expecting?" or "Who are you expecting?" How do you address a package to someone in a foreign country? What is meant by the Latin expression sine qua non? You may have to answer questions such as these every day. Of course, you aren't expected to know the answers to everything asked of you, but you are expected to know where to find the information you need.

It's smart to be right.

Chapter 9

Lesson 49

The practice material in this lesson concentrates on the shorthand principles you studied in Chapter 1.

436. BRIEF FORMS AND DERIVATIVES

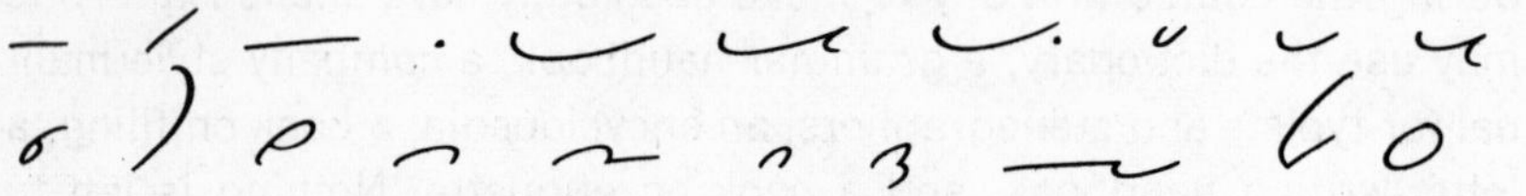

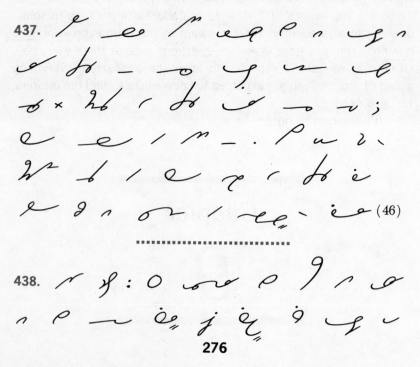

In-not, it-at, am, a-an, will-well, wills, willing, of, are-hour-our, ours.
With, have, that, can, cannot, you-your, yours, Mr., but, I.

Reading Practice

437. 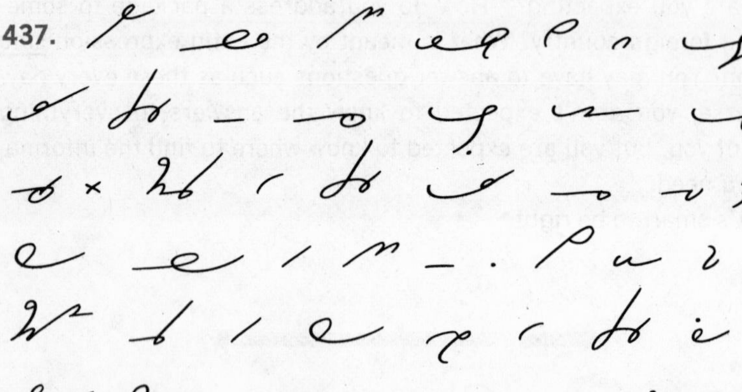

(46)

438. 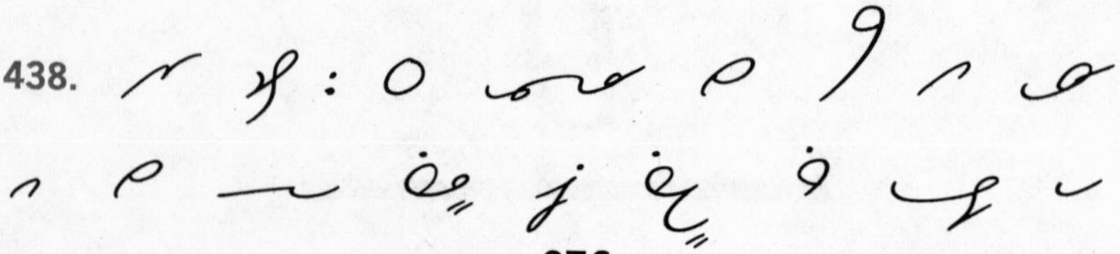

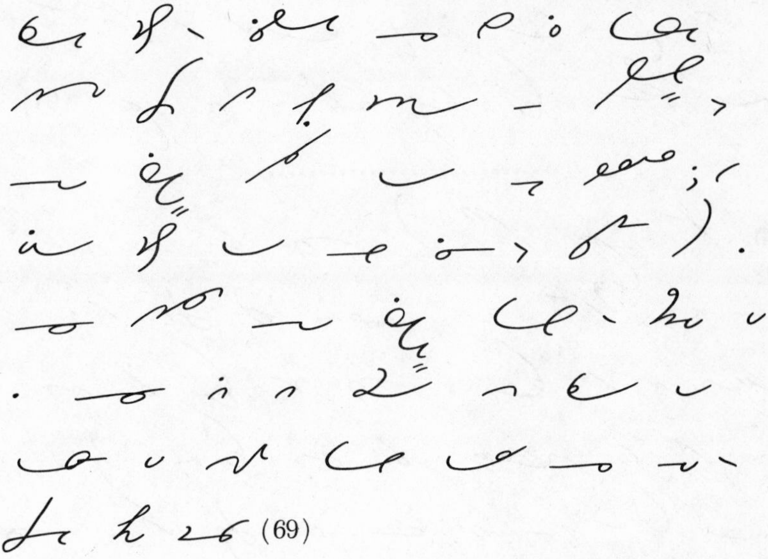

(69)

439.

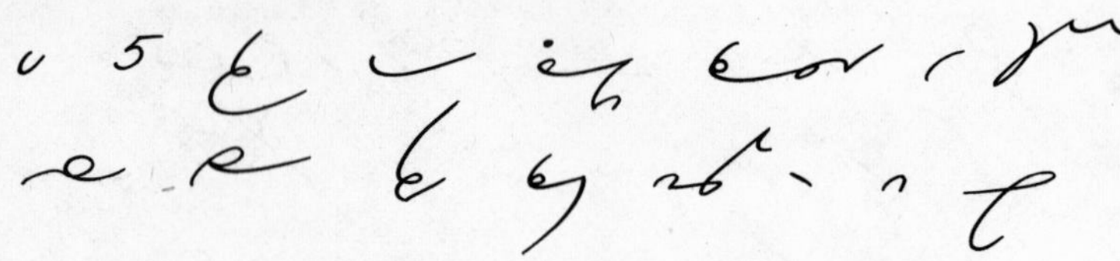

(94)

440.

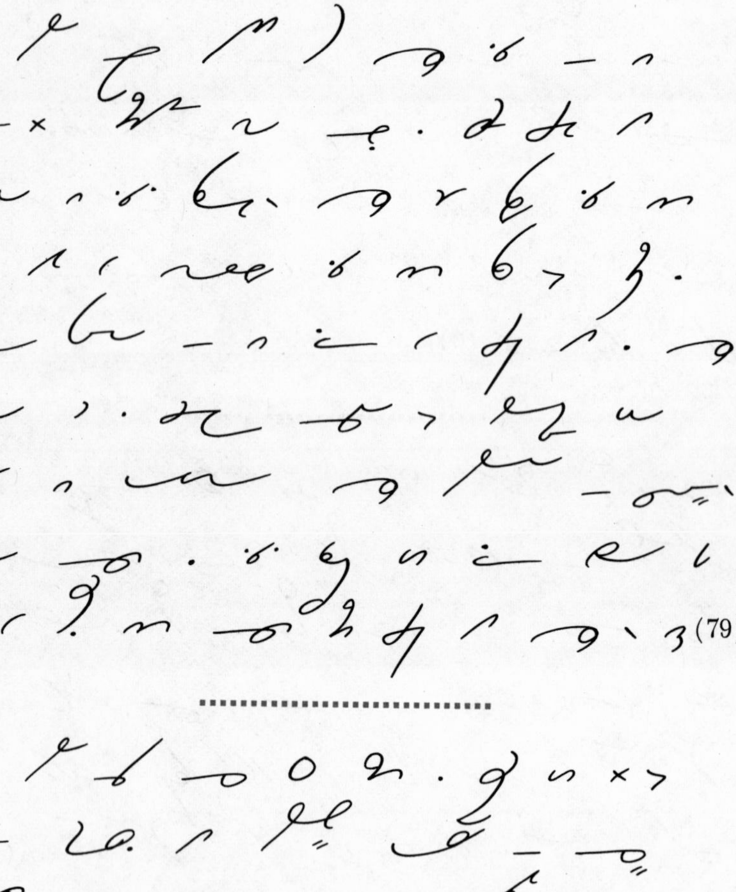

(79)

441.

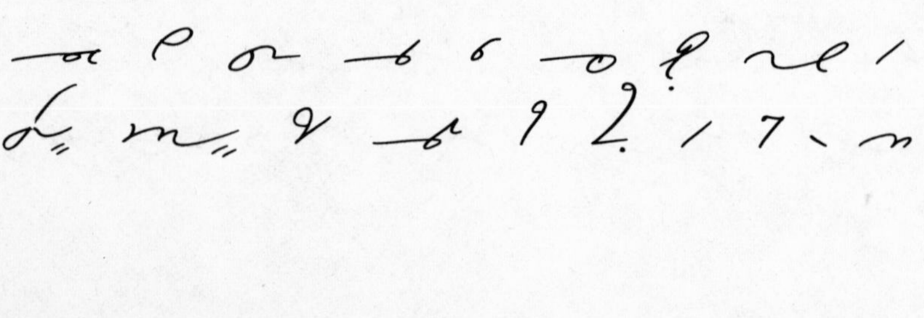

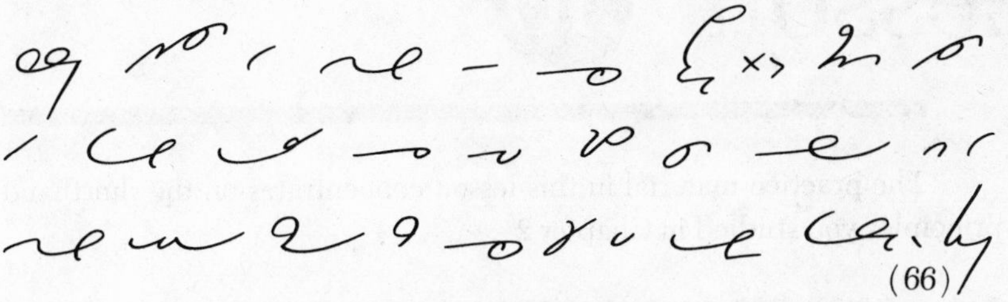

(66)

442.

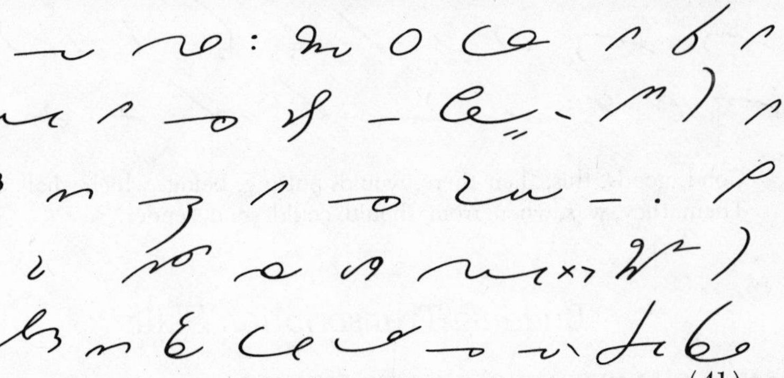

(41)

443.

(68)

Lesson 50

The practice material in this lesson concentrates on the shorthand principles you studied in Chapter 2.

444. BRIEF FORMS AND DERIVATIVES

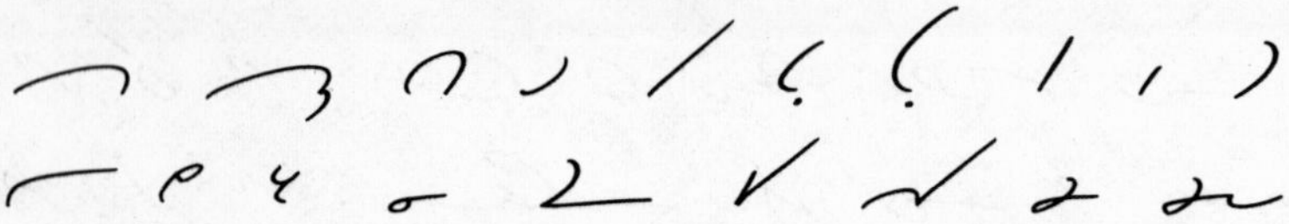

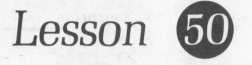

Good, goods, this, their-there, would, putting, being, which, shall, for. Them, they, was, when, from, should, could, send, sender.

Building Transcription Skills

445. BUSINESS VOCABULARY BUILDER

loath Unhappy; reluctant.

mart A market or store.

good will Kindly feeling; well wishing.

Reading and Writing Practice

446.

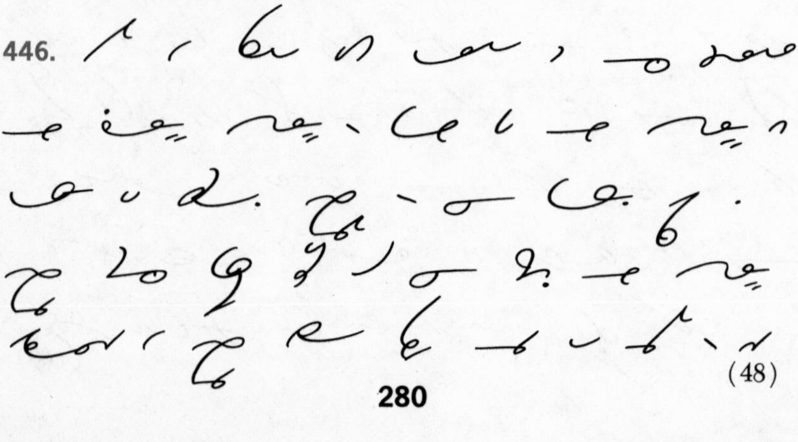

(48)

447.

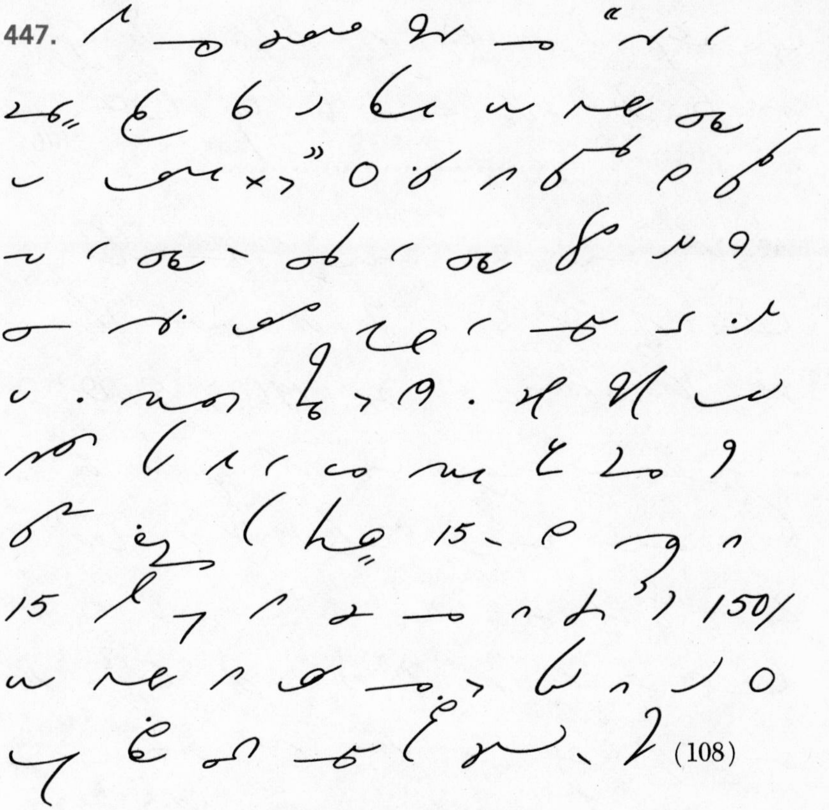

(108)

448.

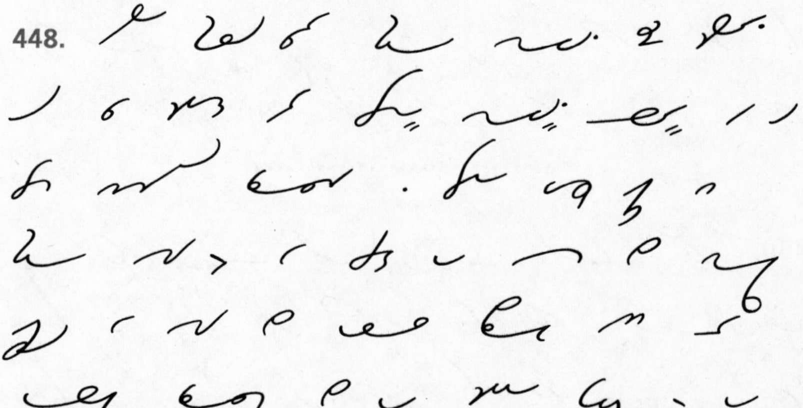

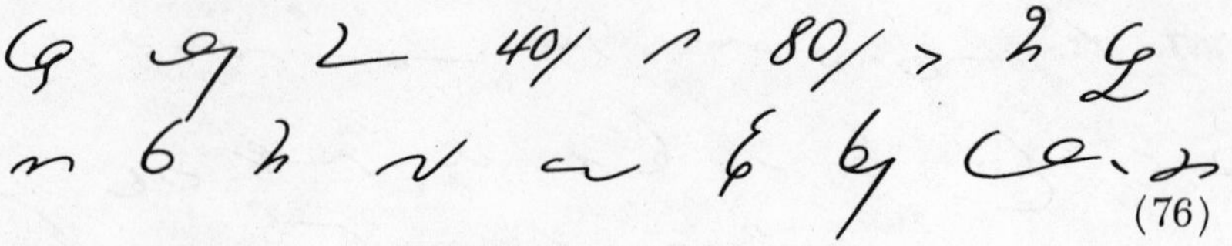

(76)

449.

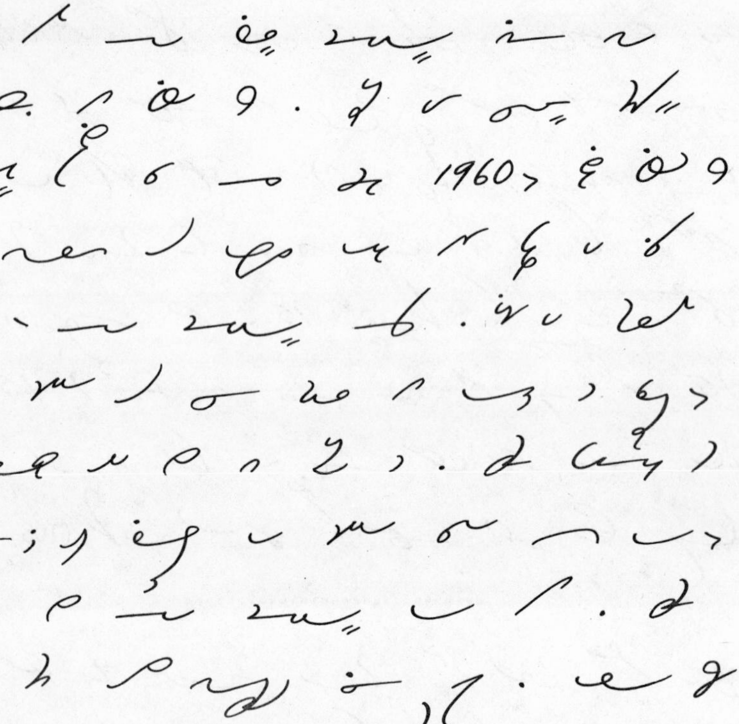

(99)

450.

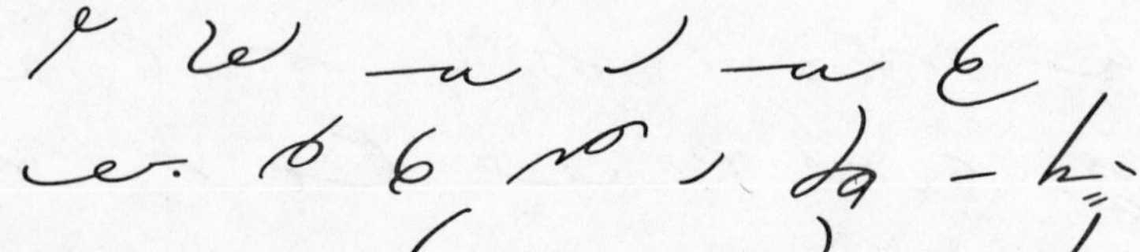

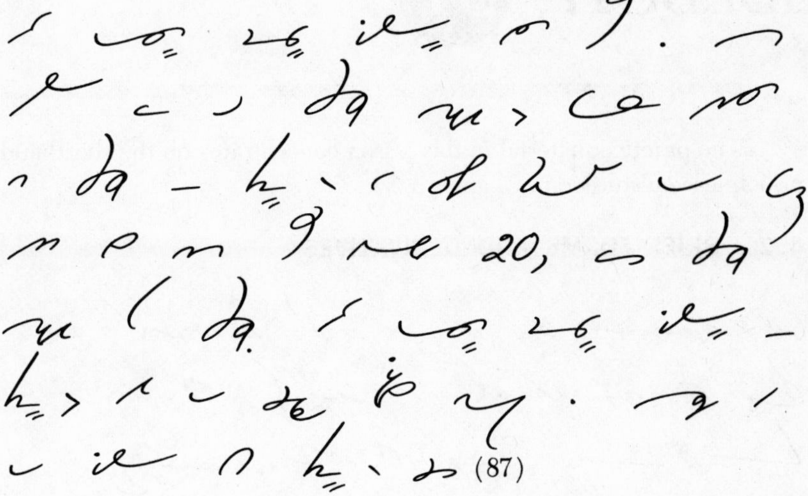

(87)

451.

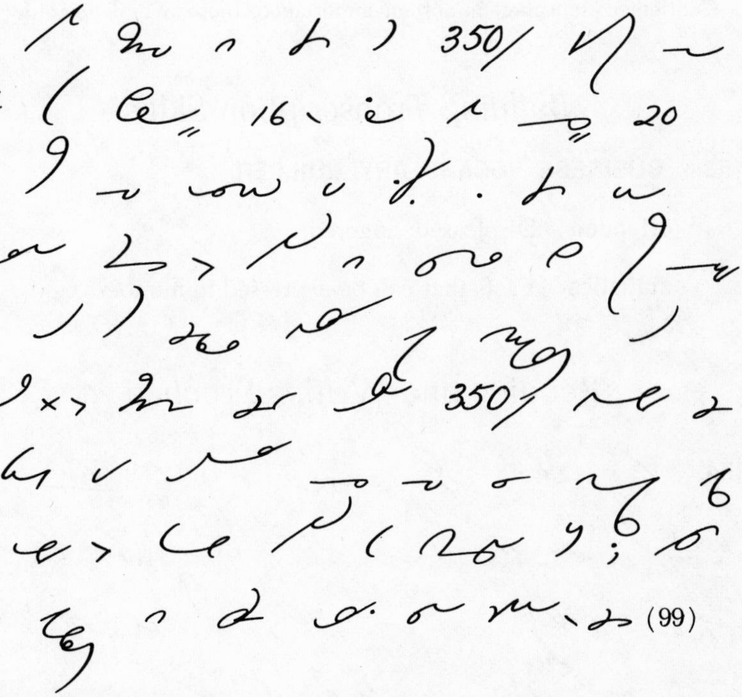

(99)

Lesson 51

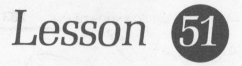

The practice material in this lesson concentrates on the shorthand principles you studied in Chapter 3.

452. BRIEF FORMS AND DERIVATIVES

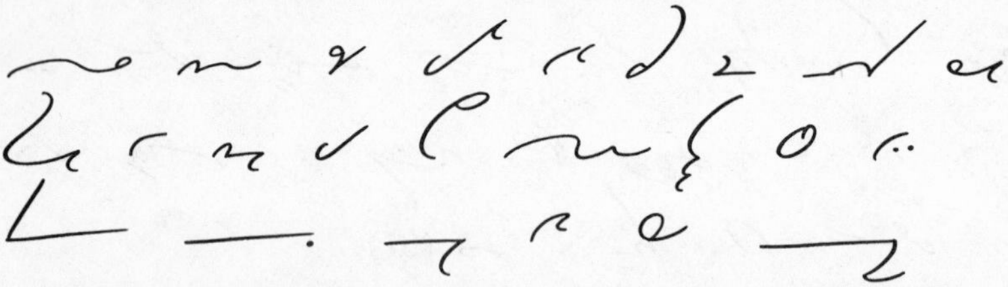

Gladly, worker, yesterday, orders, thanks, very, soon, enclosed, years.
Values, than, once, what, about, greater, businesses, why, thinking.
Gentlemen, morning, important-importance, those, where, manufacturer.

Building Transcription Skills

453. BUSINESS VOCABULARY BUILDER

offended Displeased; angered.

statistics Facts that can be expressed in numbers.

Reading and Writing Practice

454.

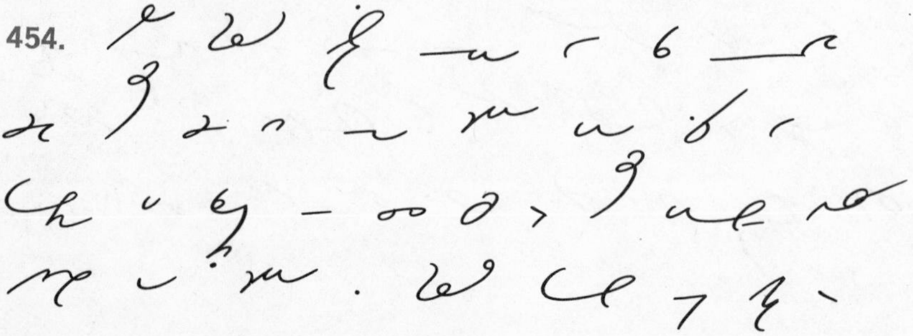

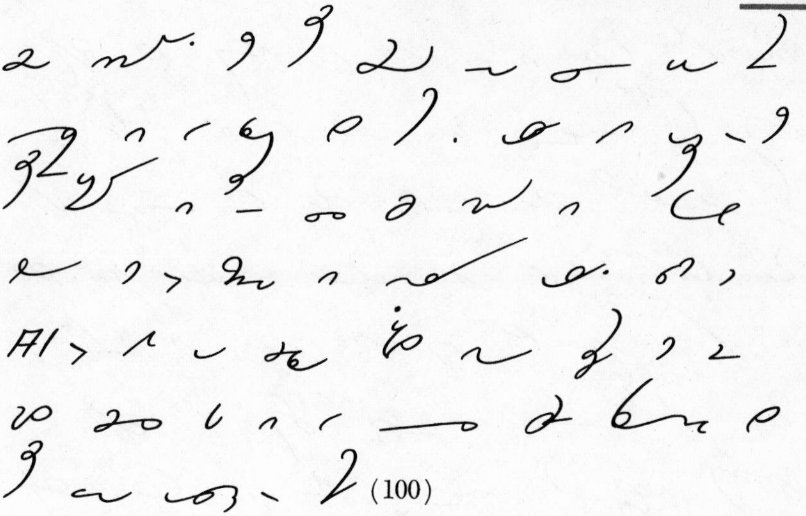

(100)

455.

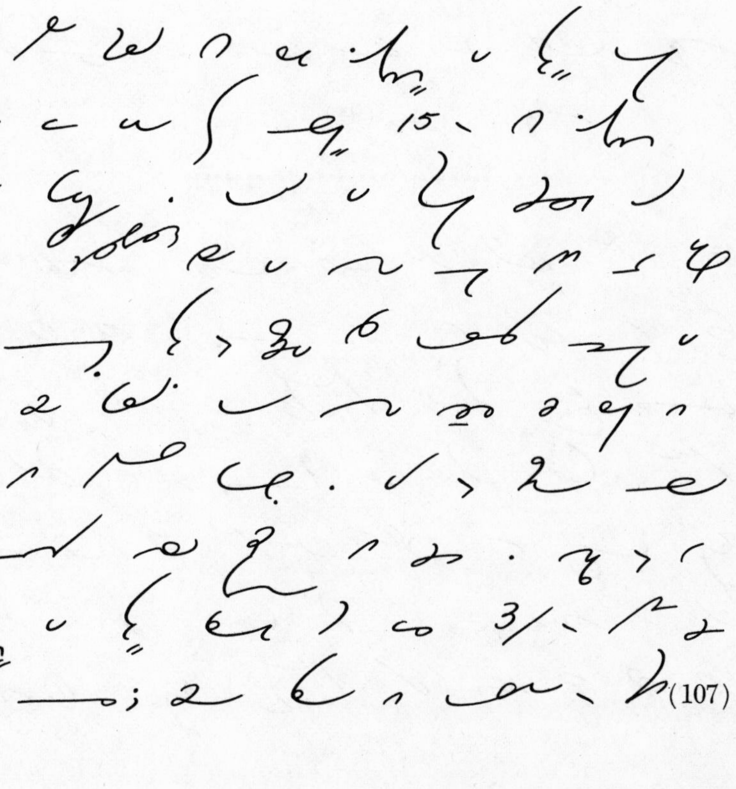

(107)

456.

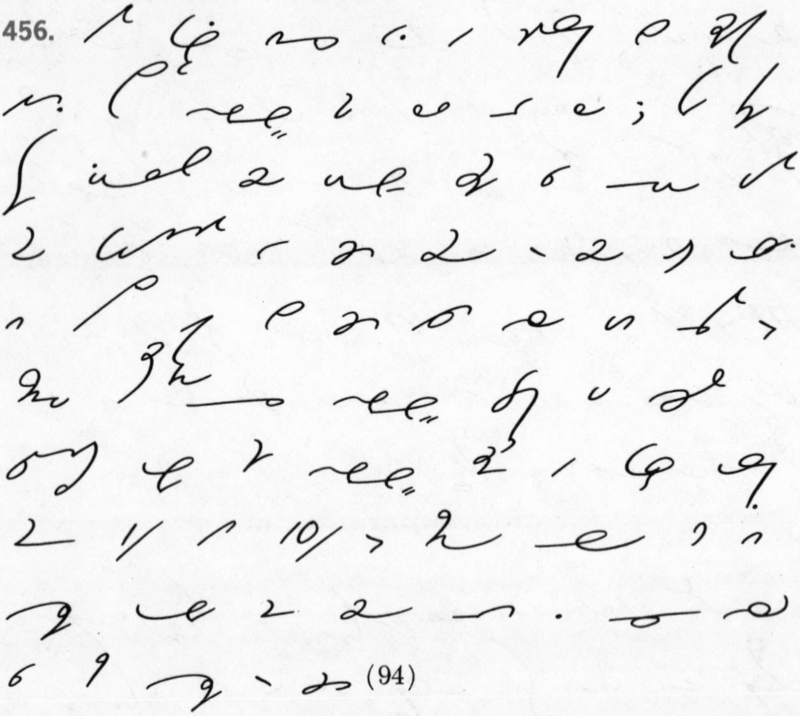

(94)

457.

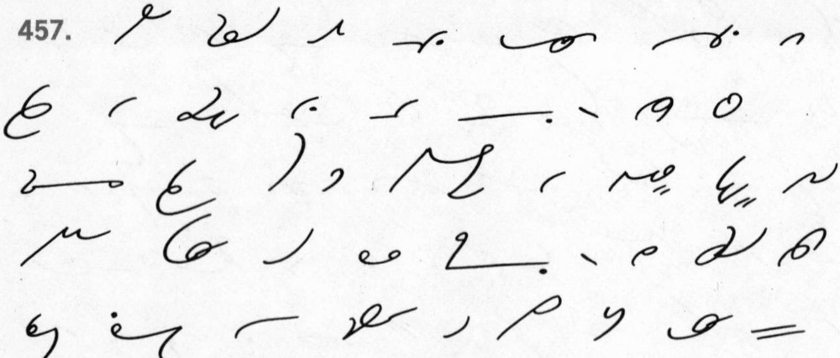

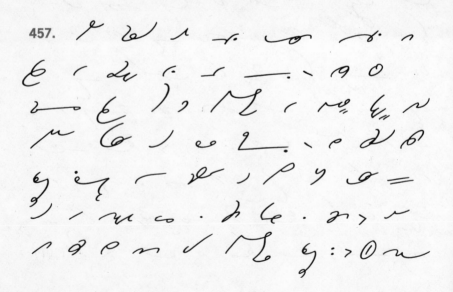

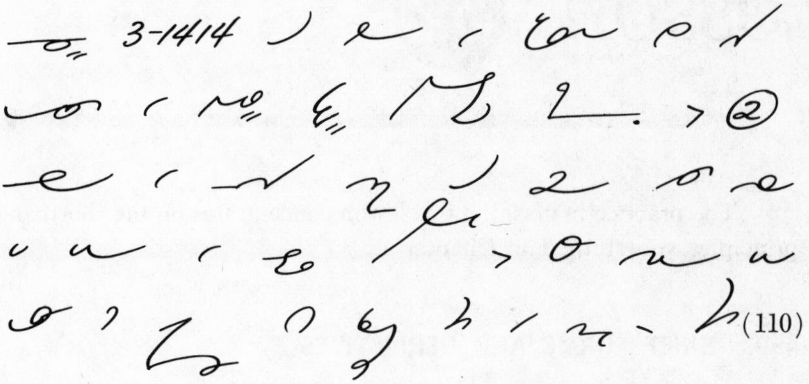
3-1414
(110)

458.

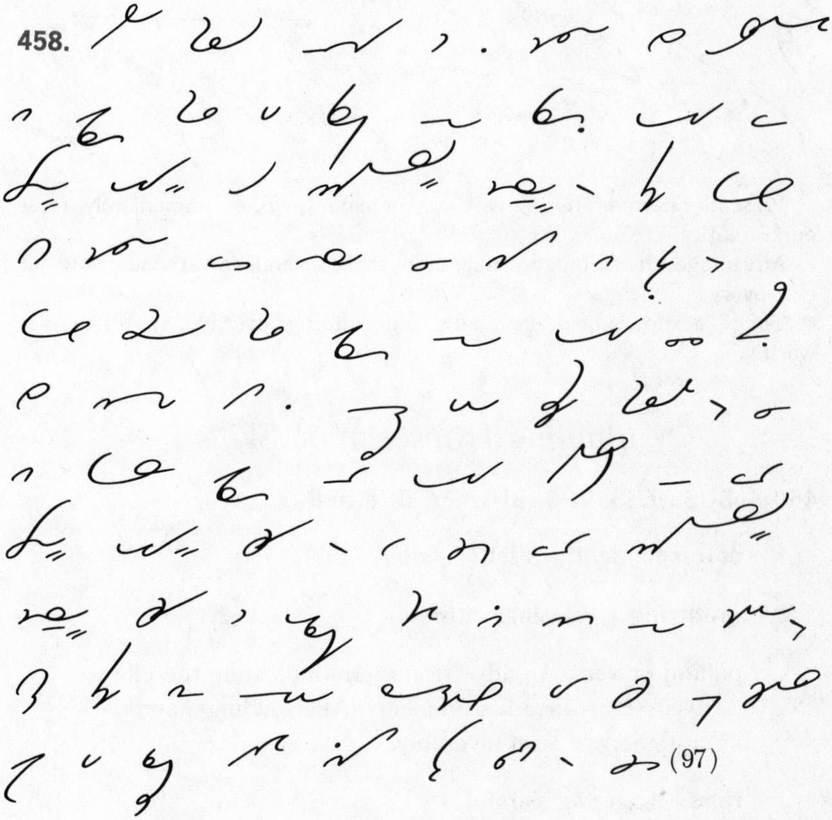
(97)

Lesson 52

The practice material in this lesson concentrates on the shorthand principles you studied in Chapter 4.

459. BRIEF FORMS AND DERIVATIVES

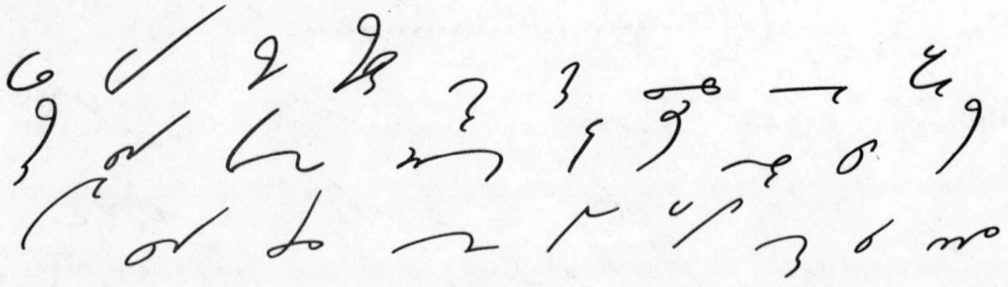

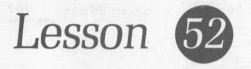

Presently, parted, after, advertises, companies, wishes, immediately, must, opportunities.

Advantages, used, bigger, suggestion, such, several, corresponds, how-out, ever-every.

Times, acknowledged, generally, gone, during, overdue, questions, yet, worthy.

Building Transcription Skills

460. BUSINESS VOCABULARY BUILDER

correspondent A letter writer.

gratifying Pleasing; satisfying.

pulling power An advertising term indicating the effectiveness of an advertisement in persuading potential customers to react favorably.

rigid Exacting; careful.

461. SPELLING FAMILIES

Words Ending in -tion

ac′tion	com·ple′tion	lo·ca′tion
ap′pli·ca′tion	con·nec′tion	mo′tion
cel′e·bra′tion	cor·rec′tion	ques′tion
col·lec′tion	il′lus·tra′tion	re·la′tion

Words Ending in -sion

con·clu′sion	di·vi′sion	pro·vi′sion
de·ci′sion	pen′sion	tel′e·vi′sion
de·pres′sion	per·sua′sion	ten′sion

Reading and Writing Practice

462.

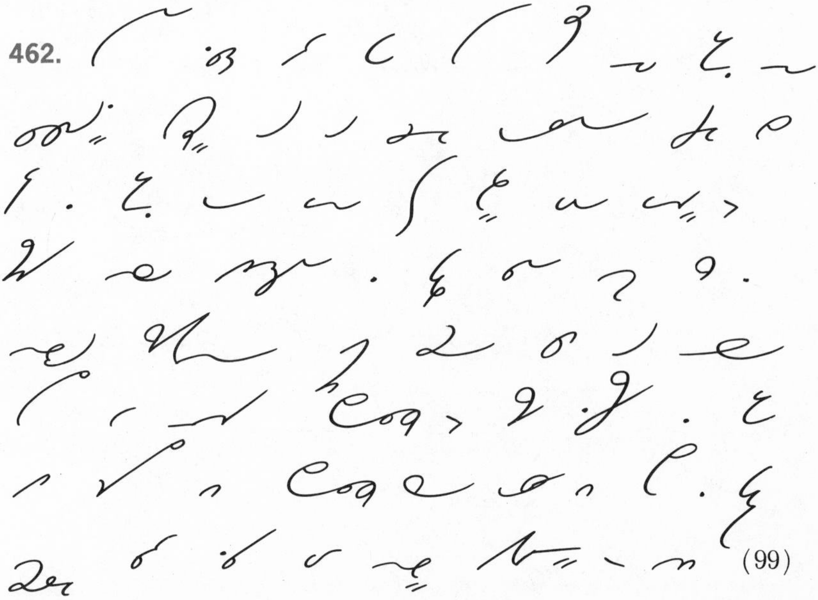

(99)

463.

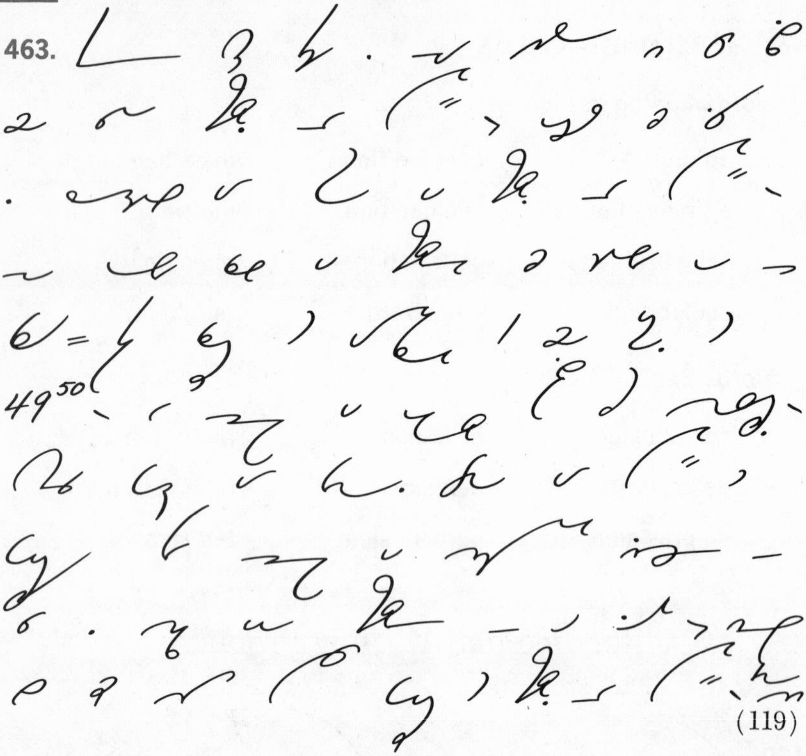

(119)

464.

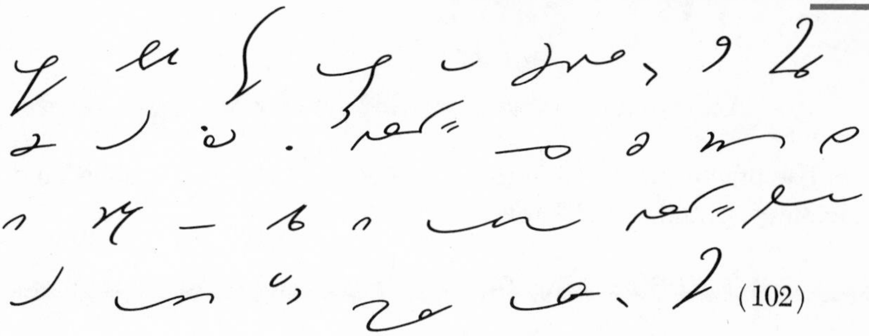

(102)

465.

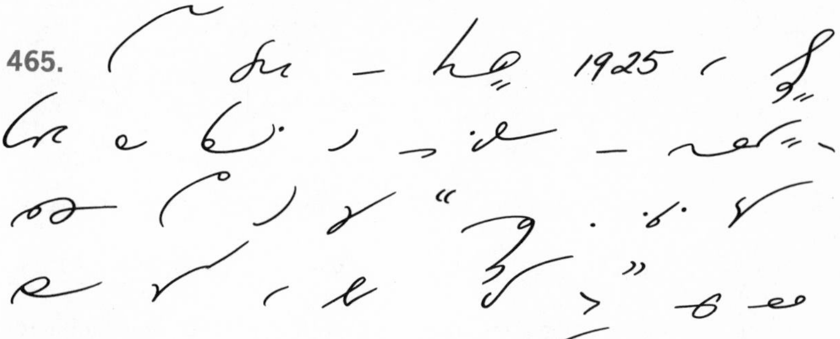

(104)

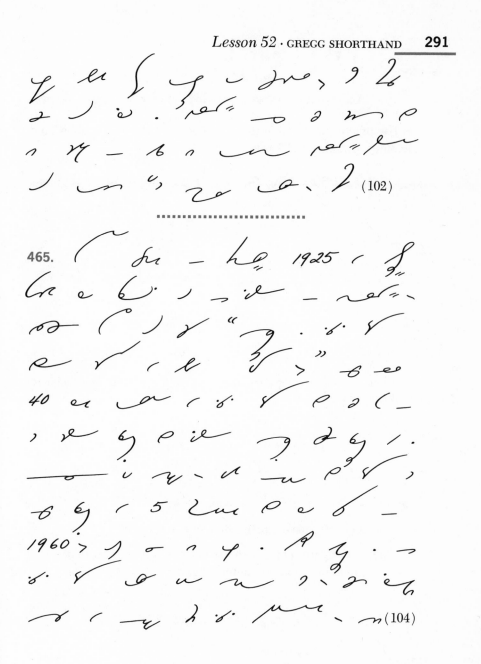

Lesson 53

The practice material in this lesson concentrates on the shorthand principles you studied in Chapter 5.

466. BRIEF FORMS AND DERIVATIVES

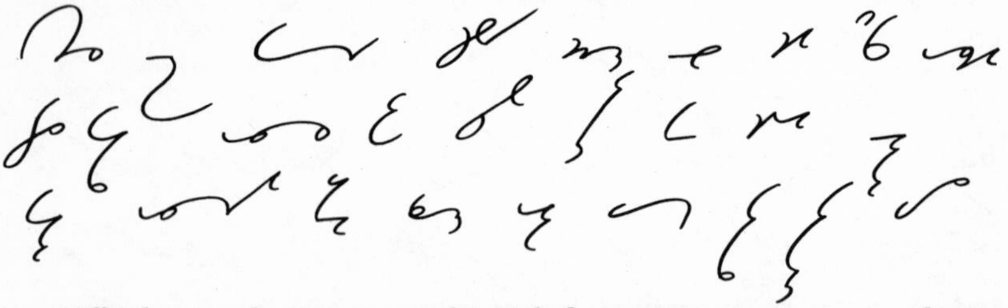

Difficulty, envelope, progressed, satisfied, successes, next, states, underpay, requests.

Particularly, probably, regularly, speaker, ideas, subjects, upon, streets, newspapers.

Purposes, regards, opinions, circulars, responsible, organization, publicly, publications, ordinarily.

Building Transcription Skills

467. BUSINESS VOCABULARY BUILDER

novel New; different; unusual.

enhance To make greater; to increase.

mailing department A department in a large firm that handles incoming and outgoing mail.

Reading and Writing Practice

468.

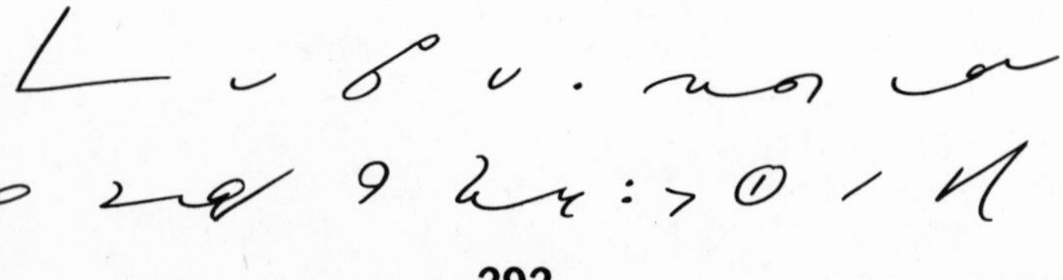

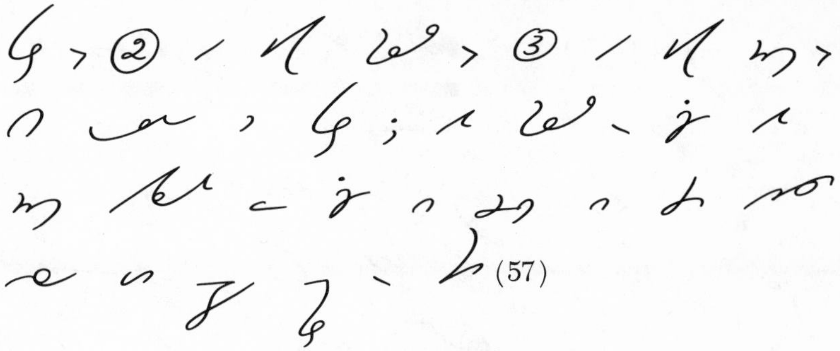

(57)

469. 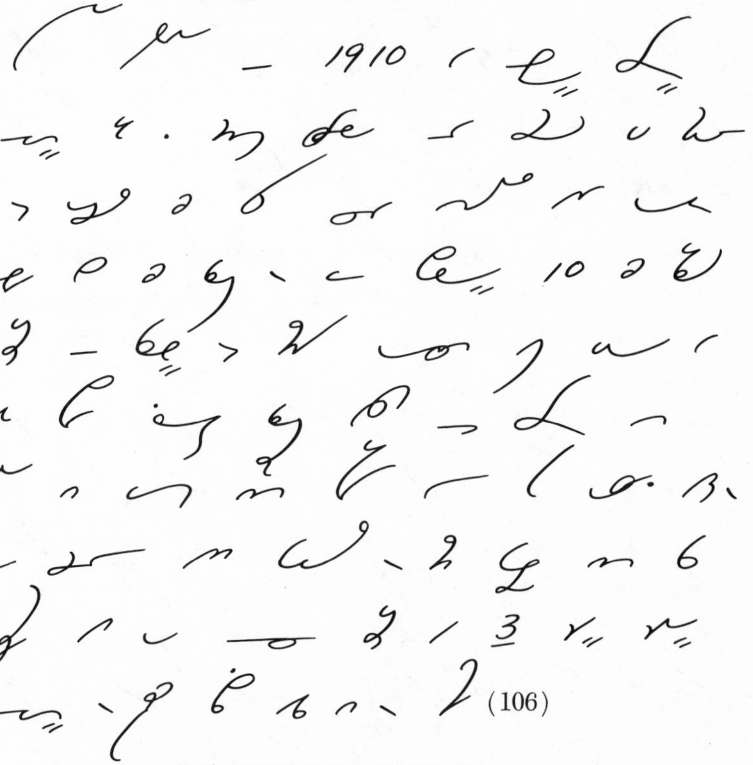

(106)

470. 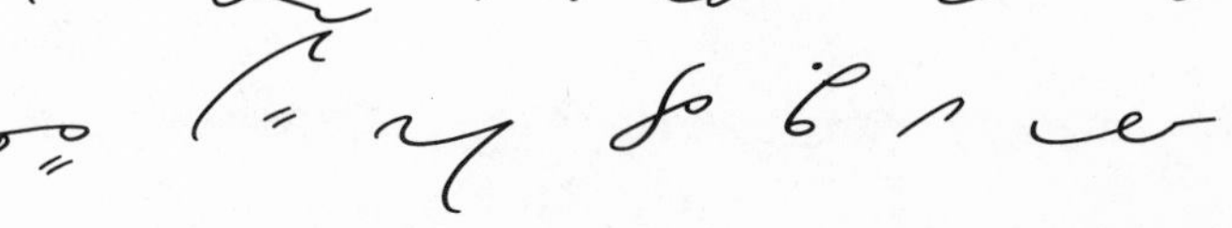

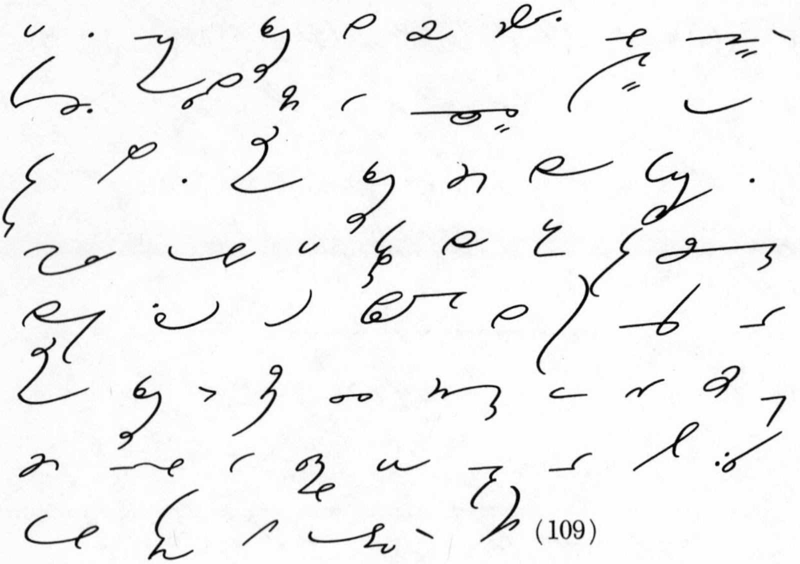

(109)

471.

(96)

472.

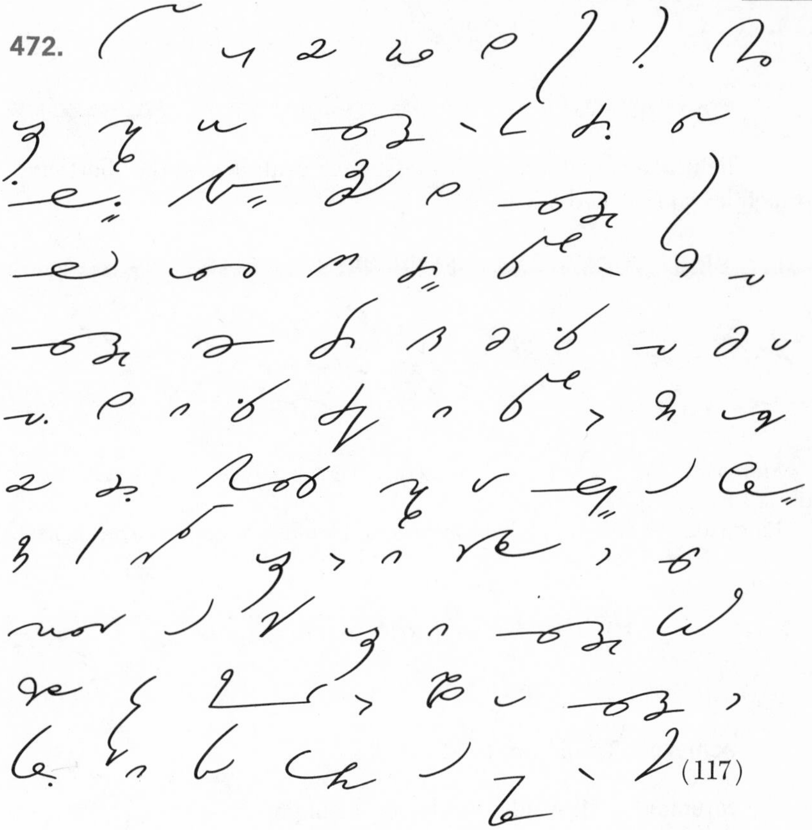

(117)

DID YOU KNOW THAT—

President Woodrow Wilson was an expert shorthand writer and that he drafted all his state papers in shorthand?

Samuel Pepys wrote his famous diary in shorthand? He wrote so legibly that students of literature had no difficulty making an accurate transcript of his notes.

George Bernard Shaw did all his composing in shorthand and then had his secretary transcribe his notes?

James F. Byrnes used his shorthand regularly while he was a Supreme Court justice, a Secretary of State, and the Governor of South Carolina?

Lesson 54

The practice material in this lesson concentrates on the shorthand principles you studied in Chapter 6.

473. BRIEF FORMS AND DERIVATIVES

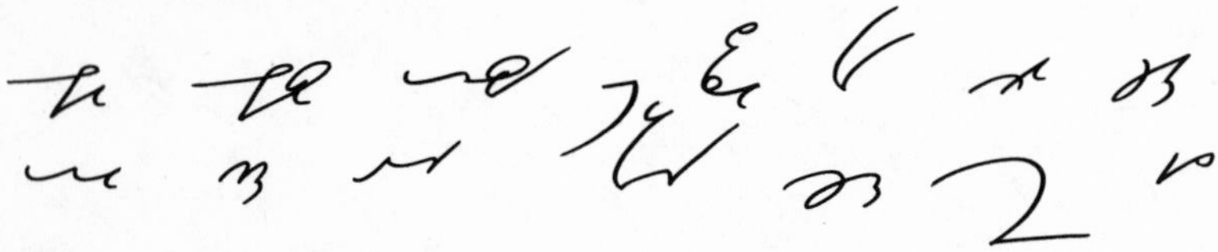

Merchants, merchandise, recognized, never, experiences, between, quantities, situations.

Railroads, worlds, throughout, objected, characters, government, shortly.

Building Transcription Skills

474. BUSINESS VOCABULARY BUILDER

achieve To obtain; to attain.

foremost Most advanced; first in importance.

hazard Danger.

refund To repay

475. SIMILAR-WORDS DRILL

Weather, whether

weather State of the atmosphere with respect to wetness or dryness, cold or heat; climate.

You can take a good picture regardless of the weather.

The game was called because of the weather.

whether Indicating a choice (often followed by *or*). Also used to introduce an indirect question.

You can take a good picture whether the sun is shining or whether it is raining.

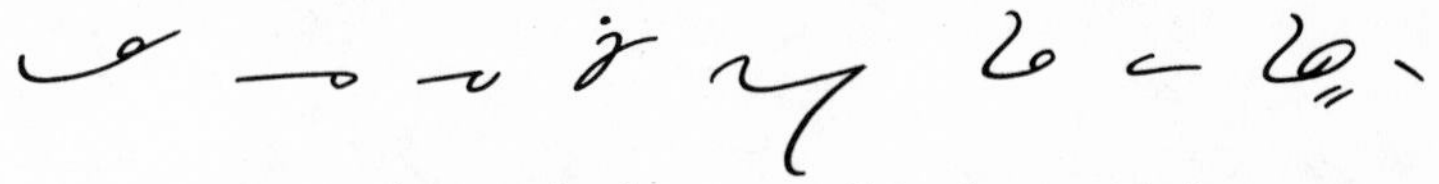

Let me know whether you will be free on Friday.

Reading and Writing Practice

476.

a·chieve′
peace

ex·pe′ri·ence

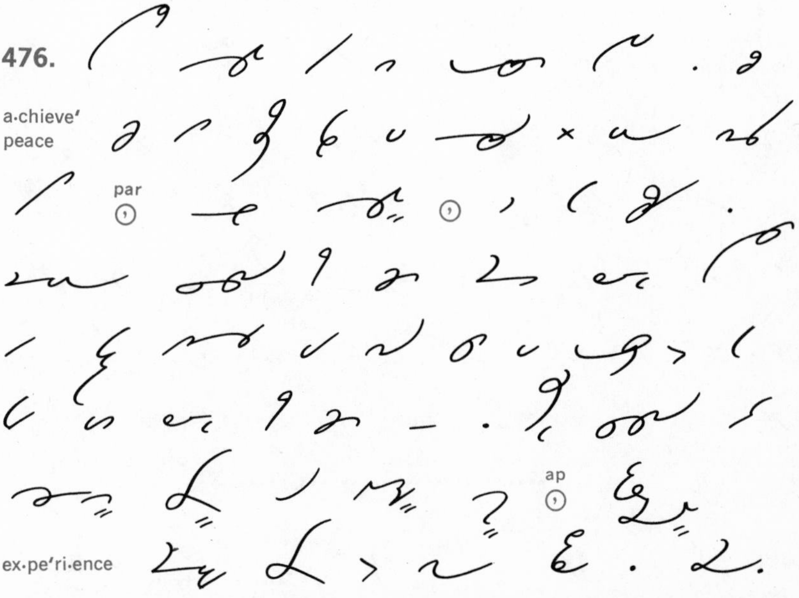
par
ap

con′fi·dence

ser

(81)

477.

un·for′tu·nate·ly
traf′fic
haz′ard

per·mis′sion
ob·jec′tion

par
par
par
par

(124)

478.

there'fore
mer'chan·dise

fig'ures
im·me'di·ate·ly

(134)

479.

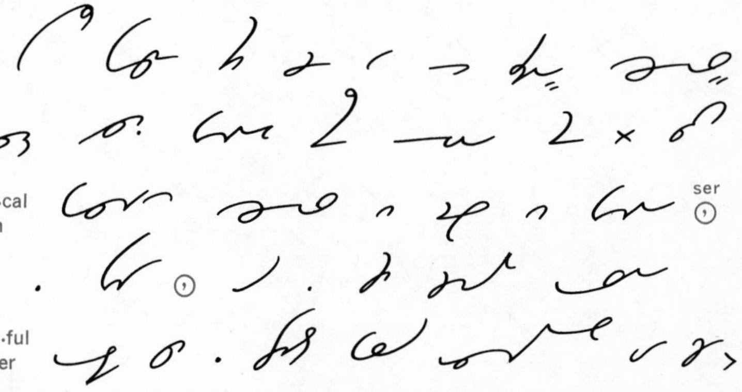

prac'ti·cal
but'ton

beau'ti·ful
weath'er

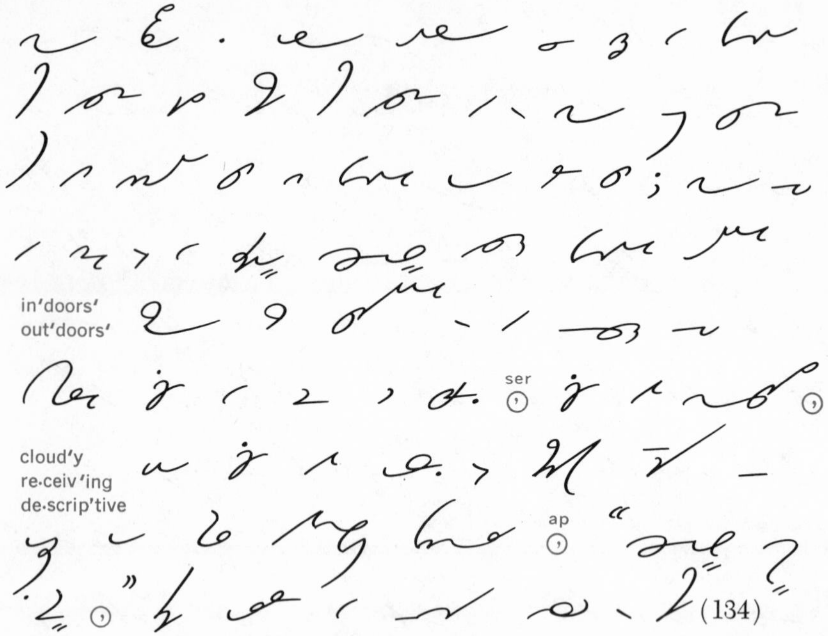

in'doors'
out'doors'
cloud'y
re·ceiv'ing
de·scrip'tive

ser
ap

(134)

480. Chuckle

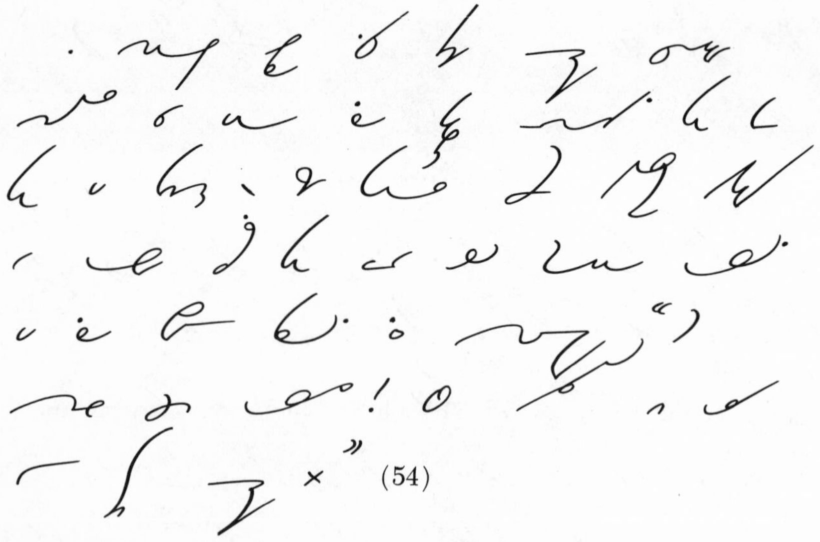

(54)

Lesson 55

The practice material in this lesson concentrates on the shorthand principles you studied in Chapter 7.

481. BRIEF-FORM DERIVATIVES

Greater, sooner, bigger, shorter, worker, sender, manufacturer.

Particularly, successfully, timely, immediately, partly, presently, gladly, purposely.

Suggested, corresponded, timed, progressed, organized, governed.

Building Transcription Skills

482. BUSINESS VOCABULARY BUILDER

clarity Clearness.

convey To tell; to impart.

aptitude Natural ability.

483. GRAMMAR CHECKUP

The Infinitive (The form of the verb usually introduced by *to—to see, to be, to have, to do.*)

Careful writers try to avoid "splitting" an infinitive; that is, inserting a word or phrase between *to* and the following word.

No

To properly do the job, you need better tools.

Yes

To do the job properly, you need better tools.

No

He was told to carefully prepare the report.

Yes

He was told to prepare the report carefully.

Reading and Writing Practice

484. Your Telephone Voice

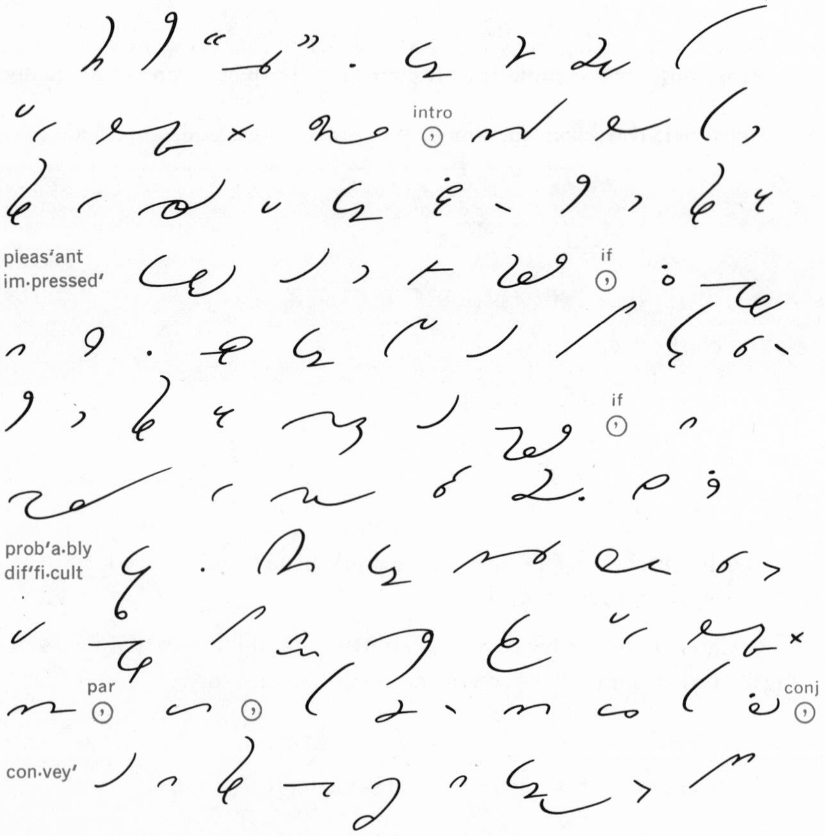
intro
pleas'ant
im·pressed'
if
if
prob'a·bly
dif'fi·cult
par
conj
con·vey'

clar'i·ty

soft'ly

choos'ing

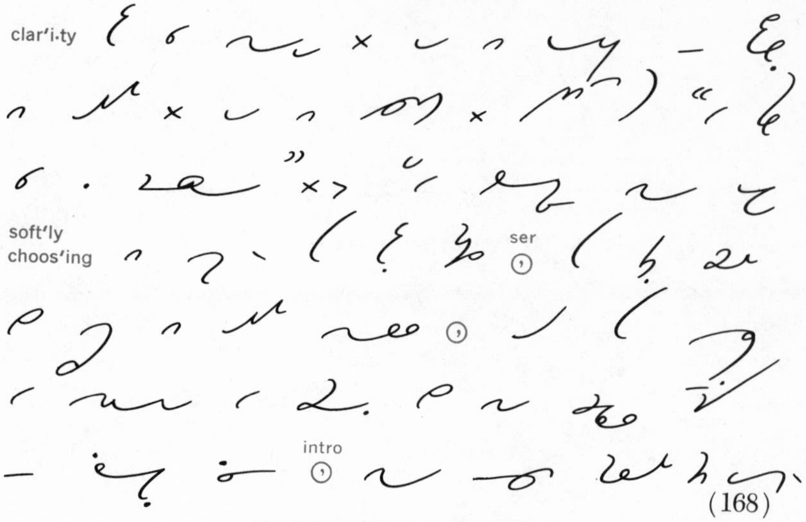
ser
intro

(168)

485.

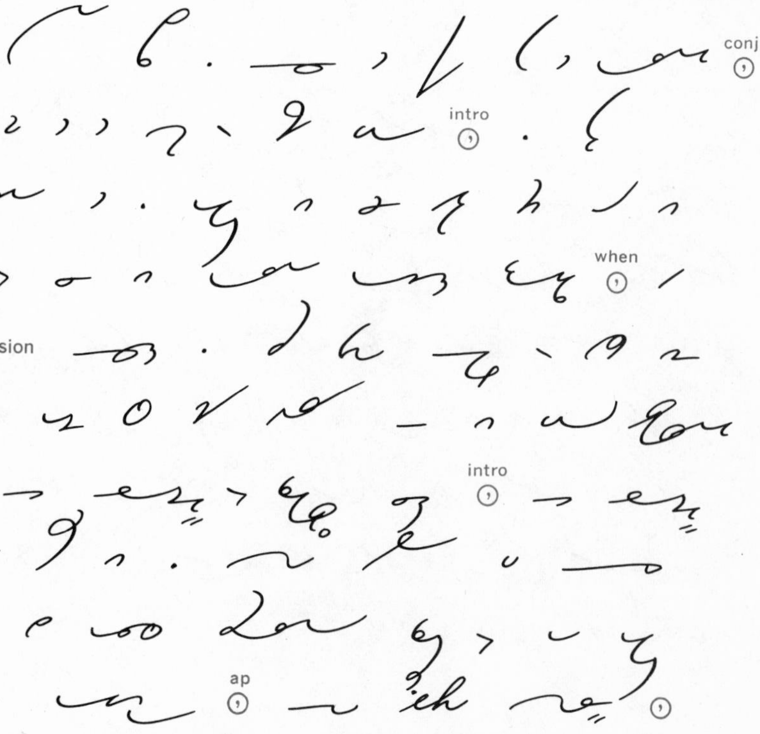
conj
intro
when
intro
ap

slop'py

im·pres'sion

(120)

486.

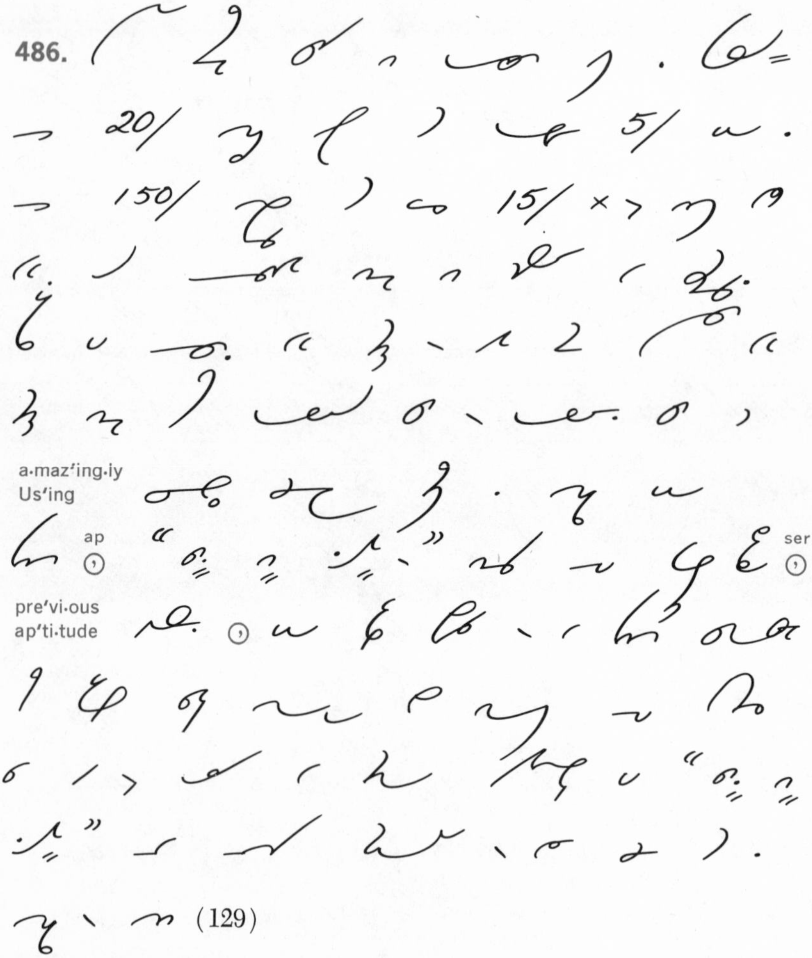

a·maz′ing·ly
Us′ing

ap

ser

pre′vi·ous
ap′ti·tude

(129)

487. Chuckle

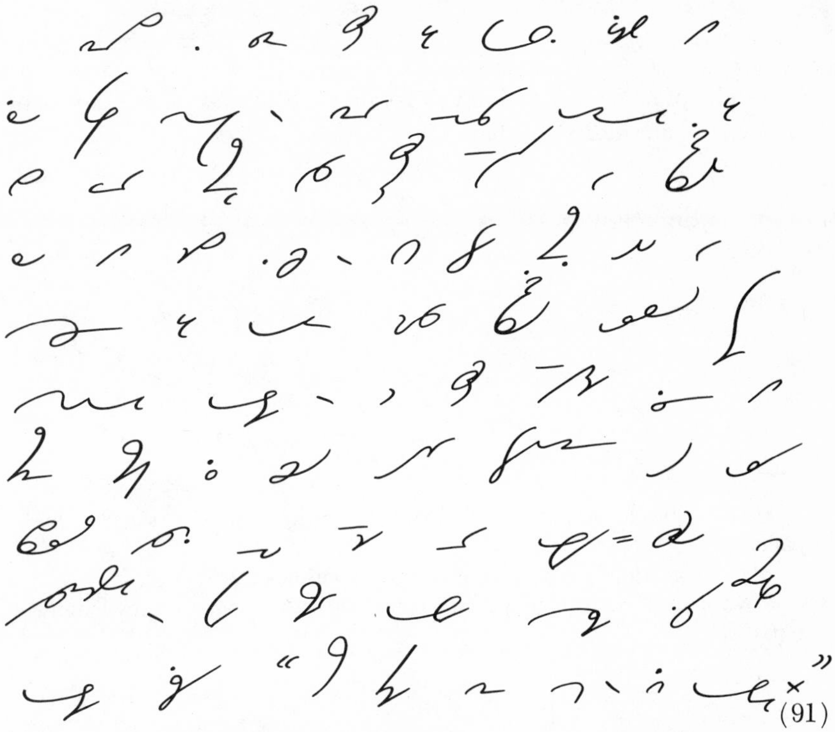

(91)

STUDY-HABIT CHECK LIST

No doubt as a conscientious student you do your home assignments faithfully. Do you, however, derive the greatest benefit from the time you devote to practice?

You do if you practice in a quiet place that enables you to concentrate.

You don't if you practice with one eye on the television and the other on your practice work!

You do if, once you have started your assignment, you do not leave your desk or table until you have completed it.

You don't if you interrupt your practice from time to time to call a friend or raid the refrigerator!

Lesson 56

The practice material in this lesson concentrates on the shorthand principles you studied in Chapter 8.

488. BRIEF FORMS AND DERIVATIVES

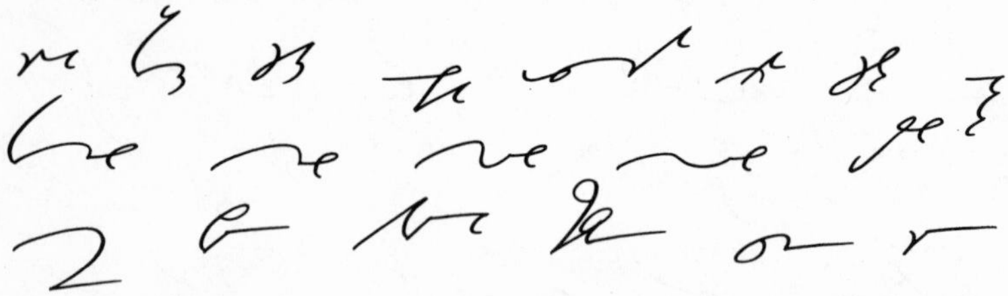

Streets, objects, situations, merchants, regards, quantities, satisfies, newspapers.

Bigness, goodness, greatness, gladness, orderliness.

Government, apartment, departments, advertisement, acknowledgment, statement.

Building Transcription Skills

489. BUSINESS VOCABULARY BUILDER

executive A person charged with administrative work in a company.

simultaneously At the same time.

accrue To come (to someone) by way of increase or advantage.

ultimately Finally; in the end.

postage meter A machine that "prints" postage on envelopes automatically.

490. COMMON WORD ROOTS

Many English words are derived from the Greek and Latin languages. Consequently, an understanding of the meanings of Greek and Latin prefixes and suffixes will often give you a clue to the meaning of words with which you are unfamiliar.

Perhaps you never heard the word *posterity*. However, if you know that *post* means *after*, you will probably be able to figure out that *posterity* refers to those who come after, or descendants.

In each "Common Word Roots" exercise you will be given a common prefix or suffix, together with its meaning, and a list of words in which the prefix or suffix is used.

Read each definition carefully, and then study the illustrations that follow. A number of the illustrations are used in the Reading and Writing Practice.

Super-: *over, more than*

supervise To oversee.

supervisor One who oversees.

superior Over in rank, higher.

supertax A tax over and above a normal tax.

Reading and Writing Practice

491.

suc·cess'ful busi'ness·men'

pat'tern ex·ec'u·tive

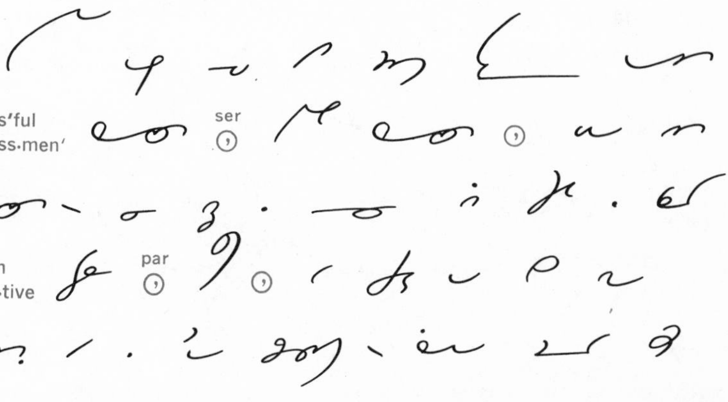

ser
par

shirk
re·spon′si·bil′i·ty

su′per·vi′sor
at·trac′tive

par
and o
when
(155)

492.

for′ward·ed
Main′te·nance

at·ten′tion
ben′e·fits
ac·crue′

as

re·duc'es
min'i·mum
ex·pense'

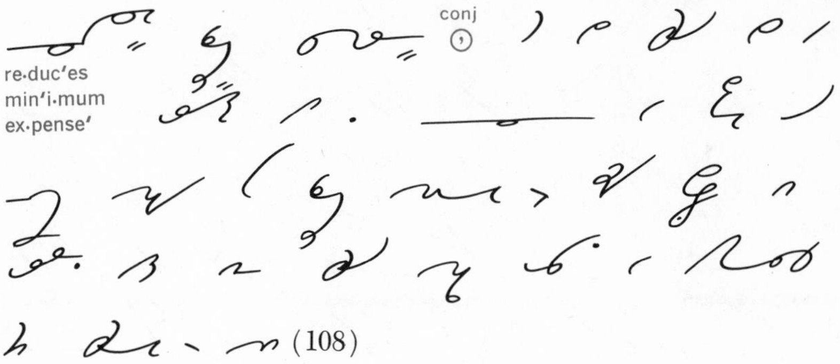
conj
(108)

493.

ser
par
conj
(119)

bur'den
fi·nanc'es

try'ing
past

for'ward
e·lec'tri·cal

494.

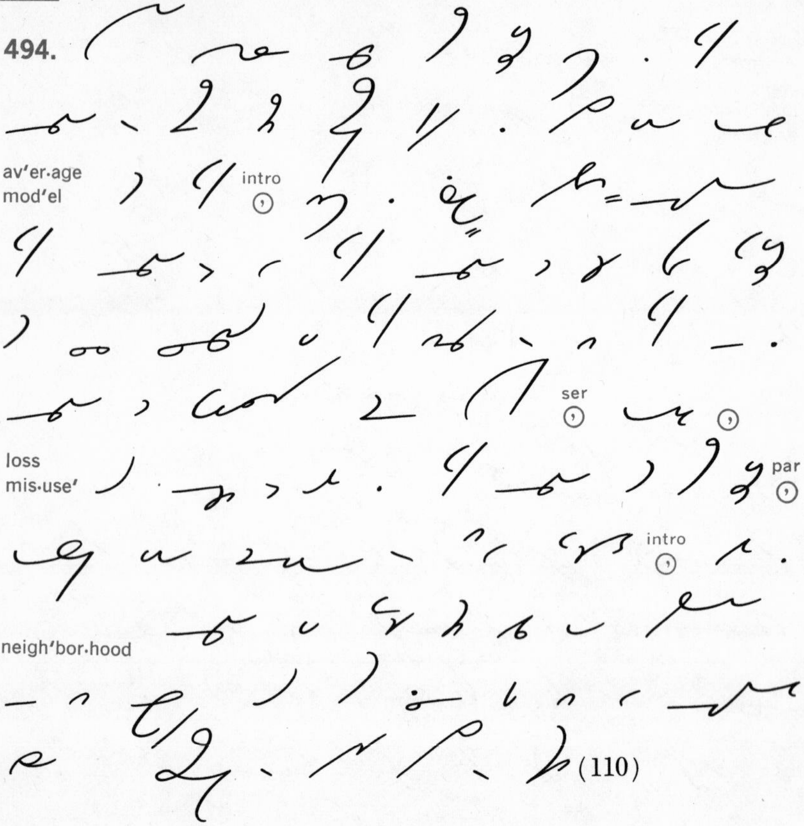
av'er·age
mod'el
intro
ser
loss
mis·use'
par
intro
neigh'bor·hood
(110)

495. Chuckle

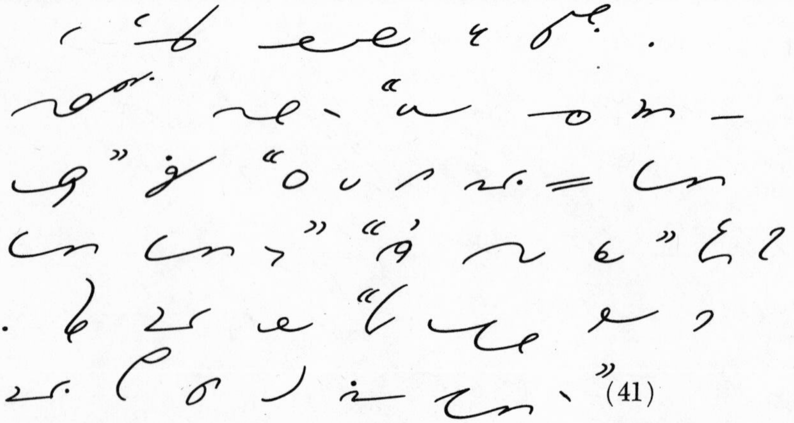
(41)

SHORTHAND AND TRANSCRIPTION SKILL BUILDING

PART 3

Going Up?

The kind of job you will get and the progress you will make in it will depend almost entirely on you. Does this sound old-fashioned? Well, it is still true. Good looks and a sparkling personality are wonderful assets to anyone; and if you are blessed with these gifts, make the most of them. But they are by no means everything. They are merely "frosting on the cake." If you manage to use your head and make the most of the talents, looks, and abilities you do have, you will make the grade in fine style.

The business executive wants his secretary to have interest and ability. With those two qualities, she can lick the world. Of course, he expects her to look smart, neat, and clean. Note that we did not say he insists that she be a raving beauty. While he is not averse to a sparkling personality and good looks, he can't afford to let these qualities influence his decision in hiring and promoting.

In a secretarial position, the opportunity to learn is unlimited. You will have an orchestra seat to all the important goings-on in your executive's domain. It has happened many times that the secretary moved into the boss's shoes when he was promoted.

Even if you don't aspire to the boss's job, your future will depend on how well he does his job. Are you skeptical? Let's examine this statement. In a typical company there are many executive promotions every year. Those promotions go to the people who have proved to be outstanding in their jobs and who "have a future." An executive can hardly be outstanding if he is saddled with inefficient secretarial help. Usually, when he receives a promotion, his secretary gets one, too. Suppose he is a department head and is promoted to the position of vice-president. Automatically his salary is increased. And the secretary to a vice-president is a more important person than the secretary to a department manager; so, she generally gets a salary increase, too. If the secretary is really good, she moves right up the ladder with her boss.

You and your boss will be a team. Your success will depend on his success. It's that simple.

Chapter 10

Lesson 57

The practice material in this lesson is "loaded" with brief forms and derivatives. Counting repetitions, it contains 222 brief forms and derivatives. If you gave proper attention to the brief forms as they were introduced, you should be able to complete this lesson in record time!

Building Transcription Skills

496. BUSINESS VOCABULARY BUILDER

speculates Wonders; thinks.

identical The same.

browse To examine casually merchandise offered for sale.

time-payment plan A charge plan offered by retail stores whereby customers may pay for merchandise in installments.

497. SPELLING FAMILIES

Words in Which Silent E Is Retained Before -ment

ad·vance'ment	**en·gage'ment**	**re·tire'ment**
ad·ver'tise·ment	**man'age·ment**	**re·quire'ment**
a·muse'ment	**move'ment**	**state'ment**
en·cour'age·ment	**re·place'ment**	

Words in Which Silent E Is Omitted Before -ment

ac·knowl'edg·ment	**ar'gu·ment**	**judg'ment**

Reading and Writing Practice

498.

sug·ges'tions
de·rive'
serv'ic·ing
lo'cal
judg'ment

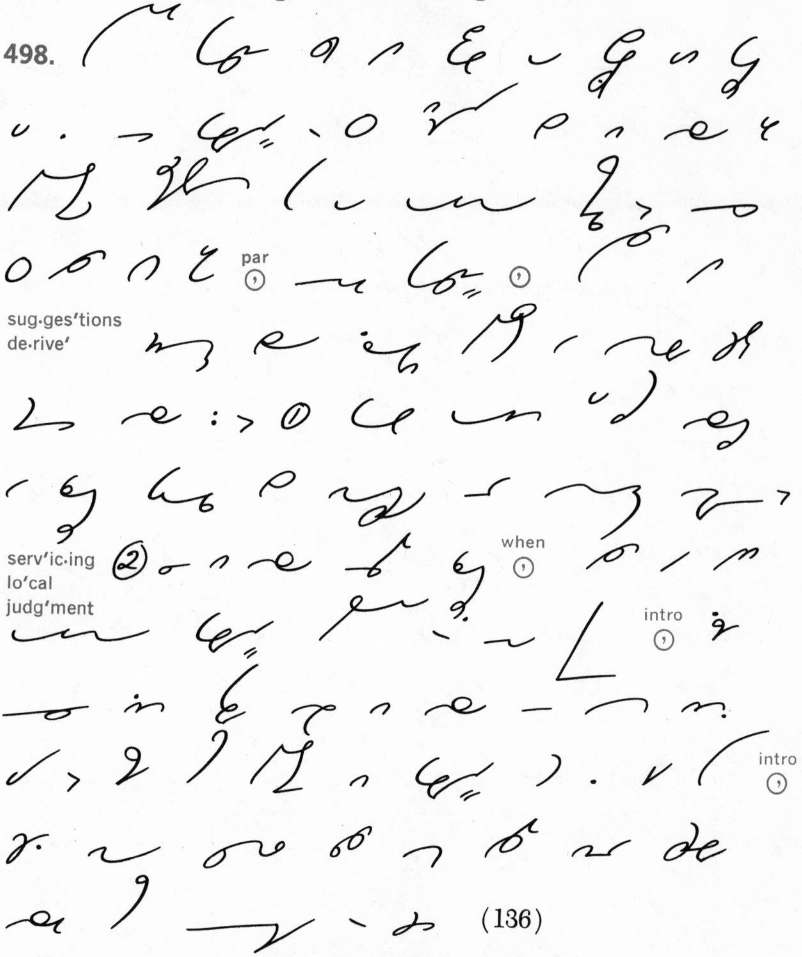

(136)

499.

yours
worn
worth'while'

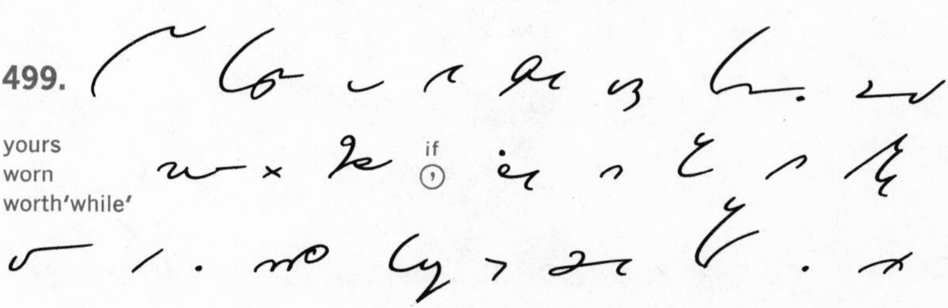

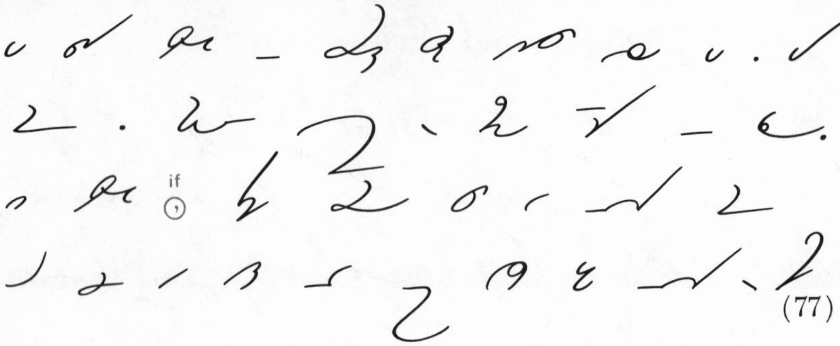
if

(77)

500.

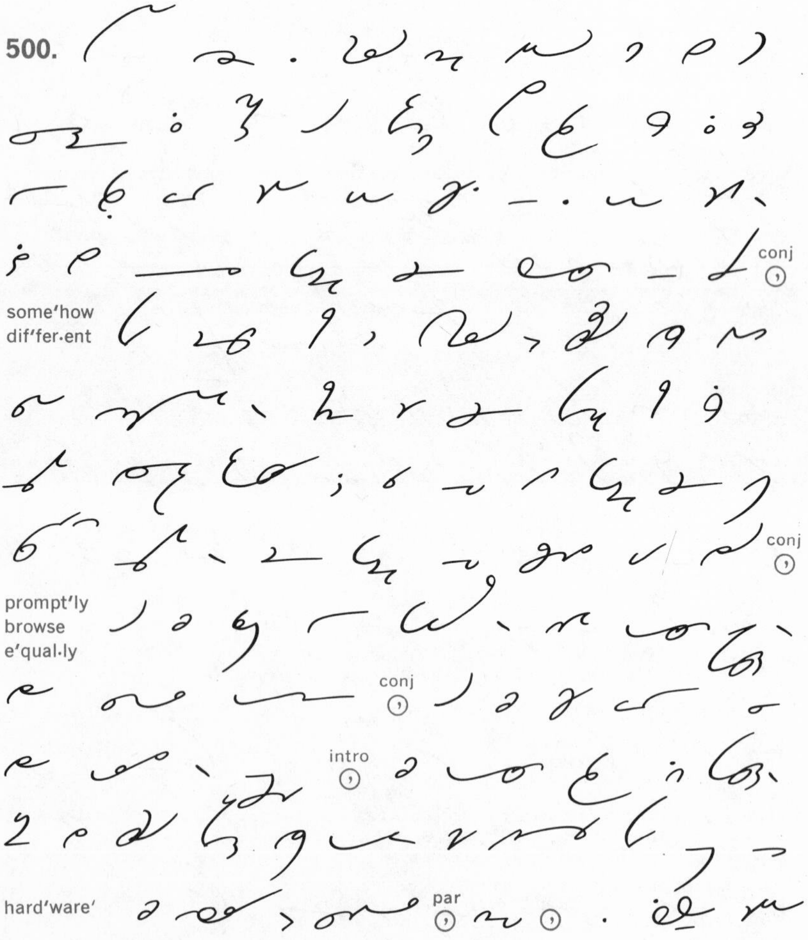
conj
some'how
dif'fer·ent
conj
prompt'ly
browse
e'qual·ly
conj
intro
hard'ware'
par

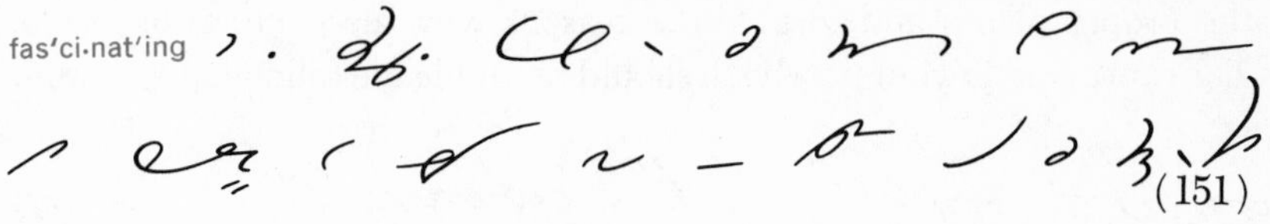
fas'ci·nat'ing
(151)

501.

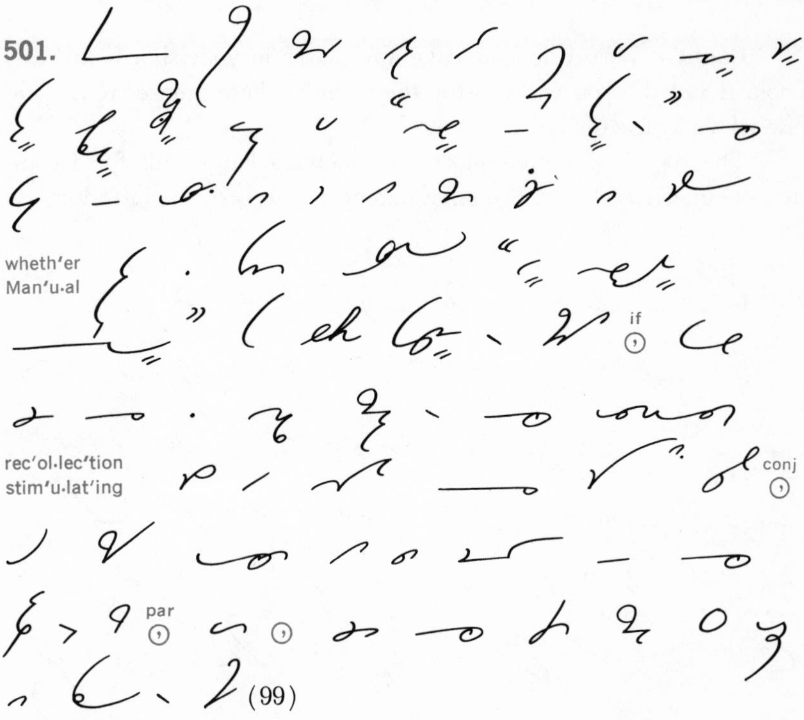
wheth'er
Man'u·al
if
rec'ol·lec'tion
stim'u·lat'ing
conj
par
(99)

502. TRANSCRIPTION QUIZ

Beginning with Lesson 57, you will have an opportunity to see how well you have mastered the nine uses of the comma that were introduced in Chapters 6, 7, and 8. Lessons 57-69 contain one letter each that is called a "Transcription Quiz." It contains several illustrations of the uses of the comma that you have studied. The commas, however, are not indicated in the printed shorthand. It will be your job, as you copy the letter in shorthand in your notebook, to insert the commas in the proper places and to give the reasons why the commas are used. The shorthand in your notebook should resemble the following example:

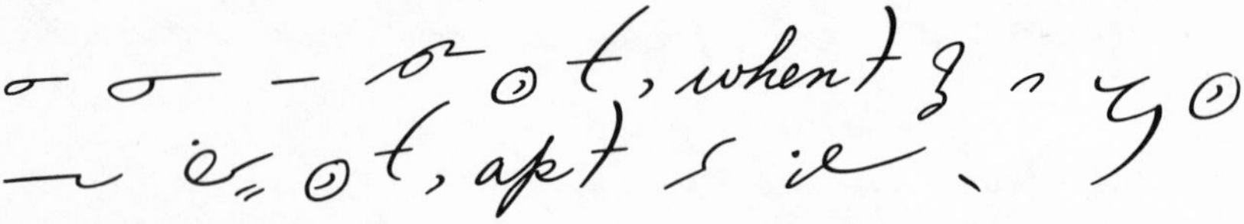

Caution: Please do not make any marks in your shorthand textbook. If you do, you will destroy the value of these quizzes to anyone else who may use the book.

The correct punctuation of the following letter calls for 4 commas—1 comma *as* clause, 2 commas parenthetical, 1 comma introductory.

(114)

Lesson 58

This lesson is designed to increase further your ability to use the frequent phrases of Gregg Shorthand. It contains several illustrations of all the phrasing principles. Altogether, there are 79 phrases, counting repetitions.

Building Transcription Skills

503. BUSINESS VOCABULARY BUILDER

brochures Pamphlets.

stationery Writing supplies, such as paper, envelopes, pens, pencils, and so on. (Do not confuse with *stationary,* which means "fixed; not moving.")

confidential Private.

credit card A means of identification issued by business firms to their charge customers.

504. GRAMMAR CHECKUP

Sentence Structure

Parallel ideas should be expressed in parallel form.

No

I hope our relationship will be long, pleasant, and *of profit* to both of us.

Yes

I hope our relationship will be long, pleasant, and *profitable* to both of us.

No

As soon as we receive the necessary information, your account will be opened and *we will ship your order.*

Yes

As soon as we receive the necessary information, your account will be opened and *your order will be shipped.*

It is especially important to keep parallel all ideas in a tabulation.

No

Her main duties were:

1. Taking dictation and transcribing
2. Answering the telephone
3. *To take care* of the files

Yes

Her main duties were:

1. Taking dictation and transcribing
2. Answering the telephone
3. *Taking care* of the files

Reading and Writing Practice

505.

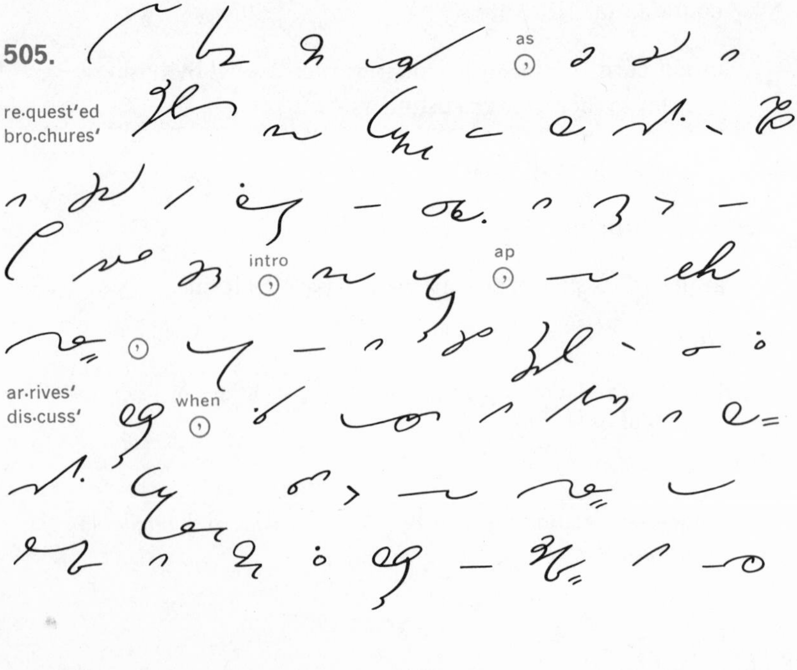
as
re·quest'ed
bro·chures'
intro
ap
ar·rives'
dis·cuss'
when

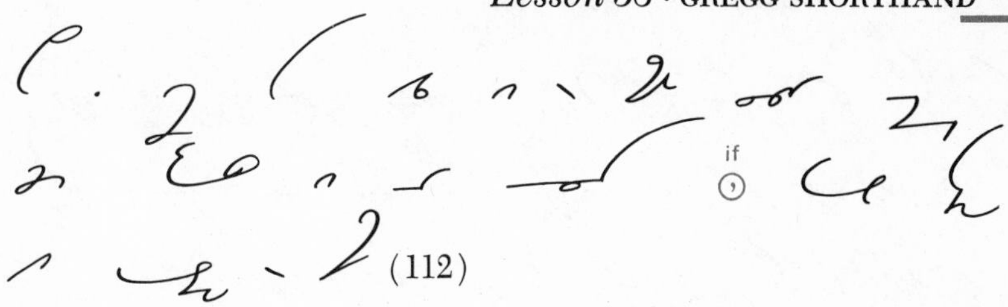
if

(112)

506.

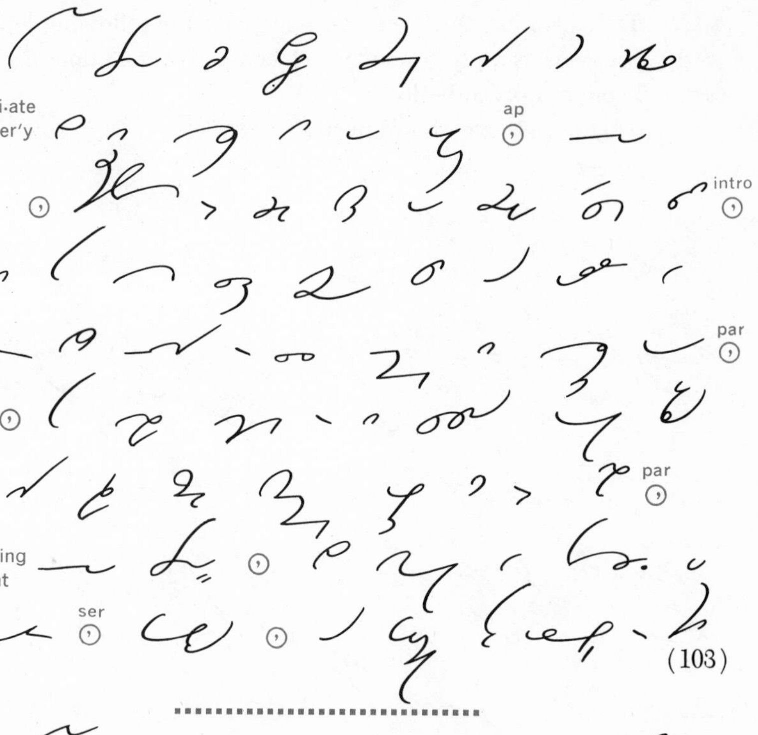
ap
intro
par
par
ser

ap·pre'ci·ate
sta'tion·er'y

be·gin'ning
pleas'ant

(103)

507.

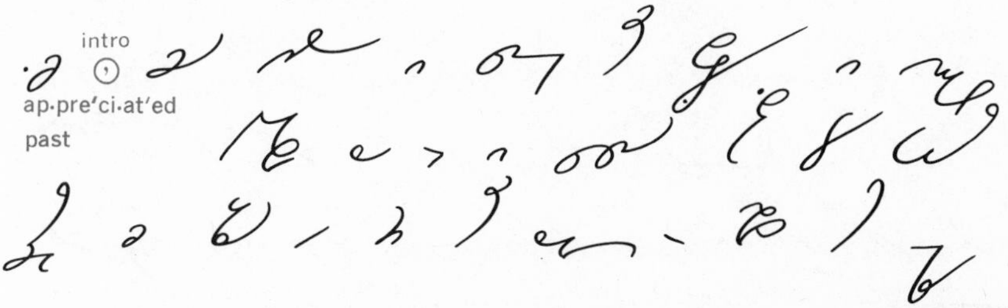
intro

ap·pre'ci·at'ed
past

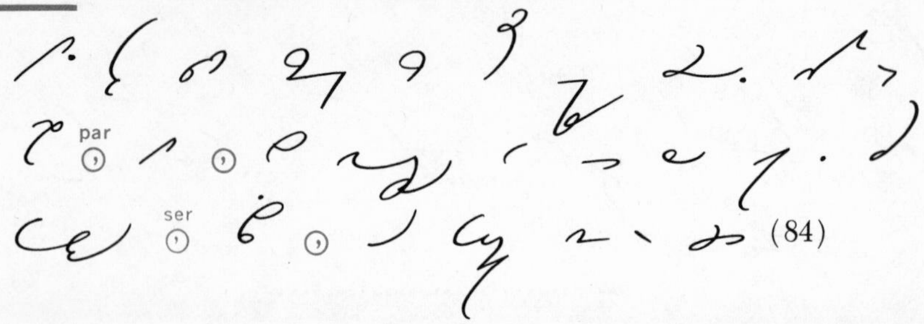
par
ser
(84)

508. Transcription Quiz. To punctuate the following letter correctly, you must supply 5 commas—1 comma conjunction, 2 commas series, 2 commas parenthetical.

No marks in the textbook, please!

(86)

509. Chuckle

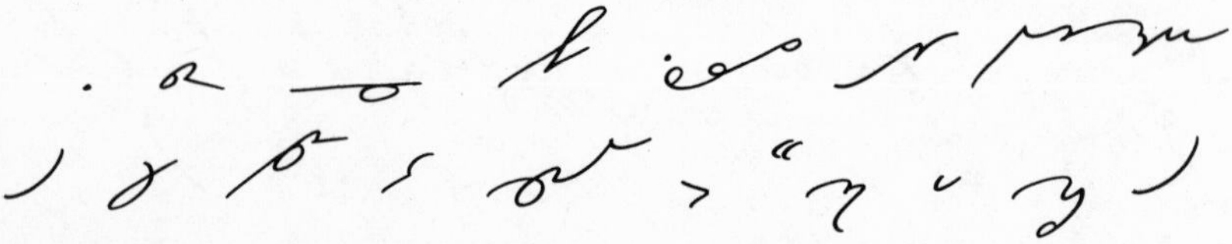

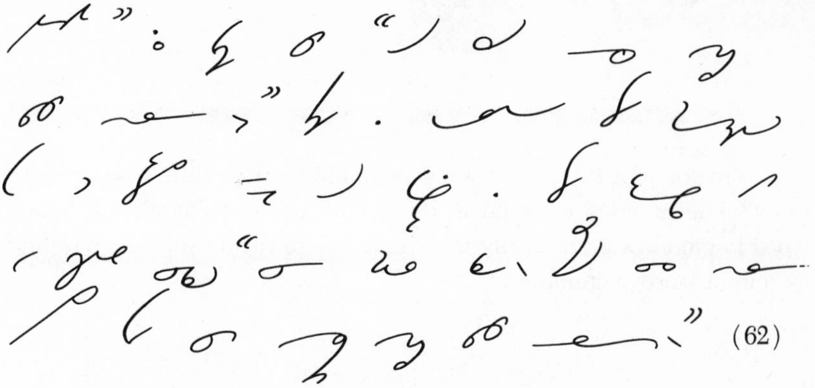

(62)

PHRASING AND SHORTHAND SPEED

Occasionally, students gain the impression that phrasing is the key to shorthand speed and that the more a writer phrases, the faster he will write. Consequently, they try to phrase as many combinations of words as possible and sometimes even devise phrases of their own.

This practice may seriously reduce a writer's speed rather than increase it. Why? A phrase is valuable only if it can be written without the slightest hesitation. If the writer must pause for even the smallest fraction of a second in composing or thinking of a phrase, that phrase becomes a speed handicap.

The phrase that can be written without hesitation is the one that has occurred again and again in the writer's practice work, so that it has impressed itself permanently on his mind. If you have been reading and copying each Reading and Writing Practice faithfully, you have encountered the common phrases of the English language many times. These phrases will come to you naturally when you take dictation.

If you have the feeling that you should be phrasing more, dismiss the matter from your mind. Simply continue to read and copy faithfully each Reading and Writing Practice, and your ability to phrase will take care of itself.

Lesson 59

Are some of the joined word beginnings still a little hazy in your mind? The practice material in this lesson will help fix all the joined word beginnings more firmly in your mind. In this lesson you will find 58 joined word beginnings.

Building Transcription Skills

510. BUSINESS VOCABULARY BUILDER

financial statement A statement prepared by a business firm showing its financial condition or progress.

via By way of.

express A method of shipping merchandise by rail, truck, and plane.

discount An amount deducted from a customer's bill when prompt payment is made.

ensue To follow.

511. SPELLING FAMILIES

Words Ending in -ence

com·mence'	**ev'i·dence**	**neg'li·gence**
con'fer·ence	**ex'cel·lence**	**oc·cur'rence**
con'fi·dence	**ex·per'i·ence**	**ref'er·ence**
dif'fer·ence	**in'de·pend'ence**	**vi'o·lence**

Words Ending in -ance

ac·cept'ance	**as·sist'ance**	**bal'ance**
al·low'ance	**as·sur'ance**	**cir'cum·stance**

ig′no·rance	**in·sur′ance**	**re·li′ance**
in′stance	**per·form′ance**	**sub′stance**

Reading and Writing Practice

512.

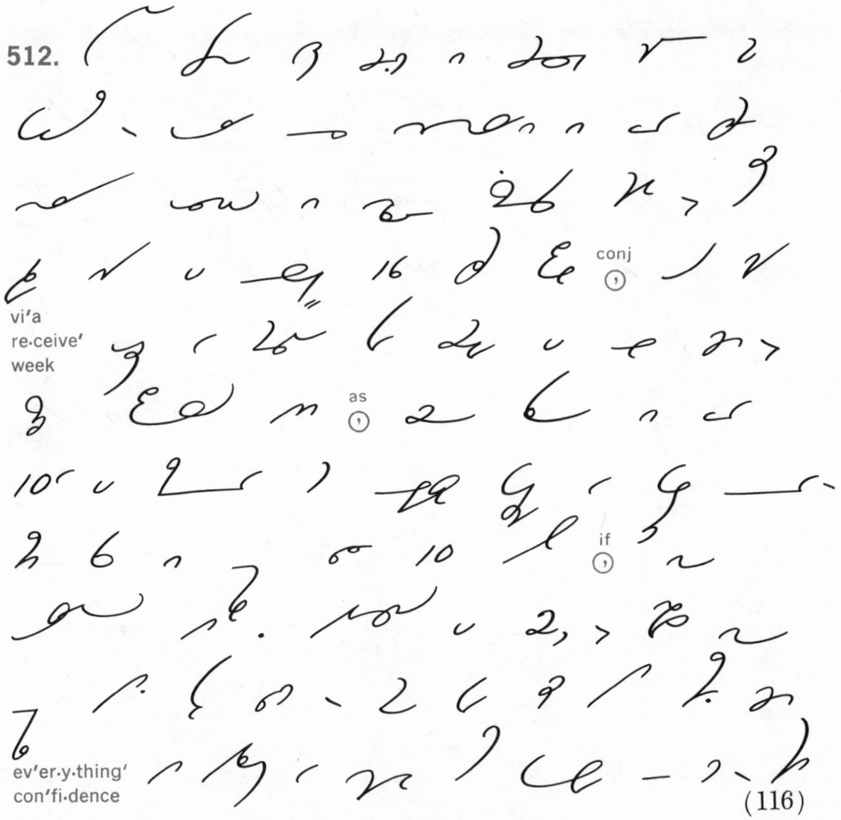
conj
as
if

vi′a
re·ceive′
week

ev′er·y·thing′
con′fi·dence

(116)

513.

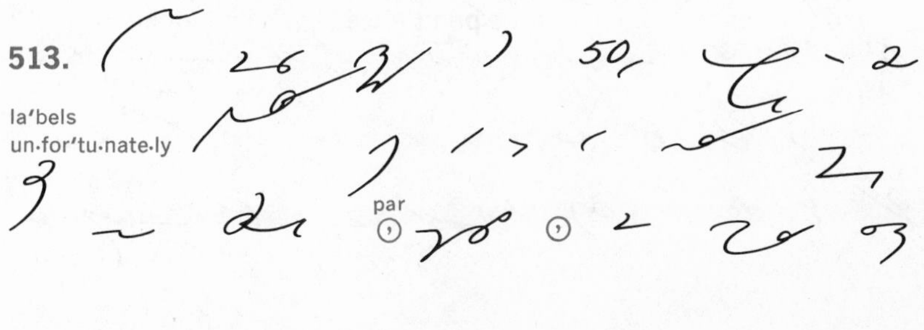
par

la′bels
un·for′tu·nate·ly

ex′cel·lent
fi·nan′cial·ly

un·doubt′ed·ly
im·me′di·ate·ly

conj
intro
when

(139)

514.

for′mer
sub·mit′ted
ref′er·ence

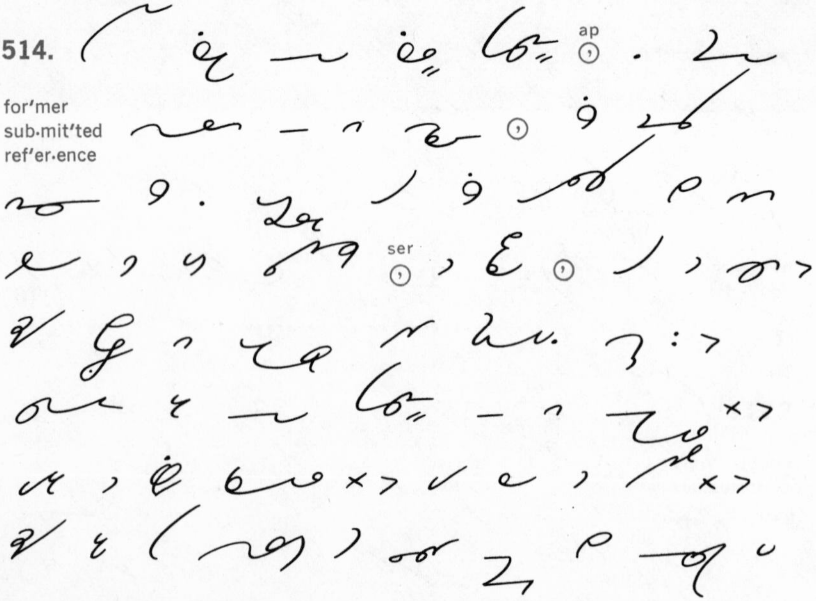
ap
ser

as·sist'ance
pro·spec'tive
em·ploy'ee

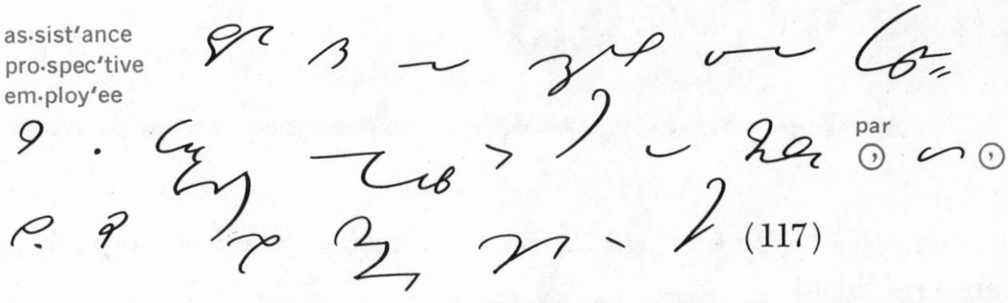
par

(117)

515. Transcription Quiz. The correct punctuation of the following letter calls for 8 commas—1 comma conjunction, 2 commas series, 4 commas parenthetical, 1 comma *and* omitted.

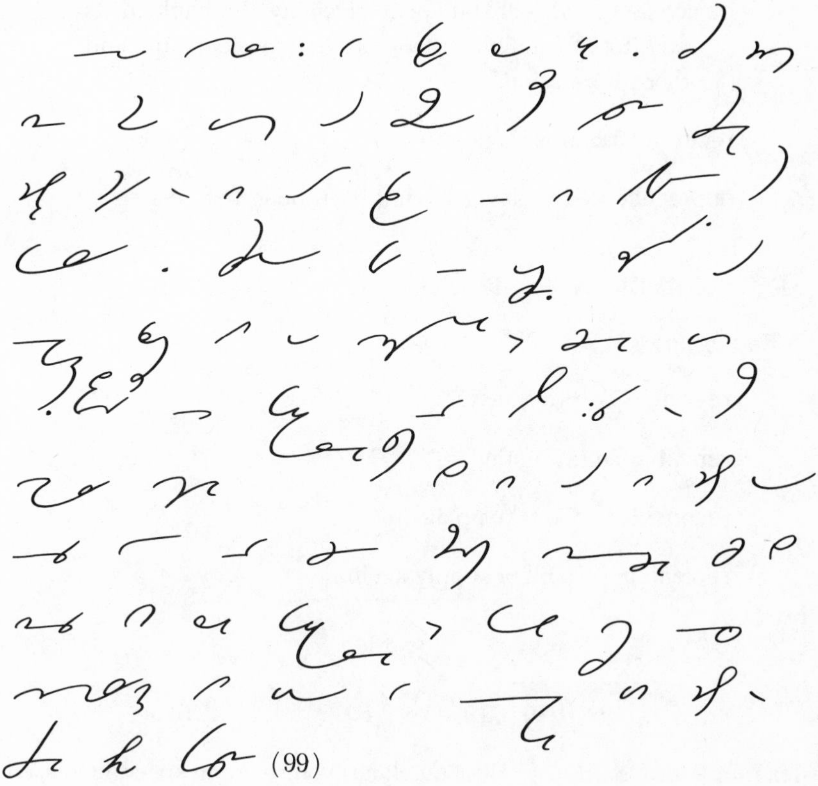

(99)

Lesson 60

In this lesson you will "brush up" on joined word endings—there are 49 of them!

Building Transcription Skills

516. BUSINESS VOCABULARY BUILDER

bank statement A statement given by the bank to its depositors to show checks written, deposits made, and other information.

recur To happen again.

unprecedented Never having been done before.

517. COMMON WORD ROOTS

Re-: *again*

reprint To print again.

repeat To say again.

reconsider To take up again.

replenish To fill or supply again.

Reading and Writing Practice

Reading Scoreboard. How much has your reading speed increased over your first score in Lesson 18? The table on the next page will help you determine your reading speed on Lesson 60.

Lesson 60 contains 470 words.

If you read Lesson 60 in	**your reading rate is**
11 MINUTES	43 WORDS A MINUTE
13 MINUTES	36 WORDS A MINUTE
15 MINUTES	31 WORDS A MINUTE
17 MINUTES	28 WORDS A MINUTE
19 MINUTES	25 WORDS A MINUTE
21 MINUTES	22 WORDS A MINUTE
23 MINUTES	20 WORDS A MINUTE

518.

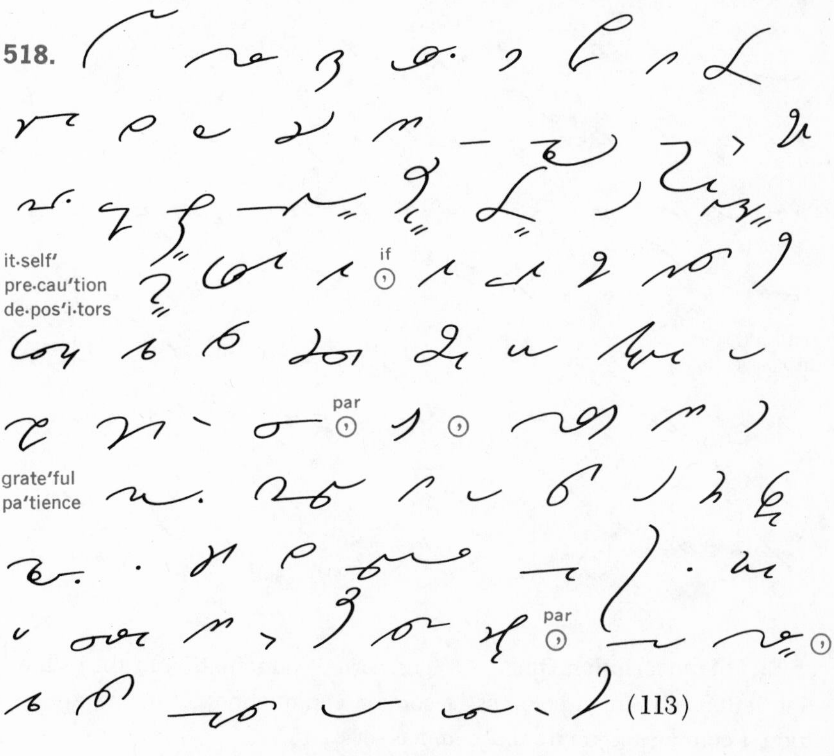
if
par
par
(113)

it·self′
pre·cau′tion
de·pos′i·tors

grate′ful
pa′tience

519.

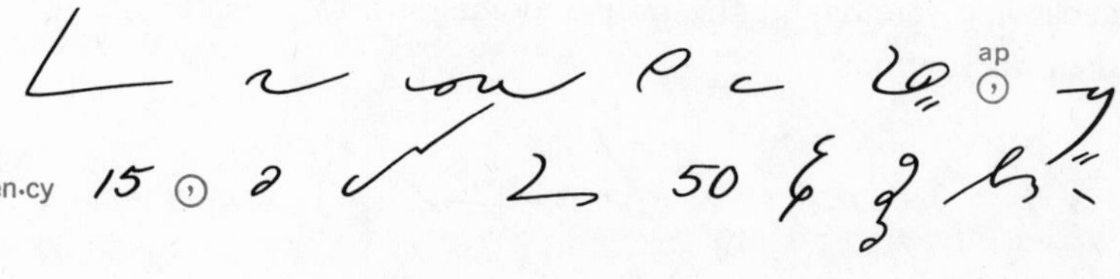
ap
15
50

re·call′
ef·fi′cien·cy

when
at·tempt'ed
truck'men
conj
when
as
sit'u·a'tion
in'con·ven'ience
par
25
25
25
10
12

(163)

520. Transcription Quiz. The correct punctuation of the following letter calls for 5 commas—1 comma conjunction, 1 comma apposition, 1 comma *and* omitted, 2 commas series.

As you copy the letter in your notebook, be sure to insert the necessary commas at the proper points and to indicate the reason for the punctuation.

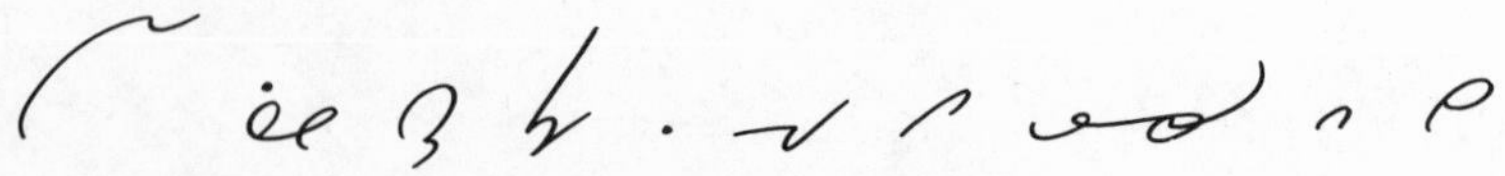

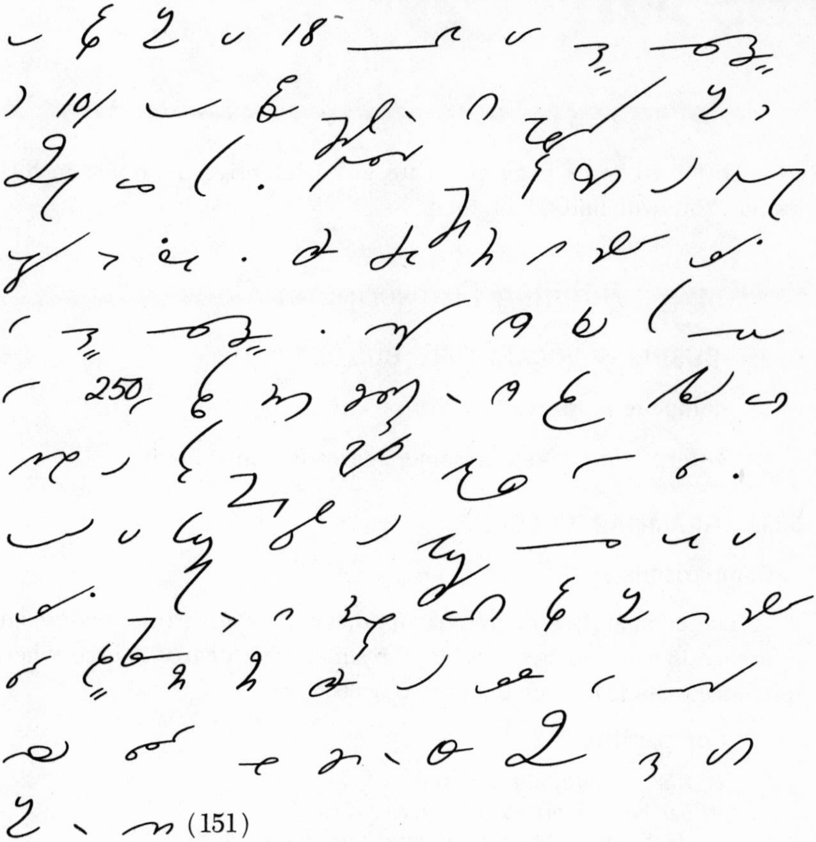

(151)

521. Chuckle

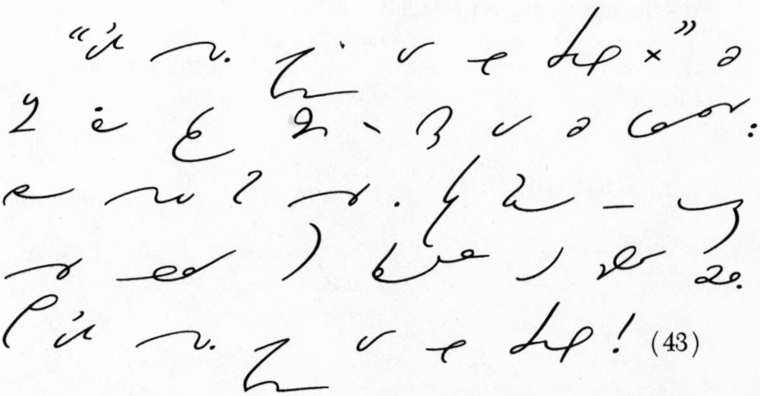

(43)

Lesson 61

Disjoined word beginnings are given intensive treatment in this lesson. You will find 31 of them.

Building Transcription Skills

522. BUSINESS VOCABULARY BUILDER

compelled Forced.

enterprising Venturesome; aggressive; imaginative.

523. GRAMMAR CHECKUP

Comparisons

The comparative degree of an adjective or adverb is used when reference is made to two objects; the superlative degree is used when reference is made to more than two objects.

Comparative

Of the two boys, Jim is the taller.
Which boy is more efficient, Jim or Harry?
Is Mr. Smith or Mr. Green better qualified to do the job?

Superlative

Of the three boys, Jim is the tallest.
Which of the boys is the most efficient, Jim, Harry, or John?
Is Mr. Smith, Mr. Green, or Mr. Brown the best qualified to do the job?

Reading and Writing Practice

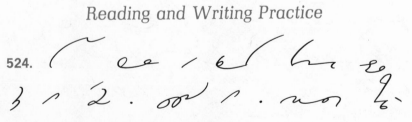

524.

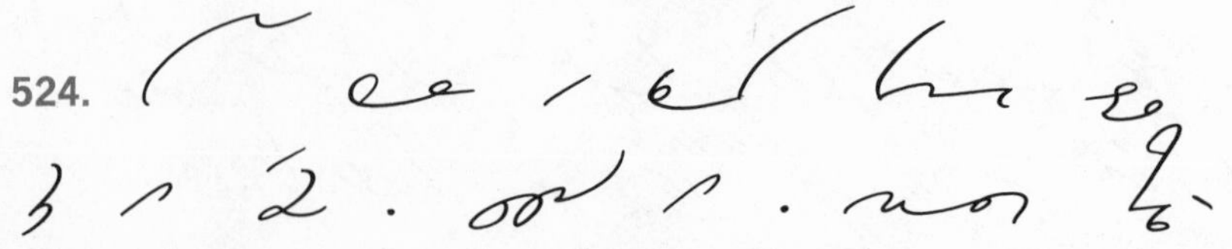

oc·ca′sions
al·ter′na·tive
com·pelled′
col·lec′tion
en′ve·lope

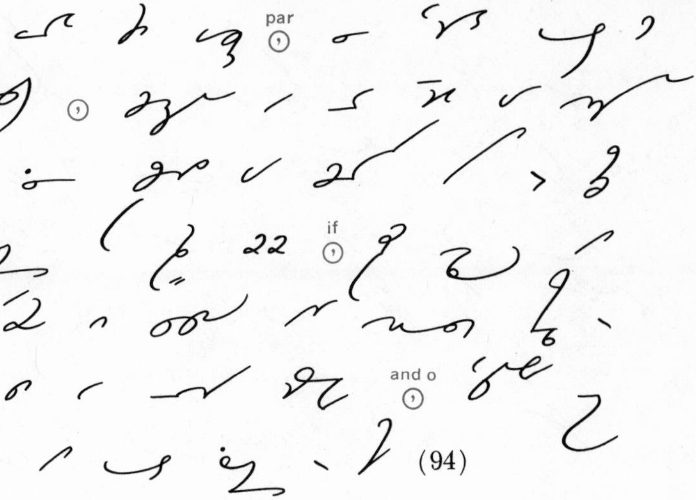
par
if
22
and o
(94)

525.

re′cent
sur′vey
sim′i·lar
com′pa·nies
sub·stan′tial·ly
o′ver·head′
is′su·ing

intro
75
intro
ser

safe'ty

conj ,

intro ,

and o ,

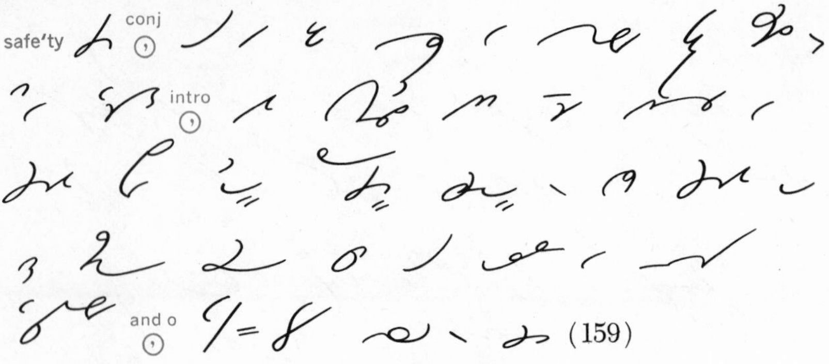

(159)

526.

ap ,

as ,

de·scribe'

ex·pe'ri·enc·es

fur'ther

as·sist'ance

if ,

(127)

527. Transcription Quiz. In the following letter you must supply 5 commas to punctuate it correctly—1 comma *when* clause, 2 commas parenthetical, 2 commas series.

(125)

Lesson 62

Do you find that you don't know the disjoined word endings as well as you would like? Then practice this lesson carefully. There are 46 disjoined word endings in it.

Building Transcription Skills

528. BUSINESS VOCABULARY BUILDER

tradition A practice carried on over a period of years.

critical Involving risk.

potential In the making; possible.

529. SIMILAR-WORDS DRILL

Past, passed

past (*noun*) A former time. (*Past* is also used as an adjective.)

The program has been very successful in the past.

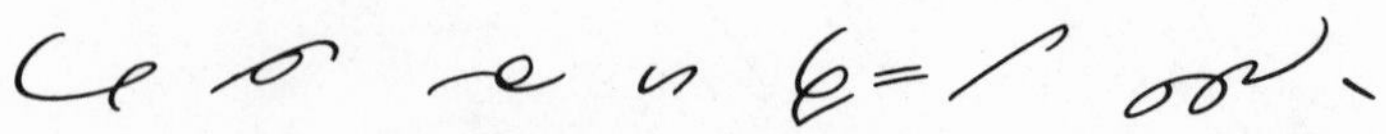

Please take care of your past-due account.

passed Moved along; went by; transferred.

I passed him on the street.

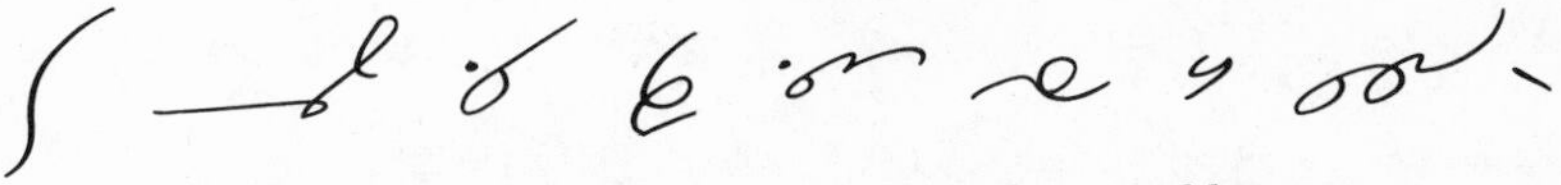

Before many days had passed, he took care of his account.

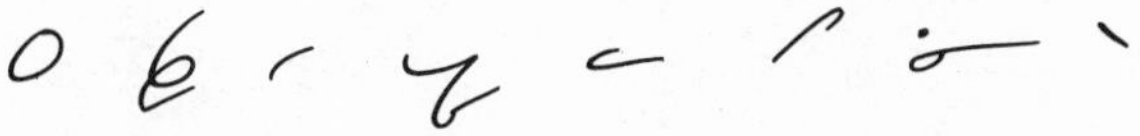

I passed the report on to him.

Reading and Writing Practice

530.

as
if
par

typ'i·cal
pro·vid'ing

(114)

531.

for'ward·ed
spon'sor·ship
ra'di·o
a·vail'a·ble
ef·fect'
fa·cil'i·ties
ad'ver·tis'ing

ap
15
intro
par
ap
ap
19
(158)

532.

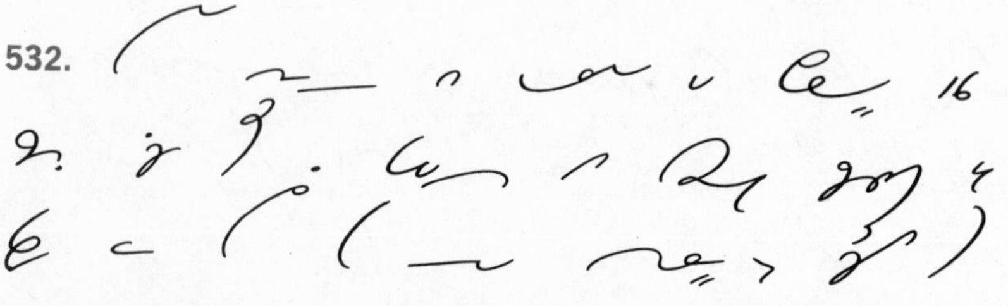
16

com'pre·hen'sive
de·vel'op
po·ten'tial
past
de·vised'
ac·cept'ed

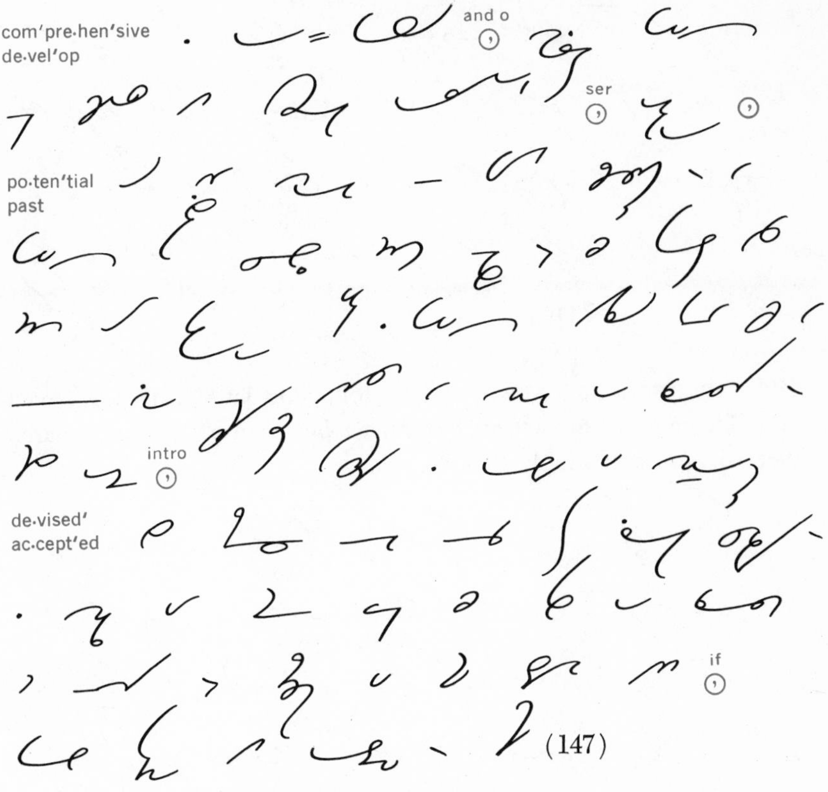
and o
ser
intro
if
(147)

533.

ex·pe'ri·ence
re'al·ize

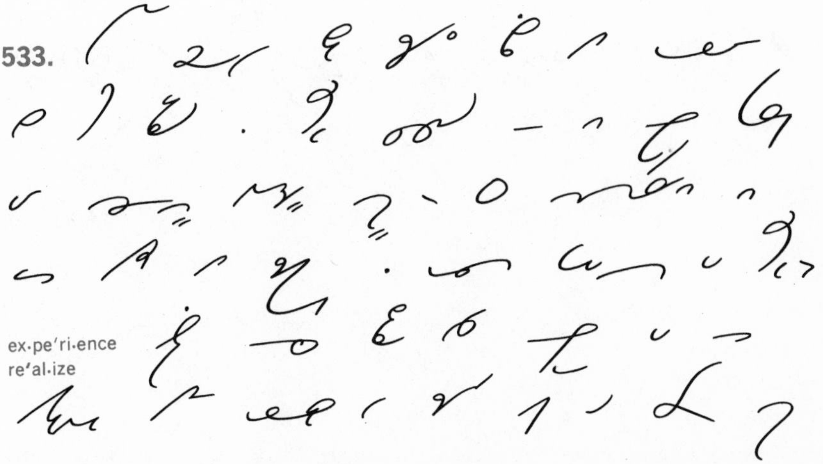

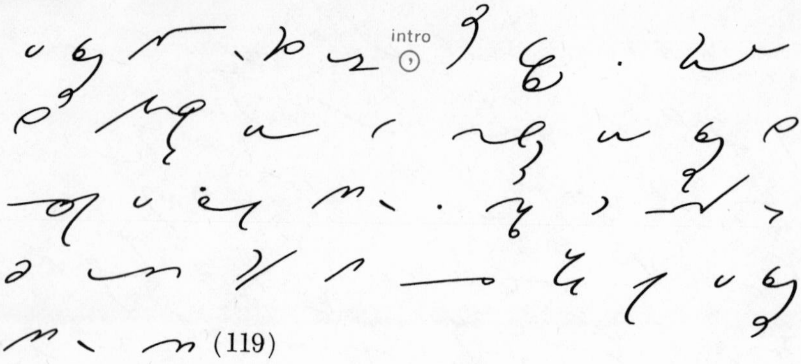
intro

(119)

534. Transcription Quiz. The following letter calls for 4 commas–1 comma introductory, 1 comma *when* clause, 2 commas parenthetical. Can you supply them?

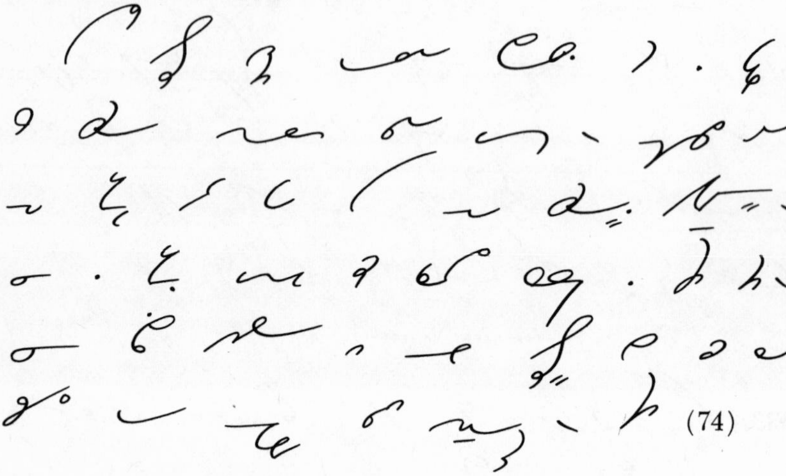

(74)

Lesson 63

Blends form a very important part of Gregg Shorthand. The material in this lesson reviews all the blends many times. In all, there are 91 words and phrases containing one or more blends.

Building Transcription Skills

535. BUSINESS VOCABULARY BUILDER

unintentionally Without meaning to.

remedy To correct; to make right.

reciprocate To repay; to return in like measure.

net worth The difference between the total assets owned by a company and its total debts and obligations.

536. COMMON WORD ROOTS

Co-: *with, together, jointly*

co-operation The act of working together.

coeducation Joint education; especially the education of boys and girls at the same school.

co-ordinate To bring together.

coherence A sticking together.

Reading and Writing Practice

537.

conj
wel′com·ing
spe′cial·iz·ing
1850
and o
intro
(92)

538.

as
30
don't
nat′u·ral·ly
when
un′in·ten′tion·al·ly
did'n't
rem′e·dy
if

ones
treas'ure

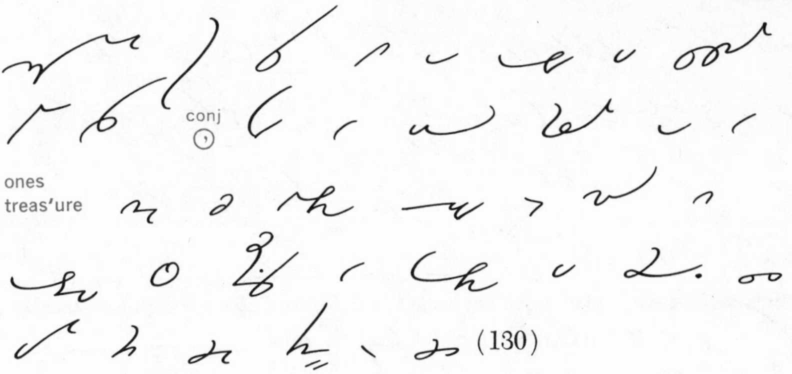

(130)

539.

Tow'els
rea'son
be·lieve'

as·sure'
re·cip'ro·cate

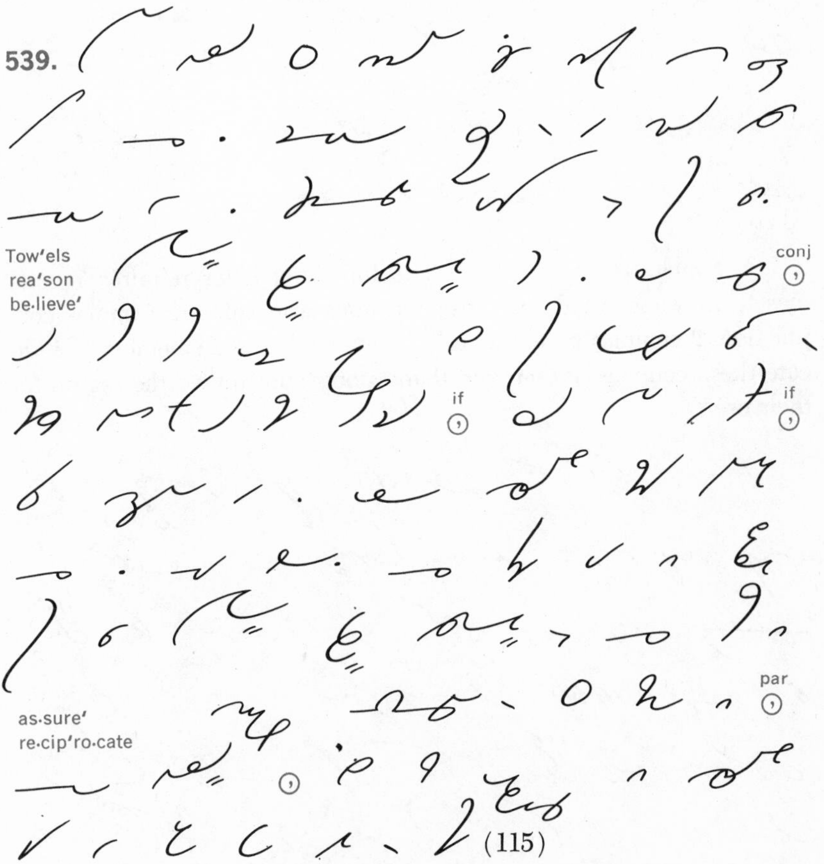

(115)

540.

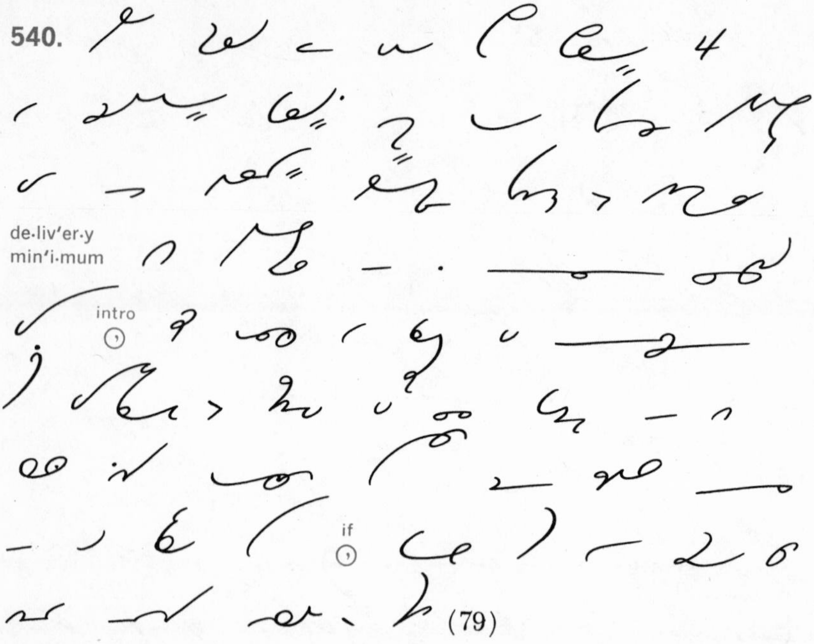
de·liv'er·y
min'i·mum
intro
if
(79)

541. Transcription Quiz. The following letter requires 7 commas to be punctuated correctly—1 comma apposition, 2 commas conjunction, 2 commas parenthetical, 2 commas series. Remember to indicate these commas in your shorthand notes and to give the reason for their use.

1950

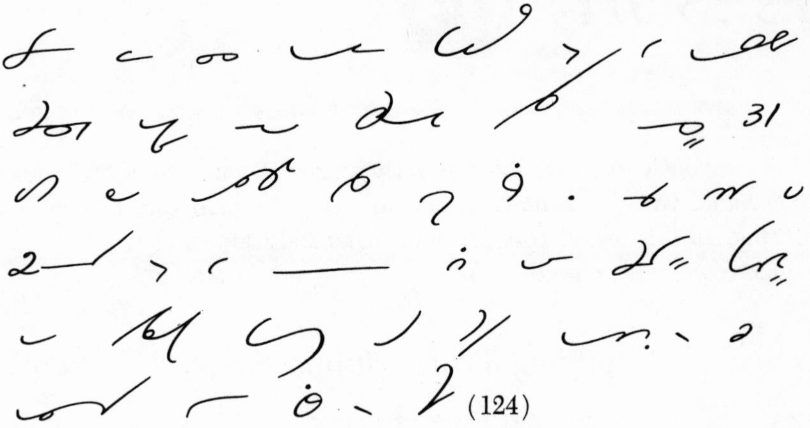

(124)

542. Chuckle

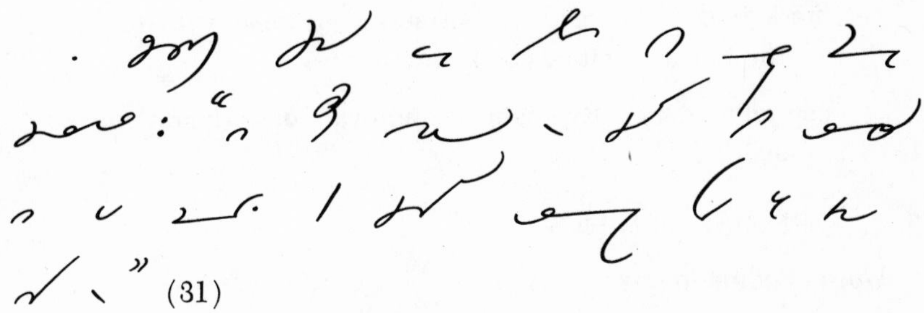

(31)

DICTATION CHECK LIST

When you take dictation, do you –

1. Make every effort to keep up with the dictator?

2. Refer to your textbook whenever you are in doubt about the outline for a word or phrase?

3. Insert periods and question marks in your shorthand notes?

4. Make a real effort to observe good proportion as you write – making large circles large, small circles small, etc.?

5. Do you write down the first column of your notebook and then down the second column?

Lesson 64

As you learned during the early stages of your study of Gregg Shorthand, vowels are omitted in some words to help gain fluency of writing. In this lesson you will find many illustrations of words from which vowels are omitted.

Building Transcription Skills

543. BUSINESS VOCABULARY BUILDER

utilize To turn to profitable use; to make use of.

marketing The field of business concerned with distributing and selling goods and services.

complimentary Expressing approval or admiration; favorable.

544. SPELLING FAMILIES

Words Ending in -ary

an′ni·ver′sa·ry	el′e·men′ta·ry	sec′re·tar′y
com′pli·men′ta·ry	li′brar′y	sum′ma·ry
cus′tom·ar′y	nec′es·sar′y	tem′po·rar′y
dic′tion·ar′y	sec′ond·ar′y	vo·cab′u·lar′y

Words Ending in -ery

bind′er·y	mas′ter·y	re·fin′er·y
dis·cov′er·y	re·cov′er·y	scen′er·y

Words Ending in -ory

di·rec′to·ry	his′to·ry	ter′ri·to′ry
fac′to·ry	in′ven·to′ry	vic′to·ry

Reading and Writing Practice

545.

sum'ma·ry
per'son·al
ca·reer'
gen'u·ine·ly
u'ti·lize
mean'while'
com'pli·men'ta·ry

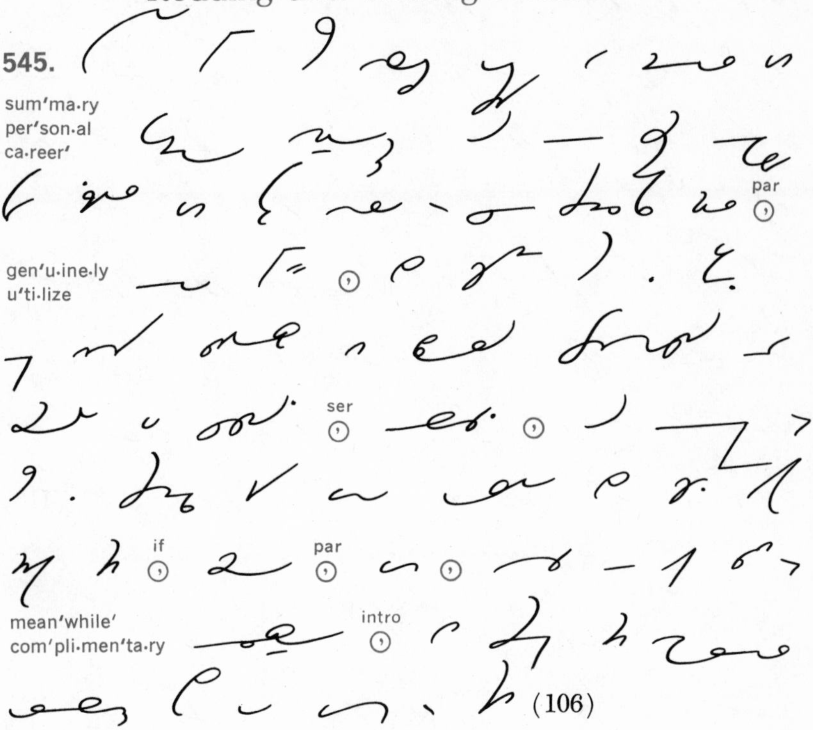

(106)

546.

pre·scrip'tion
ton'ic

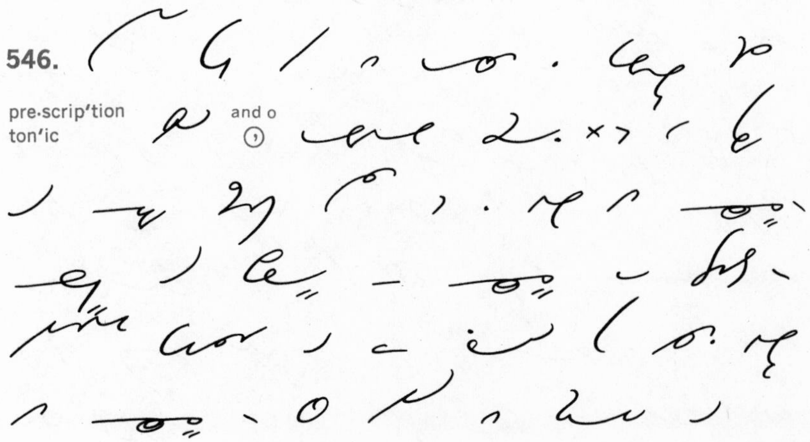

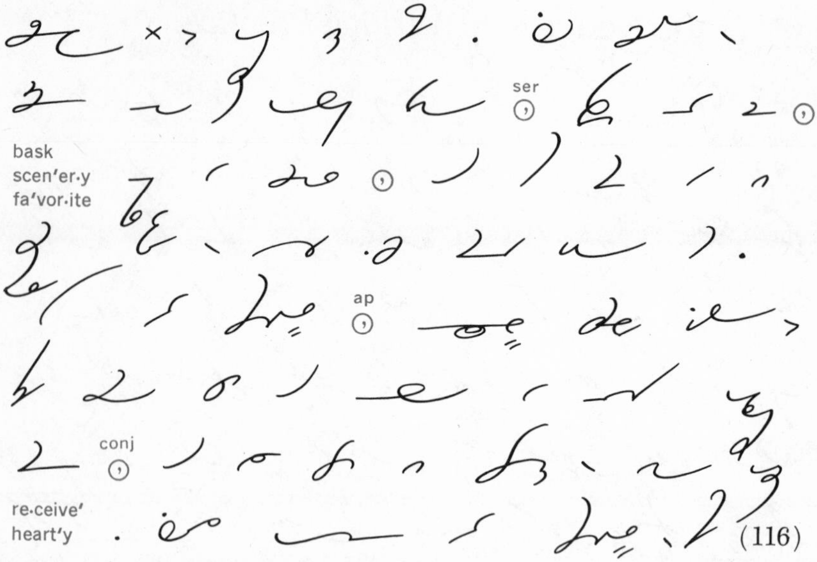
ser
ap
conj

bask
scen'er·y
fa'vor·ite

re·ceive'
heart'y

(116)

547.

when
conj
intro
intro

past
col'umns
for'eign

Christ′mas
i·de′al

as

(109)

548. Transcription Quiz. For you to supply: 5 commas—4 commas introductory, 1 comma parenthetical.

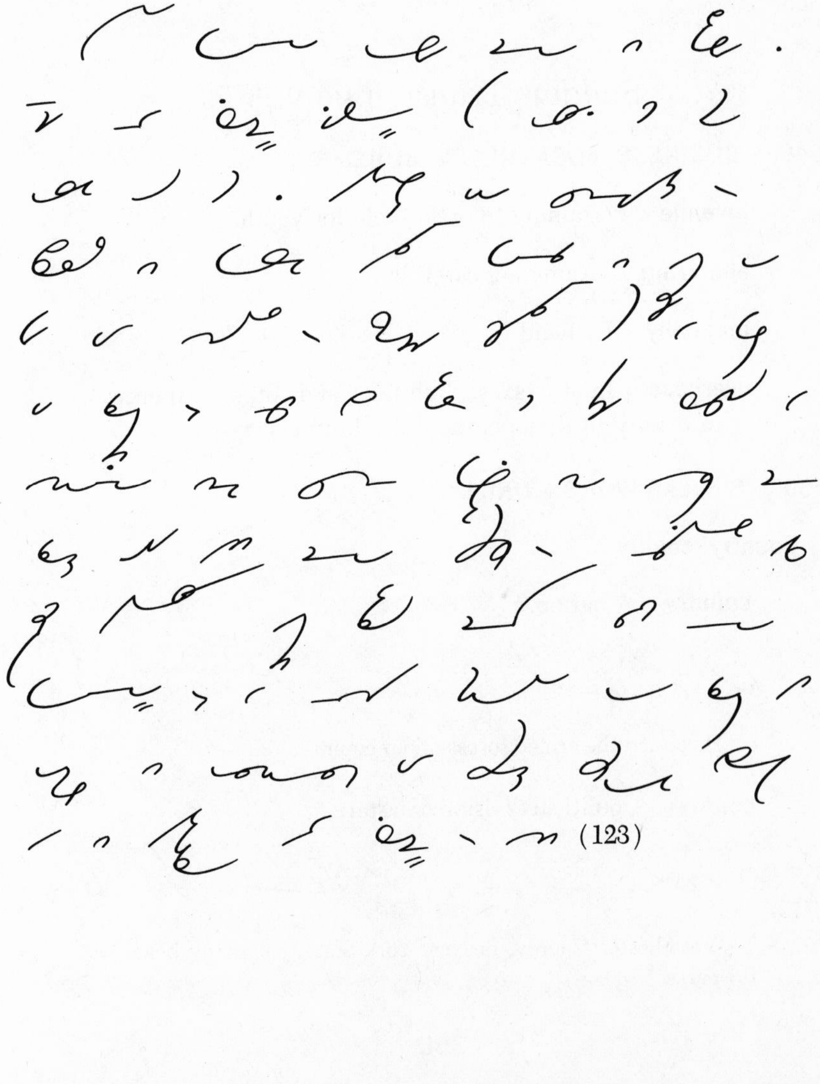

(123)

Lesson 65

You will frequently have to write numbers in business dictation. Because of the tremendous importance of accuracy in transcribing numbers, you must take special care to write numbers legibly in your notes. The material in this lesson will help you fix more firmly in your mind the various devices for expressing amounts and quantities in Gregg Shorthand.

Building Transcription Skills

549. BUSINESS VOCABULARY BUILDER

juvenile Pertaining to or suitable for youth.

analyzing Examining carefully.

manually By hand.

overhead Rent, taxes, lighting, and other expenses necessary to the operation of a business.

550. SIMILAR-WORDS DRILL

Country, county

country A nation.

He joined the armed forces of our country.

county A political division of a state.

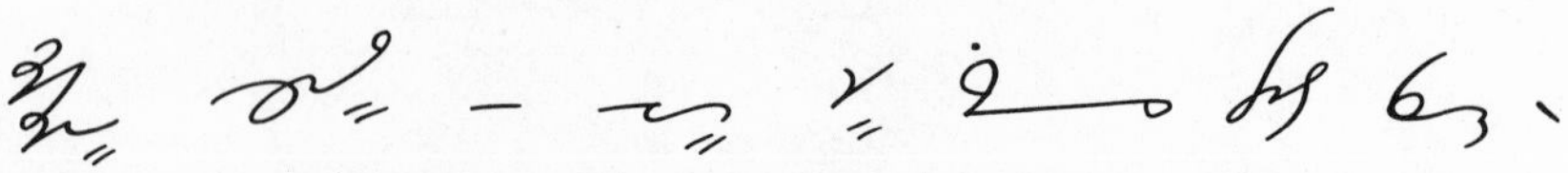

Westchester County, in New York State, has many beautiful parks.

Reading and Writing Practice

551. America's Cultural Growth

rise
past

sym'pho·ny
or'ches·tra

pho'no·graph
an'nu·al·ly

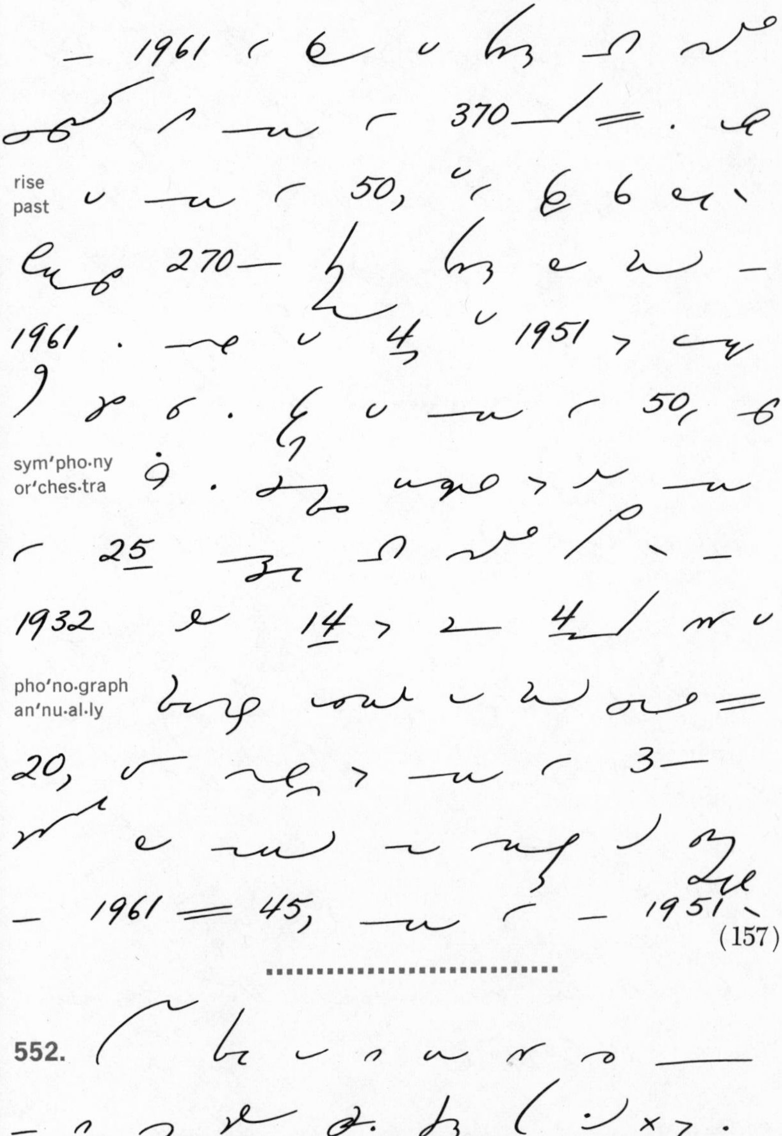

(157)

552.

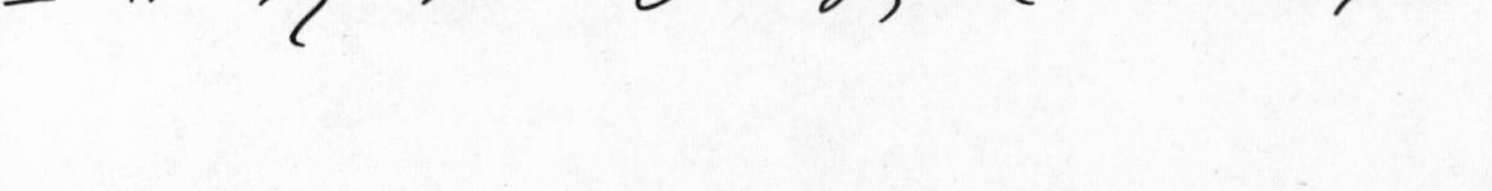

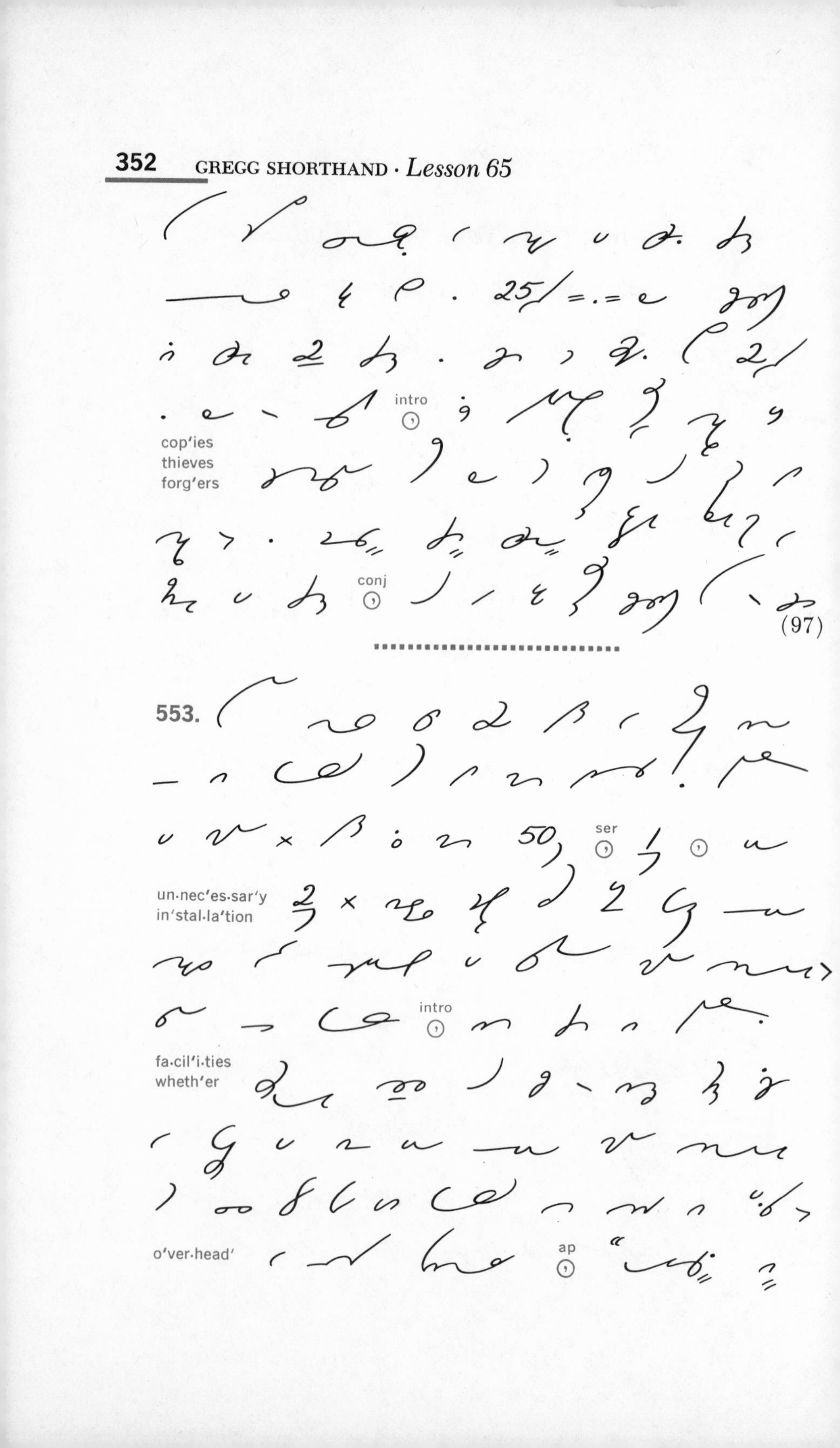

intro

cop'ies
thieves
forg'ers

conj

(97)

553.

ser

un·nec'es·sar'y
in'stal·la'tion

intro

fa·cil'i·ties
wheth'er

o'ver·head'

ap

de·scribes′ 

(104)

554. Transcription Quiz. To punctuate the following letter correctly, you must supply 8 commas – 4 commas parenthetical, 1 comma introductory, 1 comma *and* omitted, 1 comma *if* clause, 1 comma apposition.

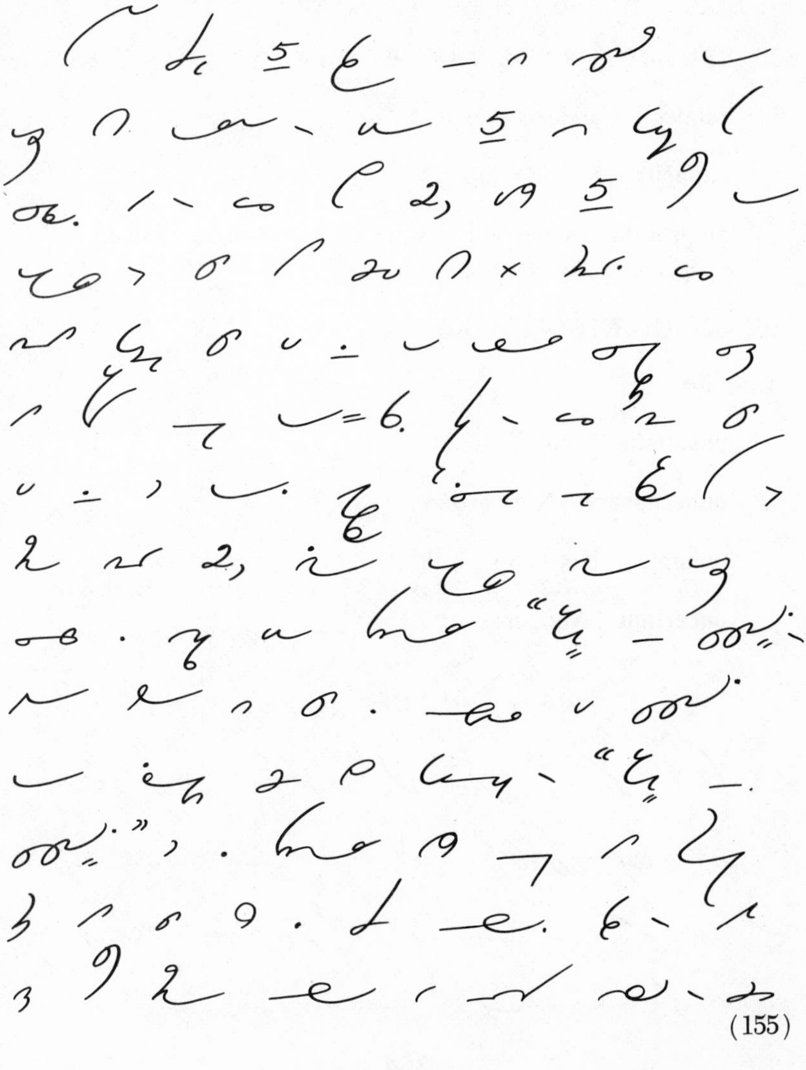

(155)

Lesson 66

This is another lesson that concentrates on brief forms. Counting repetitions, it contains 260 brief forms and derivatives.

Building Transcription Skills

555. BUSINESS VOCABULARY BUILDER

remiss Careless; negligent.

capacity Position; job.

air freight A method of shipping merchandise, usually heavy, bulky articles, by air.

556. COMMON WORD ROOTS

Un-: *not*

unsatisfied Not satisfied.

unnecessary Not needed.

unhappy Not happy; sad.

uncertain Not sure.

Reading and Writing Practice

557.

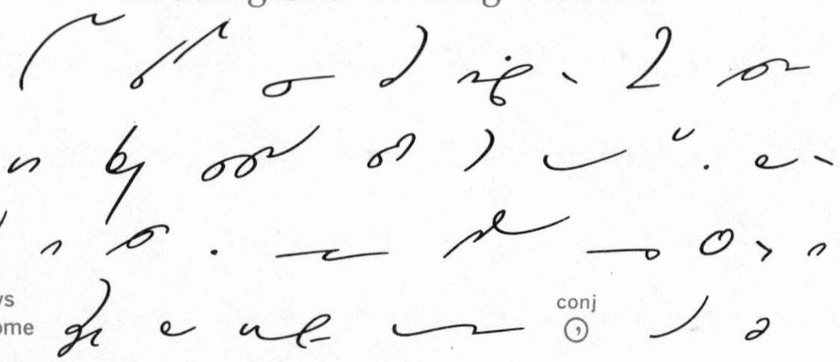

al'ways
wel'come
conj

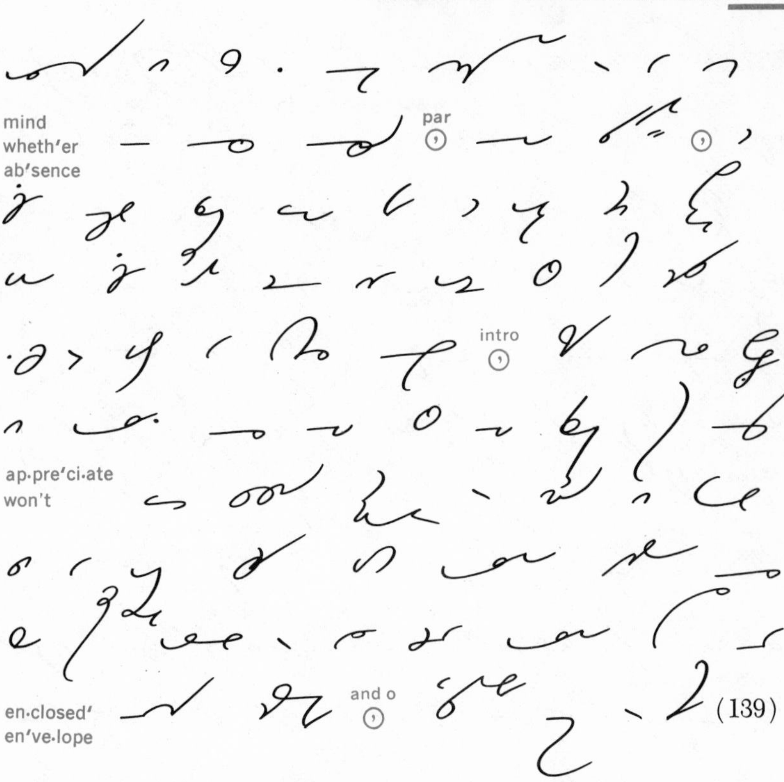

par
intro
and o
(139)

mind
wheth'er
ab'sence
ap·pre'ci·ate
won't
en·closed'
en've·lope

558.

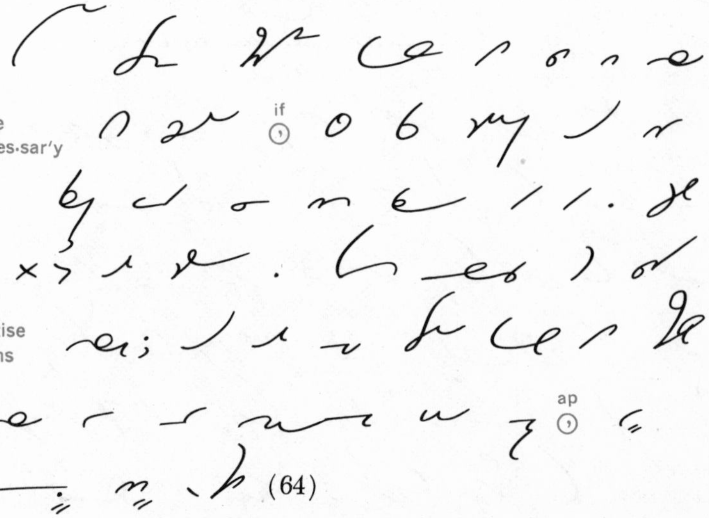

if
ap
(64)

stor'age
un·nec'es·sar'y
ad'ver·tise
col'umns

559.

conj
intro
par
(126)

of′fered
for′mer

560.

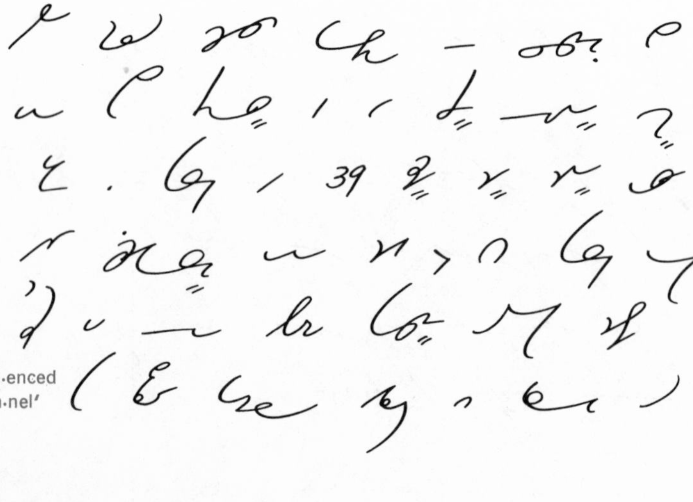

ex·pe′ri·enced
per′son·nel′

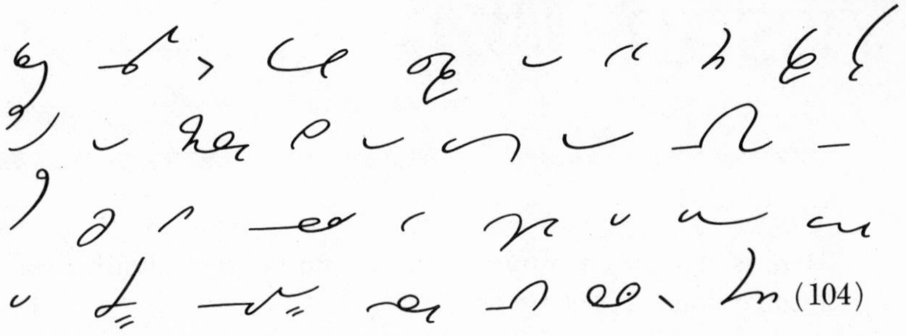

(104)

561. Transcription Quiz. For you to supply: 5 commas–2 commas introductory, 1 comma *when* clause, 2 commas series.

(130)

Lesson 67

Here is another opportunity to check up on your phrasing skill. This lesson contains 118 phrases.

Building Transcription Skills

562. BUSINESS VOCABULARY BUILDER

franchise An arrangement whereby a distributor is given an exclusive right to handle a manufacturer's products and services in a given locality.

considerate Showing thoughtfulness.

harassing Worrying.

investigate To look into.

563. GRAMMAR CHECKUP

Verbs—with "one of"

1. In most cases, the expression *one of* takes a singular verb, which agrees with the subject *one.*

> *One* of the men on the staff *is* ill.
> *One* of our typewriters *does not* work.

2. When *one of* is part of an expression such as *one of those who* or *one of the things that,* a plural verb is used to agree with its antecedent in number.

> He solved one of the *problems* that *have been* annoying businessmen for years.
> He is one of the *men* who *drive* to work.

Reading and Writing Practice

564.

o'ver·due'
pa'tient

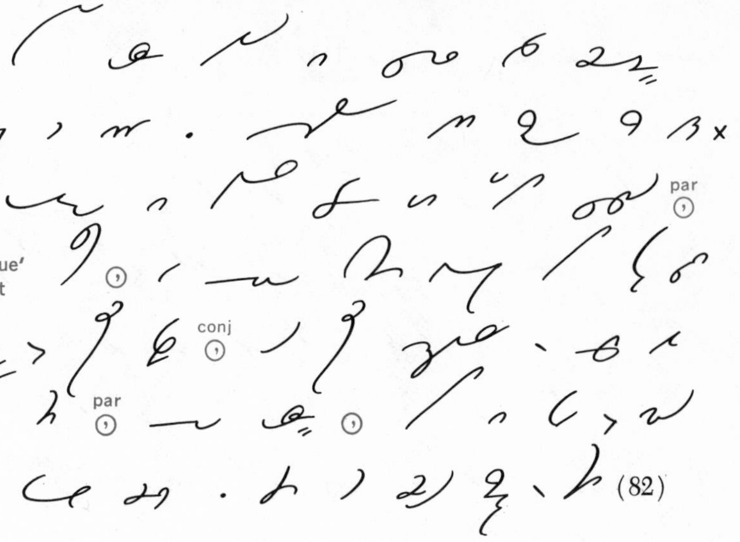
par
conj
par
(82)

565.

sea'son
ap·proach'es
be·half'
past
ma·te'ri·als

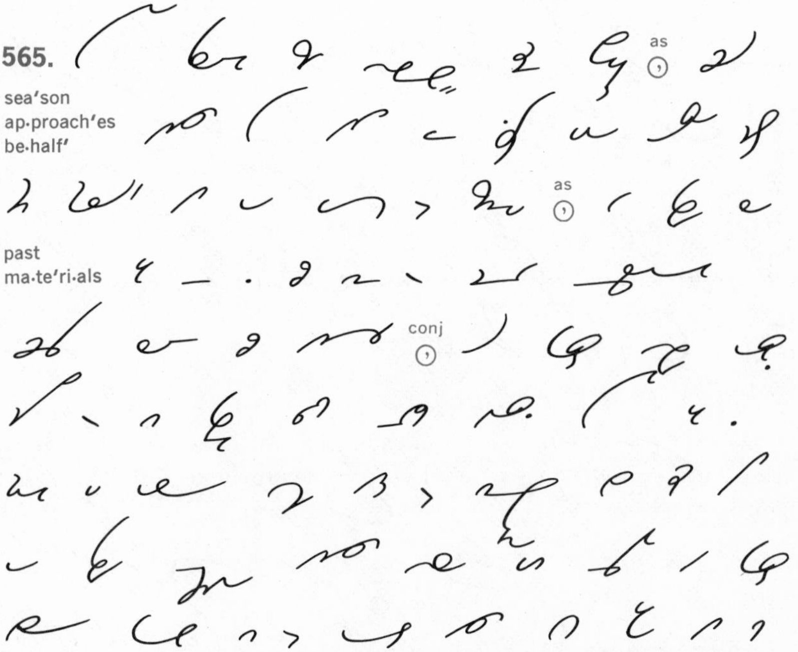
as
as
conj

Christ'mas
pros'per·ous

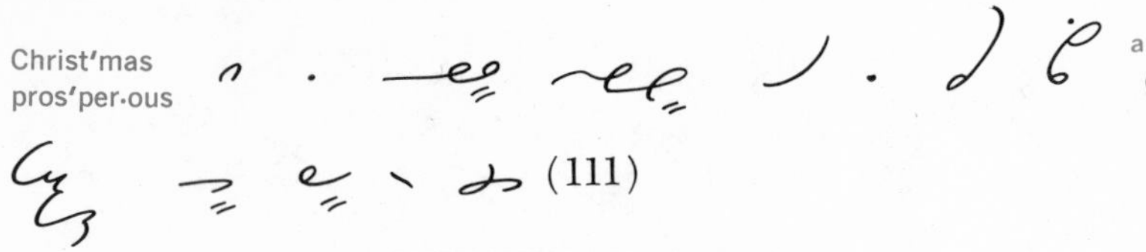

and o

(111)

566.

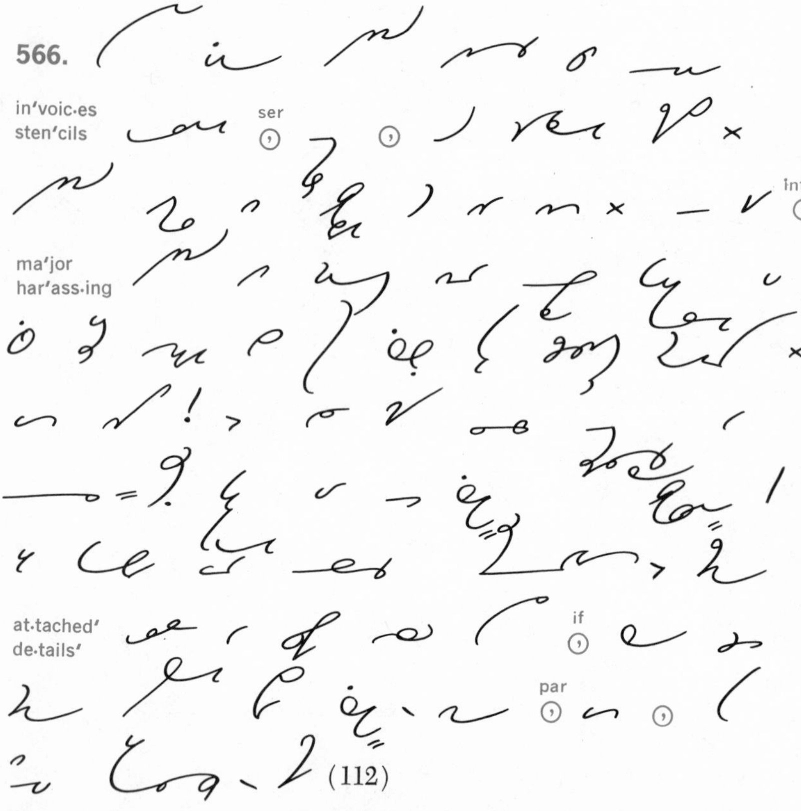

in'voic·es
sten'cils

ser

intro

ma'jor
har'ass·ing

at·tached'
de·tails'

if

par

(112)

567.

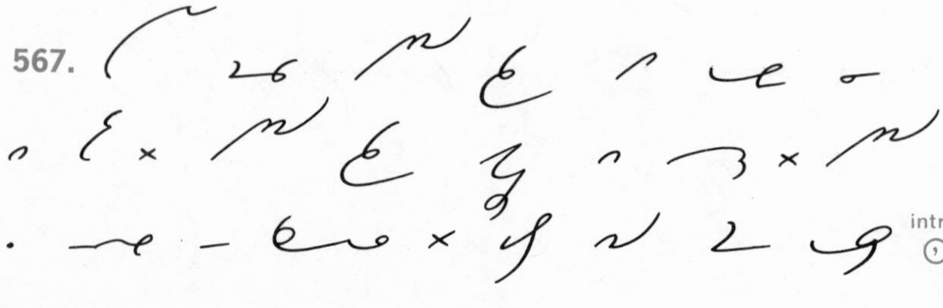

intro

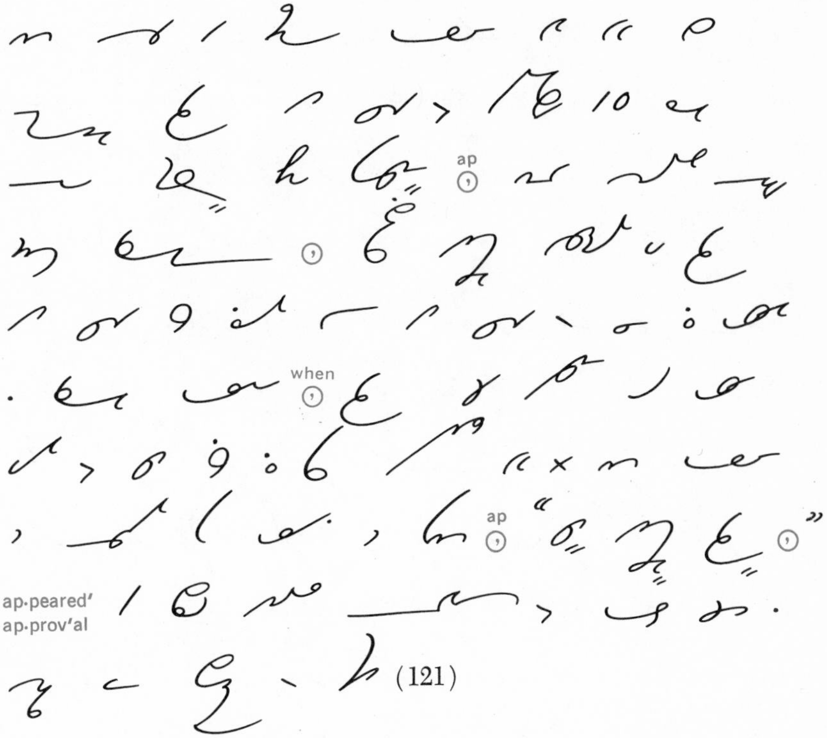
ap
when
ap
ap·peared'
ap·prov'al

(121)

568. Transcription Quiz. For you to supply: 5 commas—2 commas introductory, 1 comma *as* clause, 2 commas parenthetical.

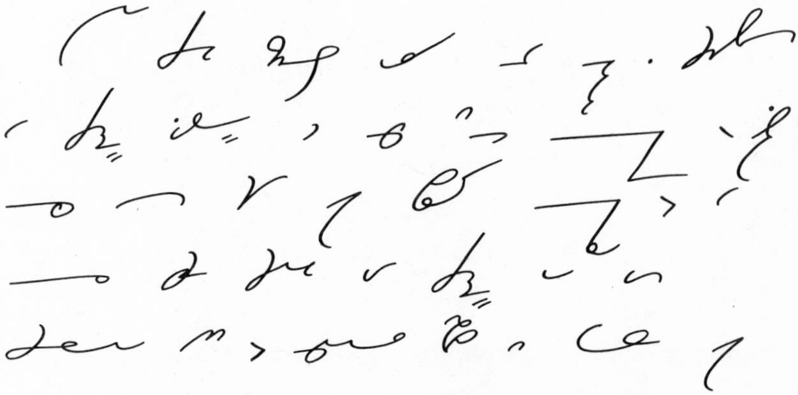

(107)

569. Chuckle

(73)

Lesson 68

This lesson contains a general review of the major principles of Gregg Shorthand.

Building Transcription Skills

570. BUSINESS VOCABULARY BUILDER

compensate To pay.

divulge To reveal; to disclose.

proficient Skillful; able.

standard This term, when referring to typewriters, means "manual" (nonelectric).

571. SIMILAR-WORDS DRILL

Assistance, assistants

assistance Help.

If we can be of assistance to you in any way, please write us.

assistants Helpers.

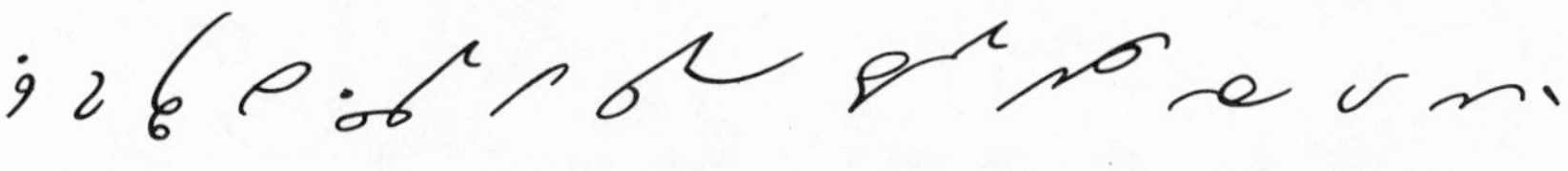

He is so busy that he needs two additional assistants to take care of the work.

Reading and Writing Practice

572.

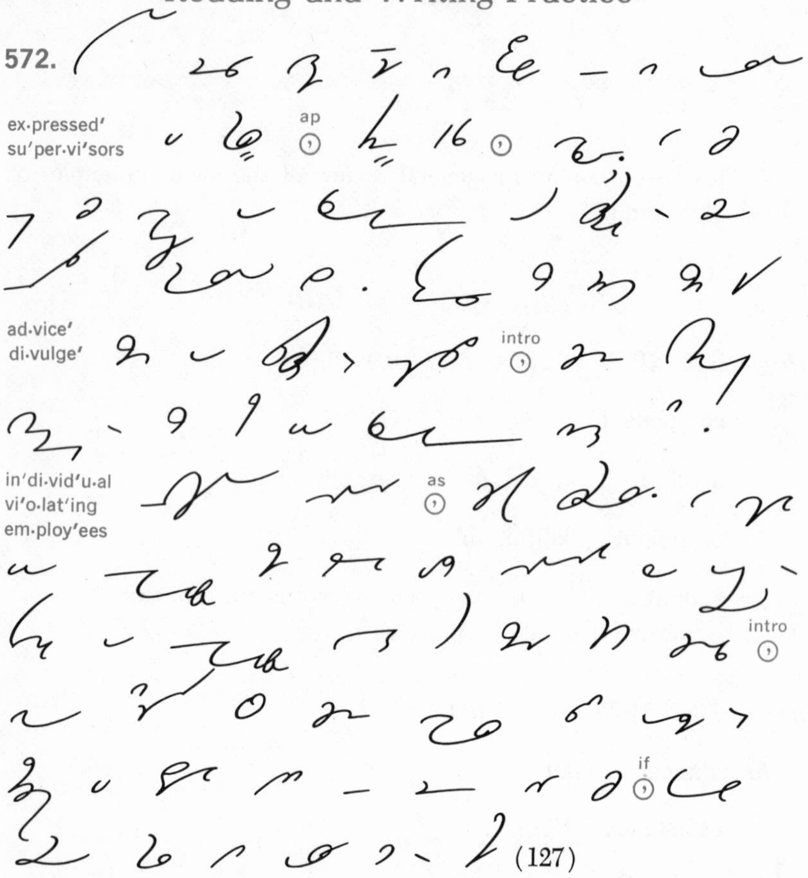
ex·pressed'
su'per·vi'sors
ap
ad·vice'
di·vulge'
intro
in'di·vid'u·al
vi'o·lat'ing
em·ploy'ees
as
intro
if
(127)

573.

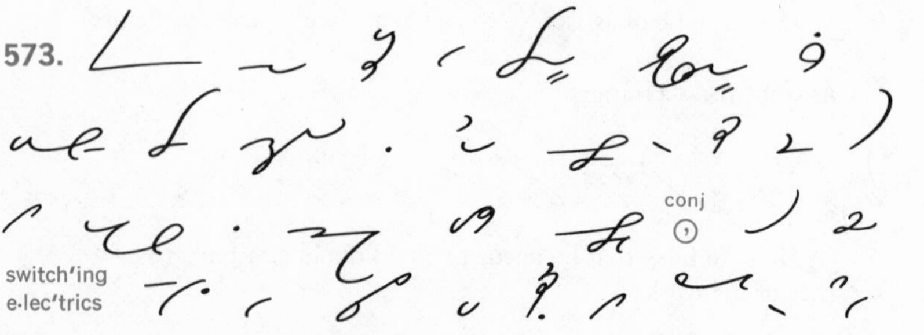
conj
switch'ing
e·lec'trics

intro
par
stud'ies
op'er·a'tor
con·ven'ience
and o
(146)

574. Transcription Quiz. For you to supply: 5 commas – 1 comma conjunction, 2 commas series, 1 comma introductory, 1 comma *when* clause.

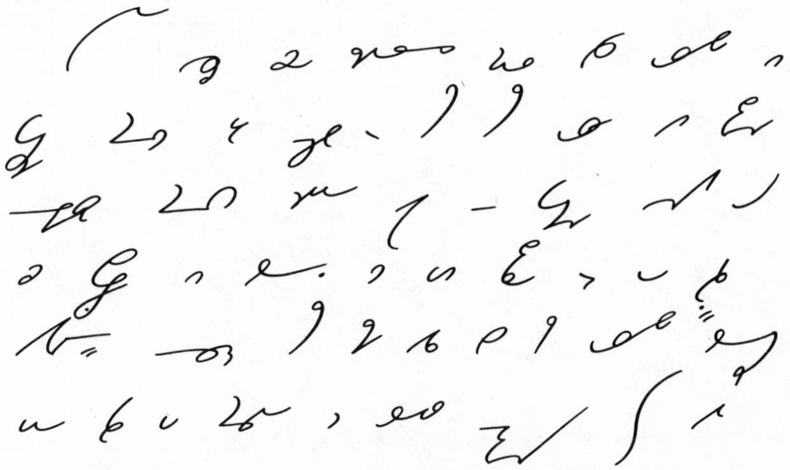

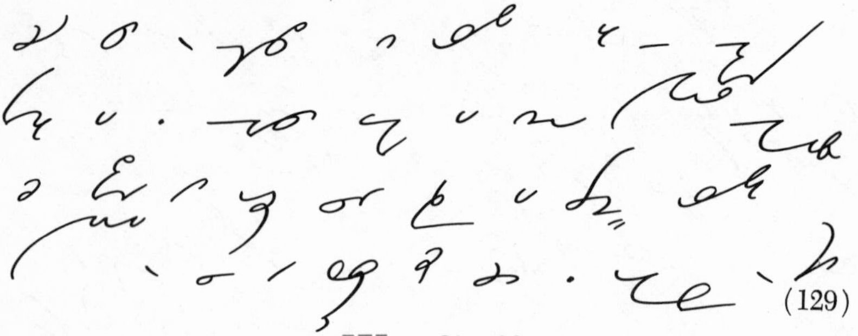

(129)

575. Chuckle

80

(104)

Lesson 69

You won't be able to refrain from chuckling as you read the Reading and Writing Practice of this lesson. It concerns an exchange of letters between a hotel manager and a guest.

Building Transcription Skills

576. BUSINESS VOCABULARY BUILDER

customary Usual.

desolated Sad; unhappy; disappointed.

establishment A place of business.

577. COMMON WORD ROOTS

Pre-: *before, beforehand*

predict To tell beforehand; to prophesy.

preliminary Coming before the main business.

premature Happening before the proper time.

prearrange To arrange beforehand.

Reading and Writing Practice

578.

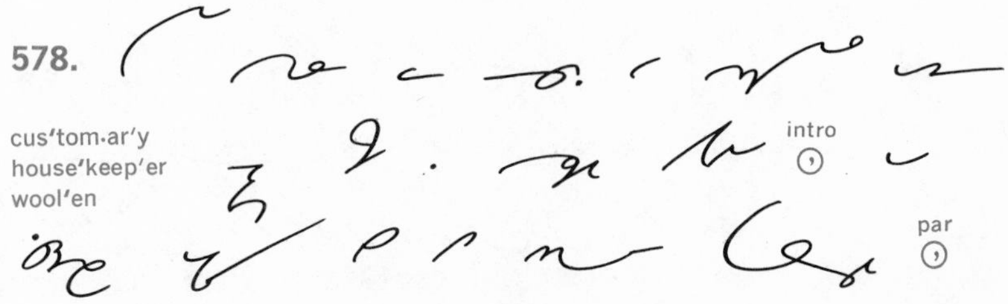
intro
par

cus'tom·ar'y
house'keep'er
wool'en

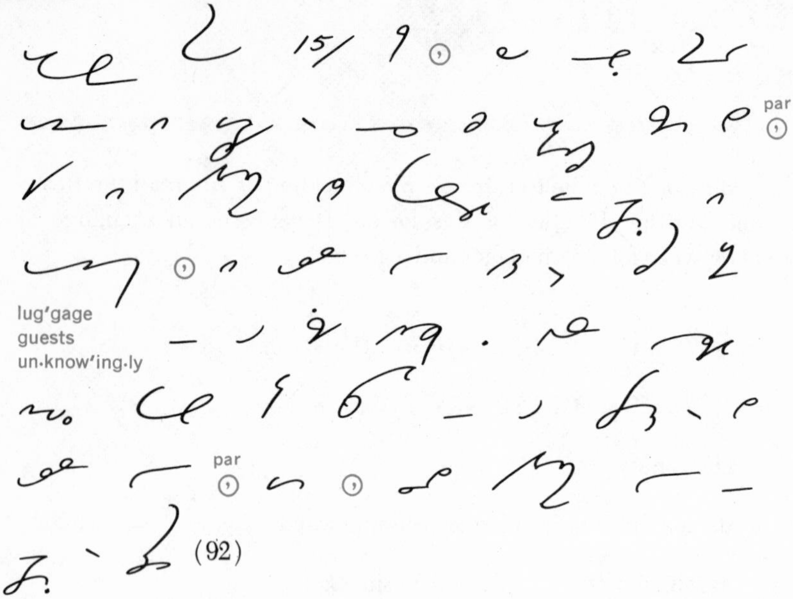

lug'gage
guests
un·know'ing·ly

(92)

579.

slight
sou've·nirs'

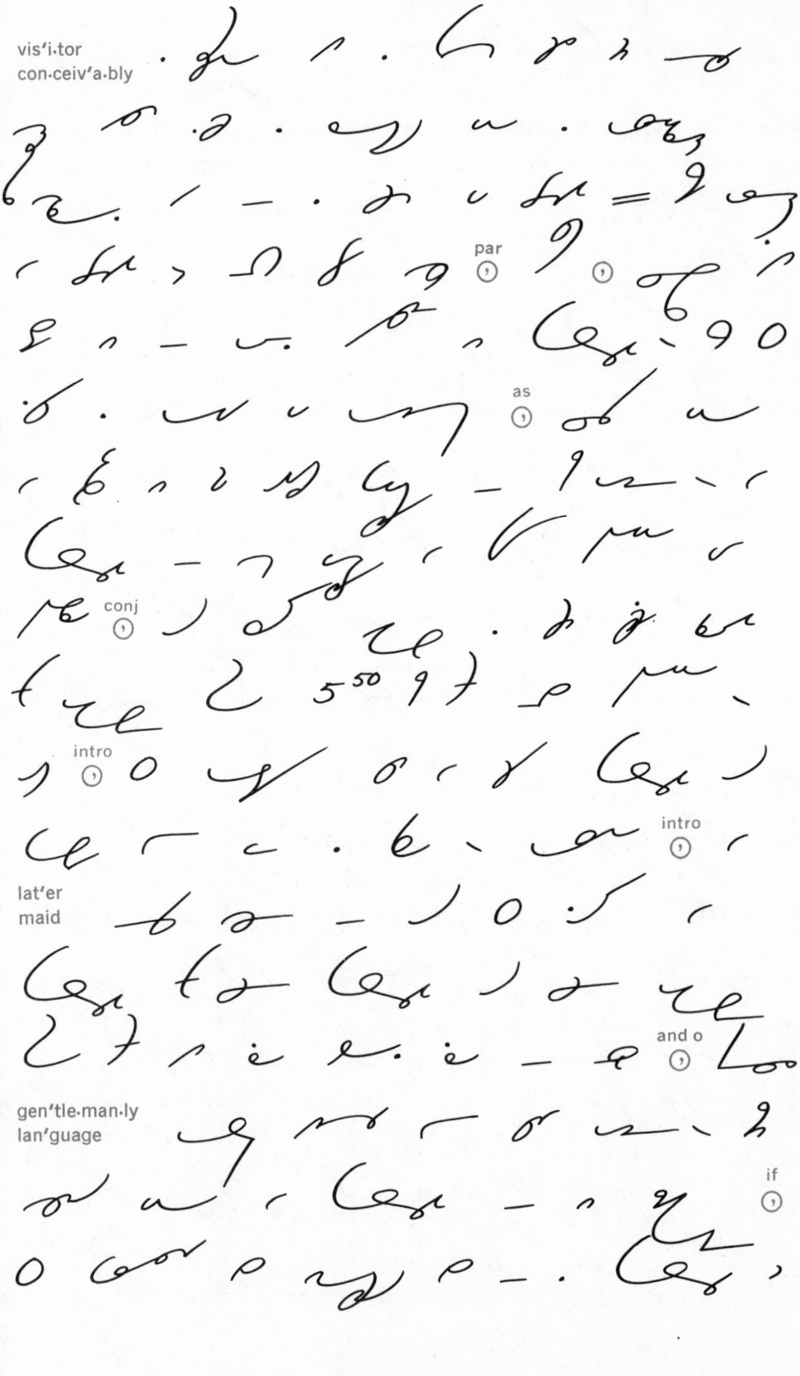

vis'i·tor
con·ceiv'a·bly
par
as
conj
intro
intro
lat'er
maid
and o
gen'tle·man·ly
lan'guage
if

(259)

580. Transcription Quiz. For you to supply: 6 commas—2 commas series, 1 comma introductory, 1 comma conjunction, 2 commas parenthetical.

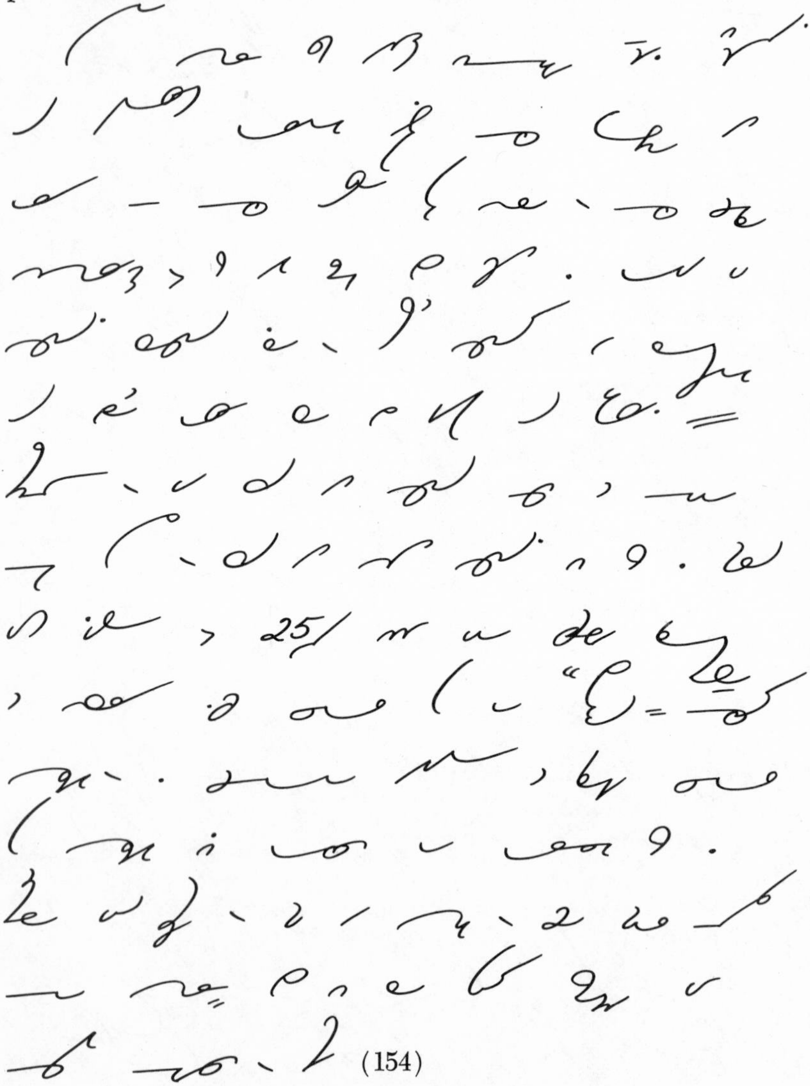

(154)

581. Chuckle

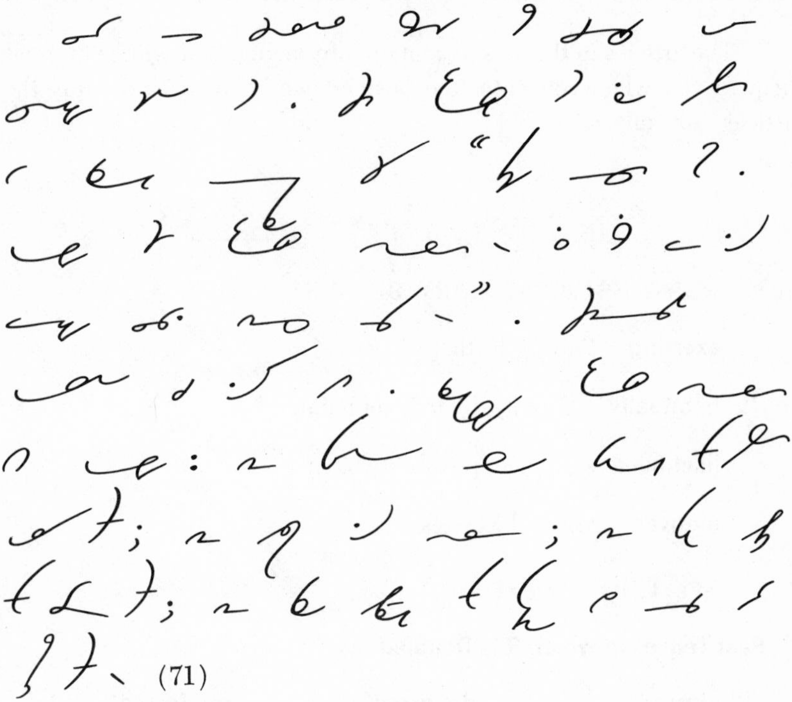
(71)

VOCABULARY CHECK LIST

Has your command of words improved since you began your study of Gregg Shorthand? It has if you–

1. Studied all the words in the Business Vocabulary Builders and added them to your everyday vocabulary.

2. Paid careful attention to the Similar-Words Drills, so that you know the difference between *addition, edition; past, passed,* etc.

3. Learned the meanings of the common word roots presented in a number of the lessons of your textbook.

Lesson 70

The articles in this lesson contain information that will be of great help to you when you enter the business world. Read and study the articles carefully.

Building Transcription Skills

582. BUSINESS VOCABULARY BUILDER

exerting Putting forth.

habitually Usually; by force of habit.

likelihood Chance; possibility.

motives Aims; objectives.

583. SPELLING FAMILIES

Past Tenses in Which R Is Doubled

blurred	**de·ferred′**	**pre·ferred′**
con·curred′	**in·ferred′**	**re·ferred′**
con·ferred′	**oc·curred′**	**trans·ferred′**

Past Tenses in Which R Is Not Doubled

cov′ered	**ma′jored**	**hon′ored**
dif′fered	**of′fered**	**suf′fered**

Reading and Writing Practice

Reading Scoreboard. Now that you are on the last lesson, you are no doubt very much interested in your final shorthand reading rate. If you have followed the practice suggestions you received early in the course, your shorthand reading rate at this time should be a source of pride to you.

To get a real picture of how much your shorthand reading rate has increased with practice, compare it with your reading rate in Lesson 18, the first time you measured it.

Lesson 70 contains 434 words.

If you read Lesson 70 in	your reading rate is
9 MINUTES	48 WORDS A MINUTE
11 MINUTES	39 WORDS A MINUTE
13 MINUTES	34 WORDS A MINUTE
15 MINUTES	29 WORDS A MINUTE
17 MINUTES	25 WORDS A MINUTE
19 MINUTES	23 WORDS A MINUTE
21 MINUTES	21 WORDS A MINUTE

584. Names

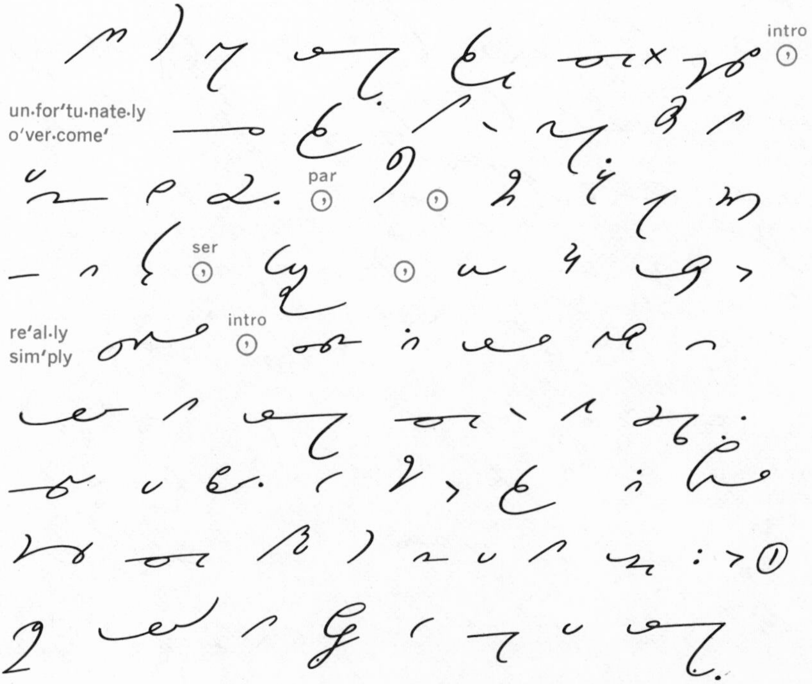
intro
un·for'tu·nate·ly
o'ver·come'
par
ser
intro
re'al·ly
sim'ply

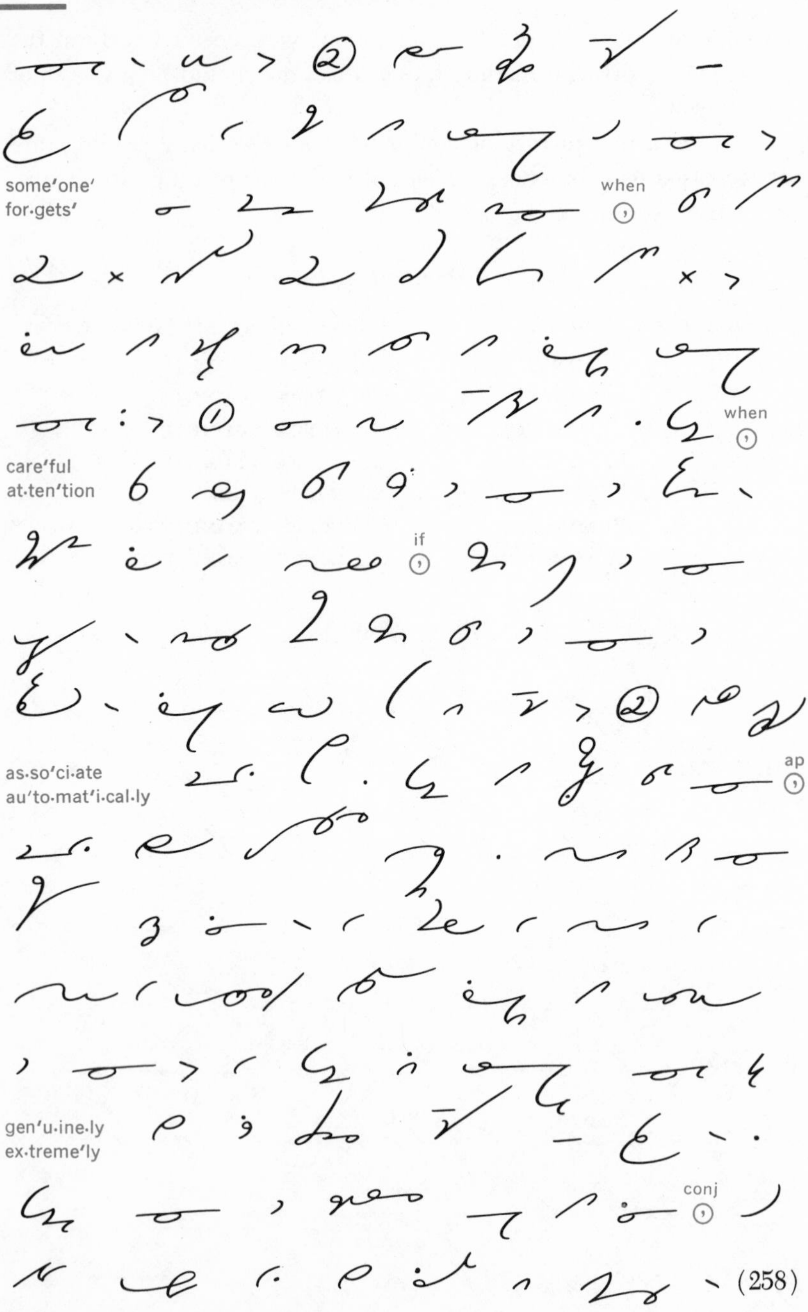
some'one'
for·gets'
when
when
care'ful
at·ten'tion
if
as·so'ci·ate
au'to·mat'i·cal·ly
ap
gen'u·ine·ly
ex·treme'ly
conj

(258)

585. Loyalty

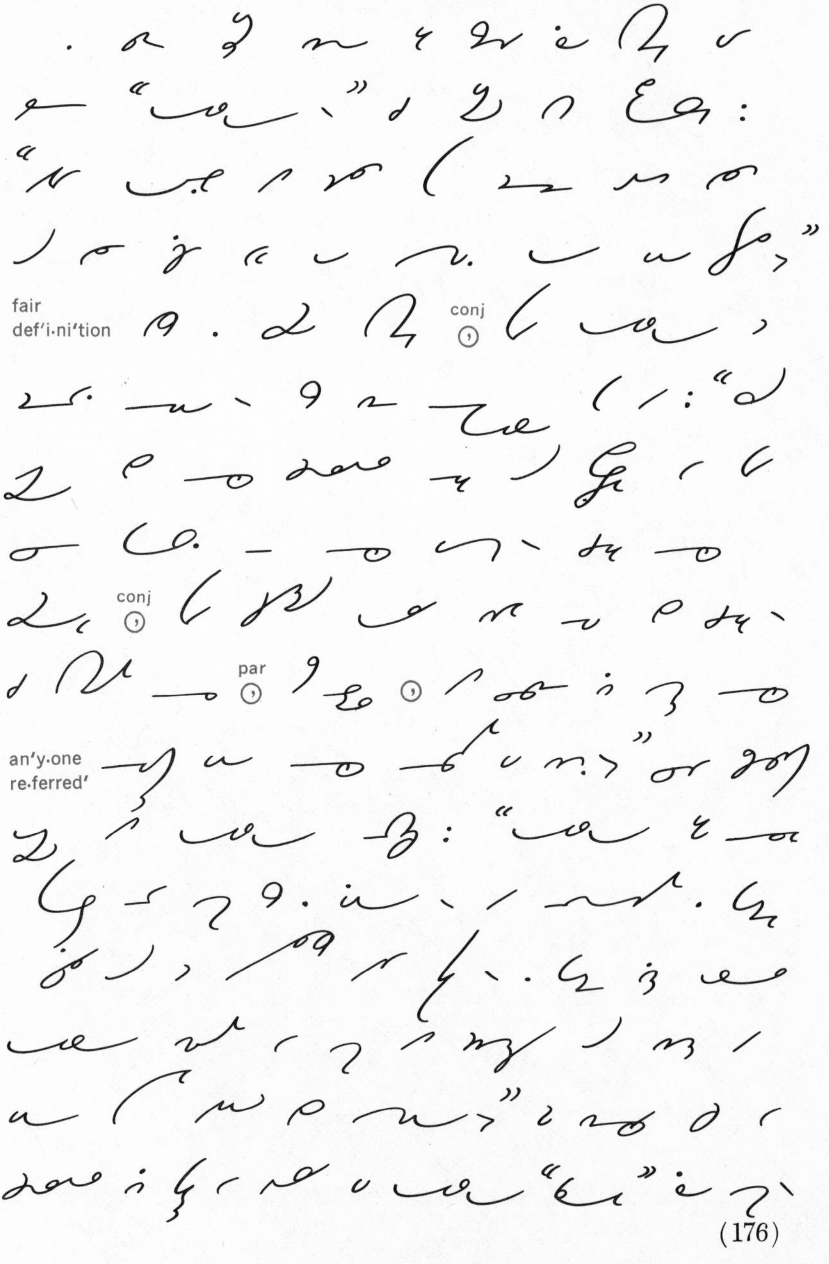
fair
def'i·ni'tion
conj
conj
par
an'y·one
re·ferred'

(176)

APPENDIX

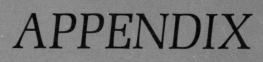

States

The abbreviations in parentheses are those recommended by the Post O
Department.

Alabama (AL)
Alaska (AK)
Arizona (AZ)
Arkansas (AR)
California (CA)
Colorado (CO)
Connecticut (CT)
Delaware (DE)
Florida (FL)
Georgia (GA)
Hawaii (HI)
Idaho (ID)
Illinois (IL)
Indiana (IN)
Iowa (IA)
Kansas (KS)
Kentucky (KY)

Louisiana (LA)
Maine (ME)
Maryland (MD)
Massachusetts (MA)
Michigan (MI)
Minnesota (MN)
Mississippi (MS)
Missouri (MO)
Montana (MT)
Nebraska (NB)
Nevada (NV)
New Hampshire (NH)
New Jersey (NJ)
New Mexico (NM)
New York (NY)
North Carolina (NC)
North Dakota (ND)

Ohio (OH)
Oklahoma (OK)
Oregon (OR)
Pennsylvania (PA)
Rhode Island (RI)
South Carolina (SC)
South Dakota (SD)
Tennessee (TN)
Texas (TX)
Utah (UT)
Vermont (VT)
Virginia (VA)
Washington (WA)
West Virginia (WV)
Wisconsin (WI)
Wyoming (WY)

Principal Cities of the United States

Akron
Albany
Atlanta
Baltimore
Birmingham
Boston
Bridgeport
Buffalo
Cambridge
Camden
Canton
Charlotte
Chattanooga
Chicago
Cincinnati
Cleveland
Columbus
Dallas
Dayton

Denver
Des Moines
Detroit
Duluth
Elizabeth
Erie
Fall River
Flint
Fort Wayne
Fort Worth
Gary
Grand Rapids
Hartford
Houston
Indianapolis
Jacksonville
Jersey City
Kansas City
Knoxville

Long Beach
Los Angeles
Louisville
Lowell
Memphis
Miami
Milwaukee
Minneapolis
Nashville
Newark
New Bedford
New Haven
New Orleans
New York
Norfolk
Oakland
Oklahoma City
Omaha
Paterson

Peoria	Salt Lake City	Tacoma
Philadelphia	San Antonio	Tampa
Pittsburgh	San Diego	Toledo
Portland	San Francisco	Trenton
Providence	Scranton	Tulsa
Reading	Seattle	Utica
Richmond	Somerville	Washington
Rochester	South Bend	Wichita
Sacramento	Spokane	Wilmington
St. Louis	Springfield	Worcester
St. Paul	Syracuse	Yonkers

Common Geographical Abbreviations

America	England	Canada
American	English	Canadian
United States	Great Britain	Puerto Rico

Index of Gregg Shorthand

In order to facilitate finding, this Index has been divided into six main sections—Alphabetic Characters, Brief Forms, General, Phrasing, Word Beginnings, Word Endings.

The first figure refers to the lesson; the second refers to the paragraph.

PHRASING

WORD BEGINNINGS

WORD ENDINGS

INDEX OF BRIEF FORMS

The first figure refers to the lesson; the second to the paragraph.

INDEX OF BUILDING YOUR TRANSCRIPTION SKILLS

The first figure refers to the lesson; the second figure to the paragraph.

BRIEF FORMS OF GREGG SHORTHAND

IN ORDER OF PRESENTATION

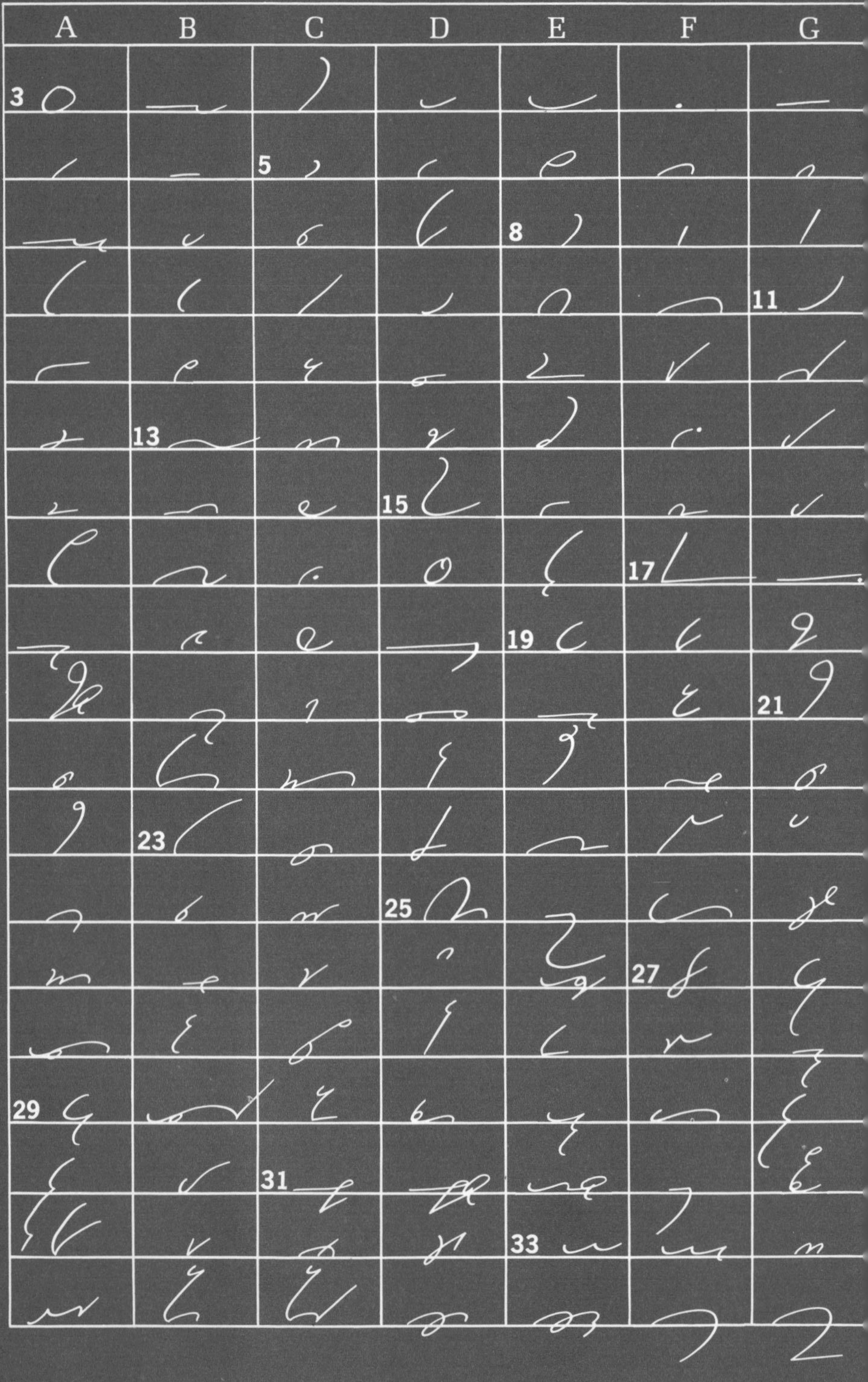

A
B
C
D
E
F
G
3
5
8
11
13
15
17
19
21
23
25
27
29
31
33